Gates County North Carolina

Deed Books A-5

- 1776-1803 -

(Volume #1)

By:
Mona A. Taylor

Southern Historical Press, Inc.
Greenville, South Carolina

Copyright Transferred 2005
To: Southern Historical Press, Inc.

All rights reserved. No part of this publication may be reproduced, stored in a retrieval system, transmitted in any form, posted on to the web in any form or by any means without the prior written permission of the publisher.

Please direct all correspondence and orders to:

www.southernhistoricalpress.com
or
**SOUTHERN HISTORICAL PRESS, Inc.
PO BOX 1267
375 West Broad Street
Greenville, SC 29601**
southernhistoricalpress@gmail.com

ISBN #0-89308-807-2

Printed in the United States of America

Notes

This book contains the earliest deeds of Gates, Co., N.C., which was formed in 1778 from parts of the counties of Hertford, Chowan and Perquimans. In 1759 the western third of what is now Gates County became a part of Hertford County but was taken from Hertford in 1779 and made a part of Gates. Before 1759 it was part of Chowan County.

Many inhabitants of the "burned" counties of Hertford, N.C. and Nansemond, Va. adjoining Gates County are mentioned in these early deeds, as well as in other books of deeds, which I have completed through 1851.

I have attempted to include all names mentioned and a full description of the land and places. An index of names and locations is included. Many names are spelled several ways but I have tried to give the most common usage. I'm sure there are errors as it was hard to distinguish between numerous letters.

I would like to dedicate this volume to my newest granddaughter, Taylor Cameron Bedard, born 31 Dec. 1986, and my other two grandchildren, Jack and Courtney Goodman.

MJT

VOLUME A
1776-84

1 29 Jul 1776--John Jones and wife, Phelishia, of Nansemond, colony of Virginia, to John Webb of town of Halifax, province of North Carolina...500 pds...parcel on NE side of Bennetts Creek in Chowan Co., which became property of said Phelishia in division of estate of Daniel Pugh, dec. and joining land whereon Ann Gibson now liveth...
Demsey Riddick   John Jones
William Riddick   Philisa (P) Jones
___is Mes__

2 20 Mar 1779--Aaron Blanshard of Chowan, planter, to his son, Demcey, deed of gift...100 acres whereon he now liveth on Wartre Swamp, beginning at a sweet gum and running up line of marked trees to corner line between Aaron Blanchard Jr. and Aaron Sr., thence along Abner Blanchard's to a corner tree line and along said line to a corner white oak between Amos Smith and Aaron Blanchard, to a corner pine and along Smith's line to a branch, to a sweet gum, to a line tree at Wartre Swamp...
Aaron Blanshard Jr.   Aaron Blanshard
Elizabeth(⩩) Blanshard

3 2 Mar 1779--Anthony Mathews to Isaac Walton...200 pds...180 acre plantation in Gates Co. on Miry Hill Pocosin, being known by name of Coles Island...
Micajah Riddick   Anthony Mathews
Sarah (●) Mathews
John (+) Morgain

4 28 May 1777--Seasbrook Wilson of Hertford Co. to James Garrett 25 pds...50 acres in Chowan Co., joining near Taylor's line, along line of marked trees to Phelps line, to corner tree and down Chowan Indian line...
George Williams   Seasbrook Wilson
James Hayes
Jacob Outlaw

5 2 Aug 1779--Persiler Lassiter to Soloman Arphan...100 pds...100 acres lying between Bennetts Creek and Catren Creek, beginning at a popular in Iron Mind Branch, along branch to Thomas Hobbs, along Richard Minchews line to a white oak; being a corner tree of Amos Lassiters and said Menchew, along said Lassiter's line...
Aaron Blanchard   Perseller (P) Lassit
Amarias Blanchard
Demcey Blanchard

6 11 Jan 1779--Jonathan Williams to James Brown, both of Hartford Co. 666 pds 13 sh and 4 pn...100 acres in Hertford Co. beginning at a hickory, a corner tree of Seasbrook Wilson and George Piland, running NW to a pine stump, to a red oak, SW to a white oak and NE to a hickory...
Robart Parker   Jonathan Williams
Robart (X)Parker

7 10 Aug 1778--John Riddick of Nancymond Co., Va. to Micajah Riddick

of Hartford Co...50 sh...100 acres whereon said Micajah now liveth and given by John Riddick, their father, in his will; plantation is in Hertford Co on N side of Middle Swamp...
Edward Doughtie
William Doughtie
Margaret (+) Doughtie
John Riddick
Mary (+) Riddick

8 2 Jan ___--Josiah Granbery to Johnathan Nichols, both of Chowan Co...25 pds...50 acres in said county beginning at Bennetts Creek road at a red oak, running to Mapel Swamp, to a mapel, a corner tree, running line of marked trees to said road and along road...
Frederick Lassiter
Jacob Norfleet
Josiah Granbery

9 1 Feb 1779--James Garrett Sr. of Hartford Co. to Jethro Meltier of Chowan Co...30 pds...50 acres in Chowan Co. beginning at a swamp at a red oak, a corner tree, up Phelps line to Oald Indian Line and down line...
George Williams
Jonathan Nichols
James Garrett

10 9 Feb 1778--John Alston, Orange Co., to Robart Parker of Hertford Co...200 pds...750 acres beginning at a pine on N side of Bennetts Creek, Jesse Brown's corner tree, along his line to Hawtree Branch, running up branch to James Hayes line and along his line to Lawrence Baker's line, along his line to George Pilands, to Seasbrook Wilson's, down his line to said creek and up creek; being plantation whereon Col John Alston formerly lived...
Wm Alston
Charles Horton
James(+) Brown
John Alston

11 20 May 1779--Hardy Jones of Edgecomb Co. to Isaac Langston... 730 pds...100 acres known by name of an Island in fork of Cypress Swamp, beginning at a corner pine tree of said Langstons and Charles Vann, standing in or near side of Cypress Swamp, up swamp by line of marked trees binding on said Vann's to a hickory, a corner, thence by line of marked trees S to another swamp, a corner pine, down swamp by line of marked trees to corner tree, N by line of marked trees; being part of a deed granted to Jacob Odom 25 Mar 1749...
Jesse Vann
Cyprian Cross
Demcy(X)Langston
Hardy (X) Jones

11 12 Mar 1778--Richard Parker of Hartford Co. to Jacob Sumner of Nancemond Co...150 pds...250 acre plantation in Hartford Co. on which said Richard lately dwelt, beginning at mouth of branch which issueth out of Elisha Parker's mill pond, running to a marked white oak, by line of marked trees binding of said Elisha's land to Va. line and along Va. line to a line of marked trees that runs into fork of Little Mare Branch and down branch to marked white oak near said mill pond and crossing pond; part of a patent granted to Richard Parker, the elder, 16 Jun 1714, and descended by right of inheritance to his grandson, Richard Parker of Nansemond Co, and by him conveyed to Richard Parker, party of these present, 14 Dec. 1751 and registered in Hertford Co.
Isreal Beeman
Jacob (J) Raby
Henry King
James (+) Jones
Richard Parker

13 7 Jan 1779--Soloman Arphen to Persiller Lassiter, both of Chowan
Co., 100 pds...50 acres in Chowan Co. between Wartre Swamp and Grate
Marsh, beginning at a post white oak in William Perce's line, running E to W corner, white oak in Rubin Lassiter's line, being a corner tree between Aaron Blanshard Jr. and said Lassiter, running to
a red oak to a mapel, a corner tree in said Percif's line...
Dempsey Blanshard   Soloman (s)Alpin
Abisha(+)Lassiter   James Alpin

14 2 Jan 1779--James Alpin to Soloman Alphin, both of Chowan Co.
40 pds...150 acres between Bennetts Creek and Catrin Creek, beginning at a white oak at Wartre Swamp in William Perse's line,
SW to a white oak in Rubin Lassiter's line and along his line to
a white oak, a corner tree between said Rubin and Aron Blanchard
Jr., to a red oak corner between Aaron Blanchard and James Alphin,
along Blanchard's line to mapel, being corner tree between said
Blanchard and Pearce, along Perses line...
Demsey Blanchard   James(+)Alphin
Abish (A)Lassiter

15 1 Sep 1779--Everard Garrett to James Garrett of Chowan Co...20
pds...20 acres on Bennetts Creek running with line of Edward Bri__
to line of Isaac ___, with his line to Jonathan Roberts line...
John Ellis   Everard Garrett
Jacob Albright

16 20 Sep 1779--John Powell to Docton Riddick...100 pds...100 acres
formerly belonging to William Phelps and sold by him to said Powell,
beginning at a pine corner tree of William Spights, running SE to an
oak, a corner tree on side of a branch and along branch NW to said
Spight's line and S nigh or joining land known as Hictoary Neck...
Jacob Sumner   John Powell
Abraham Sumner
William Hurdle

17 27 Aug 1779--William Arnell to Edward Arnell...5 pds...plantation which is part of a 200 acre grant to Thomas Milner and by him
sold to John Hubart, who by his will 15 Oct 1732 did divine the land
to his son, Mathew Hubbart, who sold to William Parker, who sold
to John Duke, who sold it to Edward Arnell Sr. and after his disease
it fell to William Arnell, heir at law; joins land of Jacob Norfleet,
Moses Hare, Thomas Parker, Isaac Benton and other land of William
Arnell and separated by a new line of marked trees to Joseph Jones
line, thence binding on his line and was formerly held by Edward
Arnell, dec. and being about 250 acres...
Thomas Parker   William Arnell
Amos(—)Parker
Noah(—)Wiggans

18 19 Jun 1779--Searsbook Wilson to James Garrett...10,000 pds...
500 acres on N side of Bennetts Creek beginning at a hickory at
bridge running along Garretts line to George Pyland's line, to James
Brown's line, then binding on George Williams line to Troy Swamp and
down swamp to Bennetts Creek and up creek...
Christ. Riddick   Seasbrook Wilson
Thomas Hunter
Jonathan Nichols

19 14 Aug 1779--Thomas Hare of Bartie Co. to Demcey Sumner...deed of gift of 150 acres joining Frances Saunders, Joseph Speight, Henry King, Cathren King and Frances Parker, running down the Deep Cypress to said Saunders line and being land his brother, Edward Hare, purchased from aforesaid Demcey and where said Demcey lives...
James Knox   Thomas Hare
John Gatling
Jesse(#)Saunders

20 5 Nov 1779--John Robarts to Jacob Eason...25 pds...100 acres beginning at a white oak, corner tree in Levi Eason's line and along his line to Henry Hobbs, to a pine in said Jacob's line; being part of a patent granted to John Arline for 500 acres 17 Nov 1733...
Joseph Riddick   John (9)Robarts
Will King

21 20 May 1779--John Duke Jr. to William Warters...100 pds...50 acres on S side of Mare Branch beginning at a warter oak in mouth of small branch at E end of an old field, W by line of marked trees to patent line...
James Bray Walters   John Duk_ Jun.
Law (+)Blade

22 15 Oct 1779--Henry Hill Sr. to Robart Taylor...60 pds...100 acres beginning at mouth of Fort Neck Branch running to Jacob Hinton's line, up branch to line of marked trees to said Taylors, along his line to Juniper Swamp and half the swamp from Taylor's bridge; being part of a patent granted to Chowan Indians and sold to said Hill by order of governor and counsel...
                                                        Henry ill Sen.
Thomas Hays
Samuel Gran Jun.
Henry (H)Hill

23 1 Nov 1779--William Hurdle to Shadrack Felton...34 pds...145 acres beginning at a pine on SE side of Warrick Swamp, running E along line of marked trees to a pine standing in patent line, that line to Deep Branch, down branch to black gum in branch, leaving branch and running line of marked trees S to a gum near run of said Swamp and down middle of swamp; is part of land belonging to Thomas Eason and given to his son, James, and by him conveyed to said Wm...
Josoph Riddick   William Hurdle
William King

24 10 Aug 1779--Hardy Cross of Nansemond Co., Va. to Demcy Oadom 21 pds 10 sh...1 acre on N side of Beach Swamp beginning at a gum near run of swamp, running a line of marked trees to a possimon corner tree, E to red oak, corner tree, S along line of marked trees to a pine...
John Bethy   Hardy Cross
James Lang
Mary Bethy

25 _____ --Cador Ohdom to John Harrell 20 pds...50 acres in Little Island, part of a patent granted to Jacob Ohdom 21 Feb 1730, beginning at a beach on S side of Cypress Swamp, down swamp along line of marked trees to a corner gum in cross swamp, Benjamin Parker's line, thence to N side of Cypress Swamp, along line of marked trees to a

pine in James Landing's line and across swamp...
William Ellis   Cader(+)Odom
William Craford

26 1 Nov 1779--William Hurdle to John Robarts...26 pds...90 acres
beginning at a pine on S side of Warrick Swamp, up middle of swamp
to a gum, corner tree of Shaderick Felton's, along his line to black
gum in Deep Branch and up middle of branch to patent line, to a marked pine, leaving patent line and running along line of marked trees
SW to a red oak in patent line; being part of land formerly belonging to Thomas Eason and given to his son, James, dec., who gave to
Jacob Eason and by him conveyed to said Hurdle... William Hurdle
Joseph Riddick
Will King

27 3 Jan 1780--John Bethy to Jesse Van_ ...300 pds...100 acres,
which he purchased of Jesse Farrow, beginning at a pine in Frances
Brinkley's line, running line of marked trees to corner pine, thence
E by line of marked trees to corner popular, to fence of said Brink-
ley's in Long Branch, up branch to John Thomas line and by line of
marked trees to a pine, SW by line of marked trees to river pecosin
swamp to corner pine and up swamp...
James Lang   John Bethy
Elisha Bathed   Mary(+)Bethy
John (+)Lang

28 8 Feb 1780--William Goodman Sen to his son, William Jr...deed
of gift of 107 acres that he purchased from his son, John, beginning in Peters Swamp at mouth of Long Branch and running up swamp to
Hennery Goodman's line, along his line to Isaac Pipkins in same paten_
along his line to mane road that leads from Suffolk to Winton and up
road to Wm. Goodman Sr, along his line to said Pipkin, bought of
Steward Pipkin, down his line to branch coming out of Long Branch
and down Long Branch; being part of patent granted to John Pipkin,
dec. 4 Apr 1720...   William Goodman
John Bethy
Henry Goodman

29 7 Oct 1776--Thomas Garrett Sr. of Chowan Co. to James Garrett
of Hertford Co...100 pds...100 acres in Hertford Co. beginning at
a hickory on N side of Bennetts Creek, crossing road and running
on Wilson's land to a corner tree, from thence along line of marked
trees to said creek...   Thomas Garrett
Thomas Garrett Jr
James Hofler

30 1 Aug 1779--Elisha Hunter to Jacob Pearce...50 pds...100 acres,
part of two tracts, one granted to said Elisha and the other to
Moses Mizell, beginning at a pine corner tree in said Mizell's line
along his line of marked trees to Abraham Eason's and along his line
to a corner, then by a line of marked trees to a red oak, a corner
on S side of Cypress Branch, then by a line of marked trees, P. (?)
Brown's, NW to said Elisha's line, then S to Cypress Branch, down
branch to a gum, then on Eason's line...
Abraham Eason   Elisha Hunter
James Bond
Moses Hill

31 22 Nov 1779--Ann Gibson of Gates Co., formerly called Chowan Co. to her son, John Webb, of Halifax...1000 pds and in consideration of a honourable maintenance and support for rest of her natural life...land formerly in Chowan Co. on NE side of Bennetts Creek and was formerly property of Daniel Pugh which said Ann received in division of his estate. Also, 14 Negroes Will, Anney, Nanny, Violet, Marquiss, Dick, Otho, Augustine, Agga, Milly, Casper, Edey, Fanny. Also china, 2 horses, 33 head cattle, 70 hogs and all other estate including accounts due, notes etc...
William Powell   Ann Gibson
William Powell Sr.
John Duke

32 14 Nov 1779--Jacob Eason to Edward Berrymon...60 pds...66 acres beginning at a pine, a corner on said Berryman's line, to Joseph Riddick's, SW by line of marked trees to a pine, a corner of said Riddick, by line of marked trees to Thomas Trotman and Ann Trotman, thence E...
Penelepy(o)Ownly   Jacob (o) Eason
John Ownly

33 12 Jan 1780--Henry Hobbs to John Robarts...200 pds...80 acres lying between Cathrin Swamp and Warrick Swamp, beginning at a white oak, a corner tree on an elbow, to a white gum in William Culley's line, down line to a line formerly belonging to James Eason, through a sandy place to white oak corner to John Eason's line and down a line of marked trees...
Guy(+)Hobbs   Henry(+)Hobbs
John Barrett

34 14 Jul 1779--Rachael Davis to John Miller...80 pds...62 acres on S side of Loosing Swamp, part of land conveyed by John Morley by several deeds of sale to Joseph Riddick, beginning at a water oak at run of swamp, John Gordon's corner tree, then running SW along his line to a pine, Joshua Small's corner tree, NE along his line to a pine in the desert and along desert to Loosing Swamp and up swamp...
Benjamin Gordon   Rachal(+)Davis
John Davis

35 23 Dec 1777--Jacob and William Hinton of Chowan Co. to John Miller of Perquimans Co...60 pds...200 acres in Perquimans Co., being plantation whereon John Harriss lived and being part of patent granted to him and John Larkum in 1695...
_____ Powell   Jacob Hinton
Benjamin Gordon   William Hinton

36 5 Mar 1778--Henry Hobs to William Colley...10 pds 5 sh...3 acres in Chowan Co. beginning at a white oak on W side of Popular Branch running to William Hurdle's line, running line of marked trees W...
William Hurdle   Henry (*)Hobbs
William Felton

37 11 Aug 1780--Thomas Langston for love and affection to his sons and daughters living in Gates Co. and to his wife, Ann... to eldest son, Isaac 20 sh; to Mary Maner 20 sh; to son Luke cow and calf; to daughter Jemmima Langston cow and calf; to daughter

Elizabeth cow and calf; to Demcy plantation whereon I live and ½ moveable estate after my desease and my wife, Ann; to Thomas my Sand Bank land, my colt and other half of moveable estate. If son Demcy should die without heirs all should fall to Thomas and if Thomas should die without heirs all should fall to Demcy...
Jesse Vann Thomas(+)Langston
James Skinner

38 28 Aug 1779--John Thomas to Noah Felton...330 pds...50 acres beginning at a marked white oak in dividing line between Thomas and Samuell Baker, running along to said Feltons binding thereon to Gum Branch, to a beach run out of percosin NW to said dividing line.
Sealey (x)Smith John ($\ddagger$) Thomas
William Felton

39 13 Dec 1779--James Eure to Lewis Sparkman...for serving three months in millita in his room...50 acres beginning at a corner pine on side of Reedy Marsh run, along William Langston's line to marked pine at end of horsepen percosin, along percosin to corner pine and along Thomas Sparkman's line and along his line to John Carter, to a corner in Reedy Marsh and is part of a patent granted to Capt Henry Baker 28 Jul 1730...
Moor Carter James($\ddagger$)Eure
Jesse Barnes

40 14 Feb 1777--John Harrell of Hertford Co. to Jesse Harrell...20 pds...100 acres, plantation of which his father, John Harrell, was possessed at Fort Island in Hertford Co., beginning at a maple, a corner tree in patent line to mane river pocosin and down pocosin to Charles Russell's line, with his line to James Brady's and along his line; part of a patent granted to John Ross 1 May 1668...
Thomas Harrell Jesse Harrell
Lemuell Harrell
Rebackah Harrell

41 6 Mar 1780--Treasury to Demcy Parker...50 sh for every 100 acres ...320 acres in Hertford Co. beginning at a pine on side of White Pot Pecosin running on Demcy Sumner's line N to a maple, said Parker's corner tree, on his line S to a white oak, thence on Christopher Riddick's line E to a red oak, to two gums on Thomas Smith's line NE...to be registered in 12 months in Hertford Co....
Richard Caswell,gov.
William Sheppard,sec.

Pages 42,43 skipped

44 25 Feb 1780--Champion Spivey to brother, Nathaniel...deed of gift of 80 acres at two pines on mane road, to a pine on NW side of Catren Creek, up swamp crossing mouth of several branches to small branch and up middle to a persimmon tree near fork, SW to black oak sapling to main road and down road; land whereon said Nathaniel lives...Said Champion is from Chowan... Champin Spivey
Moses Hill
Seth(+) Stallings

45 25 Dec 1779-James Hinton of Cumberland Co. to Isaac Harrell... 15 pds...80 acres, plantation where he formerly lived and that his

father gave him, beginning at Bennetts Creek and running down Maple Branch to fork, up another branch E to a corner tree, by a line of marked trees to Bennetts Creek road and down road...
John Bethey James Hinton
Elisha Durian
_____ Flynt

47 9 Jun 1780--John Walton to William Hinton...231 pds...78 acres on E side of Bennetts Creek, beginning at a white oak in John Webbs line, running NW by line of marked trees to a white oak in said Webb's line, along his line to a pine SE; is part of a tract granted to John Small 1776...
Elisha Hinton John Walton
Sele Hunter
William(+)Thruston

49 1 Nov 1779--James Garrett of Chowan Co. to Jonathan Robarts... 400 pds...20 acrs beginning at a pine thence running along tree line to Gordon's line...
Jethro Sumner James Garrett
John Ellis
Absolum Blanchard

50 20 Apr 1780--George Outlaw to William Freeman _00 pds...50 acres bought of Jonathan Thomas and Sarah Hinton, being formerly property of John Hinton, dec. in Indian Neck, beginning at a pine in said Outlaw's line, along line to Jacob Outlaws, along his line to James Freemans, to a corner pine, down line of marked trees which formerly belonged to Luke Sumner dec. to a black gum in a large branch, up small branch to large pine near head of branch, then along line of new marked trees...
James Sumner George (𐆑) Outlaw
James Freeman

52 3 Apr 1780--Sarah Odom and Charles King to More Carter...40 pds 100 acres of woodland ground, part of a grant of 800 acres to Henry Hackby 14 Apr 1702, beginning at a white oak on road near Scratchhall Branch, along Samuel Taylor's line, thence on Aaron Harrell's line, thence on Charles Eure's, to Thomas Piland's, thence to William Fryer's line...
George Williams Sarah(+)Odam
William(+)Fryer Charles King

53 23 Jun 1780--David Watson to Isaac Pipkin...550 pds...50 acres, part of a patent granted to him 21 Jun 1762, beginning at a pine in Gum Swamp, running W a line of marked trees to patent line, up that line to Jethro Harrells that was given out of same patent and along said Harrells to Gum Swamp and up swamp...
Jesse Vann David (D)Watson
Joseph Speght

55 5 Apr 1780--Joseph Greffin to son, Ephriam, deed of gift of 100 acres whereon said Joseph lives and 50 acres joining land of Henery Walton and Jacob Bagley at a place in the road known as Long Cossway; after his death and that of his wife, Sarah...
Kador Hill Joseph Greffin
Sarah(+)Walton

56 5 Aug 1780--Nathaniel Spivey to Charles Roundtree...120 pds...
1 acre beginning on N side of Catron Creek at cypress in swamp, N
to a persimmon tree, a corner, then on line of marked trees to a
birch, a corner tree, SW to a small red oak and along swamp...
Jacob Bagley   Nathaniel Spivey
Amos Trotman

57 14 Apr 1780--Aaron Odom to Henry Lee...200 pds...110 acres that
he purchased from Moses Hare, beginning at a corner pine of John
Duke's line and running up Short Beaverdam to the fork, thence NE
prong to maple, running along John Porter's line to said dam swamp,
up swamp and along Porter's line to Long Beaverdam Swamp...
John Bethey   Aaron(A)Ohdam
Jesse(+)Hyat

59 11 May 1780--James Parker, Sener, to William Parker S^r...20
pds...84½ acres he bought of William Jones, in fork between Rich
Thicket and Oarepeak Swamp, beginning at Joseph Jones corner on S
side of Oarepeak, running down swamp binding on Rich Thicket Swamp
and up swamp till it intersects land of said Jones and along his
line; being part of a parcel of 159 acres granted to William Jones
Sr. 7 Nov 1700 and given to his son, John, during his natural life
and after his decease to his grandson, William Jones...who conveyed
land to said James...
William Arnold   James Parker
Edward Arnold
Demcy(+)Jones

60 10 Jan 1780--John Miller to Daniell Ellis for going into service
of United States on his behalf...100 acres on side of river, being
part of patent to him in 1780, beginning at river pecosin on Arnold's
line, along his line to corner, along patent line to William Crafford
and along his line to Winns Road and along road to river and down
pecosin...
Stephen Eure   John Miller
James Landing

61 22 Feb 1781--Thomas Smith to Samuell Smith...200 pds...76 acres
part of which he took up by patent in 1780 beginning at a red oak,
Jonathan William's corner, on his line to a white oak, S to a red
oak, Jonathan Smith's corner and along line of marked trees...
Henery Smith   Thomas Smith
Jonathan Smith

62 21 Aug 1780--Isaac Benton to Moses Benton...1000 pds...170 acres
on E side of Spivey's Branch, beginning at a chesnut oak, NW by line
of marked trees to a pine, E to a white oak, S to a water oak, SE
to a water oak near water course, W to Spivey's Branch and up branch.
Jethro Benton   Isaac(+)Benton
Miles Benton

63 1 Mar 1781--Alexander Eason to Joshua Small...85 silver dollars
and 11 barrells corn...62 acres on Loosing Swamp; being part of a
patent granted to John Larcum and John Harriss and sold by them to
John Morley, by several deeds conveyed to Joseph Redding and by him
willed to his son, James, and by death of James descended to his
brother, John Redding, and by his death to his three sisters Rachal
Davis, Mary Davis and Charity Small and by said Joshua Small and wife,

Charity, ½ of 31 acres sold to William Davis and by his death descended to his son, Marmaduke, and by him willed to Rachal Davis and by her conveyed to John Miller and by Miller conveyed to Alexander Eason and by him sold to Joshua Small; beginning at a warter oak, near run of Loosing Swamp, John Gordon's corner tree, along his line to a pine, said Small's corner tree, along his line to a pine in patent line and along that line to mouth of Loosing Swamp...
Jesse Eason   Alexander Eason
James Small
Elizabeth (of)Eason

64 19 Aug 1780--William Greene to Vires Eure and Daniel Eure for said Greene's being cleared from militia man's duty for 3 mos... 30 acres beginning at hickory in Richard Greene's line, with his line to a pine corner tree on side of Mare Branch, with his line; is part of a patent granted to Henry Hackly and sold by him to said Greene...
Joseph Peal   William Greene
Soloman Greene

65 24 Jan 1781--John Freeman Jun to Jacob Outlaw...40,000 pds... 300 acre-plantation on Juniper Swamp beginning at a gum on side of swamp at bridge, running line of marked trees to a pine, corner tree in said Outlaw's line, to swamp and down swamp. Said Freeman is from Bartie Co.
James Freeman   John Freeman
Thomas Hofler
Demcy Freeman

66 17 Jan 1780--Soloman Alphin to James Gregory...2000 pds...100 acres beginning at popular on Iron Mind Branch, along branch to Thomas Hobbs line, to a white oak, a corner tree, to another white oak, corner tree of Richard Minchew and Amos Lassiter, thence up Lassiter's line...
Elisha Hunter   Soloman Alphin
Joseph (P)Alphin

67 1 Dec 1779--Elisha Hunter of Chowan Co. to Samuell Green 6 pds 20 acres beginning at a pine in said Greene's line, by line of marked trees to John Hinton's line, along his line to said Greene's...
Moses _____   Elisha Hunter
Isaac Pearce
Moses Pearce

68 29 Apr 1780--John Gatling to John Shepard...10 pds...part of a 117 acre patent granted to John Duke Jr. of Nanseymond Co. Va. 28 Oct 1702 beginning at a pine, a corner tree in Peters Swamp joining line of said Shepard, along line of marked trees to patent line or Brady's line, to Edward Hare, dec. corner tree, along Hare's line to Peters Swamp and down swamp...
More Carter   John Gatling
David Rice
John Parker

69 14 Mar 1780--Abel Martin to Thomas Brickell...36 pds...30 acres beginning at mouth of Spring Branch running to Patrick Lawler's line, along his line to John Martin's and along his line to Popular Branch

and running branch...   Abel Martin
Henry Booth   Elisabeth(+)Martin
David Martin

70 18 Nov 1780--Edward Arnold to Elizabeth Norfleet...3000pds... ___ acres in Rich Thicket Swamp and joining land of said Arnold, beginning at a chinkpen oak and gum sapling on N side of swamp, running NW to an oak then S to a willow oak, a corner tree on S side of swamp and SE to said Arnold's line...
John Arnold   Edward Arnold
Elisabeth Norfleet

71 6 Apr 1781--James Brown to Willis Brown...333 pds 6 sh 80 p... ½ of a 100 acre tract purchased of Jonathan Williams and registered in Book A p. 6 24 Nov 1779, beginning at a hickory, a corner tree of James Garrett, late Seasbrook Wilsons and George Piland, running N to a red oak then S...
                                                 James(+)Brown
George Piland
Thomas Garrett

72 8 Ju. 1779--Mills Wilkenson of Isle of Wight Co., Va. to Luke Sumner...30 pds...150 acres beginning at mouth of Orapeak Swamp, being the same which his father, Mills Wilkerson purchased of Thomas Wiggins, deed recorded in Perquimans Co...
Shadrack Wilkins   Mills Wilkenson
William Sumner
John Bab_
John Wilkenson

73 15 Feb 1781--Jethro Benton Sr to Jethro Benton Jun...100 pds... 160 acres on N side of new road beginning at a chestnuk oak on Bennetts Creek, along road to James Parker's corner tree, then W along his line to red oak, thence N to a popular in Folly Branch, down branch to said creek and down creek S...
Jethro Sumner   Jethro Benton
Josiah Benton

74 7 Jun 1780--Jesse Benton to John Benton Jun...400 pds...100 acres on Bennetts Creek, beginning at sweet gum on side of Jethro Sumners mill pond then running creek to Moses Parkers line, to Elisha Parker's, to Moses Hines, to John Benton, to a pine marked and down road...
Jethro Sumner   Jesse Benton
John Benton
Kedar Parker

75 2 Feb 1781--Aron Harrell and wife, Anne, to Samuell Brown...10 pds...15 acres out of part of deed taken out of patent granted to Hackley, beginning at a pine on Thomas Hambleton's line, to white oak corner on Deep Branch and along branch to holly, to lightwood stump, Hambleton's corner, and along line...
Charles Eure   Aaron Harrell
Thomas Hambleton   Ann(+)Harrell

76 13 Jan 1780--Thomas Norris to Peter Harrell...30 pds...50 acres on S side of Cyprus Swamp beginning at gum standing in run of mane swamp, which is now Samuel Taylor's corner tree and was formerly John Skiner's, with his line to a pond, to Steven Eure's line,

which was formerly Thomas Sparkman's and along that line to branch
and down branch; part of patent granted to Capt. Henry Baker 1 May
1728...
                   Thomas Norris
Benjamin Eure Soloman Green
Jesse Harrell Samuell Tayloe
Asa Harrell Judah Tayloe

78 16 Nov 1780--Thomas Garrett Sr. of Chowan Co. to Thomas Hofler...
10,000 pds...400 acres beginning at mouth of Gum Branch, up branch
to a branch, Capt. Aron Blanchard's line, along his line and by his
plantation at bridge, thence line of marked trees to course running
to head of Tarkil_ Branch by a pond and along Juniper Swamp to Juniper bridge, to Gum Branch and down branch...
James Freeman   Thom. Garrett Sr.
Thomas Garrett Jun.

79 8 Jul 1779--Mills Wilkenson of Isle of Wight Co., Va. to Luke
Sumner..1000 pds...tract partly in Gates Co. and part in Nancymun
Co. beginning at red oak nigh a marsh side of Henry ____, now land
of John Brinkley, on side of hill near Brinkley's house, SW binding
on land of said Sumner until it joins lands of John Randolph Wilkenson at N end of his plantation, running SW and binding on his line;
being line made between William Wilkenson, father of John R., and
Willis Wilkinson, father of said Mills in their lifetime and for a
division of thare Orapeak lands persuant to will of thar father,
William Wilkenson of Isle of Wight; which land runs down a small
deep branch till it joins patent near S end of plantation called
Thomas Wiggens, now land of Luke Sumner, running NE to marked pine
paralleling his line, now Brinkley's land, land of John Markum, now
land of John Wilkenson, till it joins land of John Brothers, E binding on Brothers land to NW corner of Brinkleys and SE, containing
500 acres and is part of 900 acrs granted to Col. John Leas of Nansemond 20 Nov 1682 and called Orapeak and purchased by Col. William
Wilkenson, who died possessed of and by his will 6 Mar 1740 gave
to his sons, William and Willis. Said William deeded land to said
Mills 20 Oct 1767 in Perquimans Co...
                  Mills Wilkenson
Shadrack Wilkins
William Sumner
John R. Wilkenson

81 5 Mar 1781--Cador Odom to John Odom...27 pds...240 acres known
as Rogers Pecosin beginning at corner pine in Richard Odom's, running along roe of marked trees, a line was dividing said land between
patent and William Frier and Charles Russell and was made dividing
line in presants of Joseph Vann, along said line to a line of Thomas
Langston, so running Langston's line to William Skiners patent, a-
long his line to a corner tree of Catherine Langston, thence running along her line; being patent granted to John Langston for 400
acres 30 Jul 1726...
                  Cadar(+)Odom
George Hargroves
Abraham Brasher

82 11 May 1781--Robart Parker Sen. to Jonathan Army Trader...40
pds North Carolina Currency viz. 100 silver Spanish milled dollars...
75 acres to be taken out of lands on which he dwells, beginning at
red oak on back of swamp, running along line of marked trees to

Bennetts Road to red oak on road and down road to Halfway Run Branch to white oak on back swamp and down swamp...
Thomas Garrett Jun.   Robart Parker
Seasbrook Wilson   Abgall Parker

83 17 Mar 1780--James Garrett to Lawrence Baker, William Baker, Elisha Hunter and John Benton, commissioners appointed for fixing place whare court prison and stocks shall be built, for any advantages he may receive...6 acres beginning at white oak on W side of Bennetts Creek, marked as corner tree, running down to a post corner E to an oak, S to an oak and W, for as long as court continues to be held...
Jonathan Robarts   James Garrett

84 7 Feb 1781--Lemuel Taylor to Richard Briggs...60 pds...100 acres beginning at a pine, corner tree in branch between James Phelps and John Briggs, down branch to Robart Powell's line to a pine in Daniel Pughs, by line of marked trees to corner tree in James Phelps line...
Moses Davis
Nathaniel Taylor   Lemuel(+)Taylor

84 5 Nov 1781--William Walton and Rachael Small to James Gregory... 500 pds...300 acres, including several tracts of land, beginning at mouth of Maple Branch, up branch to marked gum on William Cowpers line, to a red oak, a corner tree, N to James Costen's line and on his line to Jesse Spivey's line, to Thomas Walton's line and along his line to M_____ Swamp and down swamp...
John Granbery   William Walton
Rachal Garrett   Rachael Small

85 18 Aug 1781--Demcy Trotman to Henry Walton...1000 pds...7 acres beginning at a pine at corner tree in said Walton's line, along his line of marked trees, N to a pine corner and along said Walton line...
Christian Trotman   Demcy Trotman
Thomas Trotman

86 16 Aug 1781--Henry Walton to Demcy Trotman...1000 pds...7 acres beginning in Pallihial Walton's, dec. line, by path side between said Trotman and Oald Swamp bridge, then along a line of marked trees S to oak in said Trotman line, along his line and binding thereon to said Pallihial Walton's line...
Thomas Trotman   Henry Walton
Emiley(x)Trotman

87 8 Jun 1780--Richard Green and wife, Selah, to Jonathan Cullins... 12 pds...30 acres beginning at or near head of Mire_ Branch at road, along roe of marked trees on N side of said branch to William Greens and along his line to Rubin Sparkman's and along his line to Sarah Felton's, then along her line to Saron Road and along road...
Jesse Harrell   Richard Green
Asa Harrell   Selah Green
Mary Harrell

88 26 Dec 1780--Mary Ronals to her nephew, James Crafford...deed of gift of plantation where she now lives, 8 head cattle and all the rest of her estate, after her death...
John Russell   Mary (ᛣ)Ronals
Jim Vernal
James Landing

89 27 Sep 1780--William Cleaves to George Williams Jun...10 pds
10 sh...50 acres beginning at a gum in Hilly Swamp, running swamp
to a cypress in mouth of a deep branch, up branch by line of marked
trees to a corner maple in Pap Turner's line, up his line to Oald
Hilly Swamp line and along line...
Robart Parker   William Cleves
Demcy Parker   Cador Riddick
Miles Parker

90 6 Apr 1782--Henry Booth to Joseph Brown Jun...45 pds...50 acres
beginning at a pine in William Hayes line, running along said Booth's
line to a popular, a corner tree in Deep Branch, down branch and lying between a creek and Cathrun Creek and binding on S side of Bennetts Creek...
Israel Beeman   Henry Booth
Jesse Brown

91 20 Feb 1781--John Millar to Alexander Eason...85 silver dollars
and 11 bbls corn...62 acres, being part of grant to John Larcum and
John Harriss and conveyed by them to John Morley, who sold to Joseph
Riddick and by him descended to his son, James, after whose death
was divided to his 3 sisters, Rachael Davis, Mary Davis and Charity
Small. Said Small receiving 31 acres and by Joshua Small and wife,
Charity, conveyed to William Davis and at his death willed to son,
Marmaduke, after whose death it became property of Rachael Davis and
by her conveyed to said Miller. Land lies on S side of Loosing Swamp
beginning at a warter oak near run of swamp, John Gordon's corner
tree and along his line to a pine, Joshua Small's corner tree and
along his line to a pine in patent and along patent line to said
swamp and up swamp...
Jesse Eason   John (Ⱨ) Millar
Seth Eason
Moses Eason

92 29 Sep 1781--Kadar Riddick to George Williams Jun...80 pds...60
acres beginning at run of Hilly Swamp on N side of Bennetts Creek,
running up hill to a hickory, thence along a row of marked trees
to a gum, from thence a strait course to run of said creek and down
run to mouth of said swamp and up swamp...
William Cleves   Cadar Riddick
Dempsey Parker
Miles Parker

93 11 Jul 1781--Joseph Norfleet to Josiah Stallings...6 pds...70
acres known as Little Island, being part of patent granted to Jacob
Oadom for 640 acres 21 Feb 1730, beginning at corner gum in Josiah
Harrell's line in Cypress Swamp on N side and running along his line
to a corner gum on side of percosin swamp, running along river per-
cosin swamp W to a corner pine on S side of swamp, across the Is-
land by a line of marked trees to a corner gum on side of Cypress
Swamp and down swamp...
Demcy Barnes   Joseph Norfleet
Willis Wiggins

94 23 Aug 1781--Jesse Harrell to Ezekiel Jones...for serving 3 mos.

in militia service...50 acres on N side of Fort Island beginning
at a corner pine upon ma<u>ne</u> desert, to Doctor Brown's line and along
his line to corner gum, thence by line of marked trees to Thick
Neck Bridge and is part of patent granted to John Rawls 1 May 1660...
John(+)Carter   Jesse Harrell
Elisha Ellis
Moses Jones

95 7 Apr 1782--John Goodman of Edgecomb Co. to his brother, William...deed of gift...180-acre tract that William Goodman Sr. purchased of William Ashly, who took up patent 1 Mar 1719, and is in Beaverdam Swamp, beginning near Isaac Pipkin's line, running N along line of marked trees that Wm. Goodman Sr., dec. made to his son, Henry Goodman, in same patent, to John Bethey's line and along patent line to said Wm. Goodman, dec., made to Stephen ____ in same patent and along patent line to old patent line...
Henry Goodman   John Goodman
Edith Goodman

96 25 Feb 1782--William Powell to his nephew, Isaac, deed of gift...
land, tenements, Negroes Sam, Jacob, Peter, Hardy, Lydia, Charles, Jeffery, stock of horses, cattle, hogs, sheep, fowl, work tools, plantation utensils and household furniture...provided that his sister, Sarah, be gentilly maintained...
John Duk_ Jr.   William Powell
John Casey

97 20 May 1782--Demcy Parker to Elisha Cross...5 pds...50 acres on E side of Honey Pot pecosin, running W and beginning at a pine on side of White Pot Pecosin, running W a line of marked trees to Christopher Riddicks and along his line S to Demcy Odom's corner tree, thence running E, a line of Thomas Smith's, to a white oak, a corner tree, and running N...
John Bethey   Demcy Parker
James Bruter
Robart Parker

98 5 Feb 1782--John Twine of Perquiman Co. to Elisha Norfleet...25 pds...20 acres, being 5th lot of division between John Norfleet's children, given by his will, and known as an Island; beginning at a stake out of the head line running NE to line in desert and along line...
Jacob Gordon   John Twine
Thomas Twine   Pleasant(X)Twine
Jesse Twine

99 10 Jun 1782--James Sumner to John Powell...25 pds 3½ acres on N side of mouth of Orapeak, beginning at a gum on edge of swamp, running N on a ditch, being dividing line that Sumner and Wilkinson made, to a stake in ditch, E to edge of swamp...
John Barrett   James Sumner
William Ellis
James Jones alias Sketo

100 5 Jan 1782--James Gregory to Robart Taylor...5 pds...10 acres, part of tract on which said Gregory lives, on Myre Branch, along branch to a pine, being corner tree of Henry Hill, along said line

to Hinton's line and down his line to marked pine in Fork Neck
Branch and down branch...
Henry Booth   James Gregory
Himrick Hill

101 10 Apr 1782--Andrew Hambleton to Thomas Norris...10 pds...25
acres beginning at a corner pine of Charles Eure's, running John
Eure's line, cornered at red oak, N to pecosin, NE to said Charles'
line and S...
Samuell Brown   Andrew Hambleton
Thomas Hambleton

102 19 Nov 1781--Samuell Brown to William Vann...12 pds...25 acres
joining Isaac Pipkin's land, beginning at Notte Pine Swamp at Mare
Branch road at bridge, running up swamp to line of marked trees,
joining said Vann's line to a corner tree, a maple, along line of
marked trees to road and along road...
Charles Eure   Samuell Brown
Thomas Hambleton
Daniel Eure

103 6 Mar 1782--Henry Hill to James Gregory...32 pds...50 acres
lying in Indian Neck, beginning at Seasbrook Hinton's line in Gabriel Branch and along his line to Indian Road, down road to a line
between David and Henry Hill, to Gabriels Branch...
Jonathan Nichols   Henry Hill
Demcy(D)Jones

104 24 Feb 1782--Stephen Eure to Lemuell Keen...42 pds...50 acres
in Fort Island, beginning at outside pocosin at a black gum, across
to Samuell Harrell's line, to a black gum, running down Harrell's
line to William Right's line and down his line to outside pecosin
to a sweet gum and up sand pecosin; part of patent granted to John
Webb in 1723...
Jesse Harrell   Stephen Eure
James(X)Keen

105 19 Jan 1782--James Winburn and wife, Easter, of Nansemond to
Jethro Ballard...18 pds 18 sh...21 acres beginning at stake in head
line of John Norfleet's patent, thence running E to back of marsh
to patent line; was willed by John Norfleet to his daughter, Easter,
and is 11th part of tract of marsh land and is 4th division...
K. Ballard   James Winburn
William Faulk   Easter Winburn
Mary Faulk

106 20 May 1782--John Varnel to James Curle...in consideration of
his going into the service of the United States on his behalf...50
acres known as Other Island and is part of patent granted to Callum
Ross 21 Feb 1738, beginning on Gum Swamp at a gum, a corner tree,
running along line of marked trees to head of branch and down branch
to pine swamp, up swamp to Cross Swamp, to Gum Swamp...
James Landing   John (‡) Varnel
John Landing

107 14 Feb 1782--William Cleaves to Arthur Williams...12 pds...100
acres beginning at a gum on line of George Williams Jr., to Hilly
Swamp, along Williams line up swamp and along Turner's line, NE by

a row of marked trees to a pine corner tree, S by George Williams Sr. line...
George Williams   William Cleaves
Isaac Langston
Thomas Garrett

108 19 Feb 1781--Henry Booth to Jeremiah Jordon...30 pds...40 acres beginning at Spring Branch, running along road to Wore Neck Branch, up branch to Jonathan Lassiter's line and along his line to Spring Branch and down branch to road...
Thomas Brickell   Henry Booth
Josiah Jordon Jun.   Marget Booth

109 20 May 1782--Seasbrook Wilson to John Baker...400 pds...___ land on N side of Bennetts Creek lying in fork of Bennetts Creek and Sarum Creek, beginning at George Williams' line on Coles Creek, along his line to Willis and James Brown's line and along their line to Garrett's line, along that line to Pyland's line, along Pyland's line to oald patent, to hickory on Bennetts Creek Bridge, S to Sarum Creek and along patent line to said Williams line; is remainder of patent granted to John Right of Nansemond 10 Apr 1694 and conveyed by Nathaniel Right to James Wilson 23 May 1733...
Robart Parker   Seasbrook Wilson
Will. Clark

110 10 Apr 1780--Thomas Norris to Andrew Hambleton 20 pds...50 acres beginning at pond with Samuel Talors' line that was formerly John Skinners, to a corner pine standing in Will. Langston's line that's now Stephen Eure's, along Eure's line to head of pond and along pond.
Sam. Brown   Thomas Norris
Thomas Hamilton

111 20 Feb 1782--Robart Parker to John Polson...50 pds...100 acres beginning at gum on side of branch called Halfway Run, up branch NW to Bennetts Creek road and up road to a pine, corner tree,S to George Piland's line, to a white oak, a corner tree, along Piland's line to said Parker's line...
Evans Murphery   Robart Parker
Wm. Brooks

112 23 Nov 1781--John Green to son, Mathias, deed of gift...12 acres whereon said Mathias lives, on S side of Cole Creek Swamp, beginning at a pine in swamp, Samuel Eure's corner tree, that was formerly John Harris', along his line to Pine Branch, running straight course to mouth of branch near Panters Island, thence to Coles Creek and up creek...
Jesse Harrell   John (₴) Green
Peter Harrell
Asa Harrell

113 2 Nov 1781--John Powell is bound to John Norfleet of Upper Parish of Nansemond, executor of John Norfleet, dec., for 500 pds...
                                                          John Powell

114 4 Jun 1782--Peter Piland to Josiah Jordon of Nansemond...35 pds 50 acres beginning at a white oak, a corner tree adjoining Demcey Fulkes's land, W adjoining Charles Lawrence and NE to said Fulkes' line...
Thomas Brickell   Peter(+)Piland
Sarah Piland

115 2 Jul 1782--Jacob Hinton to Samuell Harrell 10 pds...40 acres beginning at a pine in Henry Hill's old patent line, N to a pine, a corner tree of John Rice's, along his line to a pine in Aaron Lassiter's line, then along his line to said Harrells and along a line of marked trees...
                                                    Jacob Hinton

116 17 Aug 1782--William Walters to James Bray Walters...50 pds... 197 acres near Mare Branch and is part of patent granted to John Lassiter 11 Nov 1719...
                                                    William Walters
Jethro Sumner
William Goodman
Benjamin Barnes

117--Received from the following for deed registration: William ___, Demcy Langston, Moses Benton, Isaac Harrell, William Culley and two for Samuell Brown; each 2=6.
Isaac Hunter's Register Book 17 Jan 1784.

                              Part 2

   The following tracts of land were sold by the Treasury of North Carolina and deeds were signed by Alex. Martin and James Glasglow, his secretary of state. Date is 1783 and the price was 50 shillings for every 100 acres.
1--To Josiah Spight...170 acres beginning at chincopin oake and holly on Holly Island, Henry King and Catrine King's corner tree, along said Henry's line N to a white oak, his and James Copeland's corner, along Copeland's line NW to Joseph Speight's corner and along his line to said Catrine's line and along her line...
2--To Demcy Trotman...119 acres on W side of Meherin Swamp, beginning at a pine on SW side of Hilly Bridge Branch in Henry Walton's line, S to a gum, SE to a red oak, Joseph Griffin's corner tree, NW to said Waltons and along his line to a pine in Jacob Bagley's line, NE to said Griffins, to said Waltons, and NE...
3--To William Baker...75 acres in Hackley Swamp, part on NE side, running to said Baker's line, down to swamp and to run, to fork whare run of Wiggens Swamp intercepts and NE...
4--To William Baker...40 acres on Knotty Pine Swamp beginning at a gum, his own corner tree, standing by side of run on S side, W to swamp and up swamp N to road and E... 18 Aug 1783
5--To Samuell Green...18 acres beginning at a black oake, said Green's and William Eason's corner, along Eason's line NW to Lassiters Branch, to Jacob Pearce's line, to Elisha Hunter's corner, down middle of branch on Hunter's line, SW to said Green's corner tree...
6--To Christopher Pearce...100 acres beginning at a gum at mouth of small branch, said Christopher and Jacob Pearce's corner tree, along W side of main pecosin to said Christopher and Moses Brigg's corner, up desert NE...
7--To Jethro Ballard...184½ acres on W side of main desert beginning at a persimmon tree at mouth of Loosing Branch on S side of Joshua

Small's corner tree N to swamp and up swamp, SW to desert, to said Small's line and N...

8--To Jethro Ballard...229 acres in Perquimans Co., back of White Oak Marsh, beginning at a cypress in desert near SE side of marsh, a corner tree in his own survey, NE to cypress near corner of marsh, in or near Generall Washington's line, N to side of desert, near Taylor's ditch, SW to his own corner tree and NW to his own line...

9--To John Green...244½ acres on SW side of Coles Creek beginning at gum, by run of creek SW to gum in Licking Root Branch, to run of Coles Creek and up creek...

10 14 May 1783--Henry Delday to son, Jesse, 50 acres, deed of gift, part of patent falling to him from Henry Delday, dec., who was part of Abram Oadom's will, runs a line of marked trees that said Delday sold to John Ra__ of same patent, then running to Goff Folly Branch and up branch...
John Ra__   Henry Delday

11--To More Carter...200 acres on E side of Meherin River beginning at a pine, black gum and holly on side of Peters Swamp and down pocosin and SE...

12--Luke Sumners...640 acres on W side of desert beginning at Peter Brinkley's corner, along his line to said Sumner's line and along his line and leaving his line S to Virginia line, along that line...

13--To Jesse Barnes...22 acres on E side of Meherin River and Gum Swamp, beginning at Swamp, S to Joseph Runnells patent and along his line to pine swamp, to William Craffords corner, along his line...

14 --William Matthews...35 acres on White Pot Pocosin beginning at a gum, Samuell Smith's corner near said Matthew's path, NW to a white oak, Edwin Sumner and Sam'l Baker's corner, along Sumner's line SW to Demcy Parker's line and along his line SW and then SE...

15--Richard Auston...64½ acres beginning at a gum in county line in Webbs Branch, Demcy Odom's corner tree, along his line to run of Beach Swamp and down swamp S and back to mouth of Webbs Branch...

16--Jesse Eason...100 acres on W side of desert beginning at a white oak in said Eason and Jacob Pearce's corner tree in Reedy Branch, to desert and along side S to said Eason and Abraham Eason's corner tree in mouth of Grate Branch, to desert and E to a gum, NE to a gum and W...

17--Jesse Eason...100 acres on W side of main desert, beginning at a sassafras, his own corner tree in Mills Riddick's line, along said Eason's line SE to a pine stump in Jacob Pearce's field, along his line to Christopher Pearce's, NW to red oake, Moses Briggs' corner in said Riddick's line and along his line S...

18--To Stephen Eure...285 acres on E side of Mehering River, beginning at a black gum at head of Painter Ridge on side of said River pocosin whare is bridge and SE side and crossing mouth of several branches to a pine, Ra__ patent corner tree, NW to Gum Swamp to a maple and two holleys on side of bridge pocosin and SE...

19--To William Hinton...830 acres on E side of Bennetts Creek, beginning at a will**ar** oak**e**, said Hinton's corner in John Bri**dg**es line, SE to a maple, said Briggs corner NE to red oak, corner in Davis**es** line, along his line to corner tree in Gum Pecosin Branch, up branch to fork, N to prong, to said Hinton's line, SE to middle of branch to Aron Lassiter's line and along his line W to red oak**e**, said Lassiters and Harrells line, to gum post in Josiah Granbery's line, to said Hinton's line...

20--John Gordon...630 acres on E side of Meherin Swamp, beginning at white oak**e**, his own corner tree, beginning in Jacob Hunter's new survey and along his line SE to a white oak, said Hunter's and David Rice's corner tree near G**ra**te Marsh, along Rice's line SE to a pine, Jacob Pe**rc**es, Thos. Hunters and Elisha Hunter's corner tree, along Thos. Hunter's line to said Hinton's corner tree and along his line to Gordon's line and NW...

21--To Demsey O**a**dom...72 acres beginning at a pine in county line in Hardy Cross line, Thomas Smith's corner tree, along said Cross line SE to run of Beach Swamp, up run S and then N to middle of Hobbs Branch and up branch W and along county line...

22--To Kedar Powell...640 acres, beginning at two gums and a maple, Joshua Small and Jesse Eason's corner tree in desert, then along Small's line N to Jethro Ballard's corner tree and along his line S to gum, to Jesse Eason's line and along his line W...

23--To Joshua Small...396 acres beginning at two pines on W side of desert, along desert NE to two gums, SE to a maple and S...

24--To Luke Sumner...377 acres in Orapeak beginning at a gum in John Norfleet's corner of SW side of swamp, up swamp NW to two yards below Norfleet's mill dam, across swamp E then S to mouth of swamp...

25--To Jacob Gordon...640 acres on W side of main desert, beginning at a red oak**e** in Seth Eason's line, along side of desert E to a wa**r**ter oak**e**, by run of Horsepool Swamp E to gum in desert, to said Eason's line and along his line...

26--To Jacob Pe**rc**e...105 acres beginning at white oak**e**, said Perce and Jess**ey** Eason's corner tree in mouth of ___ Branch, SW along side of main desert to a gum, Christopher and Jacob Pearce's corner tree in mouth of small branch, then E into desert...

27 15 Oct 1782--John Robbins to John Hare...65 pds...130 acres beginning at red oak**e** Jonathan Nichols and said Robbins corner tree, by side of road near a small branch, along Nichols line to branch and up prong NE to Kedar Hinton's path, to red oak in Joseph Parker's line and along his line to main road and along road...

Jonathan Nichols   John Robbins
Himrick Hill   Ma.(+)Robbins
Moses Hare

28 1 Aug 1782--Henry Hill to Thomas Hofler...40 pds...150 acres beginning at a maple, a corner at Richard Freeman's line, running along a line of marked trees NE to Blanchard's line, to a corner, then along his own line to William Hinton's line to said Freeman's line...

James Freeman   Henry Hill
Jethro Meltear
Jacob Outlaw

29 19 Aug 1782--Demcy Parker to Demcey Oadom...10 pds ___ acres beginning at a line of Thos. Smith's corner tree, a pine, thence running W to Christ. Riddick's line, S along his line to corner tree, a post oak, E to said Smith's line of two gums, his corner trees, then running N along Smith's line...
John Bethey   Demcy Parker
Isaac Pipkin

30 1 Nov 1782--John Shepherd to James Brady Jr...20 pds...20 acres beginning at a gum on Peters Swamp near mouth of Borgadon Branch, running up side of branch by line of marked trees to Thomas Pearce's line, along his line to said swamp and down swamp...
Thomas Burgess   John Shepherd
David Rice Best
William Vann

31 5 Nov 1782--John Thomas to Cyprian Cross...80 pds...200 acres beginning at a pine in Cabin Swamp, Francis Brinkley's corner tree, up swamp to oake, James Skinner's corner tree, along his line to a corner white oak, running Skinner's line to corner pine in Charity Ellis line and along her line to Aaron Ellis, to said Brinkley's line and running edge of sand banks along a small branch to a blac_ gum in branch and up branch and Brinkley's line to a pine, Jesse Vann's corner tree, along Vann's line, another tract of land, and along his line to side of a marsh, then running a line of marked trees to said Brinkley's...
                                          John (+) Tomas
Jesse Vann   Elisabeth(+)Tomas
John Odom
Elisha Brinkley

32 17 Sep 1781--Thomas Fullington to Alex. Eason...4 pds 10 sh...25 acres beginning at a red oake stump, a corner tree of said Fullington, along Jesse Eason's line to run of Mill Swamp, to Seth Eason's line and along his line...
David Small   Thomas (H) Fullinton
William Taylor

33 1 Aug 1782--Henry Hill to James, Benjamin, Pashents, Sarah, Nancy, Elizabeth, Darkis and Christian Robbins, Indians...5 pds...30 acres beginning at a pine corner tree in Seasbrook Wilson's line, S along a line of marked trees to dead white oake, a corner tree, at edge of Flat Pond, down pond to a sweet gum...
James Freeman   Henry(H)Hill
Thomas Hofler
Meltear Jethro

34 16 Aug 1782--Jacob Hunter to John Rice...5 pds...100 acres beginning at a pine in ___Lassiter's line, NE to Henry Hill's oald patent, S along line to pine, corner tree and W along line of marked tree...
Isaac Hunter   (unsigned)
Isaac Hill

35 5 Feb 1782--James Gregory and wife, Jane, to John Walton...80 pds...100 acres beginning at lower end of Fourt Neck Branch running branch to a popular, then along branch to Jacob Hunter's line, along branch to Bennetts Creek Swamp and along swamp...
                                          James Gregory
Robert(R)Taylor   Jane Gregory
Jethro Lassiter
Thos. Garrett

36 17 Feb 1783--Seasbrook Wilson to John Baker...10 pds...100 acres beginning at George Williams' corner, running S to corner beach, Alston's line, W to Coles Creek and up creek...
Elisha Copeland   Seasbrook Wilson
James Brady

37 6 Dec 1782--James and Jean Gregory to John Walton...50 pds... 50 acres beginning at Seasbrook Hinton's line in Gabriels Branch, along his line to Indian Town Road and down road to said branch, a line of David Hill and Himrick Hill, to Henry Hill's line, to a branch and up branch...
Thomas Hofler   James Gregory
Hardy(X)Brown   Jean(x)Gregory
Willis Parker

38 2 Mar 1782--Jethro Miltear to Evan Murphery...50 pds...two 50 acre tracts; 1st beginning at a swamp, to red oak near fence whare Thomas Taylor formerly lived, E to red oake, a corner tree, up Phelp's line to oald Indian line and down line. Second tract begins at a pine near outside of Bennetts Creek Pocosin, down side to a pine corner tree, W along line of marked trees to a hicory, a corner tree on oald Indian line and along line...
Sam. Baker   Jethro Miltear
William Baker

39 15 Aug 1783--Thomas Norris and wife, Sarah, to Benjamin Eure...10 pds...20 acres, being part of deed of Andrew Hambleton, beginning at a corner pine of Charles Eure's, running John Eure's line, corner at red oake, N to pocosin, E to said Charles and S...
Jesse Harrell   Thomas Norris
Asa Harrell
Selah Sparkman

40 1 Aug 1783--William Boothe to John Robbins...30 pds...50 acres, part of land he bought of Henry Boothe, beginning at a pine, said Robbins corner tree, on small branch that makes out of Ware Neck Branch, up branch N to a gum, said Robbins corner tree and along his line...
Jonathan Nichols   William(+)Booth
John Robbins Jun.

41 13 Jun 1783--Edward Howell to David Cross, both of Nancamond, Va. 90 pds...300 acres on Chowan River in Gates Co., being land whereon John Watson formerly lived, beginning at a pine at river bank at said Howell's line, to Benton's line, binding thereon and up river...
David Howell   Edward Howell
Michal Howell
Abel Cross

42 23 Nov 1782--Daniel Spivey to Moses Spivey...100 pds...1000 acres on E side of Chowan River, beginning at a gum in Benets Creek running SW to a white oake in Troy(?), then W to center of 3 birch in Seasbrook Wilson's corner, SW to a maple to Coles Creek, SE to Jesse Harrell's line to a cypress at mouth of Herring(?) Creek, then down Sarum Creek to Chowan River and down river to Waters Landing to E side of bounds about in Benets Creek and along creek...
James Brown   Daniel Spivey
Willis Brown

43 10 Jul 1783--William Booth to Thomas Brickell...10 sh...4 acres beginning at a corner tree on said Brickell's line, to mouth of Spring Branch, running up oald mill swamp to main road, along road to said Brickells...
Demcy Bond   William Booth

44 1 Jan 1780--John Robarts to John Barrett...300 pds...80 acres lying between Catrin_ Creek Swamp and Warrick Swamp, beginning at a white oak, a corner tree at an elbow, a white gum in William Kelley's line, down line of marked trees to line formerly James Eason's, to Jesse Eason's line and down his line to a corner pine in Jacob Eason's line and down his line and through pondy place to a white oak that formerly stood in John Eason's line and down line of marked trees...
Levi(+)Eason   John Robberts
Eddy (+)Lilley
Joseph Riddick

45 8 Jul 1783--Samuell Smith to William Hinton...40 pds...100 acres joining land of William Boyce, beginning at a gum, said Smith's corner tree in Francis Pugh's line, along said Smith's line N to patent line, to James Knight's corner tree in Jonathan William's line, through pocosin, along Knight's line N to corner pine of said Boyce's and along his line SW to said Pugh's...
William Harriss   Samuell Smith
Seth Riddick
John Rice

46 19 Jul 1783--Henry Hill and wife, Elisabeth, to Henry Griffin...164 pds...100 acres beginning at a red oake, a corner tree, to a post oake on line of children of Nan Robbins, along their line to Seasbrook Hinton's, up his line to Benets Creek road and running road to Blanchard's line and down it...
William Vann   Henry Hill
Jonathan Nichols   Elisabeth Hill
William (+)Boyce

47 17 Feb 1783--Samuell Smith to James Knight...100 pds...150 acres joining land of William Boyce, beginning at gum, Seth Riddick's corner tree in Thomas Smith's line, along Smith's line to Jonathan Williams and along his line NE to a pine, then through pocosin NE to said Boyce's, to corner pine of White Pot Land in his old line, to said Riddick's corner gum and SW...
William Harriss   Samuell Smith
John Rice

48 16 Aug 1783--Jacob Sumner and wife, Sarah, to Willis Parker, all of Nansemond Upper Parish...56 pds 5 shs...250 acres, being part of patent granted to Richard Parker 16 Jun 1714, beginning at mouth of a branch that issueth out of Peter Parker's mill pond, from thence to marked white oak, by a line of marked trees binding on said Peter's land county line and W along county line to fork of Little Mare Branch and down branch to white oake near said Peter's mill pond..
James Sumner   Jacob Sumner
William Draper   Sarah(X)Sumner
Willis Wiggens

49 13 Aug 1783--Christian Lassiter to her son, Aaron 220 acres...
deed of gift and was given to her by her father, Joseph Booth; land
binds on Isaac Harrell, John Rice and Samuell Harrell's land...
David Rice   Christian(L)Lassiter
John(X)Jones

50 11 Feb 1783--Moses Blanchard to Jacob Bagley...30 pds...78 acres
in two tracts, being part of land bought of Elisha Hunter; first
tract of 33 acres begins at forked red oak in dividing line between
said Blanchard and Bagley, NE to post oake, said Bagley and Henry
Walton's corner, along Walton's line SE to a branch and NE along
branch. Second tract of 35 acres begins at a maple on said Bagley
and Blanchard lines, NW to said Bagley and Abner Blanchard's line,
to a gum by oald road, along road...
Joseph Riddick   Moses Blanchard
Ephriam Griffin

51 23 May 1781--Thomas Tyne of Edgecomb Co. to Soloman King...600
pds...plantation he purchased of John Deloach in said Co. and all
land, Negroes and estate in North Carolina and Virginia, including
Negroes Cra___ Rose and Beck and man James...
George Dunn   Thos. Tine
Bersheba King
Catherine King
Sarah Dun_

52 16 May 1782--John Robarts to Charles Roundtree...40 pds...90 acres
beginning at a pine on SE side of Warrick Swamp, up swamp and along
middle to a gum corner of Shadrack Felton's and along his line to
Deep Branch, up middle to patent line, to a pine in line, then along
a line of marked trees SW to red oak near patent line and along line...
Nathaniel Spivey   John (h)Robards
John Roundtree

53 1 Feb 1783--James Parker to son, Amos...deed of gift of goods,
chattels, land, horses, cattle and Negroes...
William Arnold   James Parker
Josiah Brinkley

54 22 May 1782--Jeremiah Lassiter to Jethro and Timothy Lassiter...
2500 pds...100 acres beginning at David Hayes tree, a cypress, along
his line to a post oak in Indian line and along that line to a branch corner tree in Ready Branch, joining Minchews' line and down
branch to run of creek and down creek...
Bond Minchew   Jeremiah Lassiter
John Rice

55 12 Sep 1782--Peter Piland to Edward Piland...$____...100 acres,
part of patent granted to James Hambleton, beginning at Long Branch,
running up main of Sarum Swamp to white oak, W along line of marked
trees to ___ Branch...
David Umphlet   Peter(+)Piland
Job Umphlet
Thomas Robberson

56 17 Feb 1783--Henry Holland of Upper Parish of Nansemond to John
Wallis...70 pds...150 acres on N side of Chowan River near place called

Caletes Dowrey beginning on E side of river pocosin at a new marked pine in valley, running valley S to a corner tree, bargained in patent to Upaphratitus Benton, along his line and up pocosin...
John Parker   Henry Holland
Stephen Eure

57 17 Feb 1783--John Robbins to Thomas Travis...75 pds...150 acres beginning at a popular, said Robbins and Jonathan Lassiter's corner tree on side of Wier Neck Branch, SE to pine by road and along road to Lassiters line and along his line, reserving 5 acres for his own use on road joining Jonathan Nichol's line...
Jonathan Roberts   John Robbins
Kedar (A) Hinton

58 26 Feb 1783--Jesse Harrell to William Crafford...31 pds 10 shs... 50 acres known as Fort Island beginning at a maple in patent line, along his line and is part of a patent granted to John Rawls, joining Ezeciah Jones and James Brady...
James Parker   Jesse Harrell
Isaac Fryor

59 16 Feb 1783--John Robbins to Dempsey Jones 18 pds...36 acres beginning at a warter oake in John Hare's line in a small branch, NE to Kedar Hinton's path to a red oake, said Hare's corner tree in Joseph Parker's line, along Parker's line to said Hinton's, NW to white oake, then SW...
                                                    John Robbins
Jonathan Robberts
Kedar(+)Hinton

60 20 Feb 1783--Henry Booth to William Booth...225 pds...450 acres on E side of Benets Creek, beginning at a black gum in John Robbins corner in Flat Branch, up branch SW to a red oake, Jo. Brown's corner tree, down branch to said creek,to old mill race, then up race to road and along road to Wier Neck Branch, up branch to fork and along said Robbins line, up NE prong along Robbins line NE...
John Robbins   Henry Booth
Thomas Travis

61 29 Dec 1782--Henry Booth to John Robbins...30 pds...60 acres beginning at a popular, Booth and Robbins corner tree, on side of Deep Branch, along Robbins line E to Flat Branch and along run W to Deep Branch and SE...
                                                    Henry Booth
Thomas Travis   Margret Booth
Elisabeth Travis

62 --Treasury of North Carolina grants to Joseph Riddick 188 acres in Meherrin Swamp on S side beginning at forked maple in fork, said Riddick's corner, SW to a gum, James Sumner's corner, by run of swamp and down run along said Riddick's line SE to Abraham Sumner's line and along his line...   Isaac Hunter
J. Glasgow, sec.   Alex. Martin

63 12 Nov 1783--Daniel Gwin to Moses Hare...100 pds...104 acres on S side of Flat Branch and joining lands of William Ellis, Ezeciah Jones, Ann Gibson, orphans of James Jones, dec. and lands of said Hare...
                                                    Daniel(+)Gwin
Alex. Eason
Benjamin Gordon
John Small

64--Treasury of North Carolina grants to Amos Trotman...41½ acres on W side of Mehering Swamp beginning at post oake in his own line, Joseph Brinkley's corner tree, along his line to a pine, Joseph Griffin's tree, NE to dead post oake and NW to dead red oake, Demcey Trotman's corner tree...
J. Glasgow, sec.
                                       Isaac Hunter
                                       Alex. Martin

64 11 Sep 1783--Francis Saunders to Henry Speight...40 sh...2 acres on E side of Cypress Swamp of Somerton Creek in plantation where said Saunders formerly lived beginning at mouth of Grate Branch, up swamp and down branch...
Uriah Odom   Francis Saunders
Joseph Speight
Thomas Windburn

65 18 Sep 1783--Sarah and Benjamin Saunders to Henry Speight..___ 1 acre on W side of Cypris Swamp of Somerton Creek in plantation whare Joseph Ballard formerly lived opposit_ between the house and swamp joining on upper side of a small pond that has been cleared...
Joseph Speight   Sarah Saunders
Henry Saunders   Benjamin Saunders

66 ____--John Millar to Joseph Speight...$___...a third part of two places surveyed by W. Bell for said Millar when part of Heartford; first, 31 acres lies on SW side, said Speight's mill pond beginning in William Oadom's line and running side of small pond to James Copeland's line, along his line to mill pond and down pond, swamp to Parker's line and along that line to said Odom's line. Second tract of 120 acres is part of said Miller grant on Mudy Creek and river pocosin of Joseph Dickenson's corner running down pocosin and creek to William Craffords and up his line...
Francis Speight   John Millar
Henry Speight

67 17 Nov 1783--Abner Blanchard to Dempsey Blanchard...12 pds...30 acres between Bennetts Creek and Catherain Creek joining on E side of Grate Marsh, beginning at white oak on NE side of marsh, it being corner tree between said Blanchard and Amos Smith and along Blanchard's and Amos Smith's E on Blanchard's line to red oake in Ashleys path, W along line of marked trees...
Timothy Lassiter   Abner Blanchard
Samuell Brown

68 12 Apr 1783--Elisha Hunter to Demsey Bond...5 pds...20 acres of marsh land beginning at mouth of Muddy Creek, running up creek to Conellor? Ditch, crossing part of marsh to Benets Creek and down creek; land is undivided between said Hunter and Thomas Roundtree and is 2/3 part...
Jonathan Robarts   Elisha Hunter
Will Wilkings
Benjamin Saunders

The next three deeds, from State of North Carolina, are for 50 sh for every 100 acres:
69--To Jeremiah Speight...250 acres, an entry of James Cotton's, on N side of Bennetts Creek, beginning at white oak in William Harress corner tree in Morris pecosin, along Harress line NW to Francis Pugh's patent, along line SW to white oak, Henry Smith's corner, along his

line SE to center of three trees, said Harress line and NE...

70--To Jethro Miltear...250 acres on E side of Bennetts Creek beginning at pine on oald Chowan Indian line of side of pocosin, SE down side to two cypress saplings by side of run of Indian Gut, S to run of said creek, to a gum, Indian line corner tree, by run and along line...

71--To James Freeman...111 acres on W side of Caterun Creek beginning at a gum opposite mouth of Poley Branch bridge, out of swamp and up run of said branch SW, then NW to white oak, Jacob Outlaw and John Freemans line and NE...
J. Glasgow, sec.   Alex Martin

72 14 Feb 1783--William Pearce to George Lassiter...25 Spanish dollars...20 acres on W side of Watery Swamp beginning at a tree at the run, along Alphens line to blac_ jack, to head of Ready Branch, down branch to run of swamp joining said Lassiters land and down swamp...   William Pearce
Aron Lassiter
Job Riddick

73 28 Oct 1783--Demsey Odom to Henry Lee...7 pds 4 sh...110 acres beginning at Beaverdam Swamp on a line formerly called John Dukes, along that line to John Drurys, to a corner tree between said Drury, Aron Odom and Jacob Walters, up short Beaverdam swamp to fork, then down to John Webbs line to a branch making out of Beach Swamp and down said branch to a pine at head, SE to Beaverdam Swamp and down swamp...   Demsey(+)Odom
John Bethey
Thomas Vann
John Boyce

74 28 Nov 1783--William Harriss to Samuel Smith 8 pds...50 acres beginning at a pine between Jeremiah Speight and said Harriss, on said Speight's line and up line of marked trees to a pine, a corner tree, said Smith and Speight's and along line...
Seth Riddick   William Harriss
John Rice
Jonathan Smith

75 18 Nov 1783--Robart Parker Sr. to Willis Parker, both of Hertford Co...5 sh...100 acres beginning on N side of Bennetts Creek at the run, along line to warter oak on E side of main road to corner tree, along row of marked trees SE to a pine corner tree in branch and down branch to creek and down creek...   Robart Parker
George Williams
Jacob Bagley

76 20 Nov 1783--Robert Parker Sr. to Robert Jr., both of Hertford Co...5 sh...100 acres in said county, beginning at a pine in a branch, Willis Parker's corner tree, runing row of marked trees SE to back swamp, along swamp to Bennetts Creek and down creek to said Willis line.
George Williams   Robart Parker, Sr.
Jacob Bagley

77 20 Oct 1783--Jeremiah Speight to Samuell Smith...56 acres, part of a patent granted to him 18 Aug 1783, with which said Speight, Smith and William Harriss are jointly concerned, beginning at a

blazed pine in said Harriss line, along his line E to a black gum, his corner tree of new survey and along Harriss new line W to white oak, said Smith's corner and along line...
                                                Jeremiah Speight
William Harriss
Joseph Riddick

The following three deeds are from State of North Carolina for land grants and signed by Alex. Martin, governor, and James Glasgow, secretary:

78--To Thomas Hunter...250½ acres beginning at a pine in Cypress Branch, Jacob Pearce's corner tree, SW to a pine, NW to a pine, John Gordon's corner tree, SW to red oake, said Gordon's corner tree, NW to a pine in Elisha Hunter's line and along said line S to three pines, SE to a live oak and NE...

79--To Thomas Hunter...279½ acres on Snake Branch pocosin beginning at a pine, Palatia_ Walton, dec. corner tree, along his line SW to white oake, NE to gum, said Walton's corner tree in Abraham Spivey's line, along his line SW to Moses Blanchard's corner tree and along his line SE to a gum, Henry Walton's corner tree and along his line...

80--To Seth Riddick...27½ acres beginning at a pine, Christopher Riddick's corner tree in Joseph Figg's line, along his line NW to Demsey Parker's line and along his line to two gums, said Parker's corner in Thomas Smith's line and along Smith's line S to said Figgs and along his line NW...

81 25 Aug 1785--Sophia Riddick to Sir Charles Milfield: "I rec'd yours of this day in which I was sumthing surprised at the impertness of same now especially as you was writing to a person who you consider as being such an obstructor of the peace of your family. Your observations on the preceding part of your preamble that if you was not misinformed was well thought of--whoever has informed you if anyone did that I ever concerned myself in endeavoring to make a mach in your family would probably be of little satisfied to tell me so as I should have been to of seen you at your house when I set out from Hertford for that purpose as you have been so kind as to let me know you shall ever look upon me as an enemy I have little reason to suppose it would be worth my painesto inform you what I...I must confess had a fully considered the acompy of the gentlemen who I made myself so very busy in indeavoring to disgrace I might suppose ....

VOL. 1

1--State of North Carolina to Moses Hare... (Note: Descriptions and names are missing from several of the first 20 deeds and some page numbers are repeated.)

2--Guy Hill to Joseph Brinkley...2 pds...25 acres...Trotman's corner tree...   Guy Hill
____Brinkley
____rym ( )

3 25 Mar 1784--Peter Pilant to Thomas Brickle...24 pds 8 sh ___ beginning at a corner tree adjoining Demsey Phelps's land, then W to Charles Lawrences, NE and along Phelps line...
Jonathan Roberts   Peter(X)Pilant
___ Williams
3 Feb 1785

4 28 Jul 1784--Samuell Smith to Seth Riddick...20 pds...50 acres joining land of Thomas Smith beginning at a gum in said Thomas' line, through pocosin to a gum in William Boyce's line near Bakers Folly then along patent line to a pine in William Vann's line and along his line SW to a pine corner of Demsey Parker's and along his line....
Witness missing

5 12 May 1783--John Randolph Wilkinson to James Sumner...150 pds...100 acres beginning at a gum in Orapeak Swamp opposite a ditch, a former boundry between Luke Sumner and said Wilkinson, along ditch N to a corner tree between the parties, W to a large pine in White Oake Branch and along line of marked trees to a corner tree between said Wilkinson and William Matthias, being a water oak pine, to upper end of White Oak Neck and binding on said swamp...
Jethro Sumner   John R. Wilkinson
Judeah Wilkinson
Henry King
James (JJ) Jones alig Sketo
May Session 1783

7 5 May 1784--Lot Rogers to Enos Rogers...80 pds...50 acres beginning at fork of Lady of Honour Branch, up branch to Dilday's line and along that line to Goff Folle Branch, running said branch to patent line and along patent to Edw'd Warren's line and along his line...
James Arline   Lot Rogers
_____ Lang
Elisha Cross
May Ct 1784

8 8 Mar 1784--Josiah Jordan of Nancemond to Peter Pilant...35 pds 50 acres beginning at a white oake, a corner tree adjoining Demsey Phelps, W to Lawrences land, NE to neck and along Phelps line...
Thos. Brickell   Josiah Jordon Jun
May Ct 1784

9 15 May 1784--Amos Trotman to Joseph Brinkley...3 pds...3 acres, part of a plantation...
                                                       Amos Trotman
Francis Brinkley
_____ y (X) Lilley

10 3 May 1784--William Walters and Elizabeth Walters, relick of James Bray Walters, dec. to John Barg of Nancemond...60 pds...50 acres on S side of Mare Branch beginning at a water oak in mouth of small branch at E end, W by line of marked trees to patent line; said land was conveyed by said William to his son, said James Bray, who in his will 12 Feb 1784 gave to said William...
Jethro Sumner   William Walters
William Barr   Elizabeth Walters
Esther(E) Mathews
3 Feb 1785

11 11 Dec 1783--Sarah Sanders to her son, Henry...deed of gift of 50 acres given to her by her father, Henry King, dec., on S side of Cypress Swamp, beginning at mouth of Great Branch and running up branch to patent line, down to swamp...
Joseph Speight   Sarah(S)Saunders
Henry Speight   Benjamin(X)Saunders
3 Feb 178

12 23 Jun 1783--Moses Blanchard to Kedar Hill...40 pds...210 acres, whereon he resides, beginning at oak, Henry Waltons, Jacob Bagley and said Blanchard's corner tree, of land he sold said Bagley, standing by old road, along Bagley's line to Thos. Spivey's line NE to land said Blanchard bought of Elisha Hunter...
Jacob Bagley   Moses Blanchard
Mary(x) Walton

13 10 Jan 1784--John Randolph Wilkinson to William Matthias...100 acres on E side of Orapeak Swamp joining James Sumner...
Lewis Jones   John Randolph Wilkinso(
Jno. Powell   Judeh Wilkinson

14 17 May 1784--Thomas Hunter to Demcey Trotman...20 pds...50 acres beginning at a pine, Presila Walton's corner tree, along her line to read oak, her other corner tree, along her line to black gum, Simeon Stallings corner tree and along his line...
William Beremon   Thos. Hunter
Mary Walton
Aug Ct 1784

16 1 Sep 1783--Richard Bond to John Walton...30 pds...15 acres beginning at a white oak in John Jones line and along his line to a sweet gum, along line of marked trees N to a water oak and SE...
Jeremiah Speight   Richard(+)Bond
Richard Bond
Aug Ct 1784

22 24 Apr 1784--John Miller to William Crafford...9 pds 10 sh...100 acres patented to him in 1782, beginning at William Arnolds line on Wynns Rode, along road to Miller and Craffords line, across to Mud__ Creek...
William Harriss   John Miller
Jesse Barnes

23 10 Aug 1784--William Hinton to Isaac Harrell...5 pds...402 acres, including 50 acres he held by a former deed, and all part of patent granted to said Hinton 13 Aug 1753, beginning at a pine, said Hinton's corner tree in a small branch, down middle to Aaron Lassiters, along his line NW to red oak, said Lassiter's corner tree in Harrells line, to a gum and post oak in Josiah Granbery's line and along his line to said Hinton's line, and along a line of marked trees E to side of Piney Woods and along pocosin to patent line...
Absalom Blanchard   William Hinton
Monicuy Blanchard
Mourning(X)Elles
Aug Ct 1784

23 3 Jan 1784--Jonathan Trader to Peter Piland...100 silver ____...
75 acres that he bought of Robert Parker Sr. 11 May 1781...
Law. Baker   Jonathan(X)Trader
Wm Brooks
Aug Ct 1784

25 16 Sep 1783--William Wallis to Moses Jones...15 pds...50 acres beginning at a white oake, a corner tree in branch, running line of marked trees to a corner black gum in Jesse Barnes line, along his line to prong of Pine Swamp and along swamp to said branch; is part

of patent granted to William Horn 1 Apr 1723...
Jesse Harrell   William(x)Wallis
Moses(MJ)Jones
Feb Ct 1784

27 14 Apr 1783--James Skinner to John Odom...17 pds 13 sh...50
acres joining said Odom's line and part of patent to said Skinner...
Jesse Vann   James Skinner
Sarah Vann
Feb Ct 1784

29 2 Dec 1783--John Barrett to George Eason...50 silver dollars...
80 acres beginning at a corner pine joining Levi Eason's line, down
line to corner pine in Jacob Eason's line to post oak in George Eason's line, formerly John Easons, and NE...
Levi(x)Eason   John Barrett
Jacob(x)Eason
Feb Ct 1784

31 27 Dec 1783--John Felton and Elizabeth Felton to Jonathan Cul-
lens...15 pds 10 sh...5 acres, part of deed taken out of Hackleys
Patent, beginning at pine on E of road, running row of marked trees
to a pine standing in a pond and along pond to road and down road...
William Felton   John(+)Felton
William Green   Elizabeth(+)Felton
Willis Sparkman
Feb Ct 1784

33 25 Aug 1783--Amos Lassiter to James Lassiter...20 pds...50 acres
beginning on S side of Benets Creek at sipres, a corner tree between
said Amos and land of Thomas Hobbs, dec., up Urnn Mine Branch to a
popular, thence running James Gregory's line to spanish oak, being
corner tree between said Gregory and Ann Minards line, running her
line W to read oak on E side of Deep Gut Swamp and down run to Benets Creek...
Demsey Blanshard   Amos(+)Lassiter
Dinishus Minchew
Feb Ct 1784

34 21 Aug 1783--Ann Minard to James Lassiter...6 pds...50 acres
between Benets Creek and Catrin Creek beginning at a red oak on S
side of Wattre Swamp Road on E side of Deep Gut Branch, running E
to a Spanish oak, it being corner tree between said Minard and James
Gregory, running Gregory's line S to white oak, corner tree between
said Gregory and land of John Minchew's desert, along Minchew's line
SW to Deep Gut, down gut...
Dempsey Blanchard   Ann(X)Minard
Amos(X)Leasetor
Feb Ct 1784

35 24 Jan 1783--Jeremiah Jordan to Thomas Brickle...40 pds...40
acres beginning at Spring Branch and running up branch to Jonathan
Lassiter's line, down branch...
Jonathan Roberts   Jeremiah Jordan
Jethro Meltear

38 10 Jan 1777--Samuel Green of Chowan Co. to Jonathan Lassiter...

25 pds...170 acres beginning at a pine, a corner tree, running NW
to an oak, E to a great white oak and pond and S...
Seanar Lassiter   Samuel Green
Feb Ct 1784

39 15 Jan 1784--Matthias Green and wife, Zeruah, to John Felton...
75 pds 6 sh...122 acres on w side of Coles Creek Swamp, beginning
at Samuel Eure's corner that was formerly John Harriss, running to
pine near Pine Branch, to mouth of branch near Panter Island, through swamp...
Thomas(x)Felton   Matthias(X)Green
Jesse Harrell   Jeriah Green
Asa Harrell
Feb Ct 1784

41 25 Oct 1784--Edwin Sumner to Henry Griffin...20 pds...42 acres,
plantation whereon he now lives, beginning at main road,   running
line of marked trees and back to road...
Jethro Sumner   Edwin Sumner
Edward Doughtie
William Vann
Nov Ct 1784

43 5 Mar 1784--Stephen Cross and Henry Dilday Sr. to Enos Rogers...
36 pds...106 acres beginning at a marked tree at James Lang's line,
running by line of marked trees to road, down old road to Robert
Rogers' line, along this line to said Langs and along his line...
James Arline
Robert Parker   Stephen(*)Cross
Absila(+)Odom   Henry(H)Dilday

45 14 Nov 1784--Ephram Griffin and Sarah Griffin to Moses Hill...
200 pds...150 acres whereon said Hill now lives...
Kedar Hill   Ephraim Griffin
John Hofler   Sarah(X)Griffin
Guy Hill
Nov Ct 1784

47 12 May 1784--William Hunter to Demsey Trotman...5 pds...6 acres
beginning at white gum at run of Meherrin Swamp to a sweet gum,
Elisha Hunter's corner tree, down side of swamp by line of marked
trees to sweet gum, a corner tree, then to run of swamp...
John Hofler   William Hunter
Ezekiel(+)Trotman
Aug Ct 1784

49 12 Nov 1784--Ephriam Griffin to Thomas Trotman...40 pds...80 acres
beginning at a pine, Henry Walton's, then along a line of marked trees
to a red oak, Demsey Trotman's corner tree, to a pine, a corner tree
of Jacob Bagley, and along road to said Walton's line and down his
line...
Thomas Hurdle   Ephriam Griffin
John Walton
Nov Ct 1784

50 9 Apr 1784--William Harriss to Humphrey Hudgins...150 pds...374
acres on W side of Benets Creek, beginning at large red oak in head
of Wildcat Branch, near line laid off for Francis Pugh's patent,

4 or 5 chains from a pine stump and small saplings at corner of
Dukes' clearing, supposed to be Pughs, SE to red oak, SW to water oak
in Morris Pocosin, NW to a pine near Thomas Smith's corner tree,
being a corner tree of new survey to Jeremiah Speight, standing in
line of blazed trees and NE...
             William Harriss
Isaac Miller
Francis Miller
Nov Ct 1784

52 17 Jan 1783--Perselar Lassiter to Aaron Blanchard...10 pds...50
acres between Wattree Swamp and Great Marsh, beginning at post white
oak, being line between Soloman Alphen and William Perce, running
to corner red oak between Reuben Lassiter and said Blanchards line,
then along Blanchard's line to red oak, being corner tree between
said Persiller and said Blanchard...   Persiler(x)Lassiter
Rachal(x)Lassiter
Demsey Blanchard
Nov Ct 1784

53 26 Oct 1784--Elisha Parker to James Pruden...40 pds...100 acres
at Gum Branch, beginning at a marked pine in small branch running
to land of William Trevathan's line and along his line...
Isaac Miller   Elisha Parker
John Parker
Mary Parker
Nov Ct 1784

55 16 Feb 1784--John Eure to Samuel Taylor...4 pds...6 acres on N
side of Sypris Swamp beginning at Taylor and Norris' corner gum,
running Norris line to path and along path that goes over swamp and
running down swamp; is part of a patent granted to William Horn 22
Jan 1713...
Stephen Eure   John(x)Eure
Benjamin Eure
Nov Ct 1784

57 15 Dec 1784--John Walton to William Hinton...32 pds...32 acres
of timber pecosin beginning at a sweet gum in John Webb, dec. line,
Richard Bond's corner tree and along his line N to a red oak thence
S and along Webb's line...
William Harriss   John Walton
Jethro Sumner
Thomas Hofler

59 5 Oct 1784--Moses Davis, planter, to John Davis...100 pds...100
acres between lines of Thomas Fullington, Soloman Briggs and Jesse
Eason's land, along their lines down Bayles Swamp...
Jesse Eason   Moses Davis
Josiah Briggs
Nov Ct 1784

60 5 Oct 1784--John Davis to Moses Davis...100 pds...185 acres beginning at a pine in branch that is a line of William Hinton and
Josiah Granbery, running NW to main road by line of marked trees,
down road NE to John Walton's line, to said John Davis line, to
corner of Soloman Briggs and William Walton...100 acres is from
deed of Moses Hambleton and 85 acres from Joseah Granbery...
Jesse Eason   John Davis
Josiah Briggs
Nov Ct 1784

62 5 Oct 1784--Demsey Trotman to Ephriam Griffin...50 pds...80 acres beginning at a pine, his own corner tree, along line of marked trees to a red oake, formerly Joseph Griffins, to a pine in Henry Walton's line and along his line to Jacob Bagley's corner pine and along line of marked trees...
Thomas Trotman   Demsey Trotman
John Walton
Nov Ct 1784

63 17 May 1784--Israel Beeman to James Hays...60 pds...100 acres on N side of Bennetts Creek, being patent granted to William Swann 8 Mar 1705/6 beginning at mouth of Hawtree Swamp on Bennetts Creek, up swamp to head of Little Hawtree and through swamp to Bennetts Creek...
William Vann   Israel Beeman
Caleb Savage
May Ct 1784

65 1 Aug 1783--William Booth to Jonathan Nichols...30 pds...50 acres beginning at oak in Flat Branch, John Robbins corner tree, up branch SW to a branch that makes out of Wyer Neck Branch and N along Robbins line...
John Robbins   William (X)Booth
John Robbins Jr.
William(x)Perse

67 13 Nov 1784--Caleb Savage of Nansemond Co., Va. to John Gatling 50 pds...150 acres beginning at Ready Marsh at a pine, a corner tree, NW to Robert Thomas, to a corner tree of Edward ____, with his line to Odom's line, to said branch and on W side of said marsh, being a tract purchased of James Baker 17 Jan 1775...
Sam (S) Cunningham   Caleb Savage
Philip Lewis
John Parker
Feb Ct 1785

68 9 Apr 1784--Kedar Odom to Philip Rogers 12 silver dollars...50 acres beginning at Hardy Williams at main road, along his line to Long Branch and up branch to old path, then up path to main road...
William Vann   Kedar(X)Odom
William Warren
Edward Warren
Feb Ct 1785

70 10 Jan 1785--James Parker to Samuel Thomas...25 pds...50 acres, part of patent granted to Benjamin Parker 21 Feb 1738, beginning at a corner gum in branch, joining Demsey Harrell's line running into Gum Swamp and down swamp to line of marked trees and out of swamp to branch and up branch...
George Hargroves   James Parker
Amelia(x)Hargroves   Ruth(x)Parker
Feb Ct 1785

72 13 Sep 1783--Samuel Harrell to Jesse Harrell...12 pds...50 acres called Fort Island, beginning at a water oak in Great Branch and up branch by line of marked trees to main river pecosin, to corner gum and is part of patent granted to John Webb 1 Apr 1723...
William Crafford   Samuel Harrell
Demsey Harrell
Feb Ct 1785

73 16 Feb 1785--Richard Felton to Stephen Piland...9 pds...149 acres beginning at a gum in Stephen Rogers' line, to a corner oake, running E on Thomas Pilands to a corner gum and along his line...
Thomas(X)Piland   Richard(+)Felton
Asa Harrell
Feb Ct 1785

75 28 Apr 1784--James Copeland Sr., James Winborn and Zachariah Copeland to Joseph Speights...40 sh...2 acres on Chowan River at Gutt Landing and running up river...
Elisha Copeland   James Copeland
Henry Speight   James Winborne
Henry Jones   Zachariah Copeland
Feb Ct 1785

76 6 Dec 1784--James Braddy to Israel Beeman...100 pds...125 acres, part of a patent granted to William Parker for 250 acres 2 May 1706, beginning at a gum on Flatt Branch out of Mills Swamp that makes Hoop Pocosin on W, N to patent line and along patent to Rogers' line and along Rogers' line to Mills Swamp and up swamp...
Mills Lewis   James Brady
Kimbell Pratt
John Lewis
Feb Ct 1785

78 2 Aug 1784--Jesse Benton to Kedar Parker...80 pds...100 acres beginning at a swamp gum in Mare Branch, running SE along line of marked trees to a white oake, NW to a pine near a parth, to Jesse Benton Jr.'s line (or orphen of John Benton, dec.), along line to Mare Branch...
Jethro Sumner   Jesse Benton
Edwin Sumner
Peter Parker
Feb Ct 1785

80 23 Dec 1785--Thomas Smith to Jonathan Smith...50 pds...100 acres beginning at white oake at side of White Pot Swamp, to a red oake corner tree of Samuel Smith and Jonathan Williams, SW along Smith's line to patent line and along that line to red oake and NE to white oak in George Williams line and on his line SE to swamp...
Isaac Miller   Thomas(+)Smith
William Cleavs
Samuel Smith

82 15 Jan 1785--Daniel Holland, Henry Harrison and Henry Norfleet, all of Nansemond Co., Va. to John Brashar...18 pds...77 acres beginning at a marked gum in Gum Swamp, running SW along patent line to a hickory corner tree, SE to small swamp called Juniper, that issueth out of Gum Swamp, bonding on John Folk and down Juniper Swamp; patented by Jacob Odom 1740 and since several conveyances...
Demsey Langston   Daniel Holland
William Hughs Sen.   Henry Harrison
Feb Ct 1785   Henry Norfleet
                                                   Anna(+)Harrison
                                                   Elizabeth(+)Holland
                                                   Henry Holland

83 1 Nov 1784--Abraham Norfleet Sr. and wife, Sarah, of Chowan Co. to James Jones...40 pds...50 acres, which was formerly held by Lewis

Skinner by patent 20 Apr 1711 and known as Wolfpit Neck, lying at head of Loosing Swamp; by said Skinner conveyed to John Foreman in 1713 and by him sold to Elizabeth Norfleet, mother of said Abraham; bounded between land which formerly belonged to Francis Duke and bought out of same patent on Reedy Branch, running by or near said Skinners plantation...

Jacob Gordon
William Hurdle
Seth Eason
William Ellis
Feb Ct 1785

Abraham Norfleet
Sarah Norfleet

84 9 Feb 1785--Jesse Eason to Christopher Pearce...3 pds...13 acres beginning at a red oak in said Pearce's line, along his line to Moses Briggs and late Mills Riddick's line, along Riddick's line to a black gum sapling, a corner tree, and by line of marked trees; part of a patent granted to said Eason 18 Aug 1783...

Jacob Pearce
Abraham Eason
Feb Ct 1785

Jesse Eason

86 13 Nov 1784--Nicholas King to son, Henry...200 pds...400 acres beginning at two gums and water oake, corner tree of Samuel Williams and John Kitor__ line, bounding on Kitor__ line to white oake, a corner tree of Aron Odom and on Odom's line to a small branch that leads to Beech Swamp, up branch to a pine of John Waters' line, along his line to a red oak, which is now post near said Williams road, thence along Demcy Odom's line S to white oake, corner tree between said Odom, King and John Bethay, along line formerly Jesse Bethay's to Jonathan Williams line, thence along Demsey Williams line to a marsh pine at road and along said Williams line...

Jesse (‡)Wiggens
Thos. Allen Moore
Feb Ct 1785

Nicholas(∧)King

87 19 Feb 1785--Demsey Parker to Isaac Parker...2 pds 10 sh...25 acres beginning at Note Pine Swamp at mouth of branch, running up branch to William Van_'s line, along line of marked trees to black gum, a corner tree, along line of marked trees joining Sumner's line, to a red oake, a corner of said Demsey's, and along line of marked trees to the bottom and down bottom to swamp and down swamp...

Miles Parker
Daniel Parker
Mary Parker
Feb Ct 1785

Demsey Parker
Elee(X)Parker

89 2 Dec 1784--John Felton to Noah Felton...47 pds...100 acres beginning at mouth of branch, called Norwest Branch, up N side and binding on marked beach, along line of marked trees of patent line to Norwest Branch to Middle Swamp...

Stephen Harrell
John(X)Jones
Feb Ct 1785

John Felton

90 1 Dec 1784--Charles Lawrance to Thomas Brickell...30 pds...50 acres on Bennetts Creek, beginning at white oake, a corner tree adjoining Demsey Fulks' land, running across pecosin SW to a Spanish oak on S side of shipyard, then straight to creek and up creek

to a bushy top pine near causeway of Bennetts Creek Bridge and a-
long road to corner of said Lawrence's orchard and up road to said
Brickell's fence and along his line...
Ro. Mitchel_   Charles(C)Lawrence
Feb Ct 1785

92 22 Dec 1784--William Cleaves to Thomas Smith...25 pds...200 acres,
excepting 50 acres between said Cleaves and Smith, in White Pot Run
and adjoining said Smith...
Isaac Miller   William Cleaves
Jonathan Smith
Sam'l Smith
Feb Ct 1785

93 16 May 1785--Samuel Smith to William Boyce...40 pds...50 acres,
being part of patent made to him 27 Oct 1784, beginning in said Boyce
line and ___Pugh's patent, along Pugh's line N...
Hum. Hudgens   Samuel Smith
Henry Smith
Jonathan Smith
May Ct 1785

95 27 Oct 1784--State of North Carolina to Job Riddick...50 sh.
for every 100 acres...350 acres in Meherin Swamp beginning at a
cypress sapling on S side, Jacob Hunter's corner tree of an acre
belonging to his mill, along his line S to join James Cotten's
land, to Demcy Cotton's line, to Job Riddick's line, to land opposite run of swamp where it enters into Bennetts Creek, running a-
long his own line to Timothy Lassiter's line and along Bennett
Creek to Thomas Sumner's line and down his line to Richard Bond's
to a birch at end of Bond's Island above mouth of Watry Swamp, N
to said creek, to Meherin Swamp, to Jacob Hunter's flood gates
of his mill... No. 37
A. Pearce, P. sec.   Alex. Martin
J. Glasgow, sec.   gov.

96 27 Oct 1784--State of North Carolina to Simon Stallings...37 sh
for every 100 acres, 150 acres in Catherine Creek Swamp beginning
at a cypress on N side and joining land of Richard Walton, running
to a cypress, corner of said Walton and Nathaniel Spivey, along
Spivey's line to Champion Spivey to swamp side to Jacob Bagley's
line and along his line to Moses Hill, to Kedar Hills, to a white
oak in Guy Hobbs line, to patent line, S on Hobbs line to mouth
of small branch on S side of swamp, to Aaron Hobb's line and along
his line to Thomas Roundtree's, to Seth Stalling's line, to Hurdle's
line, to Charles Roundtrees, to a cypress above Walton's old mill
dam, crossing swamp and NW... No. 46.
A. Pearce, P. sec.   Alex. Martin,
J. Glasgow, sec.   gov.
May Ct 1785

97 25 Sep 25 Sep 1777--Abner Eason to Joseph Riddick of Chowan
Co...37 pds 10 sh...90 acres beginning at red oake corner in Rich-
ard Perces' line, to Ridge Pecosin, to swamp E and is part of a
patent granted to Jacob Docton 13 Feb 1758...
Jacob Eason   Abner Eason
John Rhoads Jr.   of Bartie
May Ct 1785

99 13 Nov 1784--Christopher Pearce to son, Isaac...deed of gift...
100 acres, ½ of 200-acre tract in main Dismal Swamp granted to him
17 Aug 1783, beginning at white oak, corner tree in said Christopher and Moses Briggs' line, S along side of swamp. Also, 50 acres
of high land beginning at white oak, corner tree of said Pearce
and Briggs, along Briggs line to Riddick's orphans line, to desert.
Sarah(SP)Pearce   Christopher(CP)Pearce
Jacob Gordon
May Ct 1785

102 21 Dec 1784--Thomas Smith to William Cleaves...25 pds...50 acres
beginning at white oak, beginning of his patent, down run of White
Pot Swamp, to George Williams' line, SE to pine in Williams' line...
Isaac Miller   Thomas(X)Smith
Samuel Smith
Jonathan Smith
May Ct 1785

104 1 Mar 1785--James Sumner to Willis Wiggens, planter, 60 pds...
250 acres, which was taken by virtue of execution to satisfy a debt
of said Wiggens and bought by Luke Sumners in Chowan in 1708, and
by his decree fell to said James; was land of Thomas Wiggens, father
of said willis, and purchased of Thomas Norfleet and registered in
Chowan. Land lies in Elm Swamp and is bounded by land of Jacob
Sumner, running to land of Thomas Fryor, along his line to land
of John Dardan and along his line to Edward Arnold, along his line
to James Knight, son of Jon___ Knight...
James Knight   James Sumner
William Arnold   Mourning(M)Sumner

106 2 Apr 1785--Willis Wiggens Sr. to James Knight...100 pds...200
acres beginning at red oak in Mill Swamp in said Knight's line, up
run to John Dardans, to William Arnolds, to white oak by side of
Bennetts Creek, down towards Virginia line, to said Knight's line
and along his line...
John Arnold   Willis Wiggens
Marget(+)Frazer   Mary(+)Wiggens
May Ct 1785

108 10 May 1785--Thomas Hunter to Simon Stallings...50 pds...50
acres belonging to him by patent, beginning at red oak and running
to Priscilla Walton's line, to Kedar Hill's line, to Abner Spiveys,
along his line to gum at head of swamp, corner tree between said
Spivey and Walton and along Walton's line...
Benja. Gordon   Thos. Hunter
Jesse Eason
May Ct 1785

(Note: The next deeds, ending with 134, were granted by Alex. Martin, gov. 27 Oct 1784 and signed by J. Glasgow, sec.Reg. 1785)
109--To Thomas Barnes...450 acres on Bull Pocosin on E side of Chowan River, beginning at white oak and 2 pines, said Barnes and __ge
Dun's line, NW to white oak in Henry Kings and along his line S to
Demsey Barnes line, to a red oak, corner tree of said Thomas Barnes
and Edward Warren, and NW... No. 37...

111--To Jesse Eason...553 acres at mouth of Basses Swamp beginning
at a gum and pine, Joshua Small's corner tree on W side of main

desert, to Luke Sumner's line, SW along Jacob Gordons to a red oak and dead pine, corner between said Gordon and Seth Eason and N. No. 38...

113--To Moses Boyce...100 acres adjoining William Walters at a pine in his own line, NE to white oak in Walters line and SE. No. 48

114--To Abraham Sumner...640 acres in Merry Hill Pocosin and beginning on W side of Perquimans River, a corner tree of Robert Riddick's patent, SW to black gum, corner tree in John Powell's line, NW to said Sumners line, to Phillips Old Field, to Joseph Hurdle's line in desart...No. 56

115--To Docton Riddick...325 acres, part of Meherin Swamp and Bennetts Creek, beginning just below Jacob Hunter's mill, NE down side of swamp running to an elm in mouth of Cypress Swamp to run of Bennetts Creek and down creek to swamp...No. 41...

116--To Isaac Miller...15 acres beginning on E side of Stalling's Branch that issueth out of Middle Swamp beginning at white oak, William Powell and said Miller's line, SW binding on Francis Pugh's patent line to William Boyces and NW...No. 53...

118--To Jesse Eason...260 acres beginning at a gum on NW corner of a ridge known as Middle Ridge of Pasquotank Ridge in desert near Basses Swamp, running NE...No. 39...

120--To John Odom...45 acres beginning at center of 3 pines, John Van's and Benjamin Barnes corner tree along NE to hicory and SE to said Barnes and William Copelands corner tree, SW to small swamp and crossing swamp to said Odoms... No. 45...

122--To Samuel Smith...442 acres in White Pot Pocosin beginning at a maple, Boice's corner, SW to a gum in head of said pocosin, to Mathews Parth SW to a post oak in Demsey Parker's line and along his line SE to Thomas Smith's corner and along his line to Jonathan Williams' corner, to a popular and 2 sweet gums nigh the head of _____ Pond in or near Francis Pugh's patent line and along his line... No. 42...

123--To Joseph Riddick...200 acres by Greens Pocosin beginning at a gum, Riddick's own corner tree in N prong of swamp just above Little Dam, NE to a pine near Samuel Green's line, to Joseph Hurdle's line and along his line SW to said Riddick's corner and along his line to a cypress, his and Moses Pearce's corner tree, along Pearce's line to said Riddick's...No. 44...

124--To Mary Riddick...640 acres in main desert beginning at a black gum on W side above Weir Neck Branch, Moses Briggs and Mills Riddick's into desert, along Briggs line to Gordon's corner in mouth of Horsepool Swamp, along desert... No. 43...

126--To William Hinton...470 acres joining Gum Pocosin, beginning at water oak, Hinton's and Moses Davis corner, along Davis line N to Soloman Briggs corner, SE to a pine at said Briggs and Thomas Fullington's corner, along his line SE to Josiah Lassiter's corner tree and along his line S to a pine, said Lassiter and Andrew Harrells corner tree, along Harrell's line to Aaron Lassiter's, NW to said Hinton's patent and up Gum Branch NE...No. 40

128--To Moses Briggs...100 acres on W side of Main Desert beginning at a black gum, said Briggs and Mills Riddicks' corner tree on S side near mouth of Hickory Neck Branch, S to Moses and Christopher Pearce's corner tree in small branch in desert, along their line NW...No. 40...

129--To George Dunn...9 acres on E side of Chowan River joining Henry King and Joseph Speight...No. 51...

131--To George Dunn...389 acres beginning at An Hill Pocosin in Henry King's line at an ash, his corner tree, along his line to a white oak, Joseph Speight's corner tree, N to white oak and red oak, Thomas Barnes corner and along Barnes line N to King's desert line and S... No. 49...

132--To Joseph Riddick...640 acres on W side of desert, Abraham Sumner's corner, along desert NE to William Eason's, E to Sumners and along his line NW... No. 50...

134--To Peter Harrell...199 acres in fork of Chowan River and Cypress Swamp, being land of said Harrell's line by deficiency of his former patent and resurveyed, beginning at run of said swamp where his patent line joins run, along his former line and down side of pocosin...No 55...

135 13 Jul 1785--Andrew Hambleton to Israel Beeman...100 pds...125 acres beginning at a pine, a corner tree in William Umphlett's and running along Charles Eure's line, along row of marked trees to John Eure's line of marked trees to bent of Little Sypris, down Sypris to Hawtree Branch and up run to head...
Stephen Shepherd   Andrew Hambleton
Rachael Beeman
Aug Ct 1785

137 16 Aug 1785--James Sumner, Esq. to Ezekiel Trotman...180 pds... 375 acres, 125 of old patent and 250 by entry, on NE side of Meherin Swamp, being land that formerly belonged to Luke Sumner, dec., beginning in Elisha Hunter's line in middle of said swamp, to Joseph Riddick's line and along his line to his new survey, to a forked maple in N prong of swamp, to Samuel Green, dec. line and along that line to head of Deep Run in place called Old Brakes, along Green and Hunters line to Elisha Hunter's ditch and down ditch...
Jo. Riddick   James Sumner
Seth Riddick
Aug Ct 1785

139 15 Jun 1785--Champion Spivey and wife, Sarah, of Chowan Co. to Jacob Bagley...105 pds...100 acres on Catrin Creek Swamp and binding on lands of Nathaniel Spivey, Thomas Spivey now in possession of Ann Spivey and John B. Walton, to corner tree of said Walton, Simon Stallings, James Walton and Nathaniel Spivey...
Thos. Hunter   Champen Spivey
Ann(x)Gibson   Sarah(+)Spivey
Aug Ct 1785

140 1 Jul 1785--Nathaniel Spivey, planter, to Charles Roundtree... 79 pds...79 acres beginning at 2 pines by road, SE on NW side of Catrin Creek Swamp, up swamp crossing mouth of several branches

to persimmon tree in fork, to oak sapling by main road...
John Roundtree   Nathaniel Spivey
Seth(X)Stallings   Elizabeth(X)Spivey
Aug Ct 1785

142 2 Jul 1785--Moses Spivey to Nathaniel Spivey...53 pds __sh
4 pn...50 acres beginning at a pine in Old Town Road, along line
of marked trees to Warwick Swamp, to William Spivey's line and
along his line to said road and along road...
Charles Rontree   Moses(+)Spivey
Jacob Bagley
___ Roundtree

143 9 Aug 1785--Samuel Smith to William Vann...2 pds...50 acres
beginning at a pine in Demsey Parker's line, NE through pocosin
to a pine in patent line near Bakers and along patent line...
Moses Kittrell   Samuel Smith
Demsey Williams
Joseph (X)Brady
16 Nov 1785

145 13 Jul 1785--Isaac Hunter to David Rice ____50 acres, part of
a patent granted to Jacob Hunter 18 Aug 1783, beginning at gum and
red oak in James Jones, dec. line and along his line to John Rice's
land, N to Aaron Lassiter's in patent line and along line...
W. Creecy   Isaac Hunter
Jas. Rice

146 6 Aug 1785--John Rice to David Rice...93 pds...100 acres, part
of a patent granted to Col. Jacob Hunter, dec. 18 Aug 1783 and con-
veyed to said Rice, lying on each side of Oysterlong Branch beginn-
ing at a line in Aaron Lassiter's line, along his line E to Henry
Hill's old patent line and W...
                                                  John Rice
William Luk   Peggy Rice
Moses Hair
W. Creecy
Aug Ct 1785

148 11 Aug 1785--Jesse Eason to Jacob Pierce...3 pds...43 acres
beginning at white oak and gum by Christopher Pierce's line to his
corner tree; part of patent granted to said Eason 18 Aug 1783...
for 100 acres...   Jesse Eason
Abner Eason
Moses Hill
Aug Ct 1785

149 13 Jul 1785--Israel Beeman to Isaac Pipkin...110 pds...105 acres
part of a patent granted to William Parker for 250 acres 2 May 1706
and beginning at a gum on branch or flatt that issueth out of Mills
Swamp that makes Hoop Pocosin, to patent line, to Rogers line and
along Rogers line to Mills Swamp, to main run...
John Pipkin   Israel Beeman
William(x)Gatling
Aug Ct 1785

150 22 Aug 1785--William Crafford to David Cross...20 pds...100
acres being part of land granted to him 29 Oct 1782 beginning at
a black gum in Gum Swamp, up patent line to Pine Swamp, along line
of marked trees...
Cyprian Cross   William Crafford
Christian Cross
Nov Ct 1785

152 19 Nov 1785--Benjamin Barnes to John Odom...8 pds...10 acres, part of a grant to William Hunter 6 Apr 1722, beginning at an ash in Demsey Barnes line, to a gum in Roberson's line, SE...
Samuel Thomas   Benjamin Barnes
Elisha Harrell
Nov Ct 1785

154 6 Nov 1785--Jesse Dilday to Jacob Walters...30 pds...50 acres beginning at a marked popular in Aaron Odom's line as he sold to Arther Willey, dec., running N to Great Branch, down branch to a line of marked trees, to line that Henry Dilday, dec. sold to John Ross in patent line, then running patent line to Gough Folly Branch...
                                                    Jesse Dilday
___son Howel
John(+)March
Nov Ct 1785

156 8 Sep 1785--John Walton of Chowan Co. to Jethro Meltier...30 pds...100 acres beginning at lower end of Fort Neck Branch, up branch to Jacob Hinton's line, to Bennetts Swamp...
Robert Parker Sen.   John Walton
Jesse(X)Brown

157 21 Nov 1785--John Walton of Chowan Co. to John Powell...65 pds 50 acres beginning in Seasbrook Hinton's line in Gabriel Branch, along his line to Old Indian Town Road, to line of David Hill and Himrick Hill, to mouth of said branch...
John Elliott   John Walton
____ Hare
Nov Ct 1785

158 17 Sep 1785--William Crafford to James Crafford...50 silver dollars...90 acres called Little Island, part of a patent granted to him 17_2, beginning at a chinapin oak in said James line, NW to a pine in Gum Swamp, across line of marked trees to side of swamp and down side...
                                                    William Crafford
James Landen
Nov Ct 1785

160 21 May 1785--William Sumner of Nansemond Co., Va. to Job Riddick...30 pds...200 acres on S side of Bennetts Creek, being part of patent made to Robert Lassiter, dec. 17 Ded 1744, who conveyed it to ____Mizell and by him conveyed to George Lassiter and by him conveyed to Thomas Sumner, joining land of Robert and Timothy Lassiter...
                                                    William Sumner
____ Costen
Jonathan Lassiter
Sarah Alphan
Nov Ct 1785

161 27 Oct 1785--Thomas Green to James Piland...34 pds...80 acres beginning at a water oak on side of run of Coles Creek opposite mouth of Licking Root Branch, up creek to Felton's line, W to fork in said branch and down middle...
John Felton   Thomas Green
Jesse Harrell
Nov Ct 1785

163 19 Nov 1785--John Odom to Benjamin Barnes...8 pds..10 acres, part of a tract granted to him 27 Oct 1784, beginning at red oak at Hunter's corner, running patent line and along line of marked trees to a hickory, Odom and Hunter's corner and along Hunter's line...
Elisha Harrell   John Odom
Samuel Thomas
Nov Ct 1785

164 8 Nov 1785--Daniel Hays to Jacob Hays...20 pds...50 acres on E side of Bennetts Creek beginning at a cypris and running a line of marked trees to line of William Hayes and along his line to said Jacob's line...
Alex'r Eason   Daniel(+)Hays
John Walton
Nov Ct 1785

166 21 Nov 1785--More Carter to Charles Eure...2 pds...30 acres beginning at a holly, corner tree of Samuel Taylor, running along Samuell Brown's line, across pocosin to said Brown and Eure's corner, along Carter's line; is part of patent granted to Henry Hackley 14 Apr 1702...
John (+) Hall   Moore Carter
Whitmel Williams
Nov Ct 1785

168 3 Nov 1785--William Freeman to Samuel Taylor, planters...___pds 10 acres beginning at oak tree on their lines, to a post oak by head of a branch by path, down branch to a sweet gum at swamp, across creek and up Taylor line...
John Walton   Sarah Freeman
John Alphund   William Freeman
Nov Ct 1785

169 13 Aug 1785--William Arnold to John Arnold...145 acres beginning at Gum Branch binding on Micajah Riddick, James Phelps and Abraham Morgan, to a new made line of marked trees dividing premises and James Pruden to a marked tree near branch; part of which land was granted to Richard Berryman 6 Aug 1719 and sold by him to John Lassitor, who sold to Adam Raby; other part was granted to said Lassitor and sold to said Adam , given to son, John, who sold the whole to Lemuel Powell and by him sold to William Trevathan, who sold to Demsey Sumner and by him sold to Edward Arnold, dec....
Charles Horton   William Arnold
James Knight   Kizia Arnold
Willis Wiggens Jr.
Nov Ct 1785

170 6 Oct 1785--Jethro Ballard to Joshua Small 10 pds...25 acres beginning at oak, corner tree in said Jethro's patent, N to a gum in run of Loosing Swamp, up swamp to water oak in Benjamin Gordon's line, along his line to swamp and down swamp; part of patent granted to said Ballard 18 Aug 1783...
John Small   Jethro Ballard
Daniel Gwinn
Nov Ct 1785

171 11 Feb 1786--George Outlaw to his son, James...deed of gift...
all his land in Old Town Neck and plantation whereon he lives, purchased of James Hofler and Jesse Garrett on SE side of Catherine Creek...
John Allen   George (+) Outlaw
____ Hunter
Jacob Outlaw
Feb Ct 1786

172 10 Feb 1786--Josiah Parker Sr. to son James...deed of gift...
100 acres on S side of Mills Swamp, which he bought of Stephen Shepherd 20 Aug 1756, beginning at a pine, a corner tree in Rogers line on S side of swamp, running Rogers line to a white oak, a corner tree on other side of pecosin, E binding on Thomas Piland's line, to a red oak, NW along line of marked trees to chickapin oak in ridge and up swamp...
Lawrence Baker   Josiah (₹) Parker
James Rice
Feb Ct 1786

174 10 Jan 1786--Jesse Barnes to Demsey Barnes...100 pds...450 acres, part of a patent to John Gay 26 Mar 1733, beginning at pine in Reedy Branch, Joseph Ballard and John Walles' corner, W along line of marked trees to Walles' corner in John Odom's line, binding on said Walles' patent line to a pine, William Everett's corner tree, along his line to another corner and S to Reedy Branch, to Jonathan Boyce's corner on William Beesley's line, up middle of branch and on Beesley's line to white oak, Beesley and Odom's corner tree, along dividing line of John Odom and Demsey Barnes and along Barnes' line back to said Branch, thence to a gum...
                                                        Jesse Barnes
John Pipkin
Abel Cross
Feb Ct 1786

175 9 Nov 1785--Will. Wallis to David Cross...20 pds...75 acres, part of tract granted to William Speight in 1719, and sold by him to Henry Holland and by him sold to John Wallis, son of James Wallis and by deed of heirship fell to said William; beginning at said Cross' new patent line, W to David Watson's line, to a line of trees marked by Joseph ____ in 1785 and up Cross' line...
Demsey Barnes   William(+)Wallis
Demsey Williams
Feb Ct 1785

177 11 Feb 1786--Benjamin Saunders to Jesse Saunders...150 pds...
350 acres beginning at dead pine, Joseph Shepherd's corner, along his line to branch that makes out of Gaul Bush Pocosin, to Jesse Saunders line and along his line to William Odom's, to John Miller's, to Flat Sypris Swamp, down swamp; part of patent to Charles Saunders in Hertford Co. 21 Jun 1762...
                                                        Benjamin Saunders
Joseph Speight
Bray Saunders
Henry Speight
Feb Ct 1786

178 6 Feb 1786--James Skiner to John Odom...30 pds...50 acres beginning at a chinapin oak, along line of trees across said land to white

oak in patent line, along that line to Robertson's line; being patent granted to John Hare...
                                                    James Skinner
John Warren
Luten Lewis
Feb Ct 1786

179 20 Dec 1785--Thomas Hamelton to William Vann...30 pds...70 acres beginning at a corner pine in Samuel Eure's line, running along Aaron Harrell's line to corner tree between Samuel Brown and said Harrell, along Brown's line to corner pine between said Brown and William Vann at Deep Branch, to a corner tree in Charles Eure's line, to James Eure's line and along his line to said Samuel Eure and along his line; a part of two patents granted to Henry Hackley 22 Jun 1722...
William Davidson   Thomas Hambleton
Lewis Sparkman
Moore Carter

180 12 Jun 1786--Isaac Hunter to Anthony Mathews...28 pds...180 acres, which he bought at public sale; property of Isaac Walters recovered by court execution by William Walters for debts by said Hunter, sheriff, and known as ____ Island...
William Luke   Isaac Hunter
Holloday Walton
Feb Ct 1786

182 20 Feb 1786--John Baker and wife, Nancy, to Elisha Norfleet... 24 pds...20 acres; being 8th lot of division of land of John and Elizabeth Norfleet's, dec. children, and given to said Bakers in their will, and known as Island and White Oak Spring Marsh, beginning at stake, running N to a line in desert and along line...
Feb Ct 1786   Jno. Baker
                                          Nancy Baker
183 9 Feb 1786--John Arnold to James Pruden...
20 pds...15 acres on S side of Gum Swamp beginning at large oak near Parker's Old Field, down branch by line of marked trees to said Pruden's line...
                                          John Arnold
Abraham Morgan
Ruth(+)Morgan
Turlington(+)Speight
Feb Ct 1786

184 1 Jan 1786--Demsey Ruckes to his son, Joseph...10 pds...100 acres in Peters Swamp, beginning at a chinakopin oak, corner tree between said Ruckes and James Brady, down small branch to main run, to another branch, to run of said Swamp and down course to William Warren's line to corner tree in Holland's line, to said Brady's...
William Davidson   Demsey Rooks
Charles Eure
Thomas Barnes
Feb Ct 1786

185 2 Feb 1786--Hezekiah Norfleet and wife, Mary, to Jacob Norfleet... 19 pds...9th lot of land of John and Elizabeth Norfleet's, dec. children in division of land given in their will, containing 20 acres and called Island and White Oak Spring Marsh. Said Norfleets are from

Nansemond Co., Va...
John Gordon Jr.   Hezekiah Norfleet
Bridget(B)Dawn   Mary(M)Norfleet
John Norfleet

186 2 Jan 1786--Samuel Green to Isaac Green...7 pds...67 acres on
S side of Sypris Swamp beginning at a gum near middle, down swamp
to Peter Harrell's line, along his line to head of Long Pond, up
pond to Samuel Taylor's line and along his line; part of a grant
to Capt. John Alston 12 Jul 1725 and sold by him to Richard Green...
                                                   Samuel Green
William Davidson
____ Eure
____ Umphlet
Feb Ct 1786

188 16 Feb 1786--William King of Bartie Co. to William Walles...
____pds...50 acres on a branch that parts the stiff and sandy land
along Demsey Barnes' line, to a pine, a corner tree, along John
Odom's line to a pine on John Varnal's line to hickory in branch...
Richard Arnold   William King
Morgan Dwyer
Feb Ct 1786

189 13 Jan 1786--John Norfleet and wife, Judah, of Nansemond Co.
to Jacob Gordon...35 pds...20 acres, their lot of land of John
and Elizabeth Norfleet, dec. given to their children in their
will; known as Island and White Oak Marsh beginning at a stake
and running NE to a line in desert and back to stake in head line...
Elisha Norfleet   John Norfleet
James Norfleet   Judah Norfleet
Feb Ct 1786

190 13 Feb 1786--Peter Piland to Edward Piland...13 pds...50 acres
at mouth of Jack's Branch, formerly called the Bridge Branch, running
up branch to Sarum Creek to a pine and running line of marked trees
to Mill Path, crossing Long Branch to a water oak and down branch...
William(X)Williams   Peter(X)Piland
Stephen (X)Piland
Feb Ct 1786

192 13 Apr 1786--Jethro Sumner, sheriff, to Syprian Cross by writ
of Fi Fa issued from court by Law. Baker, C.C. against John Ellis
by Jesse Barnes...26 pds 10 sh 11pn...94½ acres on Cabin Swamp and
is part of a larger tract conveyed to said Ellis by Thomas Barnes,
binding on lands of Aron Ellis and others...
Law Baker   Jethro Sumner
May Ct 1786

194 19 Sep 1785--George Eason to Timothy Lassiter...100 pds...107½
acres, part of larger grant to Lewis Conners of Norfolk Co. and John
Keyton of Nansemond Co. in 1695, formerly property of Thomas Barnes,
dec. and willed by him to his son, William, and by him sold to said
Eason, on S side of Bennetts Creek and known by Maiden Hair Neck,
beginning at said Lassiter's line at a branch and running nearly as
his cartway leads SW to said Eason's field, SW to a pine in Richard
Bonds's corner near main road and along his line NE to a pine, to
Job Riddick's and Lassiter's corner tree, to said branch and down...
Job Riddick   George Eason
Isaac Costen
May Ct 1786

196 17 May 1786--William Booth to Demsey Jones Jr...73 pds...100 acres near Bennetts Creek Bridge beginning on S side of road leading to creek at an oak, NE to Old Field near path and SE...
Joseph Jno. Sumner
William Gordon
May Ct 1786
William Booth
Elizabeth(+)Booth

198 6 Apr 1786--Dinishus Minchew and his mother, Hannah, to Demsey Bond...125 pds...206 acres beginning at a pine in Robert Riddick's line on N side of Indian Swamp to a marked white oak, along a line of marked trees to a pine, a corner tree between said Minchew and George Lassiter Sr., along Lassiter's line to Augustus Minchew, along their line to Cader Hinton's, from there running Joseph Parker's line to white oak in a small branch that makes out of Indian Swamp, down branch to run of said swamp...
Demsey Blanshard
Rich'd Bond
May Ct 1786
Dinishus(X)Minchew
Hannah(X)Minchew

200 8 Apr 1786--Demsey Bond to George Outlaw...190 pds...200 acres N side of Chatariane Creek beginning at a pine standing on a small island near side of creek opposite Blanshard's corner bridge, up creek and binding on Beaver Dam Swamp, up swamp to a cypress, a corner, by line of marked trees to a branch known as Tarkill Branch, down branch to Juniper Pecosin, to land purchased from Henry Hill, by that is to say including land purchased by Elisha Hunter of Henry Hill, dec., being tract granted to Chowan Indians...
James Foreman
____(P)Outlaw
Robert (R)Ward
May Ct 1786
Demsey Bond

201 13 Feb 1786--Moses Blanshard to John Hofler of Perquimans Co... 130 pds...210 acres, granted to Elisha Hunter in 1783, sold to Kedar Hill and bought by said Blanshard, beginning at a post oak, said Blanshard, Henry Walton and Jacob Bagley's corner tree, of land sold to said Bagley 5 Dec 1766, to said Bagley's corner tree of another piece of land said Blanshard sold to him on S side of old road joinsaid Blanshard's land, to Spivey's line to forked red oak...
Ro. Riddick
Thomas Trotman
Kedar Hill
May Ct 1786
Moses Blanshard

203 8 Apr 1786--Edward Allen and wife, Betty; Mary Reid and Catey Reid of Nansemond Co. to Henry Forest...220 pds...300 acres, Old Quarter, beginning at mouth of Watery Branch where it joins Bennetts Creek, up run binding on line of Jeremiah Speight, which was part of said patent, to mouth of another branch in Henry Smith's line, to Thomas Smith's line, to a white oak where said Smith's line makes a corner known as Soloman Alston's corner tree, binding on line which was formerly Joshua Allen's, now Sumner's, to run of Bennetts Creek and up creek...
Demsey Trotman
Jonathan Smith
May Ct 1786
Edward Allen
Betty Allen
Mary Reid
Catey Reid

206 26 Jul 1785--Samuel Smith and wife, Elizabeth to Henery Forest...
40 pds...75 acres, part of tract taken by patent by Thomas Smith in
1780, beginning at a red oak, Jonathan Smith's corner tree, running
NW to Williams' line and along line of marked trees...
Jonathan Smith   Samuel Smith
Stephen Smith
Henry Smith
May Ct 1786

208 8 Mar 1786--George Dunn to Francis Speight...5 pds...9 acres on
Flat Cypris Swamp in corner of Great Pocosin, beginning at an ash,
Henry King's corner tree, along his line to white oake, Joseph Speight's corner, along his line to center of two white oak and a red
oak, said Speight's other corner on swamp; said land was granted to
said Dunn 27 Oct 1784...
Joseph Speight   George Dunn
Rachael Lawrence
Henry Speight
May Ct 1786

209 11 Feb 1786--John Miller to Francis Speight...6 pds...62 acres
of sand banks land beginning on William Odom's line, along his line
to James Copeland's, then along his line to line of sliped trees between Joseph Speight and said Miller, to Odom's line; is part of a
grant of 92 acres made to said Miller on Speight's Mill Pond 1782...
Phillip Lewis
Tomas Wood Jr.
Jimmia Wood
May Ct 1786

210 22 Jan 1786--Elisha Copeland of Upper Parish, Nansemond Co. to
Henry Speight...75 pds...75 acres of sand banks adjoining Joseph
Speight's Mill Pond beginning at Zachariah Copeland's line in edge
of marsh running to Henry King's land on low ground and bounded by
his line...
Joseph Speight   Elisha Copeland
Francis Speight
Sol'm Freeman

211 4 Jan 1786--Thomas Brickell of Hertford Co. to William Lewis...
200 pds...82 acres, whereon he formerly dwelt, beginning at a white
oak stump near the run at forks of road, NW to Old Mill Swamp, up
swamp to Jonathan Lassiter's line and along his line...
Isaac Hunter   Thomas Brickell
John Moran
Humphrey Hudgins
May Ct 1786

212 3 Mar 1786--Elisha Parker to Peter Parker...5 sh...125 acres
whereon said Peter liveth, beginning at contry line on Mill Dam
Branch, down branch to a marked gum nigh branch, along line of marked trees to marked white oak, to branch and down branch and along
line of marked trees to Little Mare Branch to mouth of Bay Branch
to a chesnut oak, Moses Hines corner tree, binding on his land
and up Bay Branch to contry line...
Demsey Williams   Elisha Parker
Abraham Sumner
Josiah Benton
May Ct 1786

215 5 Apr 1786 Charles Vaughn and wife, Nancy, of Nansemond Co. to George Hargrove...27 pd 16 sh...100 acres beginning at a corner in patent line on W side of Gum Swamp, to a popular near John Taylor's line on W side of Juniper Swamp, along line of marked trees and up swamp to a pine, Jethro Harrell and William Vaughns corner, formerly William Harriss, along line of marked trees; being part of a patent granted to Francis Speight 27 Jul 1743...
John Harrell   Charles Vaughn
Daniel Holland
John Sanders
May Ct 1786

216 29 Dec 1785--Samuel Thomas Sr. to his son, James...deed of gift of 100 acres bought of William Powell Sr. 13 Aug 1777...
William Harriss   Samuel Thomas
William(+)Thomas
May Ct 1786

218 8 Feb 1786--James Lassitor to John Whels...28 pds...50 acres between Bennetts Creek and Cathran Creek, beginning at red oak on E side, running E on said Lassiter's line to Watrey Swamp road, to James Gregory's line and along his line to white oak, being a corner tree between Agustine Minchew and said Gregory, along Minchew's line and down run of said gut...
Amos(+)Lassiter   James Lassitor

219 22 Oct 1785--Jethro Benton Jr. to Thomas Coak and Francis Asbury, Methodist preachers...5sh...1 acre and is part of land where said Benton lives, beginning where Suffolk Road crosses Bennetts Creek Road, along Suffolk Road for length of acre, thence running E for an acre and S for an acre to Bennetts Creek...
Edward Arnold   Jethro Benton
Thomas Parker

221 23 Mar 1786--William Arnold to John Arnold...5 pds...10 acres beginning at a pine, corner between Abraham Morgan and James Phelps on said Morgan's line, to a new line of marked trees and along it to a line between said William and John, part of land, which was patented to Richard Berryman 6 Aug 1719, was sold to John Lassitor and by him to Adam Rabey, who gave to his son, John, who sold to Lemuel Powell and by said Powell to William Trevathan, who sold to Henry Smith and by him sold to Abraham Morgan, who sold to said William...
George Williams   William Arnold
John Darden
May Ct 1786

223 14 Aug 1786--Josiah Parker to Stephen Shepherd...10 pds...25 acres, being part of patent granted to Thomas Piland for 400 acres 20 Nov 1738, beginning at a white oak where said Piland corners at Miller's patent line, along Miller's line to red oake, W joining said Parker's line, by line of marked trees to post oak, S to said Piland's line...
Israel Beeman   Josiah ($\mp$) Parker
John Shepherd
Abraham Beeman
Aug Ct 1786

225 3 May 1786--Moses Hare Jr. to Moses Benton...63 pds...6 sh...200 acres whereon Peel formerly lived and binding on lands of Jethro Benton, Lem Hogens and others...
Jethro Sumner   Moses Hare
Edwin Sumner
Jas. B. Sumner
Aug Ct 1786

226 19 Jul 1786--Jacob Bagley to Demsey Trotman...125 pds...100 acres on Catheran Creek, binding on land of Charles Roundtree, land formerly belonging to Jacob Spivey, dec., lands of John B. Walton, Simon Stallings and James Walton...
Thos. Hunter   Jacob Bagley
Thomas Trotman
Aug Ct 1786

228 20 Jun 1786--Marget Colley to her father, Samuel Colley, deed of gift...17 acres in North County after death of my daughter, Marget..."
James Outlaw   Marget(+)Colley
Nathaniel Spivey

229 21 Jun 1787--Jonathan Roberts to Jethro Meltear...10 pds...5 acres beginning at white oak, corner tree, to ash in cornfield, wherein he lives, along line of marked trees...
William Gordon   Jonathan Roberts
David Harrell
Aug Ct 1787

230 6 Jun 1786--Seth Stallings and wife, Rachael, to Simon Stallings...300 pds...100 acres beginning at white oak in a large branch that issueth out of S side of Katherine Creek Swamp, said branch dividing said land from land occupied by Thomas Hurdle, up branch to Amos Hobbs line and along his line to Aaron Hobbs, running line of marked trees to said Stallings, to Seth Roundtree's, to said swamp and along swamp...
James Walton   Seth(+)Stallings
James Talor   Rachael(+)Stallings
Elijah(X)Spivey
Private examination of said Rachael may be found in Book No. 3 p. 97-98. J. Walton P.R.

232 3 Feb 1786--Mary Hill, daughter of Richard Street, to her son, Henry Hill...deed of gift...250 acres formerly belonging to said Street on W side of Hampton River beginning at mouth of small creek on W side, to Channers' line, to small creek going to Hampton Town, down creek to river and down river; ___McKinsey lived on part of land in Elizabeth Co. Va...
James Freeman   Mary(M)Hill
Timothy Freeman
Feb Ct 1787

233 16 Feb 1787--David Cross to Abel Cross...30 pds...100-ac. tract granted to William Crafford 29 Oct 1782, beginning at a black gum in Gum Swamp, up patent line to line of marked trees and up swamp...
William Gatling   David Cross
Jesse Benton
Feb Ct 1787

234 3 May 1786--Lewis Jones to David Brinkley of Nansemond...20 pds 100 acres known as The Trap, running from edge of road leading from

Suffolk E, then N to said Jones and SW...
                                                                                            Lewis Jones
Joseph Thomson   Mary(x)Jones
John Brinkley
Simeon Brinkley
Aug Ct 1786

235 8 Aug 1786--Keziah Blanshard to her brother, Joseph Alphin...
3 pds every year during her widowhood...lease of 75 acres on which
Amos Blanshard, dec. formerly lived...
                                                         Keziah(X)Blanshard
Job Riddick
Moses Lassiter
Aug Ct 1786

236 18 Aug 1787--Demsey Trotman to James Walton...25 pds...27 acres
beginning at post oak on W side of Virginia Road, NW to John B. Walton's line, along his line S to his, Simon Stallings and James Walton's corner, SE along said James line to main road and along road;
part of patent granted to Thomas Spivey for 494 acres 19 Jun 1715...
John B. Walton   Demsey Trotman
Esther Walton

237 17 Aug 1786--William Hinton to Isaac Harrell...60 pds...150 acres,
part of a patent granted to him for 478 acres 17 Oct 1784, beginning
at a pine in a branch, SE to two pine saplings, Abraham Harrell's
line, along his line W to line of Aron Lassiter, dec., N to branch...
David Harrell   William Hinton
Monijay Blanshard
Noah Harrell
Aug Ct 1786

240 18 Nov 1786--Zachariah Copeland and William Porter of Nansemond
Co. Va. to William Goodman...190 pds...3 sh...6 pn...333 acres,
which they empowered by Joseph Porter's will 20 Jun 1772, to sell,
beginning at a pine, Henry Goodman, Soloman Hiat and James Riddick's
corner, N along Riddick's line to white oak in branch coming out of
Beach Swamp and standing in Daniel March's line, W along March's line
to Jacob Walters, to Henry Lee's, to said Hiat...
Jn. Lawrence   Zachariah Copeland
Henry Goodman   William Porter
Elisha Copeland
Nov Ct 1786

242 30 Oct 1786--John Raby to Kedar Raby of Upper Parish, Nansemond
Co...10 pds...50 acres bounded by land of William Baker, Kedar Riddick, Moses Spivey and Michael Lawrence...
                                                          John Raby
Thomas Draper
Henry Meroney
Jethro Riddick
Nov Ct 1786

243 3 Sep 1786--George Gatling to Jesse Sanders...20 pds...___tract
beginning at water oak in Beaver Dam Swamp, down to mouth of Plumb
Tree Branch, up branch to a sweet gum, along line of marked trees...
John Pipkin   George (X)Gatling
Isaac Pipkin
Isaac Pipkin Jr.
Nov Ct 1786

244 15 Nov 1786--Isaac, Mary, Richard and Ann Croom of Dobbs Co. to Francis Parker...50 pds...330 acres beginning at a gum, corner tree of Henry King's, now in possession of Miles Benton, standing on Sypres Swamp, along line of marked trees to Deep Cypress Swamp, down swamp and across, up Flatt Cyprus Swamp on S side, to a gum, then running along line of marked trees near a spring opposite William Hudgins Jr.'s line N to Francis Saunders, SW to Cypress Branch near head, down branch to a former line of Joseph Ballard's and along his line...
Sherrard Barrow   Isaac Croom
Abraham Sanders   Mary Croom
Spener Caldell   Richard Croom
Nov Ct 1786   Ann Croom

246 17 Aug 1786--Jesse Spivey to Henry Harrell...133 pds 6 sh 8 pn...175 acres on N side of Watery Swamp, being part of tract conveyed by Timothy Walton to Jacob Spivey, dec., who gave by his will 18 Nov 1776 to his son, Jesse, bounded by Charles Roundtree, Demsey Costen and James Costen...
Abraham Hurdle   Jesse(+)Spivey
David Harrell
Thomas Walton
Nov Term 1786

248 ___ Jacob Pearce to Oisten Nickson...4 pds...50 acres in Dismal Swamp beginning at a gum, Christopher Creecy's corner tree on W side, then E...land was granted to said Pearce in 1783...
William Bereman   Jacob Pearce
Benjamin Bereman
Reuben Nixon
Nov Ct 1786

251 24 Oct 1786--John Harrell to Cyprian Cross...17 pds 5 sh...70 acres, part of tract granted to Francis Speight, beginning at a pine, corner tree in patent line, along line to George Hargroves and along his line to Jesse Vann's and along Vann's line to patent line...
John Odom   John Harrell
Samuel Thomas   Ann(X)Harrell
Elizabeth Brinkley
Nov Ct 1786

252 25 Dec 1786--William Vann and Samuel Brown to Charles Eure...43 pds...35 acres beginning at a lightwood stump of said Vanns and Browns line, along that line to corner of Samuel Taylor's at head of Reedy Branch, down branch to white oake in branch, a corner of Aaron Harrell, to a pine in William Davidson's line and along his line and a line of marked trees to James Eure's line, W along his line to Charles Eure's and along his line...
William Davidson   William(X)Vann
Cyprian Cross   Samuel Brown
Lewis Sparkman   Mary Brown
Feb Ct 1787

253 12 Mar 1786--William Vann to William Davidson...10 pds...10 acres beginning at corner pine in Samuel Eure's line, thence by line of marked trees as Aaron Harrell's line goes to Samuel Brown's line and along his line of marked trees S to James Eure's line, E to Samuel Eure's and along his line...
Samuel Brown   William(W)Vann
Sealah Sparkman
Feb Ct 1787

255 13 Jul 1786--John Brigs to Josiah Granbery...106 pds 5 sh...two
tracts of 50 acres, being part of tract purchased from Josiah Granbery, dec., 1765; bought from Abraham Hill. One parcel lies W of
main Gates Road and other opposite on E side of and containing a
2-acre apple orchard...
Rd. Mitchell
James Baker   John (O)Brigs
25 Jun 1787

256 21 Dec 1786--John Goodman of Edgecomb Co. to Soloman King...10
pds...50 acres granted to William Skiner 11 Mar 1740 and conveyed
to William Goodman and Isaac Pipkin 1 Aug 1760, beginning at oake
on side of Winton Road, Pipkin's line, S to a gum, Wm. Goodman's
corner, E to post oak in Copeland's line and along that line N
to Winton Road...
William Odom   John Goodman
Uriah Odom
Mary(+)Lang
25 Jun 1787

258 18 Jan 1787--Peter Piland to William More...70 pds...75 acres
beginning at red oak on back swamp, running a line of marked trees
NW to Bennetts Road, to red oak, down road to Halfway Run and down
run and to back swamp...   Peter(+)Piland
Robert Parker
William Polson   Charity(+)Piland
Feb Ct 1787

259 15 Dec 1786--Edward Arnold to Thomas Parker...55 pds...70 acres
on W side of Thicket Road on S side of a new line of marked trees
issuing out of Turnip Patch, running to said Parker; part of a
patent of 200 acres granted to Thomas Miller and by him sold to
John Hubbert, who by his will 14 Oct 17_4 devised to his son, Mathew, who sold to William Parker, who sold to John Duke, who sold
to Edward Arnold, whose heir was William, who gave to the present
Edward; joins other lands of said Arnold and Parker, Moses Hare
and Elizabeth Norfleet...
John Morgan   Edw. Arnold
William Parker   Elizabeth Arnold
1 Jul 1787

260 5 Dec 1786--John Felton to Asa Harrell...40 pds...22 acres on
W side of Coles Creek, running up creek to Samuel Eure's corner tree,
a pine, thence running line to Thomas Felton's corner tree, along his
line; being all land in said John's possession...
Law. Baker   John(+)Felton
William Baker
Cyprian Cross
16 Jul 1787

263 7 Dec 1786--Jethro Lassiter of Bertie Co. and Timothy Lassiter
to Robert McCulloch...133 pds 6 sh 8 pn...100 acres beginning in
Daniel Hays line at a cypress, running along his line to a pine,
a corner tree in Reedy Branch joining Minshis line and down said
branch to run of creek and down creek...   Timothy Lassitor
Isaac Hunter   Timothy Lassitor for
Josiah Granbery   Jethro Lassitor
William Gordon
17 Jul 1787

264 15 Jan 1787--Job Riddick to James Costen...10 pds...25 acres, part of 350 acres granted to him 27 Oct 1784, on S side of Meherren Swamp, beginning at Isaac Hunters mill, along Costen's line to mouth of Keaton Branch, down branch to run of swamp and up run...
John Moran   Job Riddick
Isaac Costen
19 Jul 1787

267 20 Jun 1787--Joseph Scott and wife, Mary, of Southampton Co., Va. to Josiah Granbery...433 1/3 Spanish dollars plantation whereon James Jones, dec. formerly lived, adjoining said Granbery...
Ro. Mitchell   Jos. Scott Jr.
John Rice
20 Jul 1787

268 14 Oct 1786--Joseph Riddick to Charles M. Smith...25 pds...50 acres beginning at gum in Horsepen Swamp, across the land S to pine in John B. Walton's line, along his line to swamp binding on James Sumner's line, along his line and up swamp; land was bought of Clemmon Hill...
Sam. Smith   Jos. Riddick
Ruben Riddick
23 Jul 1787

270 13 Feb 1786--Kedar Hill to Moses Blanshard...47 pds...18 sh... 8 pn...210 acres whereon said Moses lives and sold to said Hill 23 Jul 1783, beginning at a post oak, Henry Walton and Jacob Bagley's corner tree by road, along lines appearing in deed 5 Dec 1766, to Jacob Bagley, S side of old road along Bagley and Spivey lines NE including all land said Blanshard bought of Elisha Hunter that was not sold in 1783...
Jo. Riddick   Kedar Hill
Thomas Trotman
Reuben Riddick
26 Jul 1787

271 1 Jan 1787--James Sumner to Joseph John Sumner...50 pds...land whereon said Joseph John lives, being ½ of land whereon Samuel Sumner formerly lived in Chowan Co. with life right of Patty Meroney, who was widow of said Samuel and given to her in his will...
David(+)Jones
James(+++)Jones, s of David   James Sumner
29 Jul 1787

273 4 Feb 1787--William Arnold to Abraham Morgan...45 pds...60 acres near patent line and running line of marked trees across land N and including all land on E side of dividing line; land was granted 6 Aug 1719 to Richard Bereman, who conveyed to John Lassiter, who sold to William Davis, who conveyed to Lemuel Powell, who gave to his son, John, who sold to Edward Arnold, whose heir is said William...
Edwd. Arnold   William Arnold
Mathias(+)Morgan   Kezia(+)Arnold
Feb Ct 1787

274 19 Feb 1784--Isaac Pipkin, sheriff, to John Parker...100 pds... 100 acres formerly belonging to Charles Vann, dec. beginning at red oake on S side of main Cyprus Swamp in William Jones' line, running line of marked trees to white oake on patent line, along that line to said swamp and up swamp; part of a grant to John Nichols

6 Jun 1699. Land was sold in open sale to execute court order for a debt of 58 pds 5sh against the estate of Charles Vann, dec. recovered by Elisha Copeland...
Phillip Lewis
John Pipkin
12 Aug 1787
                                        Isaac Pipkin

276 7 Apr 1787--Silas, John, James and Jesse Copeland of Nansemond Co., Va. to Francis Parker...5 pds...50 acres, being residue of a 350 acre patent granted to Charles Sanders, dec. 25 Jun 1762, who previously sold 300 acres to William Odom; land is on S side of Sypris Swamp...
Abraham Sanders   Silas Copeland
Mary Copeland   John Copeland
11 Aug 1787   James Copeland
                                        Jesse Copeland

278 28 Apr 1787--William Boothe to Joel Foster...250 pds...250 acres beginning at mouth of small branch that falls into Bennetts Creek, up branch to Jonathan Nichols' corner tree, along line of marked trees to Demsey Jones line and along his line to branch and along said creek binding on Abraham Riddick's land...
Isaac Miller   William Boothe
Daniel Horton
Micajah Riddick
15 Aug 1787

280 22 Feb 1787--Joseph Brown and wife, Happy, to Abraham Riddick... 56 pds...50 acres on S side of Bennetts Creek, part of patent of James Hinton, dec., beginning at pine in James Hays' line at creek side, running Hays line to red oak, corner tree, along Demsey Jones' line to William Boothe's line, to a popular, a corner tree in Deep Branch, down branch to said creek and along creek...
James Hays   Joseph(O)Brown
Henry(+)Hays   Happy(H)Brown
Wright Hays
May Ct 1787

281 13 Mar 1787--Sawyer Lawrence and wife, Peggy; George Lawrence; Thomas Cambel and wife, Nancy; Benjamin Powell, guardian to Polly Lawrence, all of Nansemond Co., to Thomas Marshall...60 pds...400 acres beginning at cypress at end of Sharps Island on E side of Bennetts Creek, along Gabrel Lassiter's line to end of Beach Island, to Bennetts Creek, to Chowan Indians line, to white oak, along Piland's line to said creek and down creek; excepting 50 acres on which Thomas Taylor formerly lived and now property of Evn Murphy, dec. and bounded by line of marked trees and Indian line...
William Brooks   Sawyer Lawrence
15 Aug 1787   George Lawrence
                                        Thomas Campbell
                                        Nancy Campbell
                                        Benj'n Powell

283 18 Dec 1784--John Goodman of Edgecomb Co. to William Goodman... 2 pds 8 sh...10 acres which was given by Henry Goodman, dec. to his son, William, dec., from whom said John heired, beginning at Wm. Goodman and Henry Goodman, dec. corner, a lightwood stump, along line of marked trees to a branch that comes out of Peters Swamp, down branch to said William's line...
Henry Goodman   John Goodman
James Lang
16 Aug 1787

285 8 Feb 1787--John and William Felton to John Piland...24 pds...
50 acres on W side of Coles Creek beginning at corner tree of James
Piland and along his line to said creek, up creek to Asa Harrell's
land, formerly John Feltons, to white oak and down line of marked
trees...
Stephen Harrell   Thomas(+)Felton
Benjamin Harrell   John(+)Felton
18 Aug 1787

286 13 Sep 1745--Thomas Hilton and James Bennett, Chowan Indian,
of Chowan Co. to Aaron Blanshard of Chowan Co...150 pds...400 acres
in Indian Neck between two creeks, Bennetts and Catherine, that issue
out of N side of Chowan River, beginning at a pine in said Blanshard's
land, along his line to Thomas Garrett Sr, along his line to a corner
tree in Juniper Branch, up branch and along line of marked trees to
land formerly occupied by Henry Bonner, late of county, to Bennett's
Creek near lower end of Indian Old Field, to tract now in possession
of Jacob Hinton, along his line to Juniper Branch to a maple in Merry
Branch to said Blanshard's land...
Ephriman Blanshard   Thomas (h) Hilten
Samuel Mansfield   James(‡B)Bennett
Benjamin Blanshard
26 Sep 1745 Gab. Johnston

289 1 Aug 1787--Demsey Trotman to Charles Roundtree...30 pds...30
acres beginning at black oak corner tree in side of main road, to
a pine in back line, along John B. Walton's line to a black oak,
corner tree of James Walton's, back to said road...
John Roundtree   Demsey Trotman
Seth Roundtree
15 Nov 1787

290 8 Oct 1785--Andrew Hamilton to William Davidson...$65 or 12 pds...
50 acres beginning at gum in middle of pond, along Samuel Taylor's
line to a corner pine then along Betsy King's line to a corner pine
of Stephen Eure's, along his line to head of pond and down middle
of pond, on edge of Sand Banks...
Samuel Brown   Andrew Hambleton
William(+)Vann
Mary(+)Brown
Aug Ct 1787

292 15 Aug 1787--Robert Fisher of Nansemond to John Anderson, mariner...15 pds...50 acres, being part of land granted to James Maney,
dec. in 1740 and purchased by said Fisher's father, Thomas, from
Samuel Brown, beginning on side of Chowan River joining line of marked trees belonging to Henry King, the elder, dec., to a pine on side
of branch and down branch to a marsh on edge of sand hills, to a gum
in patent line and along line to said river and along river...
Jethro Darden   Robert( )Fisher
Elisha Darden
15 Nov 1787

293 6 Jan 1787--John Norfleet to Elisha Darden...23 pds...20 acres
on White Oak Spring Marsh, which fell to him from his father, John,
who devised his land to his sons and daughters...
Sally Darden   John Norfleet
Esther Darden
Charles Hedgpeth
Aug Ct 1787

295 6 Jun 1787--James Sumner to Jacob Powell...2 pds 18 sh 4 pn...
72 acres, part of a larger tract of Luke Sumner, dec. on S side of
Loosing Swamp, beginning at black gum in David Jones' line, across
swamp to maple on S side and down swamp to said Powell's, to a sweet
gum above Harris and Larkum's corner, SW to said Powell's new patent,
to said swamp and down swamp binding on said James' line...
Kedar Ballard   James Sumner
William Ellis
Aug Ct 1787

296 17 Aug 1787--Richard Bond to William Hinton...40 pds...48 acres
beginning at a gum, said Hinton's corner, and along his line...
Reuben Riddick   Richard Bond
James( )Jones
Aug Ct 1787

298 15 Aug 1787--Israel Beeman to James Hays...40 pds...160 acres,
being part of grant to William Swann 27 Mar 1708, beginning at popular in said Hays' line, corner tree, in Great Hawtree Branch, along
branch E to Robert Parker's line, to a sweet gum, corner tree, along
James and Cader Riddick's line E to said Hays and on his line to head
of Little Hawtree Branch, to corner oak in Willis Brown's line and
along his line to said Hays...
Christ. Riddick   Israel Beeman
Isaac Miller
Aug Ct 1787

299 15 Aug 1787--James Hays to Seth Riddick...264 pds...160 acres
N side of road that goes to Col. Law. Bakers, being part of patent
granted to William Davis, beginning at corner tree, a post oak, in
Robert Parker's line, NW to Col. Baker's line, along his line to a
sweet gum in Moses Spivey's line, E along his line to black gum
near Hop Pocosin, to corner tree in James Riddick's line, along
his line S to said Parkers and W...
Christ. Riddick   James(+)Hays
Isaac Miller
24 Dec 1787

301 21 Feb 1787--Joseph John Sumner to Jethro Sumner...41 pds 10 sh...
250-acre plantation whereon he lives, being ½ of land where his father,
Samuel Sumner formerly lived, beginning at swamp side of William Arnold's line with row of apple trees to W door of house, through entry and up road that leads to Brothers by Virginia line to bounds
of land...
William Arnold   Joseph Jno. Sumner
Willis Wiggens
Aug Ct 1787

302--The next 3 deeds were made 24 Oct 1786 from the Treasury of
North Carolina to William Crafford and registered 17 Feb 1788 by
J. Glasgow, sec. and Richard Caswell, gov., with a price of 10 pds
for every 100 acres: 220 acres NE side of Chowan River beginning at
black gum on side of river just below Speight's Creek, running NW to
patent corner on main river pecosin to mouth of swamp, NE down side
joining Rawls, to two gums, E along river. 25 acres on E side of
Chowan River beginning at cypress on side above mouth of Barnes

Creek, up river NW then S. Island in Chowan River just below Dr. Samuel Brown's Cosway beginning at a sypres on E side of island, up S side and across creek, down N side and containing 62 acres...

306 1 Mar 1787--William Davidson to Elisha Harrell...350 or 15 pds 50 acres on edge of Sand Banks beginning at gum in middle of pond, along Samuel Taylor's line to corner pine of Betsy King's line to Stephen Eure's, along his line to head of pond...
Stephen Eure   William Davidson
Mills Eure
Peter Harrell
Feb Ct 1788

307 18 Feb 1788--Richard Mitchell and wife, Esther, to William McDonald of Edenton, merchant...desiring to settle their estate... 5 sh...several tracts of land from Warwick Plantation and devised to said Esther from her father, James Sumner, including 50 acres bought from John Freeman 10 Oct 1700, 100 acres conveyed by John Brinkley and wife, Nancy 8 Nov 1744, 50 acres bought from Richard Walton and wife 4 Oct 1762, 100 acres conveyed by Thomas Garrett 12 Oct 1763, 50 acres remaining from 100 sold to Samuel Taylor. Also 75 acres adjoining deeded from Martin Hurdle to said Sumner, dec. 19 Oct 1763. Said Mitchells to retain use during their lives...
Simon Stallings   Rich. Mitchell
Seth Roundtree   Esther Mitchell
Feb Ct 1788   William McDonald
Jno. Baker attested said Easter signed
deed of her own free will.

Note: 311-315 repeat of same deed.

315 18 May 1787--William Morris to Henry Goodman...30 pds...50 acres beginning at a pine running Moses Kittrell's line to Great Branch, down middle to corner oak of Jesse Harrell's, along line of marked trees to main pecosin...
James(X)Keen   William(+)Morris
Samuel Keen
William Goodman

316 27 Aug 1787--John Arnold and wife, Patsey, to James Pruden... 17 pds...10 sh...20 acres on E side of Gum Branch beginning at large sweet gum running line of marked trees to a dividing line between Micajah Riddick and said Arnold, to said Pruden's and along line of sweet gums...
William Draper   John Arnold
Abraham(A)Morgan   Patsey(+)Arnold
Micajah Phelps

318 29 Jan 1788--George White of Chowan Co. and Joshua and John White to Thomas White...30 pds...75 acres, their part of land left to them by their father, George, dec., beginning at mouth of branch issuing out of Warwick Swamp, up swamp and bounded by Reuben Hobbs to Spivey's line and down line; being part of patent for 500 acres granted to Thomas Garrett, Jr. 1 Mar 1718. Said Thomas White is their brother...
Jacob Spivey   George(+)White
Bethary(+)White   Joshua(+)White
                                         John White

319 17 Nov 1787--John B. Walton to Moses Davis...30 pds...100 acres beginning at furthermost of the branches S, from plantation at marked pine E to John Miller, dec. line, to Jacob Powells and along his line; land formerly belonged to Henry Hill, who gave to his son, Abraham, who with wife, Elizabeth by deed 11 Oct 1752 sold to Josiah Granbery and Edward Riddick, who sold to said Henry, who conveyed to James Jones. Said Jones sold to Tim'y Walton, who gave of his son, said John B., by will...
Thos. Hunter   John B. Walton
Jacob Bagley
Timothy Walton
Feb Ct 1788

320 19 Feb 1788--Joseph Scott Jr. and wife, Mary, of Southampton, Va. and Judith Jones, Hertford Co. to Moses Hare...90 pds...100 acres beginning at gum in Foreman Swamp, along David Jones to Flatt Branch, to a gum in said Hare's line, along his line; being land John Jones devised by his will to son, James, father of said Mary and Judith...
Jethro Ballard attested   Jos. Scott Jr.
said Mary signed deed freely.   Mary Scott
Feb Ct 1788   Judith Jones

322 18 Dec 1787--Josiah Granbery to Robert Riddick...140 pds...two tracts, 50 acres purchased by Josiah Granbery, dec. from Abraham Hill and sold to John Briggs in 1765, on W side of main Gates Road and 2 acres on E side of road and being an apple orchard...
Isaac Miller   Josiah Granbery
Micajah Riddick
Feb Ct 1788

323 10 Dec 1787--Henry Copeland to Demsey Langston...13 pds 10 sh... 100 acres beginning at hickory near run of Sypress Swamp beginning at line of marked trees, running to Jno. Parker's line, with his line to Rogers Branch and down branch to said swamp and down swamp; land was granted to Richard Ohdom 1 Mar 1718...
Luke Langston   Henry Copeland
Thomas(+)Langston
Feb Ct 1788

324 28 Jan 1788--John Arline Jr. to Moses Kittrell...18 pds...60 acres, all land which his Grandfather Kittrell gave to him in his will, lying near Dismal Pecosin beginning at pine stump in Elisha Parker's line, to Solcman Phillip's corner, along Phillip's line S to a pine in bottom, E along new line made between said Arline and said Kittrell...
Edward Drake   John Arline
William Dunsford
Feb Ct 1788

326 19 Jan 1786--John Brayshear to William Crafford 30 pds...77 acres known as Little Island and granted to Jacob Odom 17 Mar 1740, beginning at a hickory in patent line, along line to Juniper Swamp, along swamp to line of marked trees...
James Landing   John Brayshear
Robert(+)Manor
Feb Ct 1788

327 22 Jun 1788--Henry Dilday to William Gatling...12 pds...50 acres, part of a patent granted to Thomas Jernagan, dec. 2 Feb 1719, and purchased by said Dilday from Henry Goodman, beginning at a lightwood stump, corner of William Goodman, Isaac Pipkin and said Dilday, along line of new marked trees between said Dilday and Robert Rogers, dec. and patent line, down Rogers' line that said Dilday made to Stephen Cross, W along Cross' line to a patent granted to William Ashley...
William Goodman
William Gatling Jr.
Feb Ct 1788
Henry(H)Dilday
Elizabeth(X)Dilday

328 7 Jan 1787--Benjamin Harrell to Peter Piland...86 pds...105 acres at Halfway Run, beginning at white oak in branch and running line of marked trees to corner pine, to an oak, to black gum; part of a deed to Aaron Harrell and patented to George Piland by Gov. Gabriel Johnson 2 Feb 1753...
Willis Moore
William Polson
Nov Ct 1787
Benjamin Harrell
Aaron Harrell
Elizabeth(X)Harrell

330 7 Feb 1788--William Freeman to John Howbs...97 pds...50 acres beginning at marked pine at George Outlaw's line, to Jacob Outlaws, along his line to James Freemans, to a line of marked trees, which formerly belonged to Luke Sumner, dec. to black gum in large branch, up branch near head, then along line of marked trees...
James Freeman
William Valentine
William Freeman

331 21 Jun 1787--Jethro Meltier to Jonathan Roberts...10 pds...75 acres on E side of Bennetts Creek beginning at two cypress by side of run of Indian Gut, down run SW to Bennetts Creek and up run to a cypress on side of run, through pecosin to island, to a pine corner of said Roberts...
William Gordon
David Harrell
Nov Ct 1787
Jethro Meltier

332 16 Nov 1787--William Ellis and wife, Mary, to Jacob Gordon...18 pds...20 acres, third lot in division of estate of John and Elizabeth Norfleet, dec., who gave land to their children, and is known as an Island and White Oak Spring Marsh, beginning at stake in division line between Jethro Ballard and marsh, to desert and back...
John Rice
James Baker
Nov Ct 1787
William Ellis
Mary Ellis

333 13 Jan 1786--Jesse Barnes to David Cross...4 pds...20 acres, granted to him by patent in 1783, on E side of Gum Swamp, along line to Pine Swamp, to a pine, Crafford's corner, and along his line, joining Joseph Runnell's patent...
Demsey Barnes
John Odom
Cyprian Cross
Nov Ct 1787
Jesse Barnes

334 13 Jan 1787--James Parker to James Thomas...60 pds...100 acres, being part of a patent to Jacob Odom 21 Feb 1738, beginning at a

gum in gum swamp, corner of Samuel Thomas Jr., down swamp to mouth,
to a corner gum of Samuel Thomas and Stephen Eure, up Little Rigg
over mouth of Gum Swamp, along line of marked trees, across Island
to gum in Sypress Swamp, Samuel Thomas' other corner tree and up
swamp to mouth of branch to Samuel Thomas Jr. to Island...
John Odom James Parker
James Landen Ruth(+)Parker
Nov Ct 1787

335 10 Feb 1786--Charles Roundtree to Jacob Eason...50 pds...90
acres beginning on SE side of Warwick Swamp, up middle to a corner
tree of Shadrack Felton's, along his line to a black gum in Deep
Branch, up middle to patent line, SW along line of marked trees
to patent line; land formerly belonged to Thomas Eason and given
by him to his son, James, dec., who gave to his son, said Jacob,
who sold to said Roundtree...
                                                Charles Roundtree
Levy(+)Eason
John Roundtree
Nov Ct 1787

337 18 Aug 1783--Treasury of North Carolina to Demsey Costen for
50 sh for every 100 acres...470 acres beginning at oak in head of
Starffords Branch, William Cowper and William Walton, dec. corner,
along Walton's line SW to a pine, NW to a pine, James Cotten's corner, SW to a pine, Charles Roundtree's corner, N to Robert Lassiter's
line, to a maple, E to said Costen's corner in said Lassiter's line,
along Lassiter's line S to said Cowpers...   Alexander Martin,
J. Glasgow, sec.   gov.
17 Apr 1788

339 11 Jan 1788--William Crafford to Patrick Garvey of Winton, Hertford Co...8 pds...225 acres, No. 58 patented to him 24 Oct 1786, beginning at black gum on NE side of Chowan River below Speights Creek,
NW to Webbs Patent on side of river pecosin, down side, crossing
mouth of swamp, SE joining Powell's Patent, to river and along river,
reserving part of fishery held in common with said Garvey...
Feb Ct 1788   William Crafford

342 23 Feb 1789--Richard Baker to John Rochell...100 pds...150
acres, which Benjamin Baker and Abraham Cole purchased from John
Odom 23 Sep 1770, lying in part of Gates Co., formerly part of
Hertford Co., on E side of Chowan River beginning at marked pine
near Henry Copeland's land, down river to a cypris at mouth of
small creek, up creek to black gum near Main Road and bounded by
road, to marked pine, a corner tree, to black gum...
Elisha Darden   Richard Baker
John McCabe   of Nansemond Co.,Va.
Jacob Daughtree
Peter Fiveash
Nov Ct 1787

344 13 Aug 1787--Joseph Rooks to Willis Hughes...19 pds...100 acres
in Peters Swamp, beginning at a chinkapah oake, corner tree between
said Rooks and James Brady, down small branch to main road and along
another branch to run of said swamp, to William Warren's line and
up small branch to a pine, corner tree of Hollands and along Brady's
line...   Joseph Rooks
Law. Baker
James Rice
Nov Ct 1787

345 26 Oct 1787--Benjamin Harrell and James Parker of Martin Co. to John Whitehead of Southampton Co., Va...3 sh. per acre..land they patented joining Muddy Creek, beginning at gum on river running out of William Arnolds Ridge, up his line to Wynns Road, along road to Muddy Creek and down creek...
William (+)Barnes
Ruth(+)Parker
Elizabeth(+)Parker
Nov Term 1787
            Benjamin(B)Harrell
            James(C)Parker

347 20 Jul 1787--John Wright and wife, Sarah, of Southampton Co. Va. to Lewis Meredith of Hertford Co...300 pds...200 acres of land with fishery and patented by Francis Pough on E side of Chowan River where said Wright's ferry formerly was kept, beginning at a maple near river side, SE to gum then SW to a gum and NE to a pine on river...
Elkanah Walker   John Wright
Henry Wright   Sarah Wright

348 16 May 1787--Moses Hare Jr. to Jethro Sumner...112 pds...650 acres on which he now liveth, adjoining land of Thomas Parker, David Jones, orphans of James Jones, dec., William Ellis and others...
Edwin Sumner   Moses Hare
Joseph John Sumner
Nov Ct 1787

350 19 Nov 1787--Moses Hare to son, Elisha...deed of gift...75 acres whereon he liveth after his death and death of his wife, Jean, and all household and plantation utensils...
K. Ballard   Moses Hare
Charles Jones
Nov Ct 1787

351 20 Jul 1787--Jeames Wright and wife, Jane, of Hertford Co. to John Wright of Southampton...40 pds...200 acres formerly patented by Francis Pugh on E side of Chowan River, where said Wrights Ferry was formerly kept, beginning at maple near river, running SE to a gum, SW to a gum, NW to a pine on river line and up river...
Henry Wright   James Wright
 Lewis Meredith   Jane Wright
Feb Ct 1788

352 20 Feb 1788--William Crafford to Francis Speight...$62...12½ acres of low ground on Chowan River granted to him 24 Oct 1786 beginning at cypress on side of river a small distance above mouth of Barnes Creek, up river NW to patent line...
Edward Gatling   William Crafford
Demsey Barnes
May Ct 1788

353 19 May 1788--John Rice and wife, Peggy, to Josiah Granbery... 250 pds...100 acres left to them in will of his father 17 Jan 1764, bounded on S by Isaac Hunter, E by David Rice, N by Harrells and said Granbery and W by land formerly belonging to James Jones, dec...
Benjamin Gordon   John Rice
Aaron Lassiter   Peggy Rice
John Gregory
May Ct 1788

355 25 Feb 1788--Judith Jones of Hertford Co. to Josiah Granbery...
260 pds...one undivided half of 160 acres that John Jones purchased
of John Per__ recorded in Chowan Co. 18 Dec 1737 and bequeathed to
his youngest son, Josiah, who dying under lawful age without issue
became the property of the eldest brother, James Jones, who bequeathed to his daughter, said Judith, beginning at oak in side of
Meherrin Swamp, N along line of marked trees to other land of said
Granbery, E along his line to John Rice's line, SW on his line to
said swamp, now Hunters Mill Pond, down mill pond and swamp...
Isaac Hunter   Judith Jones
Plea_ Jordan
May Ct 1788

357 13 May 1788--Jethro Meltear to Ephran Morris...65 pds...100 acres
beginning at lower end of Fork Neck Branch, up branch to Jacob Hun-
ters and along his line to Bennetts Creek Swamp and down swamp...
Jonathan Roberts   Jethro Meltear
Demsey(+)Jones
May Ct 1788

358 17 Jan 1788--Samuel Green to Uriah Eure...22 pds 10 sh...22 acres
joining said Green's own land on Cypress Swamp, beginning near gap
at red oak, corner tree between David Lewis and said Green, W along
line of marked trees to mouth of small branch, down run to said
swamp, to mouth of Mirie Branch and down branch to corner pine between Rubin Sparkman and said Green and along Green's line; part
of a grant to Henry Hackley 22 Jun 1722...
Thomas Norris   Samuel Green
Isaac Green
Daniel Eure
May Ct 1788

359 25 Mar 1877--Job Riddick to Isaac Costen...4 pds...25 acres on
S side of Meherrin Swamp beginning at a cypress at mouth of branch
and along side of swamp to said Riddick's line, up run of mill to
Keetons, along Keeton's Branch to cypress; part of a patent of 150
acres granted to him in 1784...
James Costen   Job Riddick
May Ct 1788

360 7 May 1788--Job Riddick to Samuel Harrell...42 pds...150 acres
on S side of Bennetts Creek, part of patent granted to him 27 Oct
1784, beginning at Thomas Sumner, dec., up line to line formerly
between said Sumner and Timothy Lassiter on side of said branch,
down side joining other lines to Richard Bond's line and along his
line to birch at end of Bond's Island just above mouth of Watery
Swamp, then NW to run of Bennetts Creek and up creek opposite Sumner's line, then E...   Job Riddick
____Riddick
William Arnold
Francis Speight
May Ct 1788

362 1 Jan 1788--Abner Blanshard to Samuel Brown...90 pds 2 sh...
100 acres on E side of Great Marsh and being part of marsh, beginning at red oak on NW side at path, corner tree between said Abner
and Aaron Blanshard, running line of marked trees to a water oak
in Beaverdam Swamp, down swamp to a pine and along line of marked
trees...
Amariah Blanshard   Abner Blanchard
Gabriel Martin   Ann E. Blanchard
May Ct 1788

363 16 Jan 1788--Samuel Green to David Lewis...25 pds...25 acres on Cypress Swamp beginning at a pine, corner tree in Uriah Eure's line, N along his line to William Greens and along his line; being part of a grant to Henry Hackley 22 Jun 1722...
Uriah Eure   Samuel Green
William Davidson
William Davidson, Jr.
May Ct 1788

364 10 May 1788--Henry Copland to Isaac Langston...32 pds...62 acres known as Island in fork of Cypress Swamp and Sand Banks Swamp, beginning at a pine, corner tree of Dempsey Langston and John Parker on N side of Cypress Swamp, running Copeland's own line to a corner white oak on N side of Sand Banks Swamp, to Cypress Swamp and up to said Dempsey's line and as his line goes; being part of a patent granted to Jacob Odom 25 Mar 1749...
William Davidson   Henry Copeland
Luke Langston
Thomas Langston
May Ct 1788

365 1 Jul 1787--Amos Lassiter to Israel Minard...$20...20 acres on N side of Deep Gut, beginning at white oak, up a branch that maketh out of Gut, along line of marked trees to a pine, corner tree between aforesaid parties, running line of marked trees to Kedar Hunters, across a road called name Jothom Lassiters, to Minard's own line, toward Deep Gut...
Demsey Blanshard   Amos(X)Lassiter
Aaron Blanshard
May Ct 1788

366 (The next deeds are from North Carolina Treasury for 10 pds for every 100 acres. Signed by Richard Caswell, gov. and J. Glasgow, sec.)
24 Oct 1786--To James Skinner 122 acres E side of Chowan River beginning at red oak, Cyprian Cross corner tree in Benjamin Barnes' line, along his line NW to center of three pines, to Jonathan Boyce's line and along his line NE to oak, Hare's old patent, along line S to white oak, said Cross' corner tree along his line...
12 Nov 1788

368 24 Oct 1786--To Jesse Barnes and Cyprian Cross...120 acres on E side of Chowan River and Gum Swamp beginning at a pine on SW side of swamp, a corner tree of Speights Old patent, John Harrell's corner running along patent line, now Harrells and Vaughns, SE to a gum by run of Gum Swamp NE side of swamp, up swamp to holly, James Landing's corner and along his line to James Curl's land, binding on swamp to James Craffords and along his line to said Barnes new patent W to run of Gum Swamp, down middle binding on John Odom's line to gum, said Odom's corner tree in said Landing's patent and along Odom's line S...
12 Nov 1788

370 24 Oct 1786--To David Cross...165 acres on E side of Chowan River beginning at a bunch of hollys on side of river at a point below said Cross' house binding on pecosin and crossing mouth of Poly Bridge Branch to a pine in Jethro Benton's line and along his line to river and up side...
14 Nov 1788

371 24 Oct 1786--To Benjamin Barnes...263 acres beginning at sweet gum, William Hunter's patent corner tree in Demsey Barnes field, along patent line SE to a red oak, another corner tree of patent, in William Gatling's line, along his line and Goodman's NE to red oak and gum, Edward Warrens and Thomas Barnes, dec. corner tree, along Barnes new patent line N to said Demsey's corner tree near Hill Pocosin and along his line...# 72
18 Nov 1788

372 24 Oct 1786--To Moses Kittrell...930 acres on W side of Northwest Branch, beginning at a water oak in branch, W to a white oak, William Mathews corner tree, along his line SW to a hickory, SE to a hickory, William Powell's corner tree, and along his line to William Boyce's and along Boyce's new patent line to a pine in White Pott Pocosin and Bakers Folly, said Boyce and Samuel Smith's patent, binding on said Smith's to said Mathews to a white oak, Edwin Sumner's corner tree and along his line N to Watering Hole Branch W to said Kittrells, N along his line to a pine on Mery Hill Pocosin then SE to a branch and down run...# 63
10 Dec 1788

373 6 Aug 1788--Joel Foster to Humphrey Hudgins of Gloschester Co Va...75 pds...127 acres beginning at a beach and chinkepen tree on side of Bennetts Creek just above Hinton's Old Landing, SE to a small gum and ash in Jonathan Nichols line, along his line NW to a popular, Abraham Riddick's corner tree in a branch and down branch to Bennetts Creek...
                                                                Joel Foster
Isaac Miller
John Hudgins
Humphrey Hudgins
Aug Ct 1788

(Deeds 374-Book 2 10 from the North Carolina Treasury for 10 pds for every 100 acres are signed by Rd. Caswell, gov. and J. Glasgow, sec. Book 2 10-12 are signed by Sam Johnston, gov.)

374 24 Oct 1786--To Benjamin Harrell...250 acres on E side of Chowan River beginning at a holly, William Arnold's corner tree, SW to riverside and up river to mouth of Muddy Creek and up creek NE...
18 Feb 1789

375 11 Oct 1776--To James Sumner...100 acres beginning at black gum on N side of Loosing Swamp in David Jones' line, across swamp S to Jacob Powell's line, to sweet gum sapling just above said Powells and Sumners corner white oak to said Powells new patent, S to his old patent and along line NE to swamp, to John Miller's line, to Benjamin Gordens, to run of swamp, to John Gordon's corner tree...
1788   # 81

376 ____ To Elisha Hunter, Samuel Green and Abraham Green...367 acres beginning at a red oak, corner tree of Nicholas Hunter's near said Abraham's plantation, with William Hunter's, dec. line N to a branch in William Lassiter's patent line and along his line E to main road, N to said Elisha's patent corner, N to another corner tree, S to said Samuel's, to William Eason's line, to a glade, along Eason's line S to Joseph Riddick's corner, to Ezekiel Trotman's corner, NW...
10 Jul 1788

Book 2

Treasury of North Carolina to the following:

2 24 Oct 1786--To Moses Eason...56 acres on W side of main desert beginning at a pine in James Norfleet's line on E side of road, along his line E to a pine S to a white oak in John Gordon's line and along his line SE to a white oak, Gen. Washington's corner tree, along his line NW to a sapling, said Norfleets and Jethro Ballard's corner, along Ballard's line NW to main road and along road... No. 70

3 24 Oct 1786--To William Freeman...120 acres beginning at mouth of branch on S side of Catherine Creek Swamp beginning below said William and Demsey Freeman, dec. line, to Samuel Taylor's line to said creek and NE...# 70

6 24 Oct 1786--To Samuel Taylor...15 acres on Catherine Creek Swamp beginning at gum, said Taylor and William Freeman's corner tree on S side of swamp, along Taylor's line to Seth Roundtree's, along his line into swamp, NW along run to a gum, S along said Freeman's line. # 60

7 24 Oct 1786--To Ezekiel Trotman...300 acres on N side of Meherran Swamp beginning at a maple, Elisha Hunter and said Trotman's corner tree, NE to John Hunter's corner tree and along his line NE to Samuel Green's and along his line to patent corner, E to Joseph Riddicks S to black gum in N prong of said swamp and down swamp to said Riddicks...#69

8 24 Oct 1786--To William Boice...85 acres on NW side of White Pot Pocosin beginning at a sweet gum, said Boyce and Samuel Smith's patent, along Boyce's old patent and NW to said Smith's near Bakers Folly on side of White Pot Pocosin and along Smith's line...#64

10 10 Jul 1788--To John Fontaine...6185 acres in Great Dismal Swamp beginning at a gum in James Sumner's line where Camden Co. line intersects said Sumner's and John Powell's grant, SW to a cypress, John Norfleet's patent corner, along his line to Jethro Ballard's corner in said Powell's, with his line NE to a gum, Jesse Eason's line S to Jacob Gordon's corner E to a juniper in Camden Co. line, with that line NW... # 77

11 10 Jul 1788--To Micajah Riddick...63 acres on W side of Middle Swamp beginning at a pine, William Boyce's line, corner tree in Moses Kittrell's new patent line, along that line N to Lewis Walter's, SE to Isaac Miller's, to said Boyces... #77
15 Jul 1789

13 24 Oct 1786--To Benjamin Harrell...75 acres on E side of Chowan River beginning at a gum in John Miller's patent near Wynns Ferry Road crossing road NE to a gum in Gum Swamp in James Parker's line, along his line to Stephen Eure's line and along SW to a maple, said Eure's corner, to William Arnold's corner, to John Miller's line... # 64

14 24 Jun 1788--William Davidson to Aaron Harrell...10 acres beginning at a small red oak in James Eure's line near side of small branch N by line of marked trees to Old Tarkill bed, to a pine in Capt. Eure's line and along his line to said Harrell's, SE to Samuel Eure's line, to a corner pine between Samuel and James Eure and along said James' line; part of a grant to Henry Hackley 22 Jun 1722...
James Eure   William Davidson
Stephen Harrell
Aaron Harrell
Aug Ct 1788

15 1 Jan 1789--Willis Wiggens Sr., planter, to Josiah Granbery...
60 pds...250 acres on Elm Swamp bounded by lands of James Sumner
and Thomas Frazor, dec., along Frazor's line to land of John Darden, along his line to Edward Arnold's and along his line to James
Knight, son of John Knight, as appears by James Sumner's deed to
said Wiggens...
John Sedgley   Willis Wiggens
May Ct 1789

16 16 Apr 1789--Edward Arnold and wife, Elizabeth, to Thomas Parker...27 pds...27 acres, part of patent of 200 acres granted to
Thos. Millner and by him conveyed to John Hubart, who by his will
15 Oct 1734 devised to his son, Mathew, who sold to William Parker,
who sold to John Duke, who conveyed to Edward Arnold, whose heir
at law is William Arnold, who gave to said Edward 27 Aug 1779, on
W side of Thicket Road near mouth of small branch issuing out of
Thicket Swamp, along road NW to Thomas Parker's line...
William Arnold   Edward Arnold
James Knight   Elizabeth Arnold
Mills Ellis
May Ct 1789

17 12 May 1789--Isaac Pipkin to son, John...deed of gift of 100
acres, part of patent granted to William Bentley 22 Feb 1719 beginning at a red oak on E side of main road, along line of marked trees
to water oak in a branch, down branch to Bray Warren's line and along
his line to Phillip Lewis, NW along his line to said road and down
road...
John Goodman   Isaac Pipkin
William Goodman
May Ct 1789

18 3 Apr 1789--Samuel Brown Sr. of Southampton Co., Va. to Henry
Goodman...45 pds...175 acres, which he bought of Charles Russell
19 Dec 1788, on N side of Chowan River in Fort Island, beginning
at a pine in lower end of Fort Neck, running pocosin to a branch,
up branch to a maple, thence running Samuel Eure's line, now Jesse
Harrell Jr. line, to river pocosin and along pocosin...
Randel Moore   Sam'l Brown
William(X)Gatling
May Ct 1789

19 21 Jul 1788--Job Riddick to Timothy Lassiter...6 pds...15 acres,
part of a large tract beginning at mouth of William Ashley's branch,
down branch to creek opposite mouth of Maidenhead Branch, to Samuel
Harrell's line and along his line to said Lassiters...
Jo. Riddick   Job Riddick
Aaron Lassiter
Feb Ct 1789

20 14 May 1789--Thomas Vann to Mills Lewis...25 pds...65 acres,
whereon he lives and which was granted to William Vann 1705, beginning at end of line of said patent, SE to corner gum, NE along
old line of marked trees to corner pine, N along line of other end
of patent to red oak, then SW the length of patent, bounded by William Hughes on SW, James Braddy and Joseph Holland on E, and by William Warren on NE and land of William Vann on W...
John Lewis   Thomas Vann
Edward Gatling
May Ct 1789

22 22 Nov 1788--John Anderson, mariner, of Nansemond Co. Va. to
Jesse Sanders...25 pds...50 acres, part of a tract granted to James
Maney, dec. in 1740 and purchased by Thomas Fisher from Samuel Brown,
beginning at side of Chowan River joining line of marked trees to a
pine on side of branch, to a marsh in edge of Sand Hills, along patent line to Chowan River and up river...
John Pipkin   John Anderson
Amos Dilday
Feb Ct 1789

23 28 Jan 1789--Samuel Baker to Timothy Lassiter...142 pds...118
acres, part of patent granted to Moses Kittrell, beginning at a
maple in Lewis Walters' line, along his line SE to a hickory gum
and maple, William Powell's corner in said Walter's line, to William Boyce and Micajah Riddick's corner tree, with Boyce's patent
line and NW...
Geo. Hamilton   Samuel(SB)Baker
Sarah Baker
Lewis Walters Jr.
Feb Ct 1789

25 14 Oct 1788--Lewis Outlaw to son, James...deed of gift...Negro
woman, Luce and children Sam, Nancy and Edah after decease of said
Lewis and wife, Zilphia...
Tho. Hunter   Lewis (X) Outlaw
James Outlaw
James Freeman
Feb Ct 1789

26 1 Feb 1789--James Skiner to John Odom...40 pds...95 acres, beginning at white oak and along patent line NE to said Odom's line,
SE along old patent line; is part of patent granted to said Skinner
24 Oct 1786...
Cyprian Cross   James Skinner
Joseph Smith
Feb Ct 1789

28 13 Jan 1786--Jesse Barns to Cyprian Cross...9 pds...60 acres
in Gum Swamp; being ½ of land patented by said parties...
Demsey Barns   Jesse Barns
Jesse Vann
Nov Ct 1788

29 6 Sep 1788--Nathaniel Spivey to James Outlaw...60 pds...50 acres
beginning at a pine in Old Town Road by line of marked trees, to Warwick Swamp, up swamp to line of Seth Spivey, orphan of William Spivey, dec., to said road...
Sarah Modling   Nathaniel Spivey
John White   Elisabeth(+)Spivey
Nov Ct 1788

30 10 Feb 1789--Samuel Green to Samuel Taylor...49 pds...65 acres
on Long Pond beginning at a corner pine on side of small branch on
Peter Harrell's line, along his line to a corner tree of Stephen
Eure's line to a corner pine at side of Cypress Pond and along said
Taylors line to end of Long Pond; part of patent granted to John
Aulston...
Feb Ct 1789   Samuel Green

31 27 Aug 1788--Thomas Brickell to William Lewis...200 pds...82 acres as per 1786 deed of sale but omitting boundries and now given: SE side of road leading by said Lewis, joining lands formerly belonging to Patrick Lawley, beginning at white oak stump at fork of road on Popular Branch, with Lawler's patent line to white oak formerly Jno. Martin's corner, now Jonathan Lassiter's, along line of marked trees to a corner tree near Edenton Road to Popular Branch and down branch...
David Rice   Thos. Brickett
Thomas Marshall

32 7 Feb 1789--Mickel and Edward Howell of Nansemond Co. Va., executors of estate of Edward Howell, dec. to Abel Cross...25 pds...110 acres on E side of Chowan River, plantation where John Watson, dec. lived, beginning at a maple in David Watsons line on river pocosin running James Copeland's patent E to Kings line, along his line to dividing line between John Copeland, dec. and Edward Howell, dec., along dividing line to river pocosin thence course of Windborn's deed to said Watsons; land was grant to James Copeland...
David Cross   Michal Howell
William(M)____   Edward(E)Howell
James(+)Powell
Feb Ct 1789

33 16 Apr 1789--Edward Arnold and wife, Elizabeth, to Mills Ellis...125 pds...150 acres on W side of Orapeak Swamp, beginning at mouth of branch issuing out of said swamp, along branch by line of marked trees to Thicket Road and along road to William Jones' line and along his line to road, along road to Elizabeth Norfleet's line, along her line to Edith Jones' line; being part of land formerly belonging to Edw. Arnold, dec. and fell to his heir, William, who gave to the present Edward...   Edw'd Arnold
William Arnold   Elizabeth Arnold
James Knight
Thomas Parker
May Ct 1789

34 16 Feb 1789--Abel Cross to David Cross...9 pds...40 acres on E side of Chowan River, tract whereon John Watson, dec. lived, beginning at maple in David Watson's line on river pecosin, running James Copeland's patent line E to gum in Deep Branch, up middle to other line of land and down line to river pecosin; being patent granted to James Copeland...   Abel Cross
Feb Ct 1789

35 2 May 1789--Daniel Ellis to Elisha Ellis...10 sh...50 acres in Cypress Swamp, beginning at a corner tree between said parties, up small branch to John Parker's line, along his line to William Ellis line, to a pine, corner tree, to Cypress Swamp and down run...
Jno Burgess   Daniel Ellis
Josiah(X)Stallings   Abia(X)Ellis
May Ct 1789

37 20 Nov 1788--Mordecha Perrey and wife, Sarah, to Shadrack Felton of Chowan Co...25 pds...50 acres beginning at a cypress in branch that maketh out of Warwick Swamp, known as Line Branch, along line of marked trees to old field, to a persimmon tree, corner tree in

White Oak Pecosin, NW to William Hurdle's line, E to said branch.
William Felton   Mordecai Perry
John(+)Ward   Sarah(X)Perry
May Ct 1789

38 10 Feb 1789--Francis Parker to Benjamin Saunders...5 pds 6 sh...
___acres on NE side of Reedy Branch beginning at holly at patent line,
along line to corner, N to a pine stump, Henry King's corner on his
line, SW to a white oak, to said branch near head and along branch;
being part of patent granted to Charles Saunders 25 Jun 1762...
Uriah Odom   Francis Parker
John Odom
Joseph(+)Saunders
Feb Ct 1789

40 8 Jul 1788--Samuel Thomas to Nancey Vann...30 pds...50 acres, part
of a patent granted to Jacob Odom 25 Feb 1738, beginning at corner
gum in a branch joining Demsey Harrell's line, into Gum Swamp and down
swamp to a gum, a corner tree, out of swamp, along line of marked trees
to said branch and up branch...
John Parker   Samuel(+)Thomas
Richard Barnes   Mary(+)Thomas
Ruben Harrell
Nov Ct 1788

41 10 Jul 1787--Thomas Brickell of Hertford Co. to William Booth...
100 pds...50 acres beginning at a white oak, corner tree adjoining
Demsey Phillips' line, W to Charles Lawrence's land, NW along Phillips
line...
Willis Driver   Thomas Brickell
John Warren   Acension Brickell
Nov Ct 1788

43 14 Jan 1788--Arthur Williams to Samuel Williams...60 pds, 40 pds
now and 20 pds in one year, 100 acres beginning at a gum in George
Williams line in Hilly Swamp, up swamp to Turner's line and along his
line NE, by row of marked trees to a pine, a corner tree, SW to George
Williams Sr. line...
Edw. Drake   Arther Williams
Moses Kittrell
Feb Ct 1789

43 1 Oct 1788-- Peter and Edward Piland to Hardy Brown...___pds...
60 acres beginning at pine in Jacks Branch on W side of main road,
along road to run of Long Branch near Willis Hughes, up Long Branch
and along line of marked trees to head of Jacks Branch and down...
Jesse(X)Brown   Peter(+)Piland
Wright Hays   Edward(+)Piland
Jethro Sumner
Feb Ct 1789

45 16 Feb 1789--Samuel Green to David Lewis...150 Spanish dollars...
75 acre plantation whereon he lives that he purchased of John Denby
2 Oct 1752, beginning on Cypress Swamp at Thomas Norris lower corner
tree, a pine, along his line to lands of James Eure Jr., E along
Eure's line to land of William Smyth, a red oak, S with his line to
said swamp; part of a patent granted to William Horn Sen...
Uriah(+)Eure   Samuel Green
Isaac(+)Green
Andrew Gooden
Feb Ct 1789

46 6 Nov 1788--Edward Arnold and wife, Elizabeth, to Thomas Parker...
25 pds...58½ acres on W side of Thicket Road, beginning where William
Jones and said Parker's lines join, along road N to William Arnold's
line, SW to a sweet gum, corner tree in Moses Benton's line, NE then
E; part of land William Arnold conveyed to said Edward and known as
Thicket Ferguson...
John Arnold   Edward Arnold
Richard Pope   Elizabeth Arnold
John Darden
Feb Ct 1789

48 3 Feb 1789--Joshua Small to son, James...deed of gift of 200 acres,
beginning at dead pine on desert side, W to peach tree, N to black
walnut, to mulberry tree, NW to a seedar, W to a stake near John
Gordons, to a corner pare tree, E to desert side of his line. Also,
50 acres known as Little Reedy...   Joshua(+)Small
Jethro Ballard
Seth Eason
Moses Eason
Feb Ct 1789

50 5 Jun 1788--John R. Wilkinson and wife, Judith, to Elisha Copeland
338 pds 18 sh 10 pn...300 acres whereon they reside...
Josiah Granbery   John R. Wilkinson
James Gregory   Judith( )Wilkinson
Feb Ct 1789

51 13 Feb 1789--Moses Kittrell to Samuel Baker...5 sh...deed of gift
of 312 acres on White Pot Pocosin beginning at a white oak on dividing line between them at upper end of said Baker's plantation, along
his line of marked trees SW to patent line bearing date of 1786, SE
to white oak, Edwin Sumner's corner, to a pine, Smiths and William
Boyce's corner tree near Bakers Folly, along Boyce's line to Jonathan Kittrell's patent line of 1713 and along old patent line...

Lewis Walters   Moses Kittrell
Lewis Walters Jr.
Feb Ct 1789

52 5 Nov 1788--Mary Riddick of Nansemond Co. to Seth Eason...15 pds...
100 acres beginning at a gum on hill near mouth of Mizells Mill Branch,
Moses Briggs corner tree, running W to old patent line, N along line
to 3 persimmon trees near bottom, then E to said line in desert S
to said Briggs patent and up his line...
Alex. Eason   Mary Riddick
Edward(+)Kelley
Feb Ct 1789

54 28 Oct 1787--William Odom to Hardy Howard...lifetime lease for
he and wife, Ann, land on Chowan River as far as high water mark
with privilege of timber and pasturage...for yearly rent...
John Odom   William Odom
Abraham Saunders
James Skiner
Nov Ct 1788

55 7 Oct 1784--Treasury of North Carolina to Samuel Baker...10 pds
per 100 acres...55 acres in Merry Hill Pecosin beginning at center
of 3 maples, a gum and bay, Moses Boyce's corner of his new survey,
S to a pine on Moses Kittrell's line, NW to said Bakers...
J. Glasgow, sec   Alex. Martin, gov.
27 Oct 1784

56 17 Feb 1789--Abraham Sumner to Abraham Eason...330 pds...250 acre joining line of Thomas Hurdle, Jacob Bagley, dec. and tract he now lives on known as Thomas Docton Old Place; his swamp survey of 650 acres joining Joseph Riddick, Joseph Hurdle and John Powells lines and 200 acres in Chowan Co., formerly property of James Price Jr., dec., which he willed to Mary Sumner, said Abraham's wife, joining lines of Noah Price, Josiah Small and Meedy White...
Patrick Hagerty   Abraham Sumner
Treasey Jones
Feb Ct 1789

57 1 Feb 1787--Josiah Parker to James Parker...lease for 6 years at 1 pd 10 sh per year of property whereon said Josiah lives...
James Rice   Josiah( )Parker
Josiah(+)Parker Jr.
Feb Ct 1789

60 28 Apr 1789--George Piland and wife, Catherine, to Lawrence Baker... $125...200 acres, part of patent granted to him for 930 acres 2 Feb 1753, beginning at a pine, corner tree in Coles Patent, SE to a post oak, corner in said Baker's Patent, SW to water oak in head of Halfway Run Branch, corner tree of Peter Pilands, to a pine and along line of marked trees adjoining land of William Brooks, James Bristow and said Baker...
Jacob Johnson   George Piland
Edward(+)Piland   Katherine (C)Piland
Joseph Riddick, ESQ. testified said
Katherine signed deed freely.
May Ct 1789

62 13 Feb 1789--Moor_ Carter to William Williams...26 pds...13 acres on main road beginning at water oak on Long Branch, along branch to main road, to a red oak and along road and across ridge by line of marked trees; part of patent granted to Henry Hackley 14 Apr 1702...
George Williams   Moor Carter
Jesse Harrell   Elizabeth Carter
William Davidson
May Ct 1789

63 10 Jul 1788--Mary Riddick of Suffolk, Nansemond Co., Va. to sons Mills, Nath. and David...deed of gift of all her dower rights and lands formerly belonging to Mills Riddick, dec. and swamp lands granted 29 Oct 1784 and known as Horsepool Swamp...
Christ. Riddick   Mary Riddick
Micajah Riddick
May Ct 1789

64 8 Sep 1788--Thomas Travis to Jeremiah Jordan...30 pds...50 acres beginning at a popular, corner tree, along Jeremiah Lassiter's line to a red oak, along Travis line to John Robins line...
Henry(H)Hill   Thomas Travis
Jonathan Nichols   Elizabeth Travis
Feb Ct 1789

66 19 Dec 1788--Charles Russell of Johnston Co. to Samuel Brown of Southampton Co., Va...75 pds...175 acres formerly belonging to his father, Charles Russell and given to him in a deed of gift 17 Feb 1769, on N side of Chowan River in Port Island, beginning at a pine

in lower end and running to a branch, to a maple, to Samuel Eure's
line, to Jesse Harrell Jr., to river and along river...
Stephen Shepherd   Charles Russell
Josiah(X)Parker
May Ct 1789

69 20 Jul 1789--Abraham Eason to James Gregory...154 pds.10 sh...
250 acres beginning on side of desert in Joseph Hurdle's line near
Red Hill, along his line to a post oak of Joseph Riddick's and said
Hurdle, along Riddick's line that he bought of George Eason, to a
pine, Abraham Sumner's corner of land he bought of Jacob Eason, now
property of said Riddick, to desert...   Abraham Eason
Seth Eason
Thos. Hunter
Aug Ct 1789

70 5 Jun 1789--George Hargrove to Jesse Vann...60 pds...200 acres,
part of patent granted to Capt. Francis Speight in 1743, beginning
at a corner pine tree in patent line on W side of Gum Swamp, along
line to corner live oak on said swamp, to Myry Branch and along
branch to said Hargrove and Cyprian Cross corner, formerly called
Harrells and Vaughns, along line of marked trees to Juniper Swamp...
John Odom   George Hargrove
John Vann   Amelia(+)Hargrove
Aug Ct 1789

71 12 Mar 1789--Rachael Bond to her children: Elisha H., Selah, Dem-
sey and Thomas...deed of gift of woman Rose and boy Bob...
Robert Riddick   Rachael Bond
Rich'd Bond
John B. Walton
Aug Ct 1789

72 25 Nov 1788--Jethro Benton Sr. to son, Miles...deed of gift...640
acres whereon he lives, lying on Chowan River, 180 acres whereon son,
Josiah lives, 300 acres on Cow Swamp, 7 Negro men slaves, 5 women,
3 girls, 4 boys, still and furniture, smith tools, cattle, sheep,
hogs, household goods, crop of corn, sider and brandy...
Moses(+)Benton   Jethro Benton
Benton Jones
Milley(+)Benton
Aug Ct 1789

73 16 Apr 1789--William Walters to James Matthews...200 silver dollars
150 acres in Mery Hill Pecosin bounded by Samuel Baker,Moses Boice,
said Walters and William Arnold; part of a patent of 640 acres...
Humphrey Hudgins   William Walters
William(+)Gwin
Aug Ct 1789

74 6 Mar 1789--Lewis Jones to Kedar Rabey Sr. of Nansemond Co. Va..
2 Negroes Davey and Venus to insure debt of 90 pds 5 sh. to be paid
by 31 Mar 1789...   Lewis Jones
Joseph Thomson
James Knight
Willis Wiggens
Aug Ct 1789

75 24 Feb 1789--Alexander Eason to Seth Eason...60 pds...grist mill and 2 acres on N side of Barnes Swamp on hill joining end of mill dam and running road to high water mark; being gift in will of his father, Jesse Eason...
Jacob Gordon   Alex'r Eason
Elisha Norfleet   Mary(+)Eason
Bartholomew Opdycke

76 17 Aug 1789--James Bacor Sumner to John Gatling...50 pds...80 acres, part of grant to Catherine Langston 20 Apr 1634, beginning at a pine on prong of Rogers Branch, running W to red oak in patent line, to corner pine, along line of marked trees to Rogers Branch and up branch...
                                                James B. Sumner
Aug Ct 1789

78 15 Feb 1789--Joshua Small to son, John...deed of gift...50 acres purchased of Jacob Powell, and 100 acres of desert land adjoining. Also 50 acres in desert known as Woolf Pit Ridge...
Jethro Ballard   Joshua(X)Small
Joseph Trader Morgan
Daniel(+)Gwin
Aug Ct 1789

79 13 Mar 1789--Joshua Small to son, John...deed of gift...two Negroes Mingo and Ginney, feather bed and furniture, 3 cows and calves and 2 young stears...
Jethro Ballard   Joshua Small
Alex. Eason
Aug Ct 1789

80 29 Jun 1789--Miles Walles to Jeames Outlaw...200 pds...___ acres in Old Town Neck joining land of said Outlaw and William Walles and George Outlaw's land...
George(+)Outlaw   Miles Walles
James Freeman
Aug Ct 1789

81 6 Aug 1789--Thomas Sparkman to son, Lewis...50 pds...240 acres on Cypress Swamp known as Banks of Italy, beginning at a pine on swamp, across plantation by lane of marked fence to hickory, by line of marked trees to Langston's corner tree, along Langston's line to said Lewis' line and along it to John Carter's, to Henry Copland's line, to Rogers' line and along it to swamp and along swamp; is part of two patents granted to Henry Baker 1 May 1728 and 28 July 1730...
Jesse Taylor   Thomas Sparkman
Samuel Taylor
Aug Ct 1789

82 15 Jun 1789--John Hunter to Ezekiel Trotman...10 pds...20 acres, part of large tract granted to Nicholas Hunter and Thomas Davis, beginning at a pine in Elisha Hunter's line, SE to Hunters line and W to a pine, then S...
William Hunter   John Hunter
Abraham Hurdle
Demsey Trotman
Aug Ct 1789

83 2 Aug 1788--Edward Dudley of Warrick Co., Va. to William Gatling...
14 pds 8 sh...Negro girl Lucy about 7...
John Pipkin   Edward Dudley
William Gatling Jr.
Aug Ct 1789

84 10 Jul 1788--State of North Carolina to Joseph Hurdle...10 pds
per 100 acres...368 acres on W side of desert beginning at a pine
in mouth of branch, William Eason, dec. corner tree, NW to a pine,
SW to a pine, Joseph Riddick's corner tree, SE along his line to
another pine corner tree, SE to Abraham Sumner's line, NE to Sumner's
desert patent line and NE...
J. Glasgow, sec.   Samuel Johnston, gov.

85 10 Jul 1789--David Lewis to Samuel Green...90 pds...75 acres
joining land of said Lewis, Thomas Nores and Cypress Swamp, beginn-
ing at a pine, said Norris' corner tree, N with his line to James
Eure's line, E along his line to William Smith's line to main swamp
and along run, part of a patent granted to William Horn...
Isaac Green   Davis Lewis
Pilvey Gills
Aug Ct 1789

87 18 Aug 1789--Inventory of household, kitchen furniture and books:
Black walnut chest of drawers, 3 ditto dressing tables with glasses,
3 ditto dining tables, ditto round tea table, 30 ditto chairs, ditto
desk and book case, ditto desk, ditto bofat, 8 feather beds, counter
pen, 3 blankets, 2 par sheets, bolster, two pillers to each bed, 20
pictures in fraims, 8 boles assorted, 2 ditto lots of tea cups and
saucers, 2 ditto coffe_, 4 doz Quean chany plates, doz ditto dishes,
1 doz ditto tumblers, 4 silver salts, 2 doz table and tea spoons,
knife case with doz knives and forks, 8 iron pots with hooks, 2
Duch ovens, 3 gridles, 3 gridle irons, 2 large copper kittles, 4
scillets and freying pans, 2 doz puter plates, doz puter dishes, large
family Bible, Burkett on Testament, 4 prayer books, 7 vol. vogages and
travels, 2 ditto Cook's voyages, 10 ditto Rev. line history, 2 ditto
Fordess' Sermons, 2 ditto Age Lewis XV, 4 ditto Connossury, 2 ditto
Guidiens, 8 ditto Spectator, 7 ditto Popes Work, 2 ditto Sterns
Works, 3 ditto Herveys Meditations, 1 ditto Paridise Lost, 2 ditto
Humphrey Clarks, 8 ditto Shakespeare...
                                                  Jos. Granbery
                                                  Chistr. Riddick, P.R.

87 18 Aug 1789--Josiah Granbery to Josiah Collins of Edenton...$1500
crops of corn, fodder, flax, cotton, potatoes, plantation tools, oxen,
34 head cattle, 30 sheep, 100 hogs, 3 horses, yoke of oxen and cart,
double riding chair, still, kettle, scales and weights, 200 empty
pork barrels, 3/4 seine and salt barrels...
Josiah Collins Jr.   Jos. Granbery
Alex. Miller   Josiah Collins
Aug Ct 1789

88 18 Aug 1789--Josiah Granbery to Josiah Collins of Edenton...
$3000...Negro slaves Ben, Will, Tarte, Sam, Jacob, Marrick, Dick,
Lewis, Jerry, Ned, Jim, Isaac, Jack, Tom, Myles, Juda, Benah, Liza,
Agga and child Peg, Pott, Venus and child Amy, Amy, Younger, Lueller,
Lucy and Hannah...
Josiah Collins Jr.   Jos. Granbery
Alex. Miller   Josiah Collins
10 Jan 1790

91 18 Aug 1789--Josiah Granbery and wife, Ann, to Josiah Collins
of Edenton...$4000...several tracts of land: 320 acres conveyed to
him by Thomas Gregorie and wife, Priscilla, 10 Feb 1775 and registered in Chowan Co. becoming Gates Co. after division 25 Mar 1775;
160 acres formerly property of James Jones, dec. and conveyed to
said Granbery by Judith Jones 25 Feb 1788 and Joseph Scott, the younger
and wife, Mary, 10 Jan 1787; 100 acres conveyed to said Granbery by
John Rice and wife, Peggy 19 Nov 1788...
Josiah Collins Jr.   Josiah Collins
Alex. Miller   Jos. Granbery
James Baker   Ann Granbery
David Rice   testified said Ann
signed deed freely.
24 Oct 1789

94 18 Aug 1789--Josiah Granbery to Josiah Collins of Edenton...$1500
household goods, furniture, crops, etc. listed in previous deeds
and including a bay mare...
Josiah Collins Jr.   Jos Granbery
Alex. Miller   Josiah Collins
20 Jun 1790

96 15 Oct 1789--Clement Hill to James Freeman...150 pds...320 acres
beginning at a maple on side of pecosin in Robert Taylor's line, running by line of marked trees to Horse Pen Swamp, along swamp to Charles
Smith's line, then along his line to Timothy Walton's, and along Walton's line to percosin, including his right of Juniper Swamp with all
high land...
James Walton   Clement Hill
James Outlaw   Ann(X)Hill
Nov Ct 1789

97 20 Jan 1789--Jesse Brown and wife, Mary, to Robert Parker...190
pds...90 acres beginning at a pine on Bennetts Creek, running line
of marked trees to Hawtree Branch, down branch to pine, to said creek
and down run...
Abm. Riddick   Jesse(X)Brown
Seasbrook Wilson   Mary(X)Brown
Moor Carter
Nov Ct 1789

98 4 Nov 1789--Thomas Green to Hugh and Pernal King...deed of gift
100 acres on N side of out pocosin beginning at a corner pine of
Samuel Taylor's line, with his line to Elisha Harrell's, to Stephen
Eure's and along Eure's line to out pocosin and to Eure's line again,
to said Taylors; part of patent made to John Osten 12 Jul 1725...
William Davidson   Thomas Green
John Piland
Thomas Piland
Nov Ct 1789

99 2 Oct 1789--Jacob Lassiter of Norfolk Co., Va. to John Atkinson
of Pitt Co....67 pds...Negro girls Isabelle and Fanny...
Hardy Cross   Jacob Lassiter
John Cross
Nov Ct 1789

100 8 Aug 1789--Willoughby McCoy of Norfolk Co., Va. to John Atkinson

of Pitt Co...39 pds...Negro girl Cate...
Samuel Cross   Willoughby McCoy
Mary(+)Cross
Nov Ct 1789

101 19 Nov 1758--James Bennett and John Robins, chief men of Chowan
Indians, to Edward Brisco of Chowan...5 pds...300 acres on E side
of Bennetts Creek between Indian Town and Patrick Lawley's patent
line in Chowan Co., beginning at upper end of Indian Old Field, up
to high land, down side of pecosin to Indian Gut and across...
Robert Taylor   John Robins
Nov Ct 1789   James(B)Bennett

102 14 Nov 1789--Willis Hughes to Thomas Vann...145 pds...100 acres
on Peters Swamp beginning at a chinkpen oak, corner tree between said
Hughes and James Brady, down small branch to post oak, along William
Warren's line to a pine, a corner tree, thence along Holland's line
to a red oak, to said Brady's line...
John Vann   Willis Hughes
Kedar(+)Odam   Sarah(+)Hughes
Nov Ct 1789

104 1 Feb 1789--James Skinner to Cyprian Cross...$___...27 acres,
part of patent granted to him in Oct 1786, beginning at red oak in
Benjamin Barnes line, along his line N to center of 3 pines, Barnes
corner in Jonathan Boice's line, along patent line E to a pine, then
NE to John Odom's corner and along line of marked trees to white oak,
Hare's Old Patent corner and said Cross and along his line...
John Odom   James Skinner
Joseph Smith
Nov Ct 1789

105 4 Nov 1789--Job Umphlet to Israel Beeman...34 pds 8 sh...122
acres joining lands of John Parker, Charles Eure and said Umpflet,
beginning at a small pine in Eure's line, running W as Beeman's line
goes to pine in Parker's line, along his line to small pine, corner
tree, E by line of marked trees to large white oak in Eure's line
and along his line S; part of patent granted to John Collins...
John Parker   Job Umflet
Mills Eure
Nov Ct 1789

106 7 May 1789--John Powell to Elizabeth Chaney Moroney...160 pds...
Negro Hannah...   John Powell
Kedar Ballard
Isaac Miller
Nov Ct 1789

107 10 Nov 1786--Isaac Hunter, sheriff, to More Carter...14 pds...
42 acres belonging to Thomas Green on SE side of Coles Branch be-
ginning at gum in Lickingroot Branch, down branch to Ann Piland's
line, along her line to Asa Harrells and along his line to Samuel
Eure, to said Pilands; sold by execution from court...
Robert Parker   Isaac Hunter
Edward Gatling
Nov Ct 1789

108 8 Nov 1786--Elisha Hiatt of Hertford Co. to Thomas Hiatt...20 pds...

50 acres in Soloman Hiatt's desert...
Edith Goodman   Elisha Hiatt
Sarah(+)Goodman
Nov Ct 1789

109 9 Jun 1789--John Parnall to Aaron Hobbs...13 pds...1 feather bed
and furniture, flax on ground and trunk...
Moses Hill   John Powell
Feb Ct 1790

110 19 Mar 1789--John Harrell to Samuel Thomas...13 pds 10 sh...100
acres, part of patent granted to David Watson, beginning at gum in
Gum Swamp, S with patent line to Jethro Benton's line, a corner, W
to Benton's corner pine, N by line of marked trees to Gum Swamp and
down swamp...
George Hargroves   John Harrell
William Thomas   Nancey(+)Harrell
George Hargroves
Feb Ct 1790

111 17 Nov 1789--Robert Parker Sr. and wife, Abigal, to William Boyce
260 pds...112 acres beginning at pine on Bennetts Creek, along patent
line to a gum, corner tree, in Great Hawtree Swamp, down swamp to said
creek and down creek...
Isaac Miller   Robert Parker
Henry Forrest   Abigal(+)Parker
William Cleaves
Feb Ct 1790

113 23 Aug 1788--Elisha Copland to Watson Scott, both of Nansemond
Co., Va...169 pds...300 acres whereon John Wilkenson now resides and
conveyed by him to Elisha Copeland Sr. 5 Jun 1788...
George Sparling   Elisha Copland
William Neverson
James Thorburn
Nath'l Riddick Sr.
Feb Ct 1790

114 17 Dec 1784--Israel Beeman to James Brady...priviledge of timber
on his paster land that he bought of Lewis and James Brady to insure
debt of 100 pds...
Mills Lewis   Israel Beeman
John Lewis
Kimbell Pratt
Feb Ct 1790

115 9 Oct 1789--John Odom to Henry Copland...9 acres beginning at
pine stump on riverside, NE to marked gum, N to river and down river,
land granted to Robert Hardy in favor of Jeremiah Jackson 30 Jan 1755
...for 35 acres on E side of Chowan River beginning at pine in patent
line joining said Odom's land, SE to corner of patent; grant to John
King in Apr 1720...
William Harriss   John Odom
Jesse Vann   Monica Odom
Feb Ct 1790

116 15 Feb 1790--James Brady to Eborn Sears...water and timber on 58
acres in return for building plant and improving fences,land begins

at a pine in Peters Swamp, along line of marked trees to new road,
to Poplar Branch and down branch to William Warren's line and along
his line to said swamp and up swamp...
John Pipkin   James Brady
James Landen
Feb Ct 1790

117 18 Jan 1790--Mills Skinner to William Crafford...80 pds...50
acres of patent granted to Jacob Odom 21 Feb 1738, beginning at corner gum in branch, Demsey Harrell's line, running to Gum Swamp, to
ash, corner tree, down swamp and along line of marked trees to said
branch and down branch...
Jesse Vann   Mills Skinner
Demsey Harrell   Ann Skinner
Feb Ct 1790

118 25 Dec 1789--Ann Carter to Isaac Carter...20 pds...Negro girl
4 years old...
Edward Gatling   Ann(+)Carter
Jesse Vann
William Warren
Feb Ct 1790

119 16 Aug 1789--Josua Small to his daughter, Mary Gwin, and her
son, William Gwin...deed of gift...150 acres known as Morley's
Point, beginning at corner percosin tree on desert side on Jethro
Ballard's line, N along his line to run of Loosing Swamp, up run to
John Gordon's line, S to dividing line between land on which he lives
and said point, E along line of marked trees to desert, to back line
of new patent and N...
James Small   Joshua Small
David Small
Hezekiah Jones
Feb Ct 1790

120 5 Oct 1789--Seth Riddick, sheriff, to Patrick Hegerty...40 pds
1 sh 6 pn...200 acres whereon Will. Dunsford lives adjoining lines
of Samuel Baker, Moses Kittrell and Jonathan Williams; sold by court
execution against Abraham Sumner and Abraham Eason brought by Thomas
Newby for 118 pds in debts...
William Harris   Seth Riddick
Julia Riddick
Feb Ct 1790

121 28 Nov 1788--Abraham Hill of Rowan Co. to Kedar Hill...80 pds...
his part of 82 acres on swamp that maketh into Catherine Creek and
formerly belonging to their father, Guy Hill, dec...
Thos. Hunter   Abraham Hill
Simon Stallings
Himbrick Hill
Feb Ct 1790

123 15 Dec 1789--Henry Hill to Edward Brisco...20 pds...50 acres
on E side of Bennetts Creek and is ½ of plantation whereon he lives
and joining Gordon's line...
Willis Parker   Henry(H)Hill
Thomas Marshall
Feb Ct 1790

124 14 Jun 1789--William Williams to James Brown...$___...13 acres, part of a patent granted to More Carter 14 Apr 1752, beginning at main road, running W by line of marked trees to water oak in branch, up branch to main road and up road...
William Brown   William Williams
Robert Doughtry
Feb Ct 1790

125 16 Aug 1789--Joshua Small to his daughter, Mary Gwin, and her son, William, and daughter, Charlotte...deed of gift of Negroes Bob and Liddy, feather bed and furniture, cows and calves; after death of said Mary, William to receive said Bob and Charlotte to receive said Liddy...
David Small   Joshua(X)Small
Hezekiah(X)Jones
Feb Ct 1790

126 28 Jan 1789--Henry Dilday to Henry Eborn Sears...20 pds...50 acre plantation beginning at lightwood tree, corner of Joel Goodman and William Gatling, along Goodman's line to lightwood stump, corner of Isaac Pipkin, along his line to corner tree of William Goodman and said Gatling and along his line...
James Brady   Henry(H)Dilday
Lemuel(+)Collins
Mary(ııı)Brady
Feb Ct 1790

127 15 Nov 1789--Jesse Jones to Eborn Sears...30 pds...33 acres beginning at oak in Peters Swamp, along Burgess line to William Warren's, along his line to swamp and along run; said land was purchased of John Ellis...
James Braddy   Jesse(X)Jones
Robert Douglass   Ruth Jones
Feb Ct 1790

128 13 Dec 1789--Edward Briscoe to Henry Hill...20 pds...50 acres, ½ of plantation whereon he lives, on E side of Bennetts Creek pecosin, up creek to Olde Indian Patent, along line of marked trees to Gordon's line, to white oak, a corner tree, and along line of marked trees...
Willis Parker   Edward(EB)Brisco
Thomas Marshall
Feb Ct 1790

129 17 Dec 1789--Mary and Osiah Harrell to Demsey Harrell...25 pds 66 acres called Long Ridge on N side of Cypress Swamp in place called The Islands, beginning at corner pine in patent line, along line and river pecosin swamp to John Odom's line, by line of marked trees to a gum on Cypress Swamp and up swamp; is part of a patent of 640 acres granted to Jacob Odom 15 Feb 1738...
John Odom   Mary(+)Harrell
Milley(+)Harrell   Osiah(+)Harrell
David Harrell
Feb Ct 1790

131 16 Feb 1790--William Boyce to Timothy Lassiter...130 pds...224 acres, binding on Isaac Miller Sr., Micajah Riddick and said Lassiter

and bought of Samuel Baker. Land was possessioned by said Baker, William Vann, James Knight, William Hinton and Jeremiah Speight...
John Warren   William(X)Boyce
William Baker
Feb Ct 1790

133 6 Dec 1789--Willis Sparkman to Reuben Sparkman...10 pds...16½ acres on Cypress Swamp and is ½ of their mother's third of land joining land of which said Willis is possessed, beginning at chinkapen tree on side of said swamp, through plantation to persimmon tree, along middle of pond and by line of marked trees to a pine in Felton's line on main road and along Felton's line...
Ruth Harrell
Jesse Harrell   Willis(+)Sparkman
Feb Ct 1790

134 12 Feb 1790--Henry King and wife, Phereby, to Thomas Smith of Upper Parish, Nansemond Co., Va...100 pds...400 acres beginning at 3 gums and a water oake, corner of Samuel Williams and John Kittrell, along Kittrell's line to white oak, corner of Demsey Odom, and along his line to a small branch running to Beach Swamp, to a pine of John Waters, along his line to red oak, now scarfaced post, near said Williams road, S along Odom's line to white oake, corner tree between said Odom, said King and Robert Parker, along Parker's line to Jonathan Williams' line, to a marked tree at road and along Williams' line...
                                           Henry King
John Bethey   Phereby(+)King
Elisha Cross
Abel Cross
Feb Ct 1790

136 17 May 1790--Seth Eason, sheriff, to Samuel Pitman of Halifax Co...31 pds...250 acres belonging to Willis Wiggins Sr. and Willis Wiggens Jr. and sold by court execution from Halifax Superior Court issued by Benjamin Crowell against said Wiggens for 99 pds 6 sh and 11 pn and witnessed by Lovatt Burgess, clerk. Said Eason acted as deputy under late Seth Riddick, dec. and since has obtained office of high sheriff. Said Wiggens land joins Jacob Sumner, dec., Thomas Frazar, dec., John Darden, Edward Arnold, James Knight and Virginia line...
Jas. B. Sumner   Seth Eason
Patrick Hegerty
May Ct 1790

138 18 Jan 1788--Thomas Young of Halifax Co. to Elisha Benton...90 pds...100 acres adjoining land of said Benton, Ann Gibson and others...
Miles Benton   Thos. Young
Joshua(X)Jones
May Ct 1790

139 30 Dec 1789--James Cole of Nansemond Co., Va. to John Rochell of Southampton...100 pds...150 acres, ½ of land bequeathed to him by will of Abraham Cole, dec. and lying in Gates Co, formerly part of Hertford Co., beginning on E side of Chowan River at marked pine near Henry Copland's land, down river to cypress at mouth of small creek, to forked maple, thence to black gum near main road, bounded

by road, to a marked pine, a corner tree, to a black gum...
John Giles   James Cole
Mary Green
Elender Giles
May Ct 1790

141 9 Oct 1789--Henry Copland, planter, to John Odom, planter...
exchange of 35 acres, beginning at pine in patent line, with line
joining Odom's own land, SE to a pine, a corner, SW crossing patent,
was a grant to John King April 1720...for 9 acres on E side of Chowan
River beginning at a pine and running NE down river...
William Harriss   Henry Copland
Jesse Vann
May Ct 1790

142 6 Jan 1790--Jethro Ballard, David Rice and Timothy Hunter, executors of will of James Sumner, dec. to Joshua Small...125 pds 12
sh...150 acres in desert known as the Ridges about 1 mile E of Jesse
Eason's plantation, beginning at holly near Eastmost ridge, NE to a
juniper and binding on main swamp, to include 2 small islands, SW to
main swamp; is land granted to Luke Sumner by Earl of Granville, and
after death of said Luke fell to his brother, said James...
James Norfleet   Jethro Ballard
Charel Jones   David Rice
May Ct 1790   Timothy Hunter

144 3 Mar 1790--Abraham Saunders and Charity Saunders, widow of
Francis Saunders, dec., to Jesse Saunders...60 pds...100 acres on
W side of Somerton Creek, beginning at red oak near swamp, corner
tree of John Hook's land, running line of marked trees to marked
pine, another corner of Hooks, to John Minchew's land and along his
line to swamp and up main run...   Abraham Saunders
William Odom   Charity Saunders
Bray Saunders
May Ct 1790

146 24 Apr 1790--Soloman King appoints his friends, David Darden,
John Lee and Jethro Sumners, as trustees to his grandchildren, child-
ren of his daughter, Abigail Vollentine, for 20 years to hire and let
out for profit five Negroes: Simon, Meals, Phelles, Jack and Eden.
Also, 7 head cattle, 7 sheep, 20 hogs, dest, 2 tables, 2 chests, 6
Windsor stools, 2 iron pots, 2 bed, parcel of puter, earthen ware,
glasses and all household goods on his plantation that he purchased
of Jacob Minchew...   Soloman King
William Oadham
Uriah Oadham
John Landen
May Court 1790

147 17 May 1790--John Rochell and wife, Judith, of Southampton Co.,
Va. to Mathew Wills...$50...150 acres, ½ of tract on E side of
Chowan River opposite Meherren River, beginning at marked pine in
Henry Copland's land, down river to cypress at mouth of small creek,
up creek to black gum near main road, along road to black gum; land
formerly held by John Odom, who conveyed to Benjamin Baker and Abra-
ham Cole 22 Sep 1770, and said Benjamin conveyed his half to said
Rochell 23 Feb 1787, and said Cole devised his half to his son, James,
who sold to said Rochell 13 Dec 1789...
Open Court   John Rochell
May 1790   Judith Rochell

149 18 May 1790--Bond and Zaccraiah Menchew to Robert McCulloch...
16 sh...1 acre beginning at black gum on E side of run of Reedy Branch, up branch to white oak, E to white oak, N to pine and W...
Willeford Horton   Zacra Menchew
John Pipkin
May Ct 1790

150 17 Oct 1789--William Green to Stephen Harrell...42 pds...28 acres on S side of Lickingroot Branch, beginning at a pine, corner tree in David Lewis and Uriah Eure's lines, along Eure's line by line of marked trees to hicory, to Richard Green's line, to black gum in said branch and back to Lewis' line...
Thomas Felton   William Green
John Felton
May Ct 1790

151 16 Apr 1790--Isaac Harrell to his son, Noah...deed of gift...80 acres beginning at Bennetts Creek road, running down branch W to a corner tree, by roe of marked trees to a water oak on said road...
Samuel Harrell   Isaac(X)Harrell
Isaac Harrell Jr.
May Ct 1790

152 14 Apr 1790--Thomas Langston to his brothers, Luke and Demsey... deed of gifts after his decease: 169 acres in Edgecomb Co., all blacksmith tools, money due, tarkil_ on Sand Banks land and wearing apparrel to said Luke; whole estate within and without dores to said Demsey.
John Odom   Thomas Langston
John Parker
Charel(+)Rooks
May Ct 1790

153 12 Apr 1790--James and Benjamin Robins and George and Joseph Bennett, chief men and representatives of Chowan Indian Nation, to William Lewis and Samuel Harrell...$100...400 acres contained in Chowan Indian patent made 4 Apr 1724, beginning with Patrick Lawler's patent line near Bennetts Creek, along his line to a pine, his corner tree, to Ephriam Blanchard's corner, along line to a pine, his other corner, through a savanah and along patent to white oake in Aaron Blanchard's fence, to Catherine Creek at mouth of Indian Swamp and down creek to Chowan River and up river to mouth of Bennetts Creek...
Thomas Marshall   James(R)Robins
Permelia Marshall   Benj'n(+)Robins
May Ct 1790   George( )Bennett
                                                    Joseph(+)Bennett

154 21 Jan 1790--Henry and Ann Forrest to Zadoc Hinton...225 pds... 300 acres, called Old Quarter, beginning at mouth of Watery Branch, where it joins run of Bennetts Creek, up run binding on Jeremiah Speight's, which was part of same patent, to mouth of another branch in Henry Smith's plantation, by his house and up his line to Soloman Alston's corner tree, on a line formerly Joshua Allens, now Sumners, to run of Bennetts Creek and up creek...
Thomas Marshall   Henry Forrest
James Banrone   Anna Forrest
May Ct 1790
William Baker testified said Anna
relinquished her rights.

156 13 Mar 1790--Richard Bond and wife, Mary, to Demsey Jones...75 pds...50 acres beginning at a maple, corner tree between said land and said Bond, along line of marked trees to Indian Swamp, being a line between said land and John B. Walton, down swamp to marked gum, to Beaverdam Swamp, to large branch and up run...
William(+)Briscoe   Rich'd Bond
Elisha Hance Bond   Mary Bond
May Ct 1790

157 21 Apr 1790--Priscilla Lassitor Jr. to Aaron Blanchard Jr. deed of gift...feather bed and furniture and chest; to granddaughter, Absalah Blanchard...feather bed and furniture, loom and gear, linen wheel, chest, 2 dishes, 2 basins, 3 puter plates, earthen dish, 6 earthen dishes, 3 head cattle and mare colt...
Aaron Blanchard   Priscilla(+)Lassitor
William Bond
May Ct 1790

158 23 Apr 1790--Aaron Lassitor to Isaac Harrell...15 pds...30 acres beginning at red oak in said Harrell's line, N along line of marked trees to corner tree, SE to a white oak on a branch and along branch, up Harrell's line; is part of land on which said Lassitor lives...
Jos. Granbery
David Rice   Aaron Lassitor
Timothy Lassitor
May Ct 1790

159 21 Jan 1790--Zadoc and Leah Hinton to Henry Forrest...225 pds... 200 acres beginning at hickory in Willis Parker's line, along his line to William Hinton's line, along his line to Cherry Morris' line, to Robert Taylor's line, to Ephriam Morris' line and down Fork Neck Branch to Bennetts Creek, up creek to Roberts Mill Gutt and up gutt...
Tho. Marshall   Zadoc Hinton
James Ransone   Leah( )Hinton
May Ct 1790
William Baker testified said Leah relinquished her rights.

161 7 May 1790--Miles Benton, planter, to Abraham Morgan...30 pds... 20 acres on W side of Bennetts Creek, beginning in center of 3 gums and a maple, said Morgan's corner, E by line of marked trees and small branch NW to white oak stump corner in Pugh's Patent, N; former grant to John King 4 Nov 1707...
                                            Miles Benton
Francis Parker
Patrick Hegerty
May Ct 1790

162 26 Nov 1789--Treasury of North Carolina to Abel Cross...10 pds for every 100 acres...42 acres beginning at black gum in Pine Swamp in William Crafford's line, along patent line S to chinkapen oak, Joseph Runnell's and said Crafford's corner tree, along Runnells line SE to patent corner, N to Johny Odom's line and along his line to John Varnal's line...No. 88.
J. Glasgow, sec.   Sam. Johnston, gov.
20 Feb 1791

163 26 Nov 1789--Treasury of North Carolina to Jacob Bagley...10 pds

for every 100 acres...48 acres beginning at a pine, Daniel Stallings' corner tree in John Powell's line, along Stalling's line S to a pine in Thomas Hurdle's corner tree, thence with his line NW crossing mouth of Indian Branch to a pine, Hurdle's and Abraham Sumner's corner tree on W side of main desert, with Sumner's line to Sumner's desert patent corner tree, S to said Powell's corner tree... No. 82.
J. Glasgow, sec.
24 Feb 1791
Sam. Johnston, gov.

164 28 Nov 1789--Treasury of North Carolina to Joseph Riddick...10 pds every 100 acres...274 acres beginning at post oak, Joseph Hurdle's corner tree in Abraham Sumner's line, SW and then NW to a dead pine near Sumner's, to a cypress on side of pocosin, Abraham Perce's and Joseph Riddick's corner tree, with Riddick's line to said Hurdle's corner and SW... No. 84.
J. Glasgow, sec.
14 Feb 1791
Sam. Johnston, gov.

166 26 Nov 1789--Treasury of North Carolina to John Fontaine...10 pds for every 100 acres...3000 acres beginning at a gum, Jacob Gordon's corner tree in Jesse Eason's line, NE on Fontaine's new survey to a gum, S to Juniper Swamp, W to a gum in Mary Riddick's line, NW to said Gordon's line...
J. Glasgow, sec. No. 87
20 Feb 1791
Sam. Johnston, gov.

167 18 Feb 1789--Benjamin Harrell of Bertie Co. to William Crafford... 4 pds 16 sh 3 pn...27½ acres, part of a grant to said Harrell, beginning at a sweet gum, said Crafford's corner tree, running patent line to Gum Swamp, along line of marked trees dividing said Crafford and Moses Jones' patent line, to Gum Swamp...
Willis(+)Stallings
Jesse(+)Stallings
Aug Ct 1790
Benjamin(+)Harrell

169 16 Aug 1790--William Powell to his friend and kinsman, Micajah Riddick Jr...deed of gift...200 acre plantation whereon he lives, beginning at mouth of Middle Swamp at main run of Bennetts Creek, up run of swamp to Anthony Matthew's line, by his line to Isaac Miller's, to said Riddick's line, to main road and down road to Dobges' Branch, by line of marked trees to Bennetts Creek and up main run. Also, 6 Negroes: Sam, Jacob, Peter, Charles, Jeffery and Betty, blacksmith tools, all stock, household and kitchen furniture and all moveable estate...
Noah Felton
John Simons
Isaac Miller
Aug Ct 1790
William Powell

170 3 Aug 1789--Seth Eason, sheriff, to William Freeman...25 pds... 50 acres belonging to John Hobbs and sold to satisfy court judgment that Willis Brown obtained against said Hobbs; land in Indian Creek beginning at a marked pine on George Outlaw's line, along his line to Jacob Outlaw's line, to James Freeman's line, to a corner pine, down line of marked tree, that formerly belonged to Luke Sumners, dec. to a black gum in large branch to a large pine at head...
Jos. Riddick
James Outlaw
Micajah Riddick
Aug Ct 1790
Seth Eason

172 1 Mar 1790--Henry Hill to John White...76 pds...50 acres beginning at white oak, corner tree on Gorden's line, along line of marked trees to a pine, corner tree in Bennetts Creek pecosin, to old patent line, to Gordon's line...
William Freeman   Henry(H)Hill
Selah Freeman   Elizabeth(+)Hill
James Freeman
Aug Ct 1790

174 13 Jul 1790--Joseph Norfleet to Thomas Robertson...12 pds...240 acres, patent granted to John Langston 20 Jul 1726, beginning at corner pine of John Parker's on a branch of Robert Rogers', being formerly a corner of Richard Odom, from there along John Odom's line to Stephen Piland's line near a N corner and running said Piland's to a white oake, a corner tree, being dividing corner between John Odom and said Robertson, along Stephen Piland's line to Thomas Piland's line, to Charles Ures' line at a corner gum, along Stephen Youre's line to a corner tree on John Parker's line, formerly line of Richard Odom's, and along Parker's line...   Joseph Norfleet
Edward(X)Pilant
Gabrel(X)Marten
Aug Ct 1790

176 16 Aug 1790--Thomas Hunter to John Hofler...12 pds...50 acres on S side of Water_ Swamp beginning at Kedar Hill's corner and said Hofler's side line, NW to a pine, to John B. Walton's corner tree, with his line NE joining said Hill's line...   Thomas Hunter
Samuel Smith
James B. Sumner
Aug Ct 1790

177 2 Feb 1790--John Hunter and wife, Chloe, to William Hunter...49 pds...20 acres being part of patent granted to William Hunter in 1701, and by will of John Hunter given to his two sons, said John and William, beginning at gum in Meherrin Swamp, running to mouth of branch on W side, by line of marked trees to a sweet gum, corner tree, to William Hunter's line and to run of swamp and down...
Demsey Trotman   John Hunter
Riddick Trotman   Chloe Hunter
Aug Ct 1790

179 16 Aug 1790--Samuel Green to David Lewis...$150...75 acre plantation whereon he lives and that his father, Soloman Green, purchased of John Denby 2 Oct 1752, beginning on Cypress Swamp at Thomas Norres' line, to land of James Eure Jr., E along his line to William Smith's red oak, S to said swamp; is part of a patent granted to William Horn Sr...   Samuel Green
Jesse Vann
John Parker
Jeames Gatling
Aug Ct 1790

180 29 Jan 1790--John Hunter to Thomas Hunter...19 pds...15 acres beginning at pine saplin in said John's line, by line of marked trees and SW...   John Hunter
Robert Riddick
Simon Stallings
Aug Ct 1790

181 10 Aug 1790--Humphrey Hudgins to Easter Matthews...3 pds 4 sh...
4 acres beginning at maple near Thomas Smith's, a corner tree in new
survey, to Jeremiah Speight's, NE to road and along road...
Samuel Smith   Humphrey Hudgins
Aug Ct 1790

183 3 Jun 1790--Luke Sumner to William Ellis...300 pds...200 acre
plantation known as Folly on S side of Loosing Swamp, beginning at
marked white oake, Larcum and Harris corner, SE joining land of Jacob
Powell, dec. and Moses Davis, to marked gum by a branch, E joining
land of Soloman Briggs, by line of marked trees to John Miller, dec.
line, to Loosing Swamp and down S side to Benjamin Gordon's line,
N along line to run of swamp to high land; is land that Luke Sum-
ner the elder purchased of Col. Lemuel Riddick...
Jethro Ballard   Luke Sumner
William Hinton
Moses Davis
Aug Ct 1790

184 21 Nov 1789--Treasury of North Carolina to Jacob Gordon...10
pds per hundred acres...183 acres beginning at pine sapling on N
side of Basses Swamp in Jesse Eason's line near bridge, SE to pine,
NE to said Eason's desert patent, with his line E to William Wooley's
patent, NW to said Gordon's line to Thomas Fullington's line and N...
J. Glasgow, sec. No. 86   Sam. Johnston,
8 Apr 1791   gov.

186 24 Apr 1790--Soloman King to daughter, Martha Sumner,...Negro
man Denah, boys Peter, Isaac and Miles and girl Annaia...
David Darden   Soloman King
John Landen
John Lee
Nov Ct 1790

187 23 Oct 1790--Soloman King and Abigail and Joseph Vollentine
have appointed friends David Darden, John Lee and Jethro Sumner
as trustees to hire and use profit for 20 years of Negroes Sam,
Tom and Faney for children of said Abigail...
Isaac F. Weatherly   Soloman King
Elizabeth Tyenes   Abigail Vollentine
James(X)Bab_   Jo. Vollentine
Nov Ct 1790

188 15 Nov 1790--Isaac Hunter to Samuel Harrell...36 pds...45 acres
beginning at pine corner of said Harrell and Aaron Lassiter, E along
line of marked trees to David Rice's line, E along his line to red
oak, corner tree of said Hunter, and N...
William Harriss   Isaac Hunter
Benjamin Gordon
Nov Ct 1790

189 10 Nov 1789--Job Umflet to Stephen Eure...71 pds 4 sh...170 acres
joining land of John Parker, Joseph Norfleet and Charles Eure, beginning at large white oake in said Charles' line, W as Israel Beeman's
line goes to small pine in said Parker's line, along his line to a
blowed up pine, corner tree, along Norfleet's line, S along said

Charles' line; formerly a patent of John Collens...
William Davidson   Job Umflet
Benjamin Umflet
Elisha Harrell
Nov Term 1790

190 25 May 1790--Watson Scott of Suffolk, Va. to Luke Sumner...200
pds...300 acres whereon John R. Wilkenson, dec. lately resided and
is land said Wilkenson and wife, Judith, conveyed to Elisha Copland
with choice of redemption, for 338 pds 16 sh 10 pn 5 June 1788;
said Copeland conveyed to said Scott 23 Aug 1788 for 169 pds 9 sh
5 pn...   Watson Scott
John Lupton
James Therburn
Jethro Ballard
Nov Term 1790

192 3 Jun 1790--William Ellis and wife, Mary, to William Hinton...200
pds...174 acres near head of Loosing Swamp on SW side, beginning at
pine in Daniel Pugh's line, along James Wiggen's line to white oake
in Robert Powell's line, to his corner sowerwood tree, to said Pugh's
line; is land said Ellis bought of Moses Speght 11 Sep 1779...
Jethro Ballard   William Ellis
Moses Davis   Mary Ellis
Luke Sumner
Nov Term 1790

194 3 Jun 1790--Luke Sumner to Jethro Ballard...100 pds...150 acres
on Loosing Swamp beginning at gum at run at NW side, running W along
line of marked trees dividing tract from David Jones' land, to a gum,
crossing swamp and down S side to white oak, beginning tree of Larcum
and Harriss patent, back across swamp; is land Luke Sumner the elder
purchased of John Powell 24 Oct 1786...   Luke Sumner
William Ellis
William Hinton
Moses Davis
Nov Term 1790

195 18 Sep 1790--Thomas Robertson and wife, Margaret, to John Parker
15 pds...100 acres patent of John Langston 20 Jul 1726, beginning
at corner tree of said Parker, that was in Richard Odom's patent,
used to be a pine but fell down and present owner made corner tree
an oake, on side of Robert Rogers' branch near place where pine stood,
running John Odom's line to Stephen Pilant's, to Thomas Pilant's, to
a corner of Charles Eure's, to Stephen Eure's and along his line...
Demsey Langston   Thomas Robertson
Cyprian Cross   Margret(+)Robertson
Israel Beeman
Nov Term 1790

197 23 Sep 1790--Demsey Phelps to Henry Forrest...140 pds...120
acres on S side of Bennetts Creek, beginning at a cypress, William
Booth's corner tree, up swamp by land of Joel Foster, to William
Lewis' land, by land of Jonathan Lassiter, to David Harrell's line,
to William Gordon's, to John White, to orphans of Even Murfree, dec.
by land of Thomas Marshall to said Booth's...   Demsey Phelps
Jonathan Roberts
Ephriam Morris
Nov Term 1790

198 6 Nov 1790--Alse Owens of Bartie Co. to Henry Goodman...13 pds
10 sh...50 acres, part of a patent granted to John Rall's Jr. 1 Apr
1723, beginning at white oak near main river pocosin, running said
Goodman's line to corner maple, to main river and along run...
David Jordan   Alse(X)Owens
Elisha Jordan
William(M)Gatling
Nov 1790

200 18 Feb 1791--Joseph Riddick to his son, Reuben...deed of gift...
374 acres, including land whereon he lives and which he bought of
George Eason 26 Nov 1789 and two tracts of 50 acres each; first ad-
joining aforesaid patent, Joseph Hurdle and Samuel Green and the 2nd
in desert patent joining William Eason, dec...   Jo. Riddick
Thomas Hurdle
Shad Felton
Feb Ct 1791

201 14 Dec 1790--Pasco Turner of Nansemond Co., Va. to Henry Goodman
150 pds 10 sh...300 acres beginning at mouth of Troy Swamp at Bennetts
Creek, along swamp to end of island, S to Hinton's line and along his
line to said Creek and up creek; being all land in a patent to Joseph
John Alston 1 May 1768...
Ja. Murdaugh   Pasco Turner, ex.
Jonathan Roberts   the Rev. John Read
William Booth
Feb Ct 1791

202 23 Feb 1790--Josiah Roggerson of Perquimans Co. to Noah Felton...
92 pds...Negro woman Cherry and child Pat Henry...
Shad. Felton   Josiah Roggerson
Judith Felton
Feb Ct 1791

204 22 Dec 1790--Whereas a marrage is intended shortly to be solomn-
ized between Rachael Moore of Hertford Co. and Thomas Trotman, both
possessed of considerable property agree for Starkey Sharp of Hertford Co. to serve as trustee for 5 pds...Said Thomas agrees that
one Negro man and one Negro woman, ½ of dwelling house, 1/3 land
and use of other house belonging to him be used for said Rachael
and other property should be considered as separate...
William Moor_   Rachel Moore
Benjamin Moor_   Thomas Trotman
Feb Ct 1791   Starkey Sharp

207 15 Mar 1788--Abraham Sumner to Joseph Riddick...30 pds...90 acres
bought of Jacob Eason, beginning at hickory, John Ownley's corner
tree in said Riddick's line, along his line to Sandy Ridge Road, with
road to Abraham Pearce's line to red oak, corner tree in Riddick's
line...   Abraham Sumner
Even Jones
Reuben Riddick
Feb Ct 1790

209 12 Aug 1790--Moses Hare Sr. to Elisha Hare...5 pds...89 acres
at head of Loosing Swamp, formerly belonging to Thomas Wiggens, who

sold to James Wiggens and his heir, James Wiggens, sold to said Hare...
William(+)Arnold   Moses Hare Sr.
David Jones
James Small
Sarah(X)Brinkley
Feb Ct 1791

210 24 Nov 1790--Lewis Jones to Hugh Griffin of Nansemond Co., Va...
400 pds...200 acres joining lands of Simon Brinkley, Luke Sumner and
David Brinkley...
Robert Riddick   Lewis Jones
Morgan Overman
Elizabeth(X)Small

211 31 Jan 1790--Robert McCullock to Jethro Meltear...100 pds...100
acres beginning at Daniel Hayes line tree, a cypress, along his line
to post oak in Indian line, along that line to a pine, corner tree in
Reedy Branch, joining Minchew's line, down branch to run of Bennetts
Creek and down creek...
Abraham Riddick   Robert McCullock
William Gordon
Feb Ct 1791

212 11 Feb 1791--Moses Jones to William Wallis...12 pds...50 acres
beginning at white oake, corner tree in branch, running line of marked trees to corner black gum in Demsey Barnes' line, along his line
to a prong of Pine Swamp, down swamp to corner black gum on branch;
part of patent granted to William Hooks in 1723...
Cyprian Cross   Moses(+)Jones
John Wallis
David Cross
Feb Ct 1791

213 15 Jan 1791--William Wallis to John Wallis...12 pds...50 acres,
part of a patent to William Hooks, beginning at black gum in Pine
Swamp near said John's house, along line of marked trees to sweet
gum in William Skiners' line, along his line to black gum in said
swamp and down swamp...
Cyprian Cross   William Wallis
Moses Jones
Feb Ct 1791

214 21 Feb 1791--Jesse Saunders to Zachariah and Henry Copland of
Nansemond Co., Va...15 pds...2 acres beginning at cypress on side
of river and running along line of new marked trees to a pine, to
large pine in Kings' line, to river and down river...
Jas. Riddick   Jesse(+)Saunders
Reuben Riddick
Feb Ct 1791

215 14 Feb 1791--Zachariah Copeland and William Foulk of Upper Par-
ish of Nansemond Co., Va., executors of James Winborne, to Abel Cross
2 pds...100 acres beginning at maple in edge of pocosin near David
Watson's corn field, along his line to river, to John Copland's
line, to David Cross' line and to said Watson's line...
Hardy Cross   Zachariah Copland
James Rawls   William Faulk
James Copeland
Feb Ct 1791

216 25 Oct 1790--Joseph Riddick to James Baker...8 pds...4 acres on W side of Sandy Ridge Road beginning in Ownley's line where it crosses road, N to hickory stump near store house, binding on road and SW...
                  Jo. Riddick
Willis Brown
Jethro Meltear
Feb Ct 1791

217 19 Jan 1791--Randolph Moore to Abel Cross...6 pds...22 acres beginning at Wallis' corner tree, white oak, along his line to Demsey Barnes', to red oak, to his old patent line and to a corner pine.
Henry Goodman   Randolph Moore
Edith Goodman
Feb Ct 1791

219 1 Jan 1791--Henry Eborn Sears to Henry Dilday...20 pds...50 acres adjoining Joel Goodman, beginning at lightwood tree, corner of said Goodman and William Gatling, along Goodman's line to a lightwood stump of Isaac Pipkin's, along his line to corner tree of William Goodman's and said Gatling and along Gatling's line...
William Vann   Eborn Sears
James Brady
Liles Vann
Feb Ct 1791

220 17 Oct 1790--James Brown to Miles Parker...12 pds...13 acres beginning at red oak on roadside, down road to Long Branch, to water oak and along line of marked trees...
Lewis Sparkman   James(x)Brown
William Boys
Feb Ct 1791

221 27 Dec 1790--David Goodman to Isaac Darden of Hertford Co...60 pds...50 acres on N side of Peters Swamp, being part of tract granted to Henry (____) 28 Apr 1711, beginning at line of William Goodman in said swamp, running his line to small branch, to corner tree of said William and Isaac Pipkin, along Pipkins line to a corner lightwood post of said Pipkin and Henry Dilday, along their lines to said swamp and down...
                  David Goodman
William Goodman
John Kittrell
Feb Ct 1791

222 16 Feb 1792--Abraham Eason and Thomas Hunter, sheriff, to Joseph Hurdle...20 pds...240 acres, part of a patent granted to Abraham Sumner, beginning at Joseph Riddick's corner gum tree on side of desert, SW to a corner tree of Jeames Gregory, along his line SE to Seth Riddick's, to corner of patent...
Abraham Hurdle   Abraham Eason
Judith Hall   Thos. Hunter
Samuel Green

224 11 Jan 1791--John Wallis to David Cross...30 pds...50 acres on E side of Chowan River, and is part of plantation whereon his cousin, John Wallis, dec. formerly lived, beginning at David Cross' line and along his line to David Watson's, to Benton's old line and up Pecosin; part of agrant to William Speight 1719...
Cyprian Cross   John Wallis
Moses Jones
William Wallis
Feb Ct 1791

225 16 Feb 1791--James Arline to Robert Napper...50 pds...50 acres beginning at marked gum in Beach Swamp, running NE to red oak, SE to branch, to black gum, corner tree on Demsey Odom's line, across a neck of land; is land received by said James as only son and heir of his father, John Arline, dec...
James(+)Russell   James Arline
Mills (+)Odom
Thomas(+)Ellen
Feb Ct 1791

227 16 Apr 1791--Agreed between Joseph Spekes and William King that sute now depending in Superior Court for district of Edenton wherein said King is plantiff against said Speight, defendent, shall be discontinued and said parties agree said suit shall never be renewed by them or their heirs under penalty of 1000 pds...
Thos. Hunter   William King
Will. T. Muse   Joseph Speight
May Term 1791

227 16 May 1791--Catren Parker to Jonathan Roberts...60 pds...2 beds and furniture, 8 puter dishes, cow and yearling, cow, 9 sows, 25 pigs, 3 iron potts, 6 head sheep, dest, chest of drawers and 2 chests...
David Harrell   Cathrin(+)Parker

228 25 Oct 1790--Josiah Granbery and Josiah Collins of Chowan to Isaac Eason...45 pds...Negro Marrick...
Thos. Granbery   Jos. Granbery
May Term 1791   Josiah Collins

228 10 May 1791--Moses Hare Sr. to Moses Jr...60 pds...Negro Girl Venus...
Jethro Sumner   Moses Hare
John Darden

229 25 Oct 1791--Josiah Granbery and Josiah Collins of Chowan to Lawrence Baker...60 pds...Negro woman Jude...
Mich'l Lyunce   Jos. Granbery
Alex'r Miller   Josiah Collins

230 18 Jan 1791--Henry Blanchard of Randolph Co. to Palatiah Blanchard...70 pds...100 acres between Bennetts Creek and Catrin Creek, beginning at a pine in Richard Bond's line, along Robert Riddick's line to Long Branch, agreeable to will of Aaron Blanchard Sr...
Demsey Blanchard   Henry Blanchard
Henry Walton
May Term 1791

231 17 May 1791--Luke Sumner to Jethro Ballard...25 pds...30 acres near mouth of Orapeak Swamp and is part of patent formerly granted to Luke Sumner, beginning at gum and persimmon tree near John Norfleet's patent, along his line N to high land and E...
Samuel Harrell   Luke Sumner
William Ellis
May Term 1791

232 17 Nov 1788--Abraham Sumner to Jethro Ballard, David Rice and Timothy Hunter...145 pds...220 acres beginning at white oak running N over two small branches to Thomas Docton's head line, E by line of

marked trees to Jacob Docton's corn field fence thence E...
Seth Eason   Abraham Sumner
Miles Benton
May Term 1791

233 28 Mar 1791--George, John and Isaac Eason to Isaac Langston...
50 pds...Negro girl Philles about 17 years old...
Law. Baker   George Eason
Luke Langston   John Eason
May Term 1791   Isaac Eason

234 11 Oct 1790--John Powell to Luke Sumner...10 pds...17 acres in
White Oak Springs Marsh on N side of Orapeak beginning at a stake in
place of a cypress, formerly John Norfleet's corner, NE to ditch, then
to swamp...   John Powell
Jethro Ballard
Charles Jones
Elizabeth Riddick
May Term 1791

235 25 Feb 1791--Henry Forrest to Lawrence Baker...50 pds...75 acres,
being part of patent granted to Thomas Smith in 1780 and conveyed to
Samuel Smith, and from said Samuel and his wife, Elizabeth, to said
Forrest 26 Jul 1785, beginning at red oak in Jonathan William's cor-
ner, on his line NW to red oak, Jonathan Smith's corner, and along
line of marked trees...
Jonathan Roberts   Henry Forrest
James Hodges
William Blanshard
May Term 1791

236 25 Oct 1790--Josiah Granbery and Josiah Collins of Chowan Co.
to Moses Davis...40 pds...Negro boy Jim...
                                              Jos. Granbery
Thos. Granbery   Josiah Collins
May Term 1791

237 11 May 1791--Soloman King to John Gatling...14 pds 8 sh...48 acres,
which was granted to William Skiner 11 Mar 1740, and conveyed to Will-
iam Goodman and Isaac Pipkin 1 Aug 1760, beginning at oak on side of
Winton Road on Pipkin's line, along his line S to a lightwood post,
to William Goodman's corner, E along his line to post oak in Cop-
land's line, N to said road...
Jo. Vollentine   Soloman King
Edward Gatling   Abigail King
William Warren
May Term 1791

238 10 Aug 1790--Wright Hays and wife, Mary, to William Hays...7 pds
10 sh...10 acres, being part of tract William Hays, dec. bequeathed
to said Wright, beginning at cypress on side of Bennetts Creek, to
line between James, Wright and Jacob Hays, down fork of said creek
and down creek...
Jonathan Hays   Wright Hays
Jacob Hays   Mary(X)Hays
May Term 1791

239 18 Jan 1791--John Pipkin of Northampton Co. to Isaac Pipkin...
175 pds...part of a 100 acre patent granted to John Bently 22 May 1719

beginning at red oak on E side of main road, along line of marked
trees to water oak in branch, down branch to Bray Warren's line, to
Phillip Lewis' line, NW along his line to road...
Isaac Pipkin Jr.   John Pipkin
Stephen Rogers   Jennet Pipkin
May Term 1791

240 23 Feb 1791--James Bristow to William Doughtie...45 pds...Negro
woman Philis...
                                              James Brostowe
Jethro Sumner
William Boyce
May Term 1791

241 22 Dec 1790--Kadar Rabey to Lemuel Rabey, both of Nansemond Co.,
Va...15 pds...50 acres in Hertford Co. beginning at pine of William
Baker's line, S along line of marked trees to one of Moses Spivey's
lines, to white oak, Cader Riddick's corner, along line of trees NE
to line tree of Bucklands Patent and along line W...
                                              Cader(X)Rabey
Mary Powell   Beshbel Rabey
Sarah(+)Rabey
John Rabey
May Term 1791

242 25 Feb 1791--William Freeman and wife, Sarah, to Daniel Eure...
50 pds...78 acres in Indian Neck, which George Outlaw sold to said
Freeman 11 Apr 1780, beginning at marked pine in Outlaw's line, along
line to Jacob Outlaws, to James Freemans and along line of marked
trees, formerly belonging to Luke Sumner, dec., to large branch and
up a small branch...   William Freeman
Patrick Hegerty   Sarah Freeman
Moses Blanshard
May Term 1791

243 11 Oct 1790--Luke Sumner to John Powell...10 pds...5 acres be-
ginning at N end of Powell's dam and mill, N by line of marked trees
to a gum, S across mill swamp to road, to Powell's line and along dam...
Jethro Ballard   Luke Sumner
Charles Jones
Elizabeth Riddick
May Term 1791

245 23 Apr 1791--Josiah Lassitor to Samuel Harrell...26 pds 2 sh.
69½ acres, part of tract whereon he lives, beginning at side of road
in Thomas Fullington, dec. line, SE to gum in Nath'l Riddick's line,
SW to a pine, Abraham Harrell's corner tree, SW to William Hinton's
corner, NW to road and along road...
Jos. Riddick   Josiah(X)Lassiter
Seth(X)Lassitor
May Term 1791

246 26 Nov 1789--Treasury of North Carolina to Demsey Bond...10 pds
per 100 acres...75 acres beginning at gum in mouth of Schoolhouse
Branch on W side of Indian Swamp, to Thomas Hofler's, S across run
of Beaverdam Swamp to Timothy Walton, dec. dam, W down swamp to Richard Bond's side, to Indian Swamp...
J. Glasgow, sec. No. 89...   Samuel Johnston

247 10 Aug 1791--Treasury of North Carolina to Daniel Spivey...50 sh per 100 acres...640 acres beginning at gum on Bennetts Creek, SW to white oak in new Troy, W to center of three birch saplings in Capt. Wilson's line, to a maple in Coles Creek, to a cypress, SE a mouth of Herring Creek, down Sarum Creek to Chowan River and along river to Bennetts Creek...No. 80
                                                                       Samuel Johnston
J. Glasgow, sec.

248 25 Mar 1780--Treasury of North Carolina to William Harriss... 50 sh per 100 acres...31 acres in Hertford Co. beginning in William Powell's line on said Harriss line, SW to Powell's line... No.3
                                                                 Richard Caswell
William Sheppard, dep. sec.
2 Jan 1792

249 20 Jul 1791--Moses Hare Jr. to John Darden...60 pds...Negro girl Venus...
                                                  Moses Hare
Jethro Sumner
Humphrey Hudgins
Aug Term 1791

250 25 Oct 1790--Josiah Stallings to William Crafford...15 pds...70 acres, part of patent granted to Jacob Odom 21 Feb 1738, beginning at corner gum in Josiah Harrell's line in Cypress Swamp, to corner gum in run of river pecosin swamp, W to S side of swamp, to the Island, by line of marked trees to Cypress Swamp and along run...
Demsey Harrell   Josiah(X)Stallings
Thomas Smith
3 Feb 1792

249 (repeated) 26 Jul 1791--Joseph Norfleet to Thomas Robertson... 5 sh and maintenance for natural life...plantation whereon he lives, horses, cattle and hogs...
                                                Joseph Norfleet
Edward Pilant
Thomas Vann
Aug Term 1791

250 17 May 1790--Cyprian Cross to James Landen...7 pds...17 acres, part of patent granted to Jesse Barns 24 Oct 1786, beginning at holly at Landen's corner on N side of Gum Swamp, up swamp, along line of marked trees to near old fort, N along patent line...
Elisha Landen   Cyprian Cross
James (ϒ)Curle
Aug Term 1791

251 14 Apr 1791--Benjamin Harrell of Martin Co. to Demsey Harrell... 3 pds...37½ acres, part of patent granted to him 20 Oct 1786, beginning at sweet gum, William Crafford's corner, along line of marked trees to gum in patent line, to William Arnolds, along his line to Daniel Ellis and along his line...
William Crafford   Benjamin(B)Harrell
David Harrell
Willis(+)Stallings
Aug Ct 1791

253 22 Jul 1791--Joseph Norfleet to Thomas Robertson...100 pds...200 acres, whereon he lives, beginning at marked maple near main Sarum Swamp as appears by deed from Thomas and John Norris to William Fryer

23 Mar 1740; being corner tree of Capt. James Riddick's land, along his line to marked white oak, a corner of said Riddick's and Thomas Norris' land, to white oak, corner of said Riddick's and Thomas Pilant's, down Pilants line to Sarum Swamp, to white oak, said Pilant's corner tree, and down main run...
David(+)Pilant   Joseph Norfleet
Edward (+)Pilant
Thos. Vann

254 17 Jun 1791--Cap'n Jesse Benton to Moses Hines...50 pds...50 acres on W side of Bennetts Creek beginning at white oak, Caleb Polson's corner tree, with his line NE, and up Bennetts Creek S; being part of grant to John Benton 12 ___ 1728...
Jacob(+)Wilkins   Jesse Benton
Pa. Hegerty
Aug Term 1791

256 20 Jul 1791--Moses Hare to Jethro Sumners...110 pds...650 acres whereon he lives...
Humphrey Hudgins   Moses Hare
Jeremiah Speight
John Duke Aug Term 1791

257 1 Jun 1791--Henry Copland to Josiah Harrell...20 pds...50 acres beginning on outside swamp at said Harrell's corner tree, along his line to main run of Cypress Swamp and down run to river pecosin, to Isaac Fryer's corner tree, a maple, along his line to outside swamp; part of patent to Jacob Odom 21 Feb 1738...
John Odom   Henry Copland
Demsey Williams
Aug Term 1791

259 9 Feb 1790--William Pearce to Abner Pearce...50 pds...80 acres on W side of Watery Swamp, beginning at gum on run in George Lassitor's line, with his line up Reedy Branch to water oak in Joseph Alpin's line, with his line to Aaron Blanshard's to a maple in Colmans Branch and down middle to run of Watry Swamp and down run...
Bashford Robins   William (Ø)Peirce
John Hofler
Moses Lassitor
Aug Term 1791

260 13 Jun 1791--Miles Turner of Perquimans Co. to William Rutter... 50 pds, Negro Jenny, age 17 years...
Moore Carter   Miles Turner
William H. Boyce
Aug Term 1791

261 22 Jul 1791--Jacob Darden Jr., executor of Elisha Darden, dec. of Southampton Co., to Elisha Norfleet 15 pds 13 sh...21 acres, part of a patent granted to John Norfleet Sr., dec., who in his will devised to his son, James and after said James' death, fell to his son, John, who conveyed to said Darden; in White Oak Spring Marsh...
Jethro Ballard   Jacob Darden
K. Ballard
Charles Jones
Aug Ct 1791

262 2 Feb 1791--Thomas Travis to David Harrell...30 pds...78 acres being land said Travis had of John Robins Sr., beginning at a pine, corner tree, in Wier Neck Branch, down branch to Jonathan Nichols' line, along his line to Bennetts Creek road and along road to Jonathan Lassitor's line and along his line to Jeremiah Jordan's line...
Jonathan Roberts   Thomas Travis
Elizabeth(+)Meltear
May Term 1791

263 16 Aug 1791--Timothy Walton, planter, to Josiah Parker, planter...$150...150 acres beginning at mouth of small branch that issueth out of Bennetts Creek pecosin, known as Cruked Branch, along it to mark pine in Horsepen Swamp, down swamp to marked pine on George Outlaw's line, to juniper near Cow Bridge and up edge of reads to said Waltons; is part of land granted to Chowan Indians...
James Walton   Timothy Walton
Elisha Hunter
Aug Term 1791

265 28 Sep 1791--Treasury of North Carolina to Henry Goodman...10 pds per 100 acres...2 acres beginning at marked cypress on side of river, William Crafford's corner tree, to mouth of Barnes Creek, up creek to said Craffords and along his line SW... No. 102.
J. Glasgow, sec.   Alex. Martin,
20 Feb 1792   gov.

266 28 Sep 1791--Treasury of North Carolina to Henry Goodman...10 pounds per 100 acres...250 acres on E side of Chowan River, beginning at gum on river at William Crafford's line, up pecosin to Enos Youre's line, to Doctor Brown Garveys and Craffords corner to gum on SW side of Barnes Creek and down creek...No. 97.
J. Glasgow, sec.   Alex. Martin, gov

267 28 Sep 1791--Treasury of North Carolina to Henry Goodman and Moses Kittrell...10 pds per 100 acres...220 acres on E side of Chowan River beginning at black gum on side below Speights line, to Webbs corner tree and along Webbs Patent line to Moor Carters, N to gum on Buckhorn Creek and down creek to main river...
J. Glasgow   Alex Martin,
20 Feb 1792   gov.
268 (Same deed as one registered on page 262)

269 31 Mar 1789--John Carter to his son, James...60 pds...Negro girl Haner...   John (₤)Carter
William Davidson
Charles Eure
William Fryer
Aug Term 1791

269 25 Oct 1790--Josiah Granbery and Josiah Collins of Chowan Co. to William Harriss...150 pds...Negroes Will and Tarley...
Thos. Granbery   Jos. Granbery
Aug Term 1791   Josiah Collins

270 24 Oct 1786--State of North Carolina to George Lassiter...10 pds per 100 acres...40 acres beginning at gum by run of Bennetts Creek, Job Riddick's corner tree, along his line E to Richard Bonds' Island, up side of end of Watre Swamp to swamp that divides George

and Jonathan Lassiters land, to run of Bennetts Creek and up creek...
No. 67
J. Glasgow, sec.   Richard Caswell
2 Mar 1792

271 8 Oct 1790--James Gregory to Thomas Trotman...35 pds...28 acres
near Society Chapel beginning at Ownley's line, NW to Thomas Hurdles,
to a pine, said Ownley and Hurdle's corner, to pine near fork of
road...
James Baker   James Gregory
Thomas Hurdle
Aug Term 1791

272 12 Apr 1790--James and Benjamin Robins and George and Joseph
Bennett, chief men and representatives of Chowan Indian Nation, to
William Lewis and Samuel Harrell...$100...400 acres contained in
Indian patent 4 Apr 1724, beginning with Patrick Lawler's patent
line near Bennetts Creek to a pine, his corner tree, to Ephrahem
Blanchards, through savanah to white oak by Aaron Blanshard's fence,
to Catherine Creek, mouth of Indian Swamp and down said creek to
Chowan River...   James(R)Robins
Thomas Marshall   Benja.(x)Robins
Permelia Marshall   George(ᴧ)Bennett
May Ct 1790   Joseph(+)Bennett

273 2 Jan 1792--By virtue of resolution of General Assembly at Newborn
28 and 30 Dec. last it was agreed that William Lewis and Samuel Harrell
petition to buy 400 acres for $100 from Chowan Indians be granted...
Joseph Riddick   Alex. Martin
                                                    gov.

274 28 Dec 1791--Committee of Propersition and Grievanses reports
on petition of James Robins; appears to satisfaction of committee
that Lord Proprietors of North Carolina did grant unto the Chowan
Indian Nation a tract of land on Bennetts and Catherine Creek for
11,360 acres in 1724, the greater part has been sold by chief men
of said nation by consent of governor and counsil; the undisposed
remnants of said tract appear to be disposed off to William Lewis
and Samuel Harrell...money has been paid to above mentioned tribe
and deed has been signed by all except six Indian women, descendants
of tribe, and aforesaid purchase will in no wise affect the land
on which they now live...
J. Hunt, clk   R.M. Kinne, ch.
Feb Ct 1792

276 16 Aug 1791--Josiah Granbery and Josiah Collins of Chowan Co.
to William Baker...95 pds...Negro Agga and child Pegg...
Alex. Miller   Jos. Granbery
Nov Ct 1791   Josiah Collins

276 4 Jan 1792--Richard Baker to Joseph Rogers, Jr...15 pds...Two
year old Negro boy Jim...   Rich'd Baker
Patrick Hegerty
William Walters
Feb Ct 1792

277 28 Oct 1791--John Robins and wife, Rachel, to Thomas Travis...
88 pds...100 acres beginning at center of 2 sweet gums and a black
gum in Jeremiah Jordan's line in Wireneck Branch, down run on Jor-

dan's line in Wireneck Branch, down run on Jordon's line to David Harrell and Doctor Nichols line to John Hare's line and along his line to water oak, Demsey Jones' corner, to Kedar Hinton's, to marked red oak in his line and S...
                                        John Robins
Jonathan Nichols
John Robins   Rachel Robins
James Booth
9 May 1792

278 25 May 1791--Alexander Eason to Morning Sumner...140 pds...Negro man Ben...
James Jones(+)Sketo   Alex'r Eason
Joseph J. Sumner
Feb Ct 1792

279 3 Oct 1791--Isaac Eason to Seth Eason...40 pds...Negro man Mireca, a country born slave...
James Norfleet   Isaac Eason
Alex. Eason
Feb Ct 1792

280 28 May 1790--Willis Parker to Jonathan Roberts...120 pds...50 acres on S side of Robert's mill, beginning at corner hickory tree, along line of marked trees to William Hinton's line, along his line to Miry Branch, down run to Maple Branch, to said mill and down pecosin...
Thos. Finny   Willis Parker
Mary Finny
Feb Term 1792

281 4 Feb 1792--Abraham Pearce to William Pearce...20 pds...20 acres beginning at said William's own land, along Riddick's line to line of marked trees between said Abraham and William and along that line...
Jonathan Nichols   Abraham Pearce
John Delany
Feb Ct 1792

283 29 Aug 1791--Richard Baker to James Phelps Jr...60 pds...42 acres on E side of Northwest Branch in William Arnold's line, with his line to Micajah Riddick's and up his line to Noah Felton's and along run of Northwest Branch...
Pa. Hegerty   Richard Baker
Benjamin Baker
11 May 1792

284 30 Nov 1791--George Gatling to Jesse Saunders...20 pds...___ acres beginning at water oak in Beaverdam Swamp, along line of marked trees to sweet gum in Plumbtree Branch, to Long Marsh, to SW of main run of said swamp...
Edward Gatling   George(N)Gatling
Bray Saunders   Susaner(X)Gatling
Feb Term 1792

285 18 Jan 1792--William Doughtie to William Walters...50 pds...50 acres beginning at persimmon tree in branch in said Doughtie's line, by line of marked trees SE to gum in Mare Branch, up S side to white oak on Doughtie's line and up his line...
Pa. Hegerty   William Doughtie
Daniel Doughtie
Leah(+)Doughtie
Feb Term 1792

287 31 Dec 1791--Isaac Darden to William Goodman...73 pds 6 sh 8 pn...
150 acres on N side of Peters Swamp, being tract granted to Henry
Goodman 28 Apr 1711, beginning at line of said William's in swamp,
to small branch and along it to corner tree of said Goodman and Isaac
Pipkin, along Pipkin's line to lightwood post , corner of said Pipkin
and Henry Dilday, along Dilday's line to said swamp and down...
Joel Goodman   Isaac Darden
Soloman Goodman   Sarah(+)Darden
Henry Hill
15 May 1792

289 29 Dec 1791--Mordica Perry to Levi Eason...25 pds...50 acres
beginning at white oak, corner tree in Shadrack Felton's line, NE
to oak in Amos Hobbs' line, along his line to William Hurdle's, to
said Felton's...
Jacob(*)Eason   Mordecia Perry
Seleca Eason
15 May 1792

291 1 Oct 1792--William King, Joseph Speight, Joseph Parker and Eliz-
abeth Dwyer to Sarah Saunders...410 pds 1 sh...tract beginning at
maple on Chowan River, along straight line of marked trees to Soloman
King and Jesse Saunders' corner to Somerton Creek, to Chowan River
and along river...   William King
Jesse(‡)Saunders   Joseph Speight
Francis Speight   Joseph Parker
Henry Speight   Elizabeth Dwyer
Feb Term 1792

292 28 Mar 1785--William Sumners of Nansemond Co., Va. to George
Eason...300 pds...200 acres called Maindehead Neck...
James Costen   William Sumners
Isaac Costen
Richard Rollins
Feb Term 1792

293 28 Dec 1791--James Bristow to James Tugwell...50 pds...50 acres
beginning on E side of Knotty Pine Swamp at mouth of a branch, up
branch to William Vann's line to corner tree, formerly a maple but
now persimmon, along line of marked trees to swamp...
Demsey Parker   James Bristow
William H. Boyce
Feb Term 1792

294 13 Dec 1791--Isaac Pipkin Sr. to Richard Barnes...125 pds...120
acres, part of two patents, one granted to Roland Gwin of Nansemond
Co., Va. and the other to Richard Lawrence, beginning at maple tree,
corner of Demsey Odom's in Beach Swamp, along his line to corner tree
of Robert Parker's, along his line to gum in Long Branch, corner tree
of Phillip Rogers, down said branch to red oak in said Rogers line,
along his line to red oak, corner tree of James Bethey, James Lang
and said Rogers, down to Beach Swamp and up swamp...
Isaac Pipkin Jr.   Isaac Pipkin
Benjamin Barns
15 May 1792

296 17 Sep 1791--George Eason to Timothy Lassiter...200 pds...200
acres called Maidenhead Neck, beginning at pine in Richard Bond's

corner tree, with his line E to a pine of said Bond's and Job Riddick's corner, with Lassiter's line to head of Maidenhead Branch and down branch to Bennetts Creek Swamp and down swamp to John Keaton Jr. line and along his line...
                                                            George Eason
J. Granbery
Patrick Hegerty
William Gordon
Feb Term 1792

297 1 Oct 1791--William King, Joseph Speight, Joseph Parker and Elizabeth Dwyer to Sarah Saunders...3 acres by Henry Saunders, Feroby Parker and John Sumner's lines...
Jesse(‡)Saunders   William King
Francis Speight   Joseph Speight
Henry Speight   Joseph Parker
Feb Term 1792   Elizabeth Dwyer

297 15 Feb 1792--Cyprian Cross to John Landen...$154...153 acres, part of two patents; one granted to Jesse Barnes and said Cross 24 Oct 1786 and the other to Francis Speight 17 Jul 1743, beginning at pine, corner tree of Speight's patent and corner of Barnes and Cross patent, along line to Gum Swamp, to a gum, John Odom's corner, to black gum, said Landen's corner, down swamp and along line of marked trees to water oak, said Landen's corner, to patent line and along patent line to a pine, Jesse Vann's corner, along his line to Juniper Swamp, to Speight's patent...
                                                          Cyprian Cross
James Landen
Mills Landen
19 May 1792

299 2 Jun 1791--Thomas Trotman to James Baker...Negro girl Nancy, which he has given in his will to his daughter, Absalla Baker, and which he and said James agree is part of his estate. Also, 28¼ acres near Society Chapple, which he bought of James Gregory, beginning at Ownley's line in road, along road to Thomas Hurdle and along his and Ownley's lines...
                                                        Thomas Trotman
William Berreman
Jo. Riddick
Feb Term 1792

300 20 Feb 1792--Jacob Gordon to Seth Eason...7 pds 5 sh 10 pn...114 acres, being part of new survey made by said Gordon to secure land that hath heretofore been held by Woodley's patent, being land whereon said Eason now lives, beginning at red oak, corner tree in said Gordon's patent in dividing line between said Eason and Gordon, to white oak in branch, in Thomas Fullington's line and along his line to pine sapling on N side of Baylis Swamp just below said Fullington's corner in Harriss and Larkum's patent and along that line...
                                                        Jacob Gordon
Jethro Ballard
Alex'r Eason
Amos Dilday
Feb Term 1792

301 16 Feb 1792--James Lassitor to Samuel Harrell...20 pds...60 acres beginning at cypress, corner tree of Amos Lassitor and Thomas Holt, along line of marked trees to mouth of Iron Mine Branch, along branch S to Spanish oak, to a pine, corner tree of John Webbs, and along Webbs line to pine near main road, to red oak, corner tree in Deep Gut Swamp

and down swamp to Bennetts Creek...
Levin Dure
16 May 1792
James Lassitor

302 6 Feb 1792--Amos Lassitor and James Gregory to Samuel Harrell...
60 pds...100 acres on Bennetts Creek, beginning at popular in Iron
Mine Branch, to Thomas Holt's line to white oak, corner tree, to a
white oak, corner tree of Richard Minchew and said Lassitor and a-
long Lassitor's line...
Henry Goodman
Levin Dure
Feb Term 1792
Amos Lassitor
James Gregory

303 3 Jan 1792--Humphrey Hudgins of Mathews Co., Va. to Joel Foster
10 pds...Negro girl Philis...
Isaac Miller
John Hudgins
May Term 1792
Humphrey(X)Hudgins

304 20 Feb 1792--Timothy Walton to John B. Walton...6 pds...6 acres
beginning at Bennetts Creek road, running to a pine, SW to a maple,
to a water oak in branch, down branch binding on Fredrick Blanchard's
to mouth of branch and up branch SE to road leading to said Timothy's
house and along road E to Bennetts Creek road and along road to said
John B...
John Roundtree
Seth Roundtree
Feb Term 1792
Timothy Walton

305 31 Jan 1792--Abraham Sumner and Abraham Eason to James Gregory...
39 pds 7 sh...400 acres of desert land opposite plantation whereon
said Sumner formerly lived, beginning at a pine on side of desert
near Philips Old Field, being a corner tree of patent, along line...
Jonathan Roberts
Jesse Twine
Feb Term 1792
Abraham Sumner
Abraham Eason

306 20 Feb 1792--Capt. Jesse Benton to William Barr...50 pds...50
acres on N side of Mare Branch, beginning at post oak, Cader Parker's
corner tree, along his line to run of said Branch, to marked black
gum, NE to sweet gum in run of Deep Branch and down branch N...
Jethro Sumner
Richard Parker
Feb Term 1792
Jesse Benton

307 12 Oct 1791--Henry Copland to Isaac Williams of Southampton Co.,
Va...300 pds...100 acres on N side of Chowan River, beginning at pine
stump on river bank corner, up river to John Odom's line, on his line
to corner pine in his patent line between he and said Copland, by
line of marked trees crossing patent to lower line and down line;
being part of land granted to John King 1 Apr 1720...
John Odom
Reuben Harrell
Feb Ct 1792
Henry Copland

308 1 Oct 1791--Elisha Ellis to Charles Eure...60 pds...2 tracts,one
bought of Daniel Ellis 2 May 1700,one by James Ellis from Aaron and
John Odom 7 Sep 1751; first tract begins at gum in Cypress Swamp,

a corner tree between said Elisha and Daniel Ellis, up small branch
to John Parker's line and along his line to William Ellis' line, to
a pine, a corner tree, and running said William's line to run of
swamp and down swamp. The other tract begins at gum in Cypress Swamp,
up small branch to red oak in said Parker's line and along his line
to Rogers' line, thence up branch to Levi Lee's line and along his
line to branch and down branch to run of swamp...
Jesse Benton   Elisha Ellis
William H. Boyce
Feb Term 1792

310 4 Oct 1791--Seth Eason to James Norfleet...27 pds...10 sh...56
acres on W side of desert beginning at pine in said Norfleet's line
on E side of road, running line SE to John Gordon's line and along
his line to Gen'l Washington's corner tree, and along his line NW
to said Norfleet's and Jethro Ballard's corner and along Ballard's
line to E side of main road and along road to include patent granted
to Moses Eason 24 Oct 1786...
                                                    Seth Eason
John Cowper
Aaron Doughty
Nov Ct 1791

311 21 Nov 1791--Joseph Scott and wife, Mary, of Southampton Co.,Va.
and George Wynn and wife, Judith, of Hertford Co. to Levin Dure...
100 pds...140 acres bounded by line of Josiah Granbery and Meherin
Swamp and is land which said Joseph and Mary recovered from James
Davis, guardian to Jeames Hodges, and being land said Hodges, dec.
purchased of John Jones, dec...
                                                    Jos Scott
William Gordan   Mary Scott
Wm. Gooden   Geo. Wynns
James Gregory testified Mrs. Wynn's
signature was acknowledgement of dower.
23 Nov 1791

313 14 May 1791--William Harriss and wife, Amelia, and Samuel H.
Jimerson and wife, Peggy, to John Odom...6 pds 10 sh, 50 acres, ½
of land known as Mongses Plantation in Little Island of Chowan River
joining Demsey Harrell's line and George Wynns Ferry Road...
Humfre Hudgins   William Harriss
John Dukes Sr.   Amelia Harriss
Nov Ct 1791   Sam'l H. Jimerson
                                                    Peggy Jimerson

315 14 May 1791--William Harriss and wife,
Amelia, and Samuel H. Jimerson and wife, Peggy, to John Odom...60
pds...100 acres willed by said Odom to said Peggy and Amelia, be-
ginning at marked gum on side of Ready Marsh, along line of marked
trees to John Winborn's line, to Cypress Swamp and down swamp to
Jacob Odom's line and along line of marked trees...
                                                    William Harriss
Humfre Hudgins   Amelia Harriss
John Dukes Sr.   Sam'l H. Jimerson
Nov Ct 1791   Peggy Jimerson

317 4 Apr 1790--Seth Eason, sheriff, to Thomas Granbery...3 pds
12 sh...640 acres, property of Kedar Powell, by order of court to
pay all his debts, beginning at 2 gums and a maple, Joshua Small

and Jesse Eason's corner tree in desert, along Small's line Nw to
Jethro Ballard's corner and along his line to Jesse Eason; land was
granted to said Powell 18 Aug 1783...
Alexander Eason   Seth Eason
Elizabeth Foster
Nov Ct 1792

319 1 Oct 1791--William King, Joseph Speight, Joseph Parker, Elizabeth Dwyer and Sarah Saunders to Jesse Saunders...74 pds... 100 acres
running along Cypress Swamp to Ballard's corner...

Francis Speight   William King
Henry Speight   Joseph Speight
George Dunn   Joseph Parker
Nov Ct 1791   Elizabeth Dwyer
                                             Sarah Saunders

320 1 Nov 1791--Jacob Rabey of Nansemond Co., Va.
to Samuel Harrell...65 pds...Negro man Pompey...
Willis Wiggins   Jacob(J)Rabey
Jethro Ballard
Nov Ct 1791

321 1 Oct 1791--William King, Joseph Speight, Joseph Parker, Elizabeth Dwyer and Sarah Saunders to George Dunn...616 pds 3 sh...four
grants made to Henry King by John Sumners, Dempsey Sumners, Joseph
Speight and John King, beginning on main road leading to Maneys Ferry
at William King's corner tree, up Cypress Swamp to Thomas Barnes' corner at white oake, along said line to said Dunn's corner and along his
line to Joseph Speight's and across swamp to dogwood to main road and
along road...
Jesse(‡)Saunders   William King
Francis Speight   Joseph Speight
Henry Speight   Joseph Parker
Nov Ct 1791   Elizabeth Dwyer
                                             Sarah Saunders
322 7 Nov 1791--Demsey and Edith Rooks to James   Amelia Parker
Brady Jr....52 pds 10 sh...Negro Rose 38 years
and Negro girl Anna 11 months...
Bryant Vann   Demsey Rooks
Thos. Vann   Edith(+)Rooks
2 Jun 1792

323 12 Oct 1791--Jethro Ballard and David Rice, executors of James
Sumners, dec. to George Outlaw...160 pds...100 acres in Indian Neck
on W side of Catherine Creek, beginning at popular in head of small
branch issuing out of said creek, SW to Beaverdam Swamp and down
swamp to said creek; formerly belonged to Luke Sumner and after his
death land fell to his brother, said James...
James Outlaw   Jethro Ballard
Nancy Briggs   David Rice
4 Jun 1792

324 17 Nov 1791--Francis Speight to William Crafford...62 pds...12½
acres, ½ of patent granted to said Crafford 24 Oct 1786, beginning
at cypress on side of river small distance above mouth of Barnes
Creek, along river NW...
William Brooks   Francis Speight
Zadok Hinton
Nov Ct 1791

326 9 Feb 1790--Jacob Pearce to William Pearce...40 pds...50 acres adjoining Joseph Riddick and line known to be one in patent granted to Jacob Docton...
                 Jacob Pearce
John Hofler
William Hunter
Abraham Green

327 1 Oct 1791--William King, Joseph Speight, Joseph Parker, Elizabeth Dwyer and Sarah Saunders to Henry Speight...400 pds 1 sh..512 acres, including a patent to Henry King 10 Sep 1740 and the other a deed from Jesse Hare to said King, in Holly Island beginning at a white oak, along Thomas Speight's line to Joseph Speight's, to George Dunn's corner and along his line to Thomas Barnes, to Benjamin Barnes corner and to William King's corner...
                 William King
Jesse(*)Saunders
                 Joseph Speight
Francis Speight
                 Joseph Parker
George Dunn
                 Elizabeth Dwyer
Nov Ct 1791
                 Sarah Saunders

329 10 Nov 1791--Hardy Wills to Isaac Pipkin Sr...109 pds 10 sh... 176 acres, part of two patents, one granted to Roland Gwin of Nansemond Co. Va. and the other to Richard Lawrence, beginning at a maple, corner tree of Demsey Odom's in Beach Swamp, running his line to corner tree of Robert Parker's along his line to gum in Long Branch, to corner tree of Philip Rogers, down branch to red oak in said Rogers' line, to corner red oak of Jeames Bethey and James Lang, to said Rogers and down branch to Beach Swamp and down swamp...
Henry Goodman   Hardy Wills
James Ransom
Isaac Pipkin Jr.
Nov Ct 1791

330 17 May 1791--John Lewis, attorney of George Washington and executor of Fielding Lewis, dec. of Fredericksburg, Va. to John Cowper 1090 pds...1093½ acres, including two tracts given to Marmaduke Norfleet by his father, Thomas Norfleet, and recorded in Nansemond Co., Va., ½ of tract. having 275 acres was purchsed of William Jones in 1697 and the other of 40 acres was bought from Charles Drury 20 Jul 1721. Also, a tract granted to said Marmaduke 23 Jul 1760 for 450 acres. The three tracts are located in part of Gates County that was formerly in Perquimans Co. at a plain called White Oak Spring. Also a tract near by. All four tracts were purchased by said Washington and said Lewis 26 Apr 1766 and recorded in Perquimans Co., with deeds of survivorship, which rights said Washington does not choose to exert and authorizes said John Lewis to convey...
Demsey Copland   George Washington
Riddick Hunter   by John Lewis
Thos. Mann   John Lewis, ex.of
Arther(A)Jones   Fielding Lewis

334 18 May 1791--John Cowper to John Lewis of Fredericksburg, Va. 5 sh...1093½ acres, conveyed in above deed, to secure debt of 600 pds...
                 John Cowper
Demsey Copland
                 John Lewis
Riddick Hunter
Thos Mann
Arther(A)Jones
18 May 1791

336 18 May 1791--Received from John Cowper on order of William Fontaine of Hanover Co., Va...160 pds for the conditioned sum of 146 pds 13 sh 4 pn...which shall be considered a full discharge of within mentioned 600 pds...
C. Riddick P.R.   John Lewis
May Ct 1792

337 10 Apr 1792--Jonathan Cullens to Samuel Eure...30 pds...83 acres beginning at Pine Box Island Branch, up to head and by line of marked trees E to Great Branch and up branch...
Asa Harrell   Jonathan(#)Cullens
Nathan Cullens   Zilphia(+)Cullens
Said Zilphia was privately examined
by James Gregory
May Ct 1792

338 29 Mar 1792--Benjamin Parker and wife, Rebecca, to Caleb Savage, Nansemond Co., Va...9 pds...Negro boy Benn...
Samuel Eure   Benjamin(x)Parker
Israel Beeman
May Ct 1792

339 27 Nov 1791--John Robins Sr. and his wife, Rachel, to John Jones 69 pds...115 acres beginning at marked red oak in Kedar Hinton's line, along his line to marked white oak, Bashford Robins' corner tree, SW to run of Wireneck Branch, to a marked popular, Jonathan Lassitor and Jeremiah Jordon's corner tree in said branch and down branch to two sweet gums and a black gum, by line of marked trees...
James(B)Brown   John Robbins
Thomas Marshall   Rachal Robbins
John Robbins
May Ct 1792

341 23 Apr 1792--Soloman King has made his friends David Darden, John Lee and Jethro Sumner trustees to hire and use profit of Negro boy Abraham, feather bed, bedstead and furniture for 16 years for his granddaughters Abigail King and Rebecca King Vollentine...
William Odom   Soloman King
John Odom
May Ct 1792

343 1 Feb 1792--Richard Green to Jonathan Cullens...60 pds...156 acres beginning at gum in Great Branch, along Pine Box Island Branch to William Green's line, to a corner hickory in Uriah Eure's line and along his line to Mire Branch, N to Felton's line and along his line...
                                                         Rich'd(4)Green
Asa Harrell
Samuel Eure
Thomas Cullens

344 23 Apr 1792--John Lee of Nansemond Co., Va. to Rebecca King Vollentine...20 pds 11 sh...chesnut sorrell mare named Venus...
Uriah Odom   John Lee
Soloman King
May Ct 1792

345 26 Feb 1791--Noah Harrell to William Lewis...21 pds...Negro names Bets...   Noah(X)Harrell
Mich'l Lycune
Isaac Miller
John Riddick

346 24 Mar 1792--James Freeman to William Lewis...95 pds...Negro man
Sam about 36 years old...
                                                      Jeams Freeman
Obediah Bosworth
Jethro Benton
Aug Term 1792

347 23 Aug 1792--William Harriss and Samuel Heath Jameson to Charles
Powell...$160...Negro Ruth and her children Rachel and Ben...
Samuel Harrell   William Harriss
Aug Term 1792   Sam'l H. Jameson

348 11 May 1792--John Hunter to James Gregory...88 pds...60 acres
where he formerly lived beginning at sweet gum on run of Meherin
Swamp, up branch to maple, corner of William Hunter's, E to red
oak, corner tree of William and Thomas Hunter, back to swamp and
up run...   John Hunter
William Hunter
Senea Hunter
Aug Term 1792

349 4 Oct 1786--Treasury of North Carolina to Jonathan Lassitor...
10 pds per 100 acres...14 acres on E side of Watry Swamp beginning
at red oak, Job Riddick's corner tree in George Lassiter's patent,
along his line to water oak in Richard Bond's corner, and along his
line S to bunch of saplings in said George's patent and along patent line...No. 74.
J. Glasgow, sec.   Rd. Caswell
Christr. Riddick P.R.

350 4 Oct 1790--State of North Carolina to John Cowper...10 pds
per 100 acres...2000 acres beginning at gum in Mary Riddick's line,
Col. Fountaine's corner tree, with her line SE to a cypress, Christopher Pearce's corner tree, with his line SE to Jacob Pearce's corner, along his line SE to James Jones' line, E to juniper and N to
Fontaines' line and W...
J. Glasgow, sec.   Alex. Martin,
Christ'r. Riddick PR

351 12 May 1792--Elisha Parker to John Kittrell...2 pds. 15 sh...
3 acres beginning at a pine in branch, down branch to fork that
runs near Isaac Walter's house, up branch to said Kittrell's line
and along his line...
John Parker   Elisha Parker
Winborn Jenkins
Elisha Parker Jr.
Aug Term 1792

353 31 Jan 1792--Willis Moore to Benjamin Williams...32 pds 10 sh...
75 acres beginning at red oak on back swamp, along line of marked
trees NW to white oak, corner tree, to Bennetts Creek Road and along
road to Halfway Run Branch and down branch to white oak on back line...
George Williams   Willis Moore
Willis Brown
Aug Term 1792

354 21 Aug 1792--William Harriss to William Pugh Jamerson, his
grandson...deed of gift...___acres whereon Dr. Samuel Jamerson
now lives on S side of main road binding on lands of Humphrey

Hudgens, Samuel Smith, Jeremiah Speight and orphans of William Pugh,
to main run of Bennetts Creek and up run to Pugh's Bridge to main
road...
Jethro Sumner   William Harriss
Jesse Benton
Aug Term 1792

356 23 Jan 1792--Henry Dilday to Amos Dilday...20 pds...50 acres
beginning at corner tree of Joel Goodman and William Gatling's and
along Gatling's line to Isaac Pipkin's...
Terbeious Pervis   Henry(X)Dilday
Benjamin Cross
Timothy Rogers
May Ct 1792

357 11 Jul 1792--Luke Sumner to William Mathias...63 pds...70 acres
beginning at forked pine and holly tree in branch on said Mathias'
own line, N up branch to marked white oak, W to head of branch and
down to gum on side of Sumners mill swamp and along swamp to Lewis'
patent line...
Pa. Hegerty   Luke Sumner
Jethro Benton
Aug Ct 1792

359 13 Feb 1792--Abisha Lassitor and wife, Mourning, to James Davis
30 pds...50 acres beginning at corner tree between said Abisha and
Jonathan Lassiter, running their line to Demsey Blanshard's and Amos
Smith's line, to corner tree of Job Riddick...
Jonathan Lassitor   Abisha(X)Lassitor
Isrel Minard   Morning(X)Lassitor
Demsey Blanshard
Aug Ct 1792

Vol. 3

1 21 May 1792--Sarah Saunders, widow of Charles Saunders, dec., to
Francis Speight...$95 11 sh...sain_ place, formerly belonging to
John Minchew and whereon he lived, which Henry King purchased of
Jacob Minchew, beginning 10 ft. from hill running to Barnes old
landing at long end of marsh and 1 acre from line opposite wind-
less on Chowan River on S side of bottom and down river, also,
cartway from seine place to road...
Henry(X)Saunders   Sarah Speight
Henry Speight
John(X)Sumner
Aug Term 1792

2 1 Aug 1792--Amos Smith to George Brooks...$351...351 acres on Wat-
ry Swamp beginning at sweet gum, up run to pine corner of Demsey Blanchard's, along his line to red oak, SE to Henry Harrell's line, to
swamp...
Law. Baker   Amos Smith
William Brooks
Aug Term 1792

4 26 Dec 1791--Samuel Thomas to James Thomas...20 pds...100 acres beginning at gum in Gum Swamp, S with patent line to Jethro Benton's line, W along his line to line of marked trees to pine in said swamp and down swamp...
                Samuel(X)Thomas
Christ. Riddick
Wm. H. Boyce
Aug Ct 1792

5 15 Mar 1792--William Wallis of Orange Co. to James Outlaw...225 pds...100 acres where John Wallis formerly lived, on N side of Woineck Creek in Old Town beginning at white oak, said Outlaw's line to swamp and down run to road and up road...
James(+)Turvetan   William Wallis
George Outlaw Jr.
Aug Ct 1792

6 16 Aug 1792--Sarah and Prisillar Spivey, heirs of Moses Spivey, dec. and Jesse Spivey, their executor, to Willis Brown...61 pds...100 acres, part of a patent granted to William Daniel, beginning at gum in James Hayes' line, running his line to read oak in William Riddick, dec. line to hickory in Jno. Rabey's line, along his line to white oak in Moses Spivey's line and along his line to said Hayes...
James Piland   Sarah(X)Spivey
Thomas Marshall   Prisillar(X)Spivey
John Polson   Jesse(X)Spivey
Aug Ct 1792

7 18 Aug 1791--Bond Minchew to Jeremiah Lassiter...12 pds...40 acres on E side of Ready Branch at Bennetts Creek, along line of marked trees to pine, to road and along road; part of tract willed to said Bond by his grandfather...
William Gordon   Bond Minchew
John Eason
Aug Term 1792

9 12 Mar 1792--Edward Coffield and son, Joab and his wife, Mary, to John Hunter...125 pds...200 acres beginning at mouth of branch that issues out of S side of Bennetts Creek, up branch and binding on line of Reuben Lassiter to line of George Lassiter, along his line to white oake, corner tree of Samuel Harrell, and bounded by Iron Branch; is part of tract granted to Robert Lassiter, late of Nansemond Co., Va. 1 May 1668...
Abraham Riddick   Edward(X)Coffield
Thomas Riddick   Job(X)Coffield
Thomas Wa_fe   Mary(X)Coffield
Aug Term 1792

10 12 Jul 1792--Anderson Stroud of Orange Co. to Benjamin Gordon... 148 pds...stud horse Demascus Delefait...
William Ellis   Anderson Stroud
Nov Ct 1792

11 29 Oct 1792--Mordicai Perry to Frecric_ Eason...150 pds...deed of trust of 200 acres whereon he lives on W side of Warwick Swamp to secure debt of 315 pds 4 sh 2 pn...
Jo. Riddick   Mordicai Perry
Isaiah Riddick

12 18 Oct 1792--John Arline appoints his friend, Henry Goodman, as his attorney to sell land etc...
Henry Hall   John Arline
William Goodman

13 18 Oct 1792--John Arline to Henry Goodman...76 pds...Negro Benjamin...
Henry Hall   John Arline
William Goodman
Nov Ct 1792

14 9 Oct 1792--Mordicai Perry to Frederick Eason...315 pds...Negro boy Lade and man Sambo, formerly property of William Eason, dec...
Harmon Hurdle   Mordicai Perry
Mills Hurdle
Nov Ct 1792

15 18 Jan 1792--Timothy Walton to James Walton...5 pds 5sh...5 acres beginning at maple in Tucklow Branch on W side of Bennetts Creek Road, on run of branch and by line of marked trees to Simon Stalling's line, to said road...
John B. Walton   Timothy Walton
Miles Roundtree
Nath'l Taylor
Nov Ct 1792

17 12 Nov 1792--Zachariah Minchew to Bond Minchew...165 pds...200 acres beginning at Elisha Harrell's line pine on side of Bennetts Creek, along his line to Amos Lassiter's line and along his line to Minyard's land, to said Bond's line to Holly Tree Branch and down branch to said creek...
William Gordon   Zachariah Minchew
William Hays
Nov Ct 1792

18 9 Oct 1792--Mordicai Perry to Frederick Eason...315 pds 4 sh... Negroes Vize, Madric, Cherry, Dick and Venus and 200 acres whereon he lives, furniture, 3 head cattle, horse, saddle and bridle...
Jo. Riddick   Mordicai Perry
Thos. Twine
Nov Ct 1792

19 22 Sep 1792--John Arnold to John Simons...70 pds...100 acres on Gum Branch beginning at marked holly in Collage Branch, James Parker's corner in William Arnold's line, along Parker's line N to white oak in Benton's line, to dead pine in Merry Hill Pocosin, to James Pruden's corner, to white oak in Gum Branch in mouth of small branch known at Poket Branch, along line of marked trees to Gum Branch and William Arnold's line...
Noah Felton   John Arnold
Abraham(A)Morgan   Patsey(X)Arnold
Nov Ct 1792

21 13 Oct 1792--James Phelps to John Arnold...36 pds...30 acres beginning in Middle Swamp at red oak, corner tree in Abraham Morgan's line, on his line to corner pine in patent line, to James

Pruden's line to said Phelp's line to Middle Swamp...
John Simons   James(X)Phelps
William(X)Gwin   Trentha(X)Phelps
Nov Ct 1792

22 23 Mar 1792--Joseph Holland and wife, Elizabeth, of Nansemond
Co., Va. to Mills Lewis...90 pds...25 acres beginning at head of
Ready Branch, down branch to Knotty Pine Swamp and down swamp to
William Warren's line, along his line to Thomas Vann's line, along
his line...
Edward Gatling   Elizabeth Holland
Luten Lewis   Joseph Holland
James Rawls
Nov Ct 1792

24 13 Oct 1792--Joseph Riddick to son-in-law, Jesse Rogerson of
Perquimans Co...deed of gift...50 acres, desert land in Dismal Sw-
amp near pine noles joining James Baker's land, across patent from
SW side to NE side...
Wm. Valentine   Jo. Riddick
Rubin Riddick
Nov Ct 1792

25 27 Feb 1792--William Green to John Piland...45 pds...104 acres
beginning at hickory on Stephen Harrell's line, along his line to
Lickingroot Branch, to Great Branch and down run to Peniboa Island
Bridge, up branch to head on Jonathan Cullen's line of marked trees.
Asa Harrell   William(X)Green
Rachal Harrell
Nov Ct 1792

27 28 Sep 1791--William Evans of Hertford Co. to Cyprian Cross...25
pds Virginia or 50 pds state currency...Negro Cloe...
Lew Buren   William Evans
Priscilla Cross
William Ware Mor
Nov Ct 1792

28 12 Dec 1791--Abraham Eason and wife, Seneth, to Thomas Hunter...
210 pds...359 acres excluding 1 acre for mill formerly called Jesse
Easons mill, beginning at maple in main desert N binding on S side
of main desert to run of Great Branch, up branch to persimmon tree,
by line of marked trees to pine, formerly Mills Riddick's corner
tree, along his line to Moses Briggs, to Cypress Branch, Moses Pearces.
Elisha Hunter   Abraham Eason
Hanah(+)Walton   Aseneth Eason
Easter(X)Harress
Nov Ct 1792

30 9 Nov 1791--William Crafford to Clabourne Oysten...$75...50 acres
in Port Island, part of grant to John Rawls Jr. 1 Apr 1723, beginning
at pine in Kittrell's line, along his line to black gum, Hezekiah Jones
corner, on his line to branch and up branch...
James Landen   William Crafford
Josiah Harrell
Nov Ct 1792

31 11 Jan 1792--Henry Goodman to Elisha Cross...129 pds 5 sh...115

acres on S side of Beaching Swamp beginning at black gum, corner
tree of Robert Napers and Demsey Odom, running Odom's line to branch
and along line of marked trees in Jesse Arline's line to post oak of
said Arlines to Daniel Parker's line, to said branch and along run...
William Goodman   Henry Goodman
John Vann
Jeames(X)Bethey
Nov Ct 1792

32 1 Mar 1792--David Cross to Abel Cross...9 pds...40 acres whereon
John Watson, dec. formerly lived, beginning at maple in river poc-
osin running James Copeland's patent line E to gum in Deep Branch,
up middle to other side of said land and down line; land was granted
to James Copeland...
Henry Goodman   David Cross
Stephen Sugs
Riddick Cross
Nov Ct 1792

33 28 Sep 1791--Treasury of North Carolina to Miles Benton...10 pds
per 100 acres...3 acres beginning at pine sapling in Abraham Morgan's
line on W side of Bennetts Creek, up side binding on King's patent
to live oak , crossing creek N to chinquipen oak in Jethro Benton's
line, down E side of creek on line of said Miles to marked beech in
Pugh's line, to Morgan's line and NW...
J. Glasgow, sec. No. 103
20 Feb 1793   Alex. Martin, gov.

35 28 Sep 1792--Treasury of North Carolina to James Jones...10 pds
per 100 acres...155 acres beginning at gum in Henry Hill's patent
line where it crosses dividing branch between said Jones and Abraham
Eason, with patent line N to pine, S to pine in Richard Pearce's patent, NW to Jesse Eason's line and along his patent to sassafras in
Mills Riddick's line, to red oak in head of beginning branch...
J. Glasgow, sec.   No. 92   Alex. Martin
1793

36 28 Sep 1791--Treasury of North Carolina to William Walters...10
pds per 100 acres...50 acres beginning at white oak, Moses Boyce and
said Walter's corner tree on NW side of Merry Hill Pocosin, up pocosin binding Walter's line... No. 91
J. Glasgow, sec.   Alex. Martin
1793

37 28 Sep 1791--Treasury of North Carolina to Elisha Parker...10 pds
per 100 acres...300 acres beginning at corner oak of James Pruden's
and Isaac Walter's on side of Merry Hill Pocosin, along Pruden's line
NE to dead pine of Jethro Benton's, on his line N to pine stump, to
said Walters... No. 90
J. Glasgow   Alex. Martin
1793

38 28 Sep 1791--Treasury of North Carolina to William Crafford...10
pds per 100 acres...100 acres on E side of Chowan River beginning at
juniper sapling on low side of Joseph Dickerson's causeway in Thomas
Cotton's line, SE to head of Mud Creek, NW to said Dickerson's corner

to lower side of causeway...No. 96
J. Glasgow, sec.   Alex. Martin

39 28 Sep 1791--Treasury of North Carolina to John Odom and Cyprian Cross...10 pds per 100 acres...100 acres on side of river pocosin on Odom's line, S along his line to red oak in Henry Copeland's line, SE to Speight's patent... No. 94. Said patent represents 2/3 for said Odom and 1/3 for said Cross as surveyed by Pa. Hegerty in Oct. 1789...
J. Glasgow   Alex. Martin

41 23 Jun 1791--Moses Hare to David Rice...$100...Negro girl Venus on loan for 16 months to pay debt of said Hare...
Jethro Sumner   Moses Hare
John Darden
Feb Term 1793

42 20 Feb 1793--James Sumner to Jeremiah Benton...62 pds 10 sh... Negro slaves Isabele, Hanah and Leah...
Pa. Hegerty   James B. Sumner
Feb Term 1793

43 24 Dec 1792--Thomas Smith to Zadock Hinton...150 pds...Negro Fanny, small boys Jacob, Peter and Luke and girl Silva...
Thomas Smith   Thomas Smith
Humphrey Hudgins
Henry Smith
Feb Term 1793

44 3 Jan 1793--Pasco Turner, executor of John Reid, dec., executor of Daniel Pugh, dec., to Abraham Morgan...164 pds...Negro Violet and children Rachal, Choley, Robin, John and Silvey and Ned...sold by court order to satisfy writ of Luke Sumner in Nansemond court in Mar 1786 against said Pugh...
Joseph Jno. Sumner   Pasco Turner
Jethro Sumner
Feb Term 1793

45 11 Feb 1793--Jeremiah Speight to Zadock Hinton...45 pds...Negro Hulday...
Hum'y Hudgens   Jeremiah Speight
Samuel Williams
Feb Term 1793

46 25 Aug 1792--Seth Eason to John Darden...$30...Negro girl Lydia...
Jethro Sumner   Seth Eason
Feb Ct 1793

47 20 Dec 1792--Israel Beeman, administrator of Hardy Browne, dec. to Ludowick Brooks...75 pds 5 sh 2 pn...60 acres beginning at pine on Jacks Branch on W side of main road at a corner tree, along road to run of Long Branch, up branch and along line of marked trees to white oak in Jacks Branch and down branch...
Robert(+)Porlet   Israel Beeman
William Brooks
Feb Term 1793

49 27 Dec 1792--Thomas Robertson to Ebenezer Grayham...$500...200 acres whereon he lives on SW side of Sarum Swamp, beginning at marked maple near main swamp, as appears by deed from Joseph Norfleet to said

Robertson 22 Jul 1791, being tree of Capt. James Riddick's land, running his line to corner tree of Thomas Norris' land, to white oak, corner tree of said Riddick, Norris and Thomas Piland, down Piland's line to swamp and along run...
Lem'l Lewis　　　　　　　　　　　　　　Thos. Robertson
William Carber
Feb Term 1793

51 22 Oct 1792--William Odom to son, John...deed of gift...land whereon said William lives purchased of Sam. Lee and land to new line, and Sand Banks land purchased of Charles Saunders, on river. Also, Negroes George and Duke, bed and furniture, 2 maple tables, horse Dick, mare Dimond, ½ hogs and cattle and desk...
Jo. Vollentine　　　　　　　　　　　　　William Odom
Thos. Elem　　　　　　　　　　　　　　　Jemimah(X)Odom
Feb Term 1793

52 15 May 1792--James Powell to Levin Dure...39 pds...Negro girl Celia...
James Gregory　　　　　　　　　　　　　James Powell
Feb Term 1793

53 15 Dec 1792--Richard Bond Sr. to sons, William and Richard Jr... deed of gift...Negroes Ben, David and Diner to said William and Negroes Jack and Abram, feather bed and furniture, small desk and two chests to said Richard Jr...
David Rice　　　　　　　　　　　　　　 Richard(B)Bond
John Eason
Feb Term 1793

54 11 Feb 1793--Zadock Hinton to daughters, Oner and Nancy, deed of gifts...Small Negroes Peter and Silva, when said daughters come of age...
Hum'y Hudgins　　　　　　　　　　　　　Zadock Hinton
Sam'l Williams
William Speight
Feb Term 1793

55 13 Dec 1792--Seasbrook Hinton to Daniel Powell...30 pds...15 acres beginning at gum, corner tree in said Hinton's line, up Gabriel's Branch to a popular and along line of marked trees to Oald Indian Road and down road to said Powells...
Jonathan Roberts　　　　　　　　　　　 Seasbrook Hinton
David Harrell
Feb Term 1793

56 24 Oct 1792--John Wills to Samuel Harrell...18 pds 18 sh...40 acres between Bennetts Creek and Cathrin Creek, beginning at red oak on E side of Deep Gutt, along said Harrell's line E to side of road, called Watery Swamp and along Harrell's line to white oak, corner tree between Augustain Minchew and said Harrell and along line to Deep Gutt and up gut...
David Rice　　　　　　　　　　　　　　 John(X)Wills
Moses Hare
Feb Ct 1793

58 8 Aug 1792--Jethro Meltear to William Gordon...100 pds...100 acres

beginning at a cypress at Daniel Hayes' line, to post oak in Indian line, along Indian line to pine in Reeddy Branch, Minchew's line, down branch to run of Bennetts Creek and down creek...
Benjamin Meltear   Jethro Meltear
Edwd Briscow
Feb Term 1793

59 13 Dec 1792--James Goodman of Upper Parish of Nansemond Co., Va. to Robert Parker...60 pds...200 acres on N side of Long Branch, beginning at black gum in run, along Elisha Cross' line, down branch to Richard Barnes' line, SE along line of marked trees, Demsey Odom's line, along his line E to corner black oak and along his line...
Rich'd Barns   Robert Parker
Elisha Cross
Jonathan Rogers
Feb Term 1793

60 12 Dec 1792--Robert Parker to Demsey Odom...60 pds...115 acres beginning at black gum in run of Long Branch, Elisha Cross' line, by line of marked trees E to side of plantation, across plantation NE to post oak of Thomas Smith's and along line, down run of said branch...
Pa. Hegerty   Robert Parker
Jonathan Rogers
Feb Term 1793

62 16 Feb 1793--John B. Walton and wife, Esther, to Thomas Hunter... 500 pds...500 acres beginning in Bennetts Creek Road in Cabin Branch, Richard Bond's line, down branch to Indian Swamp and down swamp to mouth of Schoolhouse Branch, up branch to Thomas Hofler's line, with his line SW to Hinton's Path, with path to Mirey Branch and down branch to Richard Freeman, dec. line, NE to Capt. Blanchard's old patent, to Bennetts Creek road, to said swamp; except dower rights of Rachael Jones, which will end at her death...
Jo. Riddick   John B. Walton
David(X)Kelly   Esther Walton
Law. Baker testified said Esther
signed deed freely. Feb Ct 1793

64 28 Sep 1791--State of North Carolina to Abel Cross...10 pds per 100 acres...15 acres being an island in main river near David Watsons and commonly called The Dowery, beginning at marked holly in upper end of island, down E side to stake in lower end and up W side...
J. Glasgow, sec.   No. 93   Alex. Martin

65 11 Jan 1793--John Piland to Elijah Harrell...39 pds 9 sh...50 acres on W side of Coles Creek beginning at white oak, corner tree on said Harrell's line, along his line to said creek and down run to low ground...
Asa Harrell   John Piland
Mary(X)Harrell
Feb Term 1793

66 8 Aug 1792--William Gordon to Jethro Meltear...120 pds...150 acres beginning at pine stump in said Meltear's field, to Robertson's line, along his line to red oak of Briscow's, along Briscow's line to dogwood, along Henry Forrest's line to line of marked trees in Mare

Branch and down branch...
Benjamin Meltear   William Gordon
Edward(X)Brisco
Feb Ct 1793

68 18 Jun 1793--William Doughtie to Elisha Parker...20 pds...20 acres beginning at sweet gum in said Parker's line, by line of marked trees and running SE...
Jno. Kittrell   William Doughtie
Patrick Hegerty
Feb Term 1793

69 15 Oct 1792--John Landen to James Landen...exchange of 30 acres for 30 acres of a patent granted to Jesse Barns and Cyprian Cross 24 Oct 1786, beginning at holly, said James' corner, along patent line to black gum, along line of marked trees to Gum Swamp...
Elisha Landen   John Landen
Mills Landen
Feb Term 1793

71 15 Nov 1792--James Landen to John Landen...exchange of 30 acres for 30 acres of a patent granted to Callum Ross 21 Feb 1738, beginning at chinkepin oak, James Curl's corner, along line to head of a broad branch and down branch and along line of marked trees to Gum Swamp and up swamp to NE side...
Elisha Landen   John Landen
Mills Landen
Feb Term 1793

72 19 Sep 1790--Patrick Garvey of Hertford Co. to Thomas Fitt...300 pds...225 acres deeded to him by William Crafford, who was granted patent 24 Oct 1786 No. 58, beginning at black gum on NE side of Chowan River just below Speights Creek, running NE to pine in Webbs Patent corner, down river to pocosin, crossing mouth of swamp SE joining Rawls Patent to 2 gums, thence S down river; reserving to said Crafford ½ of part called the Junipers or Ridges...
Edward Kilbee   Patrick Garvey
John Gibbons
Joseph Noures
Feb Term 1793

74 24 Dec 1792--Zadock Hinton to Thomas Smith Sr...250 pds...300 acres known as Oald Quarter beginning at mouth of Watery Branch, where it joins Bennetts Creek, up run and binding on line of Jeremiah Speight, which was part of same patent, to mouth of another branch, to said Smith's line, to corner known as Soloman Alston's binding on line formerly Joshua Allen's, now Sumner's, to run of Bennetts Creek and up run...
Hum'y Hudgins   Zadock Hinton
Samuel Smith
Henry Smith
Feb Term 1793

76 13 Dec 1792--Enos Rogers to Jonathan Rogers...106 pds...124 acres beginning at prong of Long Branch, Phillip Roger's corner, up said branch binding on said Rogers' line to Sarah Rogers, orphan of Ely, to Robert Parker's line on Long Branch and up branch...
Pa. Hegerty   Enos Rogers
Dempsey Williams
Feb Term 1793

77 10 Nov 1792--Enos Rogers to Hardy Cross of Upper Parish of Nansemond Co., N.C....104 pds...130 acres beginning at pine, Joel Goodman's corner in Goffs Folly Branch, along his line to pine, Brady's corner, along Brady's line to William Warren's corner pine, E along Warren's line to head of Laidy of Honour Branch, down branch to fork, up branch to marked popular, Jacob Walters corner, along that line to pine called Ross' and along Ross' line to said branch...
Pa. Hegerty   Enos Rogers
Robert S. Benton
Feb Term 1793

78 19 Nov 1792--Even Jones to Patrick Hegerty...45 pds...Negro Silva 14 years old...
Demsey Williams   Even(X)Jones
William Kittrell
May Term 1793

78 19 Nov 1792--William Ellis to John Darden...$100...Negro girl Rose...
James Small   William Ellis
John Ellis

79 1 May 1793--James Riddick to Henry Lee of Nansemond Co., Va...264 pds 16 sh...353 acres on S side of Beech Swamp beginning at pine and running to John March's line in a branch, W to Speight's corner, SW to John Lang's corner pine, down his line NE...
Christr. Riddick   James Riddick
John Widbee
May Term 1793

81 23 Jun 1792--John Darden to Moses Hare Jr...$100...Negro Girl Venus...
Jethro Sumners   John Darden
David Rice
May Term 1793

82 1 Nov 1792--Richard Baker to Patrick Hegerty...$225...100 acres on NW Branch of Middle Swamp beginning at gum in run in James Mathew's line, along his line and Felton's line to run of branch and along branch...
Jonathan Williams   Richard Baker
Dempsey Williams
May Term 1793

83 1 Sep 1792--John Robins of Perquimans Co. to James Lassiter...55 pds...110 acres beginning at Jeremiah Jordan's corner tree, along John Jones' line to Kedar Hinton's line, up branch to Jonathan Nichols's line, along his line to Wiar Neck Branch and up branch...
Willis Brown   John Robins
Thomas Billups
May Term 1793

84 25 Feb 1793--James Bristow of Northampton Co. to Isaac Pipkin Sr...60 pds...Negro Simon about 10 years of age...
James Gatling   James Bristow
May Term 1793

85 23 Jan 1793--Joshua White to George Outlaw...64 pds...50 acres beginning at white oake corner tree in Gordon's line, along line of

marked trees to pine, corner tree on Bennetts Creek Pocosin, up
pocosin to patent line, being dividing line of lands of Mrs. Joseph Gordon and Thomas Hunter, along branch to main run of swamp
and along Isaac Hunter's patent to said Thomas and E to high land...
James Freeman   Joshua(X)White
James Walton
May Term 1793

86 1 May 1793--Isaac Hunter to Thomas Hunter...10 pds...20 acres
beginning at run of branch on E side of Meherin Swamp, being dividing line between Mrs. John Hinton and said Thomas, along branch to
main run of swamp to said Isaac's and is part of patent held by William Hunter, dec. of Nansemond Co., Va. for 100 acres 5 Nov 1694...
William Volentine   Isaac Hunter
James Small
May Term 1793

88 18 May 1793--Thomas Smith Sr. to Micajah Phelps...40 pds...100
acres beginning at gum, William Cleves' tree, on his line SW to Jonathan Smith's line and along his line...
Hy. Hudgins   Thomas Smith
Jonath. Smith
Thomas Smith Jr.
May Term 1793

90 17 Jan 1792--Rubin Sparkman to Samuel Green...87 pds...66 2/3
acres, all tract of land on Cypress Swamp, being part of John Wiggen's
patent 5 Aug 1728, beginning at chinhequin tree, running through plantation and along line of marked trees to Felton's line on main road,
to corner tree on Cullen's line...
David Lewis   Rubin(X))Sparkman
Isaac Green   Ann(X)Sparkman
Soloman Green
May Term 1793

91 28 Sep 1791--State of North Carolina to Daniel Stallings...10
pds per 100 acres...14 acres beginning at gum in Indian Branch on
W side of Meherrin Swamp, along swamp to maple in Dempsey Trotman's
line and down W side on said Stalling's land...
J. Glasgow   Alex. Martin
1793 No. 101

92 28 Sep 1791--State of North Carolina to Randolph Moore...10 pds
per 100 acres...22 acres beginning at a pine, Thomas Barns' corner
in Ballard's line, along Barnes line NW to white oak, Walters' corner and up line to Ballard's line and along his line...No. 100...

J. Glasgow   Alex. Martin
1973

93 28 Sep 1791--State of North Carolina to Patrick Garvey, William
Crafford and Samuel Brown...10 pds per 100 acres...400 acres beginning at cypress on E side of Chowan River at Dr. Brown's causeway,
up river to mouth of Barnes Creek and up creek to gum in Enos Your's
line on side of pocosin and up pocosin W to head of Little Creek and
down W side to said causeway...No. 95.
J. Glasgow   Alex. Martin
1793

95 1 Oct 1791--Miles Parker to Willis Hughes...18 pds...13 acres beginning at water oak on Long Branch, along branch to main road and along ridge...
Isaac D. Gayle   Miles Parker
William H. Boyce
May Term 1793

96 30 Apr 1793--Luke Sumner to Elisha Brinkley...200 pds...190 acres on Dismal Swamp, beginning at maple tree in Simon Brinkley's line, along his line to a pine, corner tree on main road and along road to fork and by line of marked trees...
Jethro Sumner   Luke Sumner
Henry Lee
John Brinkley
May Term 1793

97 18 Feb 1793--Joseph Riddick, justice of peace, appointed to take examination of Rachal Stallings, wife of Seth Stallings, concerning her free consent in deed for land 16 Jun 1786, registered in Book A, Folio 230-1...
Law. Baker, clerk 11 Feb 1793

98 6 Aug 1792--Nansey D. Moroney to Patty Moroney...50 pds...Negro woman Diny...
William Harriss   Nansey D. Moroney
Robert Riddick
May Term 1793

99 17 Jan 1793--Samuel Williams to Halon Williams...$130...100 acres beginning at gum in line of George Williams Jr. on Hilly Swamp, up swamp to Turner's line and along that line NE to pine, SW to said George's line...
Pa. Hegerty   Samuel Williams
Hezekiah Williams
May Term 1793

100 25 May 1793--Moses Hare to Demsey Odom...$100...100 acres beginning at sweet gum, James Jones and said Hare's corner tree, along Jones' line to a pine, Olde David Jones' corner, along his line NW to pocosin and SW by line of marked trees; being patent of 527 acres to said Hare 18 Aug 1783...
Law. Baker   Moses Hare
May Term 1793

101 19 Aug 1793--George Brooks to William Brooks...45 pds 6 sh...100 acres on S side of Coles Creek bounded by lines of James Piland and Lawrence Baker and being ½ of tract purchased by his father, William, dec. and given to said George...
Jno. Baker   George Brooks
Mack Williams
Aug Term 1793

104 19 Aug 1793--Even Jones to William Ellis...40 pds...50 acres on Basses Swamp beginning at Alexander Eason's line in branch in Mill Swamp, down swamp to Big Flat Branch, up branch to spruce pine in path to Benjamin Gordon's line and along his line...
Benjamin Gordon   Even Jones
Joseph J. Sumner
John Small
Aug Term 1793

105 9 Aug 1793--Daniel Eure to Uriah Eure...5 pds...30 acres beginning at hickory in Richard Green's line, W near course of Sarah Smith's path to pine in Soloman Green's line, with his line to corner pine on side of Merry Branch; part of grant to Henry Hackley and sold by him to said Green...
Luke Langston   Daniel Eure
Charles Eure
Aug Term 1793

107 12 Aug 1793--William Wallis to James Crafford...4 pds 10 sh...50 acres in Pine Swamp, being part and all that remains of a patent to Callum Ross and granted to said Wallis...
Cyprian Cross   William(~)Wallis
Benjamin Varnell
Moses Jones
Aug Term 1793

108 12 Aug 1793--David Cross to James Crafford...$__...22 acres granted to Jesse Barnes in 1783 on E side of Gum Swamp...
Cyprian Cross   David Cross
John Vann
Aug Term 1793

109 2 Mar 1793--Zadock Hinton to Aaron Lassiter...$150...Negro Hulday...
Samuel Harrell   Zadock Hinton
Aug Term 1793

109 19 Nov 1792--Patrick Hegerty and wife, Elizabeth, to Even Jones...45 pds...50 acres on Basses Swamp beginning in Alexander Eason's line in branch of Mill Swamp, down swamp to Big Flat Branch, up branch NW to Benjamin Gordon's line and along his line to said Eason's...
Dempsey Williams   Patrick Hegerty
William Kittrell   Elizabeth Hegerty
Aug Term 1793

111 9 Nov 1793--John Baker to George Williams...25 pds...50 acres of swamp land on E side of Coles Creek beginning at hickory, Piland's corner on swamp, binding said Williams' line W to creek and up run...
Pa. Hegerty   Jno. Baker
Malico Streetor
Feb Term 1794

112 27 Jan 1794--James Ransom to Phillip Rogers...50 pds...Negro woman Woddy...
Elizabeth King   James Ransom
William Goodman

113 28 Jan 1794--Hardy Eason to George Eason...49 pds 1 sh...Negro Cheary and child Dick...
James Baker   Hardy Eason

114 28 Jan 1794--Henry Copeland and wife, Sarah, to Benjamin Barnes...75 pds...150 acres, part of two patents, one granted to John Nichols 6 Jun 1699 and the other to William Skinner 11 Mar 1740, beginning at a chinquipen oak, corner tree of Elisha Harrell, John Parker Jr. and Isaac Langston, along Langston's line of new marked trees to a pine in Isaac Pipkin's line, corner of said Langston's line,

along Pipkin's line to main road, crossing road and along line of
marked trees to white oak in said Barnes' line, to John Odom's line
to his corner pine and along his line...
James Knox   Henry Copeland
Miles Gatling   Sarah Copeland
William Goodman testified said Sarah
relinquished her dowry freely. Feb Term 1794

116 11 Oct 1793--William Baker to William Matthews...$75...__ wood-
land beginning at red oak on side of Suffolk Road, running NW by line
of marked trees to pine of Demsey Williams' and along his line to pine
of Isaac Walters', along his line to pine in path and down path to
Bray Baker's line...
Pa. Hegerty   William Baker
Benjamin Baker
Anthony Matthews
Feb Term 1794

117 23 Mar 1792--Joseph Holland Jr. and Joseph Holland Sr. of Nansemond Co., Va. to Mills Lewis...75 acres that John Odom left to his
daughter, Elizabeth, in his will 16 Oct 1770, to insure debt of 500
pds; land begins at head of Ready Branch, down branch to Knotty Pine
Swamp to William Warrens and along his line to Thomas Vann's line and
along Vann's line to said Lewis' line and down his line...
Edward Gatling   Joseph Holland
Luten Lewis   Joseph Holland
Feb Ct 1794

118 15 Feb 1794--James Norfleet to Abraham Norfleet of Chowan Co...
$160...Negro boy Peter...
John Cowper   James Norfleet
Chris. Cowper
Feb Term 1794

119 15 Feb 1794--Josiah Parker and wife, Omy (Oma) to James Parker...
25 pds...37½ acres beginning on S side of Mills Swamp at live oak,
corner tree on James Riddick's line, along his line to Shephard's
line and along that line to red oak, new line made by said Josiah
and James and along new line...
Christopher Gayle   Josiah(X)Parker
Rob.(X)Parker
Samuel Smith
Feb Term 1794

120 26 Nov 1793--Henry Copeland and wife, Sarah, to Isaac Langston...
15 pds...50 acres, part of patent granted to William Skinner, dec. 11
Mar 1740, beginning at white oak in branch near Isaac Carter's path,
a tree of Elisha Harrells and John Parker's, along Parker's line to
Spanish oak in John Gatling's, to said Carters and along his line
to sweet gum, corner tree of Isaac Pipkin's and along Pipkin's line
to line of marked trees and along that line...
John Odom   Henry Copeland
Benjamin Barnes   Sally Copeland
Luke Langston
William Goodman testified said Sally
relinquished her dowry freely. Feb Term 1794

122 16 Nov 1793--Henry Copeland and wife, Salley, to John Odom...$250
100 acres beginning at red oak, said Odom's line, along patent line

to hickory, corner of Isaac Langston's and along line of marked trees dividing said Langston and aforesaid land to corner gum in run of Cypress Swamp and up swamp to live oak of said Odom's line; being part of a patent granted to Jacob Odom 25 Mar 1749...

Ruben Harrell   Henry Copeland
John Harrell   Sally Copeland
William Goodman testified said Sally
relinquished her dowry freely. Feb Term 1794.

123 19 Feb 1794--Charles Lawrence of Northampton Co. to William Baker 77 pds 10 sh...Negro woman Sarah and girls Winney, Rozilla and Venus...

Jethro Ballard   Charles Lawrence
David Rice
Feb Term 1794

124 26 Nov 1793--Henry Copeland and wife, Salley, to Isaac Langston... $25...50 acres beginning at pine of Demsey Langston's, E side of marsh, along said Demsey's line to Stephen Rogers' line and along his line to a pine, corner tree of said Rogers' and Lewis Sparkman and along Sparkman's line to John Carters and along his line; part of patent granted to Henry Baker 28 Jul 1730...

John Odom   Henry Copeland
Benjamin Barnes   Salley Copeland
Luke Langston
Feb Term 1794 William Goodman testified said Sally signed freely.

126 12 Sep 1793--Henry Forrest to William Lewis...90 pds 15 and 1 penny...120 acres beginning on E side of Bennetts Creek Swamp at marked cypress in William Boothe's line, to post oak, corner of his and Thomas Marshall's line, along Marshall's line to Even Murfree's corner and along his line to four dogwoods in Patrick Lawley's patent, now George Outlaw's, to Jethro Meltear's corner, to David Harrell's and along his line to white oak in Jonathan Lassiter's corner to William Lewis' corner and along his line to Edenton Road...

Jonathan Roberts   Henry Forrest
Thomas Billups   Sarah(X)Forrest
Nov Term 1793

127 9 Oct 1793--John Powell of Jacob and wife, Elizabeth, to James Jones...13 pds...30 acres on E side of main road leading from Edenton to Suffolk beginning at post oak on road near Dennis' Old Plantation and along Dennis' line E to corner black oak of William Ellis, NE to main road and S...

Jethro Ballard   John Powell
William Ellis   Eliza(X)Powell
Nov Term 1793

128 18 Nov 1793--Richard Bond and wife, Mary, to Demsey Jones...75 pds...50 acres in lower part of county on E side of Indian Swamp, beginning at corner maple, down swamp, being line between said Bond and John Matthews, to Beaverdam Swamp, to large branch and down branch.

Thomas Ledsom   Richard Bond
William Goodman testified said Mary   Mary(X)Bond
signed deed freely. Nov Term 1793

129 13 Sep 1793--Luke Sumner to John Brinkley...$100...25 acres beginning at marked pine in fork of Suffolk Road and Marsh Road, said Brinkley's corner tree, to marked red oak and by line of marked trees E to branch and down branch...

Pa. Hegerty   Luke Sumner
William Ellis
Elisha Brinkley

130 26 Nov 1793--Henry Copeland and wife, Sally, to John Odom...$10
7 acres beginning at pine in Odom's line, along his line to Cypress
Swamp, down swamp binding on Elisha Harrell's line to chinquipen
oak; part of patent granted to John Nichols' in June 1699...
Luke Langston   Henry Copeland
James Knox   Sally Copeland
William Goodman testified said Sally
signed deed freely. Feb Term 1794

132 16 Nov 1793--Bray Warren and wife, Priscilla, to Henry Copeland
$800...180 acres out of a patent to Joseph Brady 9 Mar 1717, beginn-
ing in Peters Swamp, up run to mouth of Long Branch and up branch
to Isaac Pipkin's line, along his line to Phillip Lewis' line and
along his line...
John Parker   Bray Warren
John Odom   Prisella(X)Warren
William Warren
Nov Term 1793
Law. Baker testified said Priscilla signed deed freely.

133 9 Sep 1793--John Wallis and wife, Ann, to David Cross...40 pds...
75 acres, part of plantation whereon John Wallis Sr. formerly lived,
beginning at gum on S side of Pine Swamp, William King's line and a-
long his line to sweet gum, another corner tree, along swamp just below his house, to small branch, to pine near head and along line of
marked trees; land being part of Hooks Patent and one granted to Thomas Barnes 20 Jun 1765...
Will'm(W)Walters   John(X)Walles
Wo_(X) Phelps   Ann(X)Walles
Moses(X)Jones

134 15 Nov 1793--William Wallis and wife, Edith, to David Cross...20
pds...32 acres, part of plantation whereon John Walles Sr. formerly
lived and part where said William once lived, beginning at sweet gum
on said Cross' line, to William King's line and along his line to
white oak in Hooks Patent to red oak and crossing land to corner
pine and along line of marked trees to edge of Pine Swamp, to a
maple in fork near run and up run to said Cross; part of patent to
William Hooks...
Abel Cross   William Walles
Majer Phelleps   Edith(X)Walles
Benjamin Varnell
Nov Term 1793

135 6 Apr 1793--James B. Sumner to George Allen...25 pds...120
acres beginning at white oak near Cypress Pond, Thomas Smith's and
William Cleaves' line, to corner E along Cleaves' line to post oak
of Jethro Sumner's and along line of marked trees to red oak in
said Smith's and Sumners line, near side of Mile Bridge and along
Smith's line W...
Samuel Smith   James B. Sumner
Jonathan Smith
Nov Ct 1793

137 26 Nov 1793--Henry Copeland and wife, Salley, to John Odom...
$23...23 acres beginning at water oak, Odom's line, along his line
to red oak, Francis Brinkley's corner, along his line to Cross' line
to small branch issuing out of Cypress Swamp and down branch to said

Odom's line; tract is part of a patent to Henry Baker 28 Jul 1730..
Benjamin Barnes   Henry Copeland
Luke Langston   Sally Copeland
James Knox
Feb Term 1794

138 8 Nov 1793--Ann and Reuben Harrell, with consent of his wife, to Elisha Harrell...75 pds...65 acres, part of plantation granted to Francis Neusom 6 Jun 1699, beginning at head of Cypress Swamp, down swamp to red oak in William Jones' corner, along his line and is mannor plantation whereon said Ann and Reuben dwell...
Lewis Sparkman   Ann(X)Harrell
Thos. Harrell   Ruben Harrell
Nov Term 1793

139 24 Jul 1793--Clabin Aysten to Henry Goodman...30 pds...50 acres beginning at pine on river pecosin, corner tree of said Goodman, Moses Kittrell and William Crafford, along main pecosin to Kiat Jones' corner in head of Thick Neck Branch, down branch and line of marked trees to corner gum of James Brady's and said Goodman's, to said Kittrell's line and along his line; tract is part of grant to John Rawls Jr. 1 Apr 1723...
William Goodman   Clayborn(X)Ayston
William Crafford   Rachal(X)Ayston
Mary King
Nov Term 1793

140 30 Jul 1793--Elisha Brinkley to John Brinkley...38 pds 15 sh... 30 acres beginning at black gum in branch in said John's line, W on his line to fork of marsh and Suffolk Road, down road to marked pine, E by line of marked trees to water oak in branch and along run...
Pa. Hegerty   Elisha Brinkley
Levina(X)Brinkley
Nov Term 1793

141 17 Jun 1793--Bray Warren to Sarah Winbern...20 sh...yearly lease for 20 years of 30 acres in Peters Swamp where James Wills formerly lived...
James Gatling   Bray Warren
Mills Gatling
Elisha H. Bond
Nov Term 1794

142 20 Oct 1793--Jonathan Rogers to James Gatling...$114...50 acres beginning at white oak, John Lewis' corner, along his line to Stephen Rogers' corner and along his line to pine stump, Piland's corner and along Piland and John Odom's line to said Jonathan's line, to Gatling's corner white oak and on his line...
Luten Lewis   Jonathan Rogers
Patrick Hegerty
Nov Term 1793

143 19 Feb 1794--Demsey Jones to William Baker...66 pds...Negro woman Sarah and girls Winney, Rozella and Venus...
Jethro Ballard   Demsey(X)Jones
David Rice
Feb Term 1794

144 11 Dec 1793--Demsey Jones to Elisha Hance Bond...100 pds...50 acres in lower part of county, beginning at corner maple between said land and John Burlton, down swamp to Schoolhouse Branch and down side to Beaverdam Swamp...
John B. Walton   Demsey(++)Jones
Richard Bond
Feb Term 1794

145 15 Feb 1794--William H. Baker, administrator of Benjamin Baker, dec. of Nansemond Co., Va. to Absalom Williams of Southampton Co., Va. and Kedar Parker of Nansemond...lease for 10 years land known as Pumpkin Patch in Gates Co. on N side of Chowan River to establish a seine place for 1/3 of all fish caught, except what may be eaten by employees...
John Weatherby   William H. Baker,
Feb Term 1794   adm. of B.B. Baker
                                                   Kedar Parker
                                                   Absalom Williams

147 6 Jan 1794--John Carter to James Carter...$200...150 acres, part of patent to John Odom 25 Mar 1743, beginning at ellum in Licking Hole near Cypress Swamp, down side to corner hickory and along Thomas Harrell's line to red oak, corner tree in John Parker's, along his line to Licking Rute Branch to said Carter's red oak, a tree in branch and down branch to line...
John Odom   John(‡)Carter
Charles Eure
Feb Term 1794

148 24 Dec 1793--James Goodman of Upper Parish of Nansemond Co., Va. to Richard Barnes...105 pds...200 acres on N side of Long Branch, beginning at black gum in run at Elisha Cross' line, down branch to Richard Barnes' line, along his line SE, by line of marked trees to Demsey Odom's line, along his line and by line of marked trees...
Thomas Barns   James Goodman
William Warren
John King
Feb Ct 1794

149 13 Feb 1794--Jeames Phelps Jr. to James Phelps Sr...20 pds... 52 acres beginning at gum in Norwest Branch binding on William Arnold's line, to Micajah Riddick's line, along his line to Noah Felton's line, running his line to gum in branch...
Hy Hudgins   James Phelps
Christian(X)Phelps
Feb Term 1794

151 8 Oct 1793--Thomas Norriss to Mills Landen...60 pds...100 acres, part of patent to William Horn 22 Jan 1718, beginning at pine on side of marsh on main Cypress Swamp, NW to John Eure's line, to his corner white oak, along Israel Beeman's line to Charles Eure's line, with his line to James Eure's line and along his line to David Lewis' line to pine in marsh and up marsh to Cypress Swamp...
James Landin   Thomas Norriss
Edy(X)Curle   Sarah(X)Norriss
Feb Term 1794

152 15 Feb 1794--Thomas Hunter to John B. Walton...500 pds...500 acres beginning in Bennetts Creek in Cabin Branch in Richard Bond's line, down swamp and Schoolhouse Branch, up branch to Thomas Hofler's line SW to Hinton's Path to Mirey Branch and down branch to Richard Freeman, dec. line, with his line NE to Capt. Blanchard's Old Patent and along that line to Bennetts Creek...
Timothy Walton   Thos. Hunter
Micajah Blanchard
Feb Term 1794

153 23 Dec 1793--Moses Boyce to Sion Boyce...10 pds...67 acres, tract whereon said Sion now lives, beginning at a pine, William Walter's corner tree, by line of marked trees NE to black oak stump of Isaac Walters', on his line NW to pine stump and by line of marked trees SE.
Isaac Walters   Moses(X)Boyce
John Babb
Pa. Hegerty
Feb Term 1794

154 15 Oct 1793--Demsey Trotman to William Hunter...20 pds...20 acres beginning at pine, Daniel Stalling's line, to pine in Snake Branch and up branch and by line of marked trees to black gum in Stalling's line.
John Hoffler   Demsey Trotman
Christian Hoffler
Feb Term 1794

155 17 May 1794--John Darden to Joseph Hare...$80...Negro girl Lydia.
Jethro Sumner   John Darden
May Term 1794

155 18 Dec 1793--George and Betse Eason to John B. Walton...50 pds...Negro girl Rose 8½ years old...
Thos. Ledsom   George Eason
Jno. Eason   Betse Eason
May Term 1794

156 8 Apr 1794--Richard Briggs to John Riddick...47 pds 10 sh...50 acres, part whereon he lives, beginning at white oak near cornfield whereon Hardy Reid lives, being a line tree of William E. Webb's, along Webb's line to small pine, corner made by said parties, S along Webb's patent...
William Harris   Richard Briggs
Robert Riddick
May Term 1794

157 20 May 1794--Benjamin Barns to Demsey Barns...10 pds...40 acres, part of patent granted to Benjamin Barnes 24 Oct 1786, beginning at gum at William Hunter's patent corner and said Benjamin's patent, along his line S to a cross line formerly called Demsey Barnes and along line of marked trees...
John Vann   Benjamin Barnes
Isaac Pipkin Jr.
May Term 1794

159 19 May 1794--Jacob Gordon to Elisha Norfleet...20 pds...20 acres, No. 9 lot in division of land patented by John Norfleet and known as Island and White Oak Spring Marsh, beginning at stake in Jethro Ballards line and binding on land said Norfleet purchased of John Baker the main desert and along patent line...
Nath'l Riddick   Jacob Gordon
David Riddick
May Term 1794

160 3 Apr 1794--Nathaniel and David Riddick to Isaac Miller Sr...75 pds...Negro man Tom...
Jos. Granbery   Nath'l Riddick
Hy. Hudgins   David Riddick
May Term 1794

161 19 May 1794--Elisha Norfleet to Jacob Gordon...20 pds...20 acres, the 5th lot in division of land patented by John Norfleet and known as Island and White Oak Spring Marsh, beginning at stake in Jethro Ballard's line and along patent line...
Nath'l Riddick   Elisha Norfleet
Jno. Gordon
May Term 1794

162 22 Feb 1794--Demsey Odom to Elisha Hare...30 pds...100 acres, part of patent granted to Moses Hare for 527 acres 18 Aug 1783, beginning at sweet gum, James Jones and Moses Hares corner tree, along Jones line NE to David Jones' corner pine, NE along his line, running to pecosin SW to said Demsey's gum, along line of marked trees...
Sam'l Smith   Demsey(X)Odom
Pa. Hegerty
James Small
May Term 1794

163 2 Dec 1793--Jethro Ballard, David Rice and Timothy Hunter, to comply with James Sumner, dec. will, to Richard Mitchel...2 pds 9 sh... 100 acres formerly belonging to said Sumner, on N side of Catherine Creek beginning at mouth of Muddy Gutt, up gut NE to the Junipers S to Cathrine Creek near upper part of marsh and along creek...
Jethro Benton   Jethro Ballard
Charles Moore   David Rice
Luke Sumner

165 18 May 1794--Richard Bond and wife, Mary, to John B. Walton...500 pds...440 acres beginning at Amarias Blanchard's line where it crosses road in a beach, along line near roadside to said Walton's line and down branch to Demsey Jones' line, with his line to Beaverdam Swamp and up swamp to said Blanchards...
Jeremiah Speight   Rich'd Bond
Isaac Carter   Mary(X)Bond
Jethro Sumner testified said Mary signed deed
willingly. May Term 1794.

167 9 Oct 1793--Henry Hill to Demsey Jones...100 pds...50 acres in lower part of county in Jordens Neck, beginning at James Robins' corner tree, a white oak, along line of marked trees to John Walton's line, to Oald Indian Patent and along patent line to Henry Griffin's and along his line to pine corner, along line of marked trees...
John Darden   Henry(H)Hill
Theresa(X)Darden
May Term 1794

169 12 Feb 1794--Soloman Phillips of Edgecomb Co. to Demsey Odom... 60 pds...200 acres whereon he formerly lived...
Teberus Purvis   Soloman Phillips
Britian Odom
Benjamin(X)Odom
May Term 1794

170 12 Nov 1793--John Kittrell to Isaac Walters...4 pds 16 sh...4 acres beginning at pine in branch, down branch to Elisha Parker's line and along line of marked trees...
Willes Kittrell   Jno. Kittrell
William Kittrell
Winburn Jenkins
May Term 1794

171 22 May 1793--William Lewis and Samuel Harrell to Holloday Walton $110...100 acres on road that leads from Bennetts Creek Bridge to Josiah Granbery's and Chowan Indian Patent in Ready Branch, up branch to pine in Cader Hinton line, W by line of marked trees...
Levi Eure   William Lewis
Charles Eure   Samuel Harrell
May Term 1794

172 14 Jan 1794--Zachariah and Henry Copeland to Jethro Sumner, all of Upper Parish, Nansemond Co., Va...20 pds...2 acres beginning at a cypress on side of river and along line of marked trees to pine on side of low ground, along line of large pines in King's line, along that line to river; to use for cutting timber on land of Jesse Saunders and use of fishery for curing fish as given in deed from said Saunders to them 21 Feb 1791...
Lawrence Saunders   Zachariah Copeland
R. Hunter   Henry Copeland
Demsey Sumner
May Term 1794

174 7 Apr 1794--James Walton to George Outlaw...25 pds...140 acres, part of patent purchased by Henry Hill 7 May 1742, beginning at gum on Catherine Creek, running creek to cypress and including low lands and islands...
Seth Roundtree   James Walton
Charles Powell
May Term 1794

175 21 Oct 1793--Luke Sumner to James Knight...63 pds...Negro man Demsey...
Stephen Majen   Luke Sumner
Demsey Knight
Josiah Brinkley
May Term 1794

176 18 Dec 1792--David Cross and wife, Penelope, to John Rochell...60 pds...5 acres, part of tract purchased of Edward Howell, later found to be erroneous and taken up by patent 14 Oct 1786, beginning at stooping pine on E side of Chowan River joining land of said Cross, to corner tree near mouth of gut and down gut to river and up river... Also to have cartway across land where it joins David Watson's line and privilege of taking earth to build seine place and sufficient timber for fishery, causeway and firewood...
Jo. Vick   David Cross
William Watson   Penelope(X)Cross
Sarah(X)Darden
May Term 1794

178 17 Nov 1794--John B. Walton and wife, Esther, to Richard Bond...500 pds...440 acres beginning at Amaris Blanchard's line, where it

crosses road, along a branch to Demsey Odom's line, to Beaverdam
Swamp and down swamp to said Blanchard's line, along his line...
Thomas Ledsom   John B. Walton
Demsey(X)Jones   Esther Walton
Nov Ct 1794

179 17 Dec 1793--Treasury of North Carolina to John Arnold...50 sh
per 100 acres...75 acres on Collage Branch, James Parker's corner,
along his line NW to a pine in Merry Hill Pecosin, James Pruden's
corner tree, along his line SW to chinqipen oak in said Arnold's
line, on his line to Berreyman's patent and SE to Collage Branch...
J. Glasgow, sec.   Rich'd Dobbs Speight
                                             Gov.

180 14 Nov 1792--Seth Eason to John Knight of Nansemond Co., Va.
$200...Negro man Joseph...
John Gordon Jr.   Seth Eason
John Reading
Nov Term 1794

181 28 May 1794--Luke Sumner to Daniel Franklin of Nansemond Co.,
Va...61 pds 7 sh 6 pn...150 acres being chiefly in Gates Co., be-
ginning at marked pine in Wilkerson's line, NW to pine of Jacob
Brinkley's and on his line to Kelley's Branch and down run binding
on Mill Swamp on E side to Polly Branch, up branch to Elisha Brink-
ley's, along his line to Hugh Griffins and on his line to David
Brinkleys, to sweet gum in his brother's line, W to Wilkersons
and S...
John Brothers   Luke Sumner
Pa. Hegerty

182 3 Feb 1794--William Baker, son of Sam'l, to William Lewis...50
pds...Negro boy Sam...
Jno. Baker   William Baker
Thos. Marshall
James Moore
Aug Ct 1794

182 7 Aug 1794--Elisha Norfleet of Nansemond Co., Va. to John Ben-
ton, son of his wife...deed of gift...Negro boy Jacob...
Jethro Sumner   Elisha Norfleet
Robt. Benton
Aug Ct 1794

183 5 Sep 1794--Robert Nappier to William Dilday...$36...50 acres
beginning at gum on Beach Swamp in Demsey Odom's line, on his line
to gum in Elisha Cross' line, binding his line and running branch
to pine, by line of marked trees NW along fence to said swamp and
down swamp...
Richard R. Smith   Robert Napier
Pa. Hegerty
Nov Ct 1794

184 26 Jan 1792--Joseph Riddick to James Baker...13 pds 15 sh...75
acres on SE corner of patent and Joseph Hurdle's line, part of a
patent of 640 acres and known as Pine Noles...
Wm. McKesend   Jo. Riddick
Jesse Rogerson
Aug Term 1794

185 26 Nov 1793--State of North Carolina to Cyprian Cross...10 pds per 100 acres...200 acres where he lives beginning at two pine saplings on N side of Edenton Road, Francis Brinkley's line, SE to pine near pocosin, NE to red pine on Long Branch and along branch to Hare's patent on Cabin Swamp and down swamp. No. 112...
J. Glasgow, sec.   Rich'd Dobbs Speight

186 26 Nov 1793--State of North Carolina to Benjamin Barnes...10 pds per 100 acres...27 acres beginning at table of 3 pines, William Everett's patent corner, along his line SE to pine in Ballard's Patent line, along that line to Demsey Barnes' corner and along his line...No. 108.
J. Glasgow, sec.   Rich'd Dobbs Speight

187 26 Nov 1793--Treasury of North Carolina to Seth Eason...10 pds per 100 acres...45 acres on S side of Basses Swamp, down run to white oak in Col. Jesse Eason's desert patent on Vinard Point, along new survey S. No.104.
J. Glasgow, sec.   Rich'd Dobbs Speight

188 25 Jun 1794--Abner Roundtree and wife, Sarah, and Priscilla Spivey to Lawrence and John Baker...25 pds...their rights in 650 acres received from the will of Moses Spivey, dec. on E side of Chowan River, beginning at mouth of Sarum Creek, down river to Waters Landing at cypress, to Bennetts Creek and up it to Sarum Creek...
William(X)Parker   Abner(X)Roundtree
Samuel(X)Brown   Sarah(X)Roundtree
Aug Ct 1794   Priscilla(X)Spivey

189 19 Aug 1794--William Crafford to Jesse Vann and Benjamin Barnes... $62...Seine Beech and ½ of 25 acres, patented by William Crafford in 1785 or 1786, on E side of Chowan River beginning at cypress on river small distance from mouth of Barnes Creek, up run NW...
John B. Walton   William Crafford
Luke Langston
Aug Term 1794

190 21 Aug 1794--John Baker to Thomas Hunter, chairman of county court of pleas and quarters sessions...5 pds...1½ acres whereon courthouse stands, beginning at stake, NE from large white oak at Baker's fence, E from storehouse and NE...
James Gregory   Jno. Baker
William Goodman
Aug Ct 1794

191 15 Nov 1790--Henry Forest to Demsey Phelps...100 pds...55 acres on E side of Bennetts Creek beginning at red oak sapling by Forest's opening, SW to walnut at Tar Landing, NW to said creek and down to mouth of Fort Neck Branch, up branch to pine in fork of path...
Willis Brown   Henry Forest
Jonathan Smith
Aug Ct 1794

192 10 Aug 1794--Henry Copeland to John Odom...$40...70 acres beginning at main public road leading from Winton to Suffolk, to Phillip Lewis' line to William Warrens's land, along his line to Benjamin and Thomas Barnes' lines, to white oak by line of marked tree to said road and down...
William Harress   Henry Copeland
Joseph Jno. Holland
Aug Ct 1794

193 28 May 1794--Luke Sumner to Kedar Ballard...$40...45 acres known as Corapeak, beginning at marked gum in branch in Jethro Ballard's line on side of swamp, along swamp N to run and S on said Kedar's line...
Joseph Jno. Sumner   Luke Sumner
Pa. Hegerty

194 7 Aug 1794--Job Felton to Uriah Eure...3 pds 10 sh...15 acres beginning at pine in Sarum Creek Road, a corner tree between said Job and Joel Felton, down marsh and by line of marked trees to Jesse Harrell's line, to branch and up branch to road and along road...
Luke Langston   Job(X)Felton
Jacob Johnson
Samuel Green
Aug Ct 1794

195 14 Nov 1792--Seth Eason to John Knight of Nansemond Co., Va...$200...Negro man Joseph...
John Gordon Jr.   Seth Eason
John Redding
Nov Ct 1794

196 21 Jul 1794--James Knight to John Darden...12 pds...20 acres beginning at red oak in William Arnold's line, to Jesse Wiggens line in run of Elum Swamp...
D. Knight   James Knight
William(X)Mathes
Nov Ct 1794

196 7 Jun 1794--David Rice to Abraham Riddick of Nansemond Co., Va. 64 pds...Negro woman Venus...
Jethro Sumner   David Rice
James B. Sumner
Nov Ct 1794

197 30 Oct 1794--Mills, Nathaniel and David Riddick to Moses Briggs...$1200...373 acres on S side of Horsepool Swamp, being part of tract belonging to orphans of Mills Riddick, dec. beginning at black gum sapling, David Riddick's corner tree on side of desert, along desert S to black gum of said Briggs, to Pearces' line, to Eason's line, to Briggs line and over road, along patent line to said David's corner tree in patent line...
James Gordon   Mills Riddick
Richard(X)Briggs   Nath'l Riddick
Nov Ct 1794   David Riddick

198 1 Nov 1794--Demsey Sumner of Nansemond Co. Va. to Soloman King 6 sh...2 acres, part of land he purchased of David ____ on N side of Deep Branch, joining said King's land, beginning at pine in said branch, NE along line of marked trees...
Jethro Sumner   Demsey Sumner
Teresa Sumner
Ann Streator Sumner
Sarah Sumner
Nov Ct 1794

199 19 Nov 1794--Henry and Himrick Hill to William Lewis...$100...214 acres, their part of tract Henry Hill, dec. willed to his children

and known as Junipers, which he purchased from the Chowan Indians 26 May 1748, and containing 640 acres in pocosin of Bennetts and Catherine Creeks...
Jo. Riddick Henry(H)Hill
Nov Ct 1794 Himrick Hill

200 27 Jun 1794--Levin Dure to Josiah Granbery...100 pds...140 acres by line of said Granbery and Meherrin Swamp and is land that Joseph Scott and wife, Mary, received of James Davis, guardian of James Hodgers and being land that James Hodgers, dec. purchased of John Jones, dec...
John Eason Levin Dure
Elisha Twine
John Granbery
Aug Ct 1795

201 26 Sep 1794--Renthy Phelps to Clem R. Mathews...6 bbls. of corn yearly for rent of farm left to her by her husband, James Phelps, dec.
Anthony Mathews Renthy(X)Phelps
Elizabeth Mathews
Nov Ct 1794

201 20 Oct 1794--Elizabeth Costin to her son, William Harress, deed of gift...Negro woman Hanner...
John Cunningham Elizabeth Costen
Peggy Jemeson
Nov Term 1794

202 3 Nov 1794--Demsey Jones and wife, Rachael, to John B. Walton... 200 pds...her right of dower that fell to her at death of Aaron Blanchard, dec. on S side of Bennetts Creek Road beginning at road in Cabin Branch, down branch to Indian Swamp and down swamp to mouth of Schoolhouse Branch and up branch SE to Oald Field, to said creek road and along road...
Rich'd Bond Demsey(‡)Jones
Elisha Hance Bond
Nov Ct 1794

202 30 Aug 1794--John Jones and wife, Christian, of Perquimans Co. to David Harrell...117 pds 10 sh...115 acres beginning at marked red oak in Kedar Hinton's line, on his line SW binding on Lassitor's line to run of Wireneck Branch, to marked popular in Jonathan Lassitor and Jeremiah Jordon's corner line, on Lassiter's line to center of two sweet gums and a black gum and by line of marked trees...
Jonathan Roberts John(X)Jones
Christian Roberts
Nov Ct 1794

204 24 Feb 1794--Thomas Vann to William Baker...50 pds...100 acres formerly owned by Demsey Rooks Sr., beginning at black gum, corner tree between William Warren Sr. and said Vann, along line of marked trees to small branch and up branch to corner pine, along line of marked trees to Mills Lewis' line and along his line to corner oak of James Brady's, along Brady's line to Peters Swamp, along swamp to Mills Swamp and down run...
Anthony Williams Thos. Vann
Bryant(X)Wisler
Nov Ct 1784

205 20 Oct 1794--Elizabeth Costen to grand daughter, Peggey Jemison...
deed of gift...Negro boy Ben...
John Cunningham   Elizabeth(X)Costen
William Harress
Nov Ct 1794

206 4 Feb 1792--Stephen Eure to Lemuel Keen...5 pds...40 acres,
part of grant to him 8 Aug 1783, beginning at corner black gum, down
side of pecosin to Samuel Thomas' line, a black corner tree and a-
cross pecosin...
John Parker   Stephen Eure
Mary(X)Britianham
Nov Ct 1784

207 18 Nov 1794--Demsey Jones and wife, Rachael, to John B. Walton...
100 pds...50 acres in lower part of county in Indian Neck, beginning
at James Robins' corner white oak, along line of marked trees to
said Walton's line, to Old Indian Line, to red oak, corner tree in
Griffin's line and along his line and by line of marked trees...
Abraham Hurdle   Demsey(‡)Jones
Rich'd Bond   Rachael Jones
Nov Ct 1794

208 26 Nov 1793--State of North Carolina to Jesse Vann...10 pds per
100 acres...200 acres beginning at pine on side of pocosin near road
that leads from Winton to Suffolk, N to Edenton Road and Cyprian
Cross's corner, along his line SE to outside pecosin to a pine,
NW to dead pine on Long Branch, Gatling's corner, SE to pine in
Cool Springs and S on pocosin...
J. Glasgow, sec. No. 109   Rich'd Dobbs Speight

209 10 Aug 1772--Amos Smith of Hertford Co. to James Phelps, also
of Hertford...60 pds...55 acres in said county, beginning at gum on
side of Middle Swamp, along Micajah Riddick's line to white oak,
along Edward Arnold's line to pine, corner tree, along said Smith's
line to aforesaid swamp and along swamp...
William Powell   Amos Smith
John Duke Jr.
Abraham(X)Morgan

210 26 Nov 1793--Treasury of North Carolina to Thomas Barnes...10
pds per 100 acres...180 acres beginning in center of 3 oaks, said
Barnes and George Dunn's corner, along Dunn's line NW to pine, Richard Barnes' patent corner, along his line to Horse Swamp and up
swamp to said Barnes and Warren's corner, along Warren's line SE
to Barnes line...
J. Glasgow, sec.   Rich'd Dobbs Speight,

211 9 May 1794--John Baker, sheriff, to John Docton of Nansemond Co.,
Va...194 pds...500 acres formerly belonging to Benjamin Baker, dec.
and sold by court order to satisfy writ against said Benjamin by
William Hutches, guardian of Ethelred Britt, for debts; said land
begins at line that divides North Carolina from Virginia on N side
of Sumerton Creek and down creek to Chowan River, up river to black
water and along black water to said dividing line...
James Miller   Jno Baker
Lewis Sparkman
May Ct 1795

212 10 Mar 1795--Micajah Riddick Sr. to Moses Hines...$100...Negro
man Harry...
William Harress
Daniel Riddick   Micajah Riddick
May Ct 1795

213 23 Mar 1795--Ebenezer Grayham to James Gatling...$560...200
acres, whereon he lives and which he bought from Thomas Robertson
7 Dec 1792, on SW side of Sarum Swamp, beginning at corner maple
of James Riddick's line, to marked white oak, corner of said Riddick's and Thomas Norress' land, to corner of said Riddick, Norris
and Thomas Piland and along Piland's line to swamp...
James B. Sumner   Ebenezer Grayham
Betsey Sumner
May Ct 1795

214 28 Mar 1795--Francis Speight to Isaac Pipkin...45 pds...seine
place and one acre on Chowan River where John Menchew formerly halled
the seine, which Henry King purchased of Jacob Minchew, land beginning
at branch by spring and runs up river to Barns Old Landing at lower
end of marsh to S side of bottom, to stake on Old Field; also to
have open cartway from Seine Beach to public road...
William Gatling   Francis Speight
Sarah Pipkin
May Ct 1795

215 16 Apr 1795--Edward Berreman to James Baker...200 pds...234 acres
whereon he lives, joining land of Joseph Riddick, Thomas Trotman and
William Berreman...
Joseph Davis   Edward(X)Berreman
Seney(X)Davis

216 19 May 1794--Luke Sumner to Joseph Jno. Sumner...$45...84 acres
of woodland beginning at marked red oak on W side of Suffolk at foot
of Pitch Kittle Road near hollow bridge, down Suffolk Road NW to
pine of said Joseph's line, down Pitch Kittle Road...
Daniel Franklin   Luke Sumner
Pa. Hegerty
May Ct 1795

217 16 May 1795--William Saunders to John Lang...65 pds...221 acres
on N side of Cypress Swamp, along line of marked trees to branch and
up swamp...
John Odom   William Saunders
Uriah Odom
May Ct 1795

218 21 Oct 1794--Willis Sparkman to Nathan Cullens...10 pds...16
acres on W side of Sarum Creek Road beginning at pine at Samuel
Green's line, along line of marked trees to branch, Jesse Harrell's
line and along his line N...
David Lewis   Willis(X)Sparkman
Thomas Green   Haner(X)Sparkman
Hugh King
May Ct 1795

219 19 Mar 1795--Lodewick Brooks of Halifax Co. to Edward Piland...

75 pds 5 sh 2 pn...60 acres beginning at pine on Jacks Branch on
W side of main road to Long Branch near Willis Hughes, up said
branch to marked corner pine and along line of marked trees binding
on Dr. Graham's line to said Pilands...
William Brooks   Lodewick Brooks
Thos.(X)Piland
May Ct 1795

220 30 Jul 1794--Elisha Norfleet to John Darden...$100...Negro boy
Jim...
Jethro Sumner   Elisha Norfleet
Jesse Benton
Robert F. Benton
May Ct 1795

222 27 Aug 1794--James B. Sumner to William Hall...yearly rent for
20 years on tract on E side of Honey Pot Swamp running to broad path
leading to Joseph Figg's, by line of marked trees to swamp...
Jonathan Smith   James B. Sumner
May Ct 1795

221 19 Feb 1795--Peter Foster and Thomas Ransom of Matthew Co., Va.
to Isaac Harrell Jr...60 pds...Negro girl Nancy...
Jos. Granbery   Peter Foster
Humphrey Hudgins
May Ct 1795

221 31 Dec 1794--George Eason Sr. to Abraham Harrell...50 pds...Negro
boy Robin...
Hy Hudgins   David Harrell   George Eason
Sam'l Harrell   Theophilus Harrell
John Eason   Samuel Harrell
May Ct 1795

222 1 Mar 1794--James Hayes to William Hayes...$57...38 acres on S
side of Bennetts Creek, beginning at sweet gum in mouth of small
branch, Jack Hayes' line, on his line to corner pine in Harrell's
ling, along that line SW to branch and along branch...
Holloday Walton   James(#)Hays
Sarah Hays
May Term 1795

223 18 Jan 1795--Daniel Ellis to William Crafford...20 pds...25
acres, part of patent granted to John Miller in 1780, beginning
at small sweet gum at Black Fish Hole on Wynns Road, along E side
to William Arnold's line, along his line to corner tree in Demsey
Harrell's line and along his line...
Mills Eure   Daniel(X)Ellis
David Harrell
Demsey Harrell
May Ct 1795

224 10 Nov 1791--Elisha Norfleet to Abraham Harrell...30 pds...Negro girl Sue...
Jacob Gordon   Elisha Norfleet
Jacob Gordon Jr.
May Ct 1795

225 May Ct 1795--John James Richards of Upper Parish of Nansemond Co.,

Va. to William Doughtie...65 pds...Negro woman Lucy and her son Jim.
Humphrey Hudgens   John Richards
Amos(X)Parker
May Ct 1795

225 18 May 1795--James Davis and wife, Kezia, to James Hodges...31
pds 10 sh...50 acres on Watery Swamp beginning at corner tree be-
tween said Davis and Jonathan Lassiter, along their line to said
swamp and along run binding on lands of Demsey Blanchard and George
Brooks to corner tree of Job Riddick and up Riddick's line...
Demsey Blanshard   James( )Davis
George Brooks   Kezia(+)Davis
May Ct 1795

226 2 Feb 1795--Kedar Ballard to Isaac Harrell...$150...Negro Boy
Randal...
Jos. Granbery   K. Ballard
Charles Harrell
Feb Ct 1795

226 16 Feb 1795--George Brooks to Henry Copeland...65 pds...Negro
man Miles...
William Brooks   George Brooks
Richard Smith
Feb Ct 1795

227 13 Dec 1794--Soloman Ross and wife, Elizabeth, to Henry Eborn
Sears...25 pds 10 sh...60 acres, which he bought of Henry Dilday,
binding on Joel Goodman's line, along his line to Hardy Cross, to
Bryant Walter's and back to Goodman's line...
William Vann   Soloman(X)Ross
Bryant Vann   Elizabeth(X)Ross
Feb Ct 1795

228 22 Dec 1794--Abraham Riddick to John Simons...100 pds...200
acres beginning at run of Bennetts Creek binding on Hays line, to
a red oak on Demsey Jones line to a popular in Deep Branch, down
to mouth and along run of creek...
William Harress   Abraham Riddick
John Arnold
Feb Ct 1795

229 29 Dec 1794--David, James and John Small to William Elles...44
pds 5 sh...50 acres patented by Luke Sumners 15 Mar 1762, beginning
at holly near E end of ridge on S side, NE to juniper on N side, to
gum in patent line on E side of second ridge, by line of marked trees
S and along patent line E...
Pa. Hegerty   David Small
Edward Kelley   James Small
Feb Ct 1795   John Small

230 24 Jan 1795--William Walters to Demsey Barnes...27 pds...50
acres, part of grant to John Gay 26 Mar 1723, beginning at pine
on branch that parts stiff land from sand banks, along branch and
said Barnes line to corner pine, to John Odom's line, to pine corner,
to John Varnal's line and along his line to hickory on said branch...
Jesse Vann   William Walters
James Knox   Edey Walters
Benjamin Varnell
Feb Ct 1795

231 15 Jan 1795--James Outlaw to brother, George Jr...10 pds...deed of gift of land whereon their father, George Outlaw lives and purchased of Demsey Freeman and Jesse Garrett and given to said James by his father 11 Feb 1786; said land, lying on E side of Catherine Creek, to be given to said George Jr. after his father's death...
Thos. Hunter   James Outlaw
Seth Roundtree

231 22 Dec 1794--John Simons to John Arnold...90 pds...100 acres beginning at marked holly on Collage Branch, James Parker's corner, in William Arnold's line, along Parker's line NW to Benton's line, to water oak, corner tree in Pocket Branch issuing out of said branch, by line of marked trees...
James Pruden   John Simons
Jesse(X)Phelps   Nancy(X)Simons
Feb Ct 1795

232 10 Feb 1795--Jacob Spivey and Joseph and Lydia Taylor to William Vollentine...15 pds...2½ acres, part of land that belonged to Thomas Spivey, dec., beginning at Virginia Road on E side, running S to red oak on road that leads to desert, W along desert road to Virginia Road and N...
John Hofler   Jacob Spivey
Moses Hill   Joseph(X)Taylor
John S. Parker   Lydia(X)Taylor
Feb Ct 1795

234 11 Jan 1795--John Carter to Isaac Langston...$18...36 acres, part of grant to Henry Baker for 640 acres 28 Jul 1730, beginning at said Langston's line on river pocosin marsh, along his line to corner pine of Lewis Sparkman's and along Sparkman's line to river pecosin marsh and up marsh...
John Carter   John(X)Carter
Luke Langston
John Parker Jr.
Feb Ct 1795

235 16 Dec 1794--Silas Copeland of Nansemond Co., Va., planter, to William Gatling Sr., planter...60 pds...150 acres, part of patent of 600 acres granted to Charles Jenkins 26 Jul 1743, beginning at maple corner on edge of river swamp, by swamp to patent line, to pine on Flat Cypress Branch and up branch by line of marked trees...
William Goodman   Silas Copeland
Cyprian Goodman
Jesse Copeland
Feb Ct 1795

236 16 Feb 1795--Benjamin Eure and wife, Ruth, to Jesse Taylor... 10 pds...20 acres beginning at corner black jack of Charles Eure's, to John Eure's line, to red oak, corner tree of Israel Beeman's and along his line to white oak in pecosin, E to said Charles' line, S...
Mills Eure   Benjamin Eure
Samuel Taylor   Ruth(X)Eure
Rachael Sparkman
Feb Ct 1795

237 14 Feb 1795--William Arnold to Andrew Matthews...$____...60 acres

beginning at marked maple in Mery Hill Pecosin near head of branch and down branch...
John Arnold
Mills Elles
David(X)Benton
Feb Term 1795
           William Arnold

239 27 Nov 1794--Charles Smith to Seth Roundtree...61 pds 10 sh... 50 acres in Indian Neck, that he bought of Joseph Riddick, beginning at gum in Horsepen Swamp, S to pine in Josiah Parker's line and along his line...
Thos. Hunter
James Freeman
Feb Term 1795
          Charles Smith

239 28 Nov 1794--James Lassiter to Demsey Jones...75 pds...65 acres beginning at Jeremiah Jordan's corner tree, along John Jones' line to Kedar Hinton's line, up branch to corner gum between land and Miles Lassiter's, S down Deep Branch...
Richard Bond
Demsey(X)Trotman
Feb Ct 1795
          James Lassiter
          Mary(X)Lassiter

240 29 Aug 1794--Lemuel Keen to Josiah Harrell...$5...25 acres, part of patent granted to Stephen Eure 8 Aug 1783, beginning at black gum, said Keen's corner, to William Ruters' line to a corner juniper, with his line to Isaac Fryer's line, up outside pecosin to mouth of Cypress Swamp and across...
John Odom
James(X)Powell
Feb Ct 1795
          Lemuel(X)Keen

241 2 Feb 1795--William Walters to David Cross...20 pds...patent of William Hooks granted in 1668...
Benjamin Varnall
John(‡)Varnall
Feb Ct 1795
          William(X)Walters
          Edath(X)Walters

241 18 Oct 1793--Job Felton to Jonathan Cullins...5 pds...6 acres whereon he lives beginning at pine on main road, along Samuel Green's line to hickory corner, along said Job's old line to road and down road...
Thomas Felton
Sarah(‡)Felton
Nathan Cullens
Feb Ct 1795
          Job(X)Felton
          Sarah(X)Felton

242 26 Jan 1795--Elisha and Levina Landen to John Parker...$60...½ of 100 acres, part of patent granted to John Odom, dec. 15 Mar 1745, beginning at Little Cypress on Thomas Harrell's line, along his line to David Umphlett's line, along his line to Licking Root Branch, up branch to said Parker's, on his line to Hawtree Branch, to Israel Beeman's line to Little Cypress and down run...
Jesse Taylor
Samuel Green
Benjamin(X)Eure
          Elisha Landen
          Levina(X)Landen
Jo. Riddick attested said Levina signed deed freely. Feb Ct 1795.

244 14 Oct 1794--John Hunter to Thoflas Hunter 55 pds..60 acres beginning at Spanish oak in Iron Mine Branch, up branch by line of marked trees to white oak binding on Ruben Lassiter's line, along line of new marked trees to line between said parties...
Joseph Alphin   John Hunter
John Harrison
Feb Ct 1795

245 15 Aug 1794--Thomas Barns to William Warren...10 pds...30 acres that his father, Thomas, dec. gave to him and part of patent granted to Richard Barnes, beginning at water oak at corner tree in swamp in burnt pecosin and running Warren's line to corner gum in Reddy Branch to W side of said Warren's plantation opposite house...
James Gatling   Thomas Barnes
Feb Ct 1795

246 29 Aug 1794--James Phelps to Noah Felton...50 pds...52 acres on E side of Norwest Branch of Middle Swamp in William Arnold's line, along his line to Micajah Riddick's and with his line to said Felton's line, to N'west Branch and up branch...
John Arnold   James Phelps
Daniel Riddick
Feb Ct 1795

247 26 Nov 1793--Treasury of North Carolina to George Eason...10 pds per 100 acres...125 acres beginning at pine, said Eason's and Jacob Pearce's corner in pocosin, running Eason's line SE to pine in Henry Hill's patent, along patent NE to James Jones' line to said Jones and Col. Hunter's in Riddick's line N...
J. Glasgow No. 104   Rich'd Dobbs Speight

248 26 Nov 1789--Treasury of North Carolina to George Eason...10 pds per 100 acres...200 acres beginning at pine in Abraham Eason's and Jacob Pearce's corner, SE to Henry Hill's patent, to pine, Joseph Hurdle's corner tree, SW to Hurdles and Joseph Riddick's corner, N to dead pine, Samuel Green's corner tree, NW to said Pearces...
J. Glasgow, sec. No. 85   Sam. Johnston

249 12 Feb 1777--James Norfleet to Robert Dickens...120 pds...Negro woman ____ and her child...
Jethro Ballard   James Norfleet
Nov Ct 1777

249 26 Nov 1793--Treasury of North Carolina to Hardy Murfree and George Dunn...10 pds per 100 acres...200 acres on E side of Chowan River, beginning at cypress on side of river, Benjamin Harrell's corner, down river to mouth of Buckhorn Creek, up creek to William Arnold's line to said Harrell's line...
J. Glasgow, sec. No. 103   Rich'd Dobbs Speight

250 26 Nov 1793--Treasury of North Carolina to Abraham Riddick...10 pds per 100 acres...50 acres beginning at pine corner of Patrick Lawler's and John Odom's patent, to William Gordon's line, N along creek to Bennetts Creek...
J. Glasgow, sec.   Rich'd Dobbs Speight,
                                                gov.

251 24 May 1790--Isaac Powell of Johnston Co. does release and dis-

charge William Powell and his heirs from all manner of suits, actions, etc. against him...
James Powell   Isaac Powell
Nicholas Farmer
John Powell
Nov Ct 1795

251 18 Oct 1795--Charles King of Bertie Co. to Thomas Barnes...21 pds...Negro girl Abb...
Thomas Parker   Charles King
Nov Ct 1795

252 10 Nov 1795--Abraham Riddick to John Simons...$10...20 acres, swamp and island, on S side of Bennetts Creek beginning at maple, former line between said Riddick and James Hayes, by desert course and line of marked trees to creek swamp, along swamp to Jacob Hayes line on Deep Branch and down branch to main run of Bennetts Creek.
William(X)Boice   Abraham Riddick
Miles Boice
Nov Ct 1795

253 20 Oct 1795--William Ellis and wife, Mary, to Levin Dure...500 pds...200 acres known as Folly, being land Luke Sumner, the elder, purchased of Col. Lemuel Riddick, on S side of Loosing Swamp, beginning at marked white oak on S side, Larcum and Harress beginning tree, SE to lands of Jacob Powell and Moses Davis, N joining line of John Miller, dec. to Jethro Ballard's and Benjamin Gordon's corner, SE to swamp...
Jethro Ballard   William Ellis
Chris. Cowper   Mary Ellis
Benjamin Gordon

254 20 May 1795--Abraham Riddick to Thomas Riddick...20 sh...10 acres beginning in William Hays' line in side of Bennetts Creek swamp, up swamp to James B. Sumner's line, a desert course to main run of Bennetts Creek to line opposite William Hays...
James Hodges   Abraham Riddick
John Simons
Nov Ct 1795

255 28 Nov 1794--James Lassiter and wife, Mary, to Charles Smith... 55 pds...50 acres, formerly property of Gabriel Lassiter, dec., beginning at black gum in Cypress Branch, E by line of marked trees to Flat Branch, to corner tree of Jonathan Nichols, W to branch and down branch...
William(X)Boyce   James Lassiter
Joel Foster
Nov Ct 1795

256 31 Oct 1795--Moses Williams to Thomas Smith...60 pds...80 acres beginning at mouth of Hilly Swamp binding Hezekiah Williams' land to William Cleaves, to William Williams, to James B. Sumners, to Bennetts Creek and along creek...
William Harriss   Moses(X)Williams
Isaac Miller Sr.
Noah Felton
Nov Ct. 1795

257 24 Oct 1795--Luke Sumner and wife, Judith, to William Ellis...
$313 1/3...100 acres purchased by James Sumner from John R. Wilkinson 12 May 1784 beginning at gum on edge of Orapeak Swamp opposite large ditch, formerly boundary of said Luke and said Wilkerson, along ditch N to corner tree W to White Oak Branch, by line of marked trees on N side to Wilkersons and William Mathias, to White Oak Neck, binding on Orapeak...
Pa. Hegerty   Luke Sumner
John Cowper   Judeth(X)Sumner
Nov Ct 1795

258 20 Aug 1795--Jesse Benton to his brother, Robert F. Benton...
100 pds...125 acres on S side of Bennetts Creek, beginning at black gum, along line of marked trees to Moses Hines' line, N to gum corner and along run; is said Robert's part of land given to his father, John Benton, dec. by said Jesse...
Pa. Hegerty   Jesse Benton
Mary Benton
Nov Ct 1795

259 25 Aug 1794--John Kittrell to Demsey Williams...100 pds...80 acres beginning at pine on Watering Hole Branch, along Edward Sumner's line to gum corner of Bakers and Sumner's line, to Middle Swamp, to corner tree of William Kittrell's...
William Baker   Jno. Kittrell
Anthony Williams
Nov Ct 1795

260 31 Jan 1795--Joel Foster to Charles Smith...$65...27 acres, formerly property of James Hinton, dec. beginning at water oak in Cypress Branch, by line of marked trees to Wyerneck Branch, up branch..
Demsey(X)Jones   Joel Foster
Abraham Riddick   Rosanah Foster

261 1 Nov 1795--David Watson to Mary Beasley...5 pds...5 year lease of small house and one acre of land whereon he lives..
David Darden   David(D)Watson
John(X)Ellis
Nov Ct 1795

261 4 Nov 1794--Thomas Billups, late of Sussex Co., Va. to Demsey Langston...60 pds...Negro man Davey...
William Baker   Thos. Billups
Isaac Langston
Nov Ct 1795

262 3 Jun 1795--John Powell to Nicholas Miner...37 pds...50 acres on S side of Powell's Mill Pond, beginning at red oak near end of dam, SW to path and along path and by line of marked trees to another path, to Kicheon Norfleet's line, N to side of said Powell's pond.
Miles Benton   Jno. Powell
K. Ballard
Jethro Benton
Nov Ct 1795

263 12 Nov 1795--Henry Speight to Francis Speight...160 pds.15 sh...
112 acres called Hars' Clearing beginning at said Francis' corner, running to head of Flat Cypress and down swamp to pine and along

said Francis' line...
Phillip Lewis
Elisha(X)Realy   Henry Speight
Nov Ct 1795

263 15 Aug 1795--Isaac Harrell to Levin Dure...deed of gift...Negro
girl Pleasant, after death of his wife, Judith, Negro woman, Noll...
Samuel Harrell   Isaac(X)Harrell
Isaac Harrell

264 7 Nov 1795--Luke Sumner to John Brinkley...$36...12 acres beg-
inning at red oak in Brinkley's line, E by line of marked trees to
ditch, to corner gum of William Ellis' line, N to Elisha Brinkley's
corner and NW...
Pa. Hegerty   Luke Sumner
John Reading
Nov Ct 1795

265 15 Aug 1795--Jesse Saunders to son, Bray...deed of gift of 200
acres, plantation purchased of William Odom, on S side of Sumerton
Creek, beginning at cypress on side of creek, corner tree of Barnard
March's and said Saunders, along line of marked trees to Henry Lee's
line, to Jacob Walter's line, to John March's line and along his line
to said creek and down creek...
James Gatling   Jesse(I)Saunders
Nov Ct 1795

266 20 Apr 1795--Abraham Riddick to Bond Minchew...48 sh...30 acres
on S side of Bennetts Creek Swamp beginning in William Gordon's line,
up swamp to Elisha Hare's line, to main run, to line opposite said
Gordon's and down desert...
James Hodgens   Abraham Riddick
John Simons
Nov Ct 1795

267 6 Feb 1795--James Mathews to Jacob Pruden...$100...150 acres
known at Merry Hill Pecosin, bounded by lines of Samuel Brown, Moses
Boyce, William Walters and William Arnold...
John Hodgens   James Mathews
Isaac Miller Sr.   Sally Mathews
Aug Ct 1795

269 11 Aug 1795--Isaac Harrell Sr. to son, Isaac Jr...deed of gift
after his death...all lands and estate: Negroes Tom, Tamer, Lewis,
Hardy and Esther, 30 head cattle, 80 hogs, 10 sheep, 4 beds and furniture, horse, bridle and saddle...
Aug Ct 1795   Isaac(X)Harrell

269 25 Dec 1794--William Lewis to John Baker...34 pds...174 acres
in county of Tennessee in Cumberland Settlement, granted to him
20 May 1793, beginning at black oak and two hickorys, Lt. Abner
Lamb's, NW to hickory and SW...
Polly Glover   William Lewis
Dan'l V. Pelt
Feb Term 1796

270 16 May 1796--Dr. John Cunningham, surgeon and phsician, and Will
iam Harriss made oath that Dr. Samuel Heath Jamerson, physician, de-

parted this life at house of Thomas Smith 18 Aug 1793...
                                                        John Cunningham
                                                        William Harriss

270 15 May 1795--John Warren to William Warren...25 pds...Negro boy Jack 7 years old...
James Gatling   John Warren
John Parker
Aug Ct 1795

Vol. 4

2 10 Dec 1796--Moses Briggs to Joseah Briggs...200 pds...100 acres, part of land he purchased of Mills and David Riddick, sons of Mills Riddick, dec., lying on each side of Perquimans Road and being mostly S part of land, beginning at oak in Pearce's line, along that line to James Jones, SW to Thomas Hunter's line and along his line N to said Moses' line of land purchased of Samuel Green, NE to line of new marked trees...
Nath'l Riddick   Moses Briggs
John Riddick
Aug Ct 1796

3 17 Aug 1795--Henry Eborn Sears and wife, Mary, to Hardy Cross of Nansemond Co., Va...30 pds...50 acres whereon Soloman Ross formerly lived and sold to said Sears, beginning at dead pine on N side of Goff Folly Branch, by line of marked trees, formerly land belonging to Joel Goodman, to corner pine tree of Jacob Walters as formerly belonged to Henry Dilday, thence along line of marked trees to said Walters' land, to said Cross' line, to pine in head of said branch and down branch...
Daniel Duke   Henry E. Sears
Henry Copeland   Mary Sears
Deliah Sears
Aug Ct 1795

4 15 May 1795--John Warren to John Parker...48 pds...Negro girl Cherry, 12 years old...
James Gatling   John Warren
William Warren
Aug Ct 1795

5 19 Aug 1794--Augustine Minchew of Currituck Co. to George Lassiter Sr...48 pds...100 acres in Deep Gutt, beginning at corner tree between them in Samuel Harrell's line, along his line, down gut to Israel Minard's to white oak, corner tree between said Minard and orphans of Demsey Bond, dec., along line of marked trees...
Demsey Blanchard   Augustain Minchew
Jonathan Nichols
Moses Lassiter
Aug Ct 1795

6 21 Nov 1794--Enos Rogers of Craven Co. to Jonathan Rogers...$100...104 acres beginning at pine in James Lang's line, running strait

course by line of marked trees to road that leads to Cottons Ferry,
down olde road that comes up against Robert Rogers to said Jonathan's
own line, thence to Phillip Rogers' line and along his line to said
Lang's and on his line...
Jonathan Williams   Enos Rogers
Pa. Hegerty
Aug Ct 1795

7 20 Oct 1794--James B. Sumner to Lawrence Baker...55 pds...Negro
woman Claressa and boy child Randell...
James Gatling   James B. Sumner
Agatha Baker
Aug Ct 1795

8 27 Nov 1794--Randolph Co.: Sarah Lassiter, Green Stead, Jean Lass-
iter, Sarah Lassiter and Fredreck Nichols to Aaron Lassiter...70 pds
Negro Tom, property of Ezekiel Lassiter...   Sarah(X)Lassiter
  Charles Powell   Green Stead
Abraham Elliott   Jean(X)Lassiter
Aug Ct 1795   Sarah(X)Lassiter
                                              Fredrick Nichols

9 20 Jul 1795--Jeremiah Speight to son, William...deed of gift...
151 acres whereon he lives beginning in Timothy Hunter's line where
road crosses, along road to post oak, NW to patent line to center of
three trees, binding on Pughs and Hunters line...
Jo. Riddick   Jeremiah Speight
J.W. Voight
Aug Ct 1795

10 1 Jun 1794--John Kittrell and wife, Luize, to Jonathan Williams...
170 pds...170 acres beginning at post oak, corner tree of Isaac Wal-
ters, Demsey Williams and Demsey Odom, along Odom's line to Elisha
Parker's line and along his line to said Walters' line...
William Kittrell   John Kittrell
Standley Kittrell   Luize Kittrell
Apr Ct 1796

11 6 Jan 1794--James Carter is indebted to John and Kesiah Carter
for 150 pds whereas he agrees to not interrupt them of any privilege
of their land during their lives...
John Odom   James($)Carter
Charles Eure
Aug Ct 1795

12 8 Jan 1795--Patrick Hegerty to Noah Felton...$240...100 acres on
Northwest Branch of Middle Swamp in James Matthew's line, with his
line to Kittrell's line, to Felton's line, to run of said branch and
along branch...
Daniel Riddick   Pa. Hegerty
Micajah Riddick
Aug Ct 1795

13 13 Apr 1785--Jethro Ballard and David Rice, executers of James
Sumner, dec. to Charles Powell...25 pds 12 sh...40 acres on N side
of Chowan River and W side of Catherine Creek, beginning at George
Outlaw's corner post on river, down river to mouth of said creek and
up creek to Muddy Creek and binding thereon to Outlaws...
James Norfleet John Brothers   Jethro Ballard
John Riddick   William Ellis   David Rice
Aug Ct 1795

14 24 Feb 1795--Francis and Henry Speight to William Crafford...
$100...120 acres, part of patent granted to John Miller in 1780,
beginning at red oak, said Crafford's corner tree, along patent
line to William Arnold's line, to Dickerson's patent line and along
that line...
John Ellis
Benjamin Barns   Francis Speight
Aug Ct 1795   Henry Speight

15 29 Dec 1794--Esther Mathews to son, James...deed of gift, plan-
tation whereon she lives, bed and furniture, 3 puter dishes, 2 bas-
ins, 6 plates, pot and table...after her death...
Christr. Riddick   Esther(X)Mathews
James Pruden
Aug Ct 1795

15 21 May 1795--Thomas Billups to John B. Walton...133 pds 3 sh 8
pn...Negro man James...
Willis Brown   Thomas Billups

16 26 Nov 1793--Treasury of North Carolina to John Cowper...10 pds
per 100 acres...23 acres beginning at black gum on w side of Edenton Road to Suffolk in Marmaduke Norfleet's piney woods patent, a-
long line to white oak, Ballard's line, SE to road...
J. Glasgow, sec   Rich'd Dobbs Speight
8 May 1796

17 8 Jul 1794--Demsey Rooks Sr. to William Baker...9 pds 2 sh 7 pn...
his life estate in house and land reserved to him by Thomas Vann at
the time said Vann bought the land said Rooks lived on of Willis
Hughes, also feather bed and furniture and 12 hogs...
James Gatling   Demsey Rooks
John Vann
Feb Ct 1796

17 29 Jan 1796--William Carter to William Mathias...40 pds...Negroes
Vilet and Winney...
John Powell   William Carter
William Ellis
Feb Ct 1796

18 16 Feb 1796-- John Baker to William Baker...$2500...two tracts
first of 702 acres begins on side of Bennetts Creek just below bridge
NW to pine stump opposite tavern, NW to gum in branch joining Willis
Parker, dec., thence to George Piland's line to Willis and James
Brown's line, to George Williams, on his line to Troy Swamp, across
swamp to S side, binding thereon to Bennetts Creek and up creek;
second tract of 100 acres begins at maple, Spivey's patent, on E
side of Coles Creek, NE to white oak near three birches, formerly
Capt. Wilson's corner, then NE to chestnut oak in Troy Swamp, up
side to Coles Creek Swamp, to white oak of said Williams, W to main
run of Coles Creek and up run...
James Gatling   Jno. Baker
Anthony Williams
Feb Ct 1796

19 2 Jan 1796--Miles Turlington of Nansemond Co., Va. to James Gat-
ling 82 pds 10 sh...Negro man Jacob...
William Baker   Miles Turlington
Luten Lewis
Feb Ct 1796

20 29 Feb 1786--Lawrence and William Baker to John Parker...$100...
Negro boy Jacob, 5 years old, bought of Isaac Hunter at a sheriff's
sale...
Mills Eure   Lawrence and Will-
John Gatling   iam Baker
Feb Ct 1796

21 15 Feb 1793--Jethro Ballard, David Rice and Timothy Hunter, executers of James and Luke Sumners, dec...to Joseph Riddick...200 pds...
200 acres known as place whereon Jacob Doctorn formerly lived joining land of James Gregory, Ruben Riddick, Penelope Ownly and on E
side of Sand Ridge Road...
Law. Baker   Jethro Ballard
William Baker   David Rice
Feb Ct 1796

22 29 Oct 1795--William Lewis to Levin Dure...$100...214 acres pur-
chased of Charity Morris and David Hill, in Bennetts Creek and Catherine Creek pecosin...
Thomas Marshall   William Lewis
Kincheon Norfleet

23 10 Feb 1796--Richard Briggs to Robert Riddick...5 pds...2 acres
beginning at stake in said Brigg's line, S to corner between them
W to main road and N to ditch, E along ditch...
Hy. Hudgins   Richard Briggs
Penelope(+)Bird
Feb Ct 1796

24 12 Sep 1795--Jonathan Nichols and wife, Mary, to James Baker...$80
their part of land Henry Hill, dec. willed to his children and lying
in Bennetts Creek and Catherine Creek pecosin...
John Hare   Jonathan Nichols
David(+)Hill   Mary(XX)Nichols
Feb Ct 1796

25 7 Oct 1795--William Hays to Joseph Davis...$150...70 acres be-
ginning at water oak on N side of Bennetts Creek, along line of marked
trees to corner pine between Wright and James Hays, down run of swamp
to cypress, corner tree between said Hays, to run of creek...
James Lassiter   Will'm Hays
Edward(X)Berreman   Jacob(X)Hays
Feb Ct 1796

26 12 Jan 1796--William Lewis to James Baker...250 pds...214 acres,
purchased of Henry and Kimrick Hill, and part of tract of 648 acres
given to his children in will of Henry Hill and known as Junipers,
bought from Chowan Indians 26 May 1748; extends to Parker's line on
Cow Bridge, lying in pecosin of Bennetts and Catherine Creeks...
Jonathan Roberts   William Lewis
Thos. Marshall
Feb Ct 1796

27 12 Nov 1795--Levin Dure to James Baker...$500...214 acres in Jun-
iper Swamp purchased of William Lewis...
Geo. Gordon   Levin Dure
James(X)Small
Feb Ct 1796

28 31 Oct 1795--Samuel Smith to Moses Williams 60 pds...50 acres
beginning in William Cleaves' line binding on William Hinton's line,
along old line formerly called Francis Pugh's patent, with said line.
William Harriss   Samuel Smith
Isaac Miller Sr.
Noah Felton
Feb Ct 1796

29 28 Dec 1795--Francis Saunders to Thomas Ritter...lease of 20
acres lying on main road and joining Uriah Odom's line, for 20
years....
John Odom   Francis Saunders
Uriah Odom
Feb Ct 1796

29 26 Jan 1796--Luke Sumner to Simeon Brinkley...$200...Negro Jack.
Jethro Benton   Luke Sumner
William Ellis
Feb Ct 1796

30 15 Jul 1795--Charity Morris and David Hill to William Lewis...
$100...214 acres, part of tract of 648 acres that Henry Hill, dec.
left to his children in a place known as Junipers in pecosin of
Bennetts and Catherine Creeks, which he bought of Chowan Indians
26 May 1748...
Thom. Marshall   Charity(X)Morris
James Hodgens   David(X)Hill
Feb Ct 1796

31 28 Jul 1795--James Hays to son, John...deed of gift...120 acres
on S side of Bennetts Creek beginning at pine near side of swamp,
E to red oak, corner tree between Abraham Riddick and Demsey Jones
and said James line, by line of marked trees to William Hays and
Samuel Harrell's line, NE to pine on side of Flat Branch, to main
road, to branch and down branch...
John(X)Anderton   James(X)Hayes
Abraham Riddick
Feb Ct 1796

32 19 Dec 1795--John Varnell to Demsey Barns...S90...50 acres be-
ginning at marked hickory in Pine Swamp near mouth of Reedy Branch,
down swamp to patent line and along line...
John Vann   John(‡)Varnell
Benjamin Powell
Prudence(+)Barnes
Feb Ct 1796

33 13 Nov 1795--John and James Lang to Henry Lee...280 pds...275
acres adjoining lines of John and James Bethey...
Stephen Rogers   John Lang
Jonathan Rogers   James Lang
Hillory Willey   Elizabeth(X)Lang

34 3 Feb 1796--Stephen Rogers to John Parker...62 pds 10 sh...100
acres on S side of Cypress Swamp in river pecosin, adjoining lines
of Demsey Langston and Lewis Sparkman and is part of a patent granted

```
                            to Capt Henry Baker 28 Jul 1730...
                            Isaac Langston                          Stephen Rogers
                            Kindred Parker
                            William Umphlet
```

35 21 Jan 1796--Lot Rogers of Liberty Co., S.C. to Dempsey Odom...
$50...all his part of the estate of his mother, Zilpha Rogers, dec.
John Bethey   Lot Rogers
William Goodman
Feb Ct 1796

36 19 Nov 1795--Moore Carter to Alce and Martha Green...15 pds...42
acres whereon they liveth on SW side of Coles Creek, beginning at
gum in Lickingroot Branch, down branch to John Piland's line, to
Asa Harrell's line, along his line to Samuel Eure's line, with his
line to Ann Piland's and along her line...
George Williams   Moore Carter
Israel Beeman
Feb Ct 1796

37 20 Jan 1796--Seth Morgan to John Arnold...13 pds 10 sh...4 acres
beginning at post oak stump, running patent line to corner pine, by
line of trees to road and along road...
John Hudgens   Seth Morgan
Feb Ct 1796   Rachel(X)Morgan

38 23 Jul 1795--Abraham Riddick to James Hayes...1 pd 10 sh...15
acres on N side of Bennetts Creek beginning at mouth of Great Hawtree Branch, down main run to William Boice's opposite mouth of
said Hawtree and inclosing swamp land...
Sarah(X)Riddick   Abraham Riddick
John Simon
Feb Ct 1796

39 4 Feb 1796--Stephen Rogers to James Gatling...65 pds...100 acres
beginning at oak in Isaac Carter's line near said Rogers' line, a-
long his line to black gum, corner tree of said Carter's, NE to a
pine in Robert Rogers' line, thence along his line NW to white oak
and SW...
William Gatling Jr.   Stephen Rogers
Miles Gatling
James(+)Parker
Feb Ct 1796

40 27 Apr 1795--Richard Freeman to Charles Powell...100 pds...100
acres, plantation whereon his father, Demsey, formerly lived, bounded
by land of George Outlaw on S, by William Freeman on N and Catherine
Creek on W...
Miles Wallis   Richard Freeman
Hardy Hurdle
Martin Hurdle
Feb Ct 1796

41 13 Jan 1796--Stephen Rogers to Levy Eure...25 pds...50 acres
beginning at corner pine of John Gatling'dec. and John Parker, near
E side of branch not far from Reedy March, running E with Parker's
line to said Eure's line and along his line to little branch to Levi

Lee's line and along his line to said Gatlings...
Jesse Taylor   Stephen Rogers
Anthony Williams
Feb Ct 1796

42 16 Feb 1796--William Baker to Seasbrook Wilson...rent of cleared land W of branch that runs across patent, whereon said Wilson lives, for yearly share of Indian corn, with privilege of fence timber and firewood...
Anthony Williams   William Baker
James Gatling
Feb Ct 1796

43 29 May 1795--Asal Umphlet to William Umphlet...$17...12 acres patented by John Odom 15 Mar 1743, beginning at red oak in James Carter's line, along David Umphlet's line to said William's line, along his line to Thomas Harrell's line, with his line...
                                                Asal Umphlet
Kindred Parker
Isaac Langston
John Parker

44 20 Jul 1795--Isaac Harrell to David Harrell...500 pds...250 acres, which George Gordon, dec. bequeathed to John Gordon Jr., beginning at mouth of Mirey Branch, up branch opposite to plantation, along line from branch to Henry Forrest's line and along his line to Bennetts Creek Road and along road to Maple Branch and down branch...
Henry Meroney   Isaac(X)Harrell
Isaac Harrell Jr.
Feb Ct 1796

45 14 Mar 1796--John Baker to George Piland...$425...Negro woman Phebe and her children: Ame born 6 Feb 1789, Isaac 2 Feb 1792 and Jacob 19 Nov 1795...
William Hays   John Baker
May Ct 1796

46 19 May 1795--James B. Sumner to Jethro Sumner...750 pds...Negroes: London, Mike, Gilbert, Belender, Diner, Cale, Tizza, Paul, Chloe, Mason, Zilpha, Hanna, Penny, Sarah, Hagar and Dread. Also, stock of cattle and hogs, 2 horses, 4 feather beds and furniture, household and kitchen furniture and plantation utensils...
Jethro Ballard   James B. Sumner
William Harriss
May Ct 1796

47 1 Feb 1796--John Moran to son, John...deed of gift...502 acres in Davidson Co. on E fork of Stanton Camp Creek, that he bought of Sarah Collins, sister and heir of John Hinton, and lands he purchased of John Standen... Also to son Charles...land...
David Harrell   John Moran
Asenah Harrell

47 24 Mar 1796--Seth Eason to William Hunter...$240...Negro boy Toney...
Jacob Gordon   Seth Eason
Ezekiel Trotman
May Ct 1796

48 28 Feb 1796--William Perry and wife, Penina, of Hertford Co.
to Kedar Hinton...$2...tract in Juniper Swamp left to said Penina
by her father, Robert Taylor, dec...
Joseph Parker   William Perry
Demsey Phelps   Penina(X)Perry
May Ct 1796

48 17 Feb 1796--William Perry and wife, Penina, of Hertford Co.
to Kedar Hinton...13 pds...25 acres, left to said Penina by her
father, Robert Taylor, dec., beginning at pine in middle of Meria
Branch, down branch to brik hold, NW to Morris' line and along that
line to pine in Hinton's line...
Joshua Rayna   Joseph Parker   William Perry
Robert Perry   Isaac Taylor   Penina(X)Perry
May Ct 1796

50 12 Oct 1795--Charles Smith to Demsey Jones, son of Hardy...$20...
7 acres in Cypress Branch beginning at maple, corner tree, along
branch S to maple and by line of marked trees...
Abraham Riddick   Charles Smith
Joel Foster
May Ct 1796

51 26 Mar 1796--David Watson to Abel Cross...$500...600 acres on E
side of Chowan River, part of two patents: one granted to William
Speight in 1719 and the other to said Watson in 1762 beginning at
pine in patent line NE to Watson's patent, to Pipkin's line, along
his line to Gum Swamp, to said Cross' line, to river and down to
stake, Duke's Seine Place at upper end, and down seine place to
Cross' line...
John Vann   David(X)Watson
John(X)Ellis   Rachel(X)Watson
D. Barns
May Ct 1796

52 ___ Uriah and John Odom to Jethro Sumner...125 pds...two tracts,
the first of 100 acres was purchased by Richard Saunders of John
Lee 18 Nov 1795 in Nansemond Co., Va., beginning on upper side of
mouth of Plumb Tree Branch, along branch to head line and along patent SE to corner, where pine formerly stood, now an oak, along line
of marked trees S and up Cypress Swamp; second tract formerly surveyed by Richard Saunders 1 Apr 1717, begins at black oak tree of
John Lee, the older, NE to pine corner of Paul Pinder's, on his line
SE to said Lees and NW...
Francis(X)Saunders   Uriah Odom
Ann Saunders   John Odom
May Ct 1796

54 7 Mar 1796--James Hodges to Dempsey Jones...7 pds...50 acres
beginning at corner tree of Jonathan Lassiter's, along his line to
Watery Swamp, up swamp to Demsey Blanchard and George Brooks line,
to corner tree of Job Riddick's and along his line...
Jonathan Lassiter   James Hodges
Fredrick Lassiter
May Ct 1796

55 16 Feb 1796--Simon Stallings, sheriff, to James Baker...7 pds

12 sh...150 acres belonging to John Fontain of Virginia and sold
for taxes; land begins at John Cowper's line and runs NW...
Jo. Riddick   Simon Stallings
Jonathan Roberts
May Ct 1796

56 11 Mar 1796--George Piland to Willis Brown...100 acres beginning
at gum in William Baker's line near road, running his line to hickory
corner of said Bakers, along his line to line dividing said Piland's
land and said Brown to corner red oak, along line of marked trees
to James Brown's path and along path to road...
Seasbrook Wilson   George Piland
Thomas Fryer
May Ct 1796

57 16 May 1796--Palatiah Blanchard to John B. Walton...50 pds...50
acres binding on land of Robert Riddick and orphans of Demsey Bond,
dec. beginning at maple in said Riddick's line and running NW ...
Richard Benbury   Palatiah Blanchard
Timothy Walton
May Ct 1796

58 4 Nov 1795--Stephen Harrell to John Piland...30 pds...30 acres
beginning on S side of Licking Root Branch at corner pine in David
Lewis and Uriah Eure's line, running Eure's line and by line of marked
trees to hickory in Samuel Eure's line and by line of marked trees
to branch, to said Lewis' line...
George Williams   Stephen Harrell
Willis Piland
May Ct 1796

59 2 Feb 1795--James Jones and wife, Cloey, to James Parker Jones...
30 pds...50 acres beginning at post oak at Demsey Odom's field on E
side of main road, NE along Davis' line to Larcum and Harris line
and along that line NW to road and along road...
Jethro Ballard   James Jones
David Small   Cloey(‡)Jones
Edwd.(X)Kelly

60 11 Feb 1794--Samuel Pittman to Benjamin Crowell, both of Halifax
Co..5 sh...250 acres belonging to Willis Wiggens Jr. and Sr., pur-
chased 7 May 1790 by said Pittman as said Crowell's agent from Seth
Eason, sheriff, by execution of court to satisfy writ of said Crowell
against said Wiggens for debt. Said land was tract whereon said
Willis Sr. lived and joins Jacob Sumner, dec., Thomas Frazer, dec.,
John Darden, Edward Arnold, James Knight and the Virginia Line...
William Bachelor Demsey Knight Jr.   Sam'l Pittman
James Stewart   Samuel Sawyer
May Ct 1796

61 12 Aug 1796--William Arnold to John and William Cowper...use of
Juniper Swamp land known as Speights Ridge for pasture of horses and
oxen used in carting timber to navigation in work of said swamp...
Kinchen Norfleet   William Arnold
John Jones

61 22 Jan 1796--John Small to Joseph Hare...45 pds Negro girl Ginney.
Jethro Ballard   John Small
James Small

62 24 Feb 1796--William Baker to Joseph Brady...50 pds...125 acres beginning at red oak of William Mathew's corner tree at foot of Isaac Walters' path on roadside, along line of marked trees to Demsey William's line, on his line to Hagerty's corner, to Kittrell's line, to road and down road...
Luten Lewis   William Baker
Pa. Hegerty
Aug Ct 1796

63 11 Jul 1796--John Burges to John Vann...$200...100 acres, plantation whereon he lives, beginning at white oak on main side of Peters Swamp James Brady's corner, along his line to pine in said Vann's line, to William Warren's line and along Popular Branch to Eborn Sears...
Joseph Brady   John Burges
Henry(X)Vann   Elizabeth(X)Burges
Aug Ct 1796

64 8 Mar 1795--William Fryer of Onslow Co. to John Lewis...$225... 100 acres beginning at great road near Scratchall Branch, by line of marked trees to corner, from there to Long Branch and down branch to main road; land was purchased from John Duke...
James Gatling   William Fryer
Miles Gatling
John Parker
Aug Ct 1796

65 24 Mar 1796--Joseph Riddick to his son, Isaiah...deed of gift... 300 acres whereon he lives, beginning at red oak, Abraham Pearce's corner tree, by Abraham Hurdles and oald hog pen, S to where old line formerly crossed causeway between house and road, to James Baker's and along his line to Ownley's line, to Ruben Riddick's line, to William Pearce's line, to road to Abraham Pearces. Also, 50 acres in Green's pecosin joining William Pearce, Reuben Riddick and Samuel Green and 50 acres in desert...
James Baker   Jo. Riddick
Thomas Hobbs

66 15 Aug 1796--Mariam Whitehead, executor of John Whitehead, dec. of Southampton Co., Va. to John and William Cowper of Hertford Co... $700...250 acres on E side of Chowan River, beginning at holly, William Arnold's line, up side of Muddy Creek, NE to said Arnold's, being land Benjamin Harrell and James Parker conveyed to said John and in his will in Virginia in December 1791 empowered said Mariam to sell...
H. Murfree   Mariam Whitehead
John Foote
Aug Ct 1796

67 2 Aug 1796--George Eason to Betsey Eason...13 pds 15 sh...Negro girl Milley...
Isaac Pipkin Jr.   George Eason
John Roberts
Jethro Meltier
Aug Ct 1796

68 12 Aug 1796--William Arnold to John Cowper...$162...300 acres,

part of patent of 600 acres granted to Jonathan Parker 12 Apr 1745 and contains Juniper Swamp...
Kincheon Norfleet   William Arnold
John Jones
Aug Ct 1796

69 19 Jul 1796--Josiah Granbery to Josiah Collins, the younger, of Edenton, Chowan Co...$8480 to be paid to John Field and Co. of Philadelphia, merchant; several tracts of land, one of 320 acres conveyed by Thomas Gregory and wife, Priscilla, to said Granbery 10 Feb 1775 and registered in Chowan 15 Mar 1775; a tract of 160 acres formerly property of James Jones, dec. and conveyed by Judith Jones 25 Feb 1788 and of Joseph Scott, the younger, and wife, Mary 10 Jan 1787; a tract of 100 acres conveyed by John Rice and wife, Peggy, 9 Nov 1788; and tract of 250 acres sold by James Sumner and wife, Mourning, to Willis Wiggens 1 Mar 1785, who deeded to said Granbery in 1789 to secure debts...
Jno. Brown   Jos. Granbery
Alex'r. Miller   Josiah Collins
Aug Ct 1796

72 19 Jul 1796--Josiah Granbery to Josiah Collins of Edenton, Chowan Co...$181...140 acres that Joseph Scott and wife, Mary lately recovered of James Davis, guardian of James Hodges, and conveyed by them and George Wynns and wife, Judith, 21 Nov 1791 to Levin Dure, who conveyed to said Granbery 27 Jun 1794. Said land joins Granbery's line in Meherrin Swamp...
Jno. Brown   Jos. Granbery
Alex'r. Miller
Aug Ct 1796

73 16 Jan 1796--Luke Sumner and wife, Judith, to John Cowper...$244 and 1/6...736 acres in Great Dismal Swamp adjoining dividing line between North Carolina and Virginia, beginning in line, S to Sumner's line to Simon Brinkley's land, to William Ellis, NE to land patented by Luke Sumner, dec. 17 Feb 1761 for 300 acres, to Lemuel Powell's patent, to Thomas Wiggens land recorded in Perquimans Co. and sold by said Wiggens to Willis Wilkerson and purchased by Mills Wilkerson, his divisee...
Jethro Benton   Christr' Cowper   Luke Sumner
William Ellis   Lewis Jones   Judith Sumner
John Cowper   Aug Ct 1796

74 15 Aug 1796--Kezia Blanchard to her brother, Joseph Alpin...3 pds per year...lease of her 1/3 of 75 acres of land whereon Amos Blanchard, dec. formerly lived...
James Hodges   Keziah(X)Blanchard
Presse(X)Martin

75 19 Jan 1796--Josiah Granbery to Josiah Collins, the younger, of Edenton, Chowan Co...930 pds 2 sh 1 penny to be paid to John Field, of Philadelphia, merchant...Negroes Kitt, Jerry, Ned, Lero, Amy, Omy the younger, Lucy, Jacob, Benah and her son, Isade and her other two children...
Jno. Brown   Jos. Granbery
Alex'r. Miller   Josiah Collins Jr.
Aug Ct 1796

77 20 Jun 1796--Holloday Walton to Bond Menchew...$250...100 acres on road leading from Bennetts Creek Bridge to Josiah Granbery and part contains Chowan Indian Patent line in Ready Branch, up branch to Kedar Hinton's corner pine, along his line SW...
Jos. Granbery   Holloday Walton
Robert Riddick
Aug Ct 1796

78 12 May 1796--Isaac Hunter to Samuel Harrell...20 pds...40 acres beginning at post oak, corner tree of Benjamin Gordon and David Rice, along Rice's line...
Geo. Gordon   Isaac Hunter
Milly(X)Green
Aug Ct 1796

79 20 Feb 1796--Samuel Harrell to James Hodges...120 pds...200 acres beginning at cypress, corner tree of Amos Lassiter and Thomas Holt's by line of marked trees to Iron Mind Branch, up branch to corner white oak of George Lassiter's, formerly belonging to Augustain Menchew, along that line to Deep Gutt Swamp and down swamp to Bennetts Creek and along creek...
Jos. Granbery   Samuel Harrell
Benjamin Gordon
Aug Ct 1796

80 26 Mar 1796--John Odom to Jethro Sumner of Nansemond Co., Va... 100 pds...300 acres on Chowan River beginning at hickory, along line of marked trees to Copeland's line, to corner in marsh, running Speight's line to Parkers and along Parker's line to Saunders, along that line to river; land is part of tract granted to Charles Saunders in 1762...
Uriah Odom   John Odom
Henry Speight
Eborn Sears
Aug Ct 1796   to R. Hunter of Nansemond Co. Va.

81 20 Jul 1796--Ester Parker, executer of Elisha Parker, dec...21 pds 21 sh...300 acres granted to said Elisha in 1791 and sold to comply with will, beginning at water oak, James Prudens and Isaac Walter's corner tree on side of Merry Hill Pocosin, along line to ded pine, Jethro Benton's line, to red oak, to pine stump in William Walters' corner to pecosin and along run...
Peter Parker   Ester(X)Parker
Elisha Parker Jr.
Aug Ct 1796

82 10 May 1796--Henry Copeland to Sarah Winborn...1 sh yearly for 17 years for plantation whereon James Wills lived for her to raise as much stock as she wishes...
Ham(X)Winborn   Henry Copeland
Nov Ct 1796

83 16 Aug 1796--Sarah Winborn to Henry Copeland...$100...30 acres whereon James Wills formerly lived and conveyed to him by Bray Warren 17 Jun 1793, lying in Peters Swamp...
Bryant Saunders   Sarah(X)Winborn
Henry Lee
Aug Ct 1796

84 5 May 1796--Jesse Eason to James Gordon...40 pds...260 acres in Dismal Swamp beginning at gum on N corner of Middle Ridge or Pasquotank Ridge, running E to gum, SW and back N...
Nat. Riddick   Jesse Eason
George Gordon
Aug Ct 1796

85 16 Dec 1795--William Bond, executor, of Richard Bond, dec. to Levin Dure...112 pds...Negro man Peter...
William Harriss   William Bind
Thos. Hunter
Aug Ct 1796

85 2 Dec 1796--Jethro Sumner, justice of peace, certifies that Isaac Powell of Johnston Co. appeared and made oath that he has never executed any conveyance for lands or property of William Powell given to him by deed of gift...
                                                Jethro Sumner

86 2 Dec 1796--Isaac Powell of Johnston Co. to Micajah Riddick Jr. $600...Negroes Sam, Peter, Charles, Jeffery and Betty, household and plantation utensils on plantation whereon said Riddick now lives...
Jethro Sumner   Isaac Powell
Noah Felton
John Duke
Feb Ct 1797

87 2 Dec 1796--Isaac Powell of Johnston Co. to Micajah Riddick Jr. $600...200 acres whereon said Riddick lives, beginning at mouth of Middle Swamp at main run of Bennetts Creek, up run to Anthony Matthew's line, along his line to Isaac Miller's, to main road and down road to Dobbs Branch, to Bennetts Creek. Also tract of 60 acres adjoining Lewis Walters...
Jethro Sumner   Isaac Powell
Noah Felton
John Duke
Feb Ct 1797

88 11 Jun 1796--Mills Riddick of Norfolk Co., Va. to Levin Dure... $121...Negro girl Kitty...
David Riddick   Mills Riddick
Feb Ct 1797

89 17 Jan 1797--Reuben Hobbs to Ezekiel Trotman...275 pds...125 acres beginning at marked tree in head of branch that runs to Warwick Swamp, along Thomas White's line, to orphans of Jacob Spivey, dec. land, to Edmond Hobb's line, to swamp and down run to said branch...
Thos. Hunter   Reuben(X)Hobbs
Samuel Green
Noah Trotman
Feb Ct 1797

90 17 Feb 1797--William Freeman to John Bridgers...$200...Negro Daniel...
Thomas Trotman   William Freeman
George Freeman
Feb Ct 1797

91 17 Feb 1797--Moses Davis to Isaac Harrell Jr...100 pds...100

acres beginning at furthermost of three branches, running S from
plantation at marked pine, E to John Miller, dec. line and along
his line to Jacob Powell's line...
Samuel Harrell   Moses Davis
Henry Meroney
Feb Ct 1797

92 1 Jan 1796--David Riddick to Moses Briggs...$400...373 acres that
he and his brothers, Mills and Nathaniel, conveyed to said Briggs 30
Oct 1794; said David not being of age at that time, now of legal age,
does convey said land...
Jacob Gordon   David Riddick
Joseph Gordon
Feb Ct 1797

93 1 Feb 1797--Samuel Taylor to Joseph Taylor...125 pds...135 acres
on S side of Catherine Creek beginning at sweet gum in mouth of branch binding on William Freeman's line, S to corner tree in head of
branch, to George Outlaw's line, E to great pine near Old Town Road,
along road to red oak, Seth Roundtree's line, to popular in Catherine Creek and along main run...
Abraham Riddick   Samuel(X)Taylor
Mills Walton

94 23 Sep 1796--Jesse Eason to Levin Dure...36 pds...Negro boy Ben-
jamin...
Nicholas Minor   Jesse Eason
Christopher Gayle
Feb Ct 1797

95 29 Oct 1796--Joseph Davis to William Hays...$128...3 sh 11 pn...
70 acres on N side of Bennetts Creek beginning at water oak, running
line of marked trees to corner pine between Thomas Riddick and Wright
Hays, down run to swamp, to cypress corner tree between Wright and
James Hayes, down run of creek...
Jos. Granbery   Joseph Davis
Samuel Harrell
Feb Ct 1797

96 20 Feb 1797--Jacob and William Hayes to Mills Fields...65 pds...70
acres on N side of Bennetts Creek beginning at water oak near creek,
running line of marked trees to corner pine between Thomas Riddick
and Wright Hayes, down run of swamp to cypress, corner tree between
Wright and James Hayes, down run of swamp to creek and down creek...
Aaron Hobbs   Jacob(X)Hayes
Bond Minchew   William Hayes
Feb Ct 1797

97 2 Feb 1797--Dempsey Jones Jr. to John Simons...8 pds...4 acres
beginning at red oak, corner tree between John Hayes and said Jones,
along his line and by line of marked trees S to persimmon tree in
Deep Branch, down branch and by line of marked trees to said Simons'
line.
Sarah(SR)Riddick   Demsey(DJ)Jones
Abm. Riddick
Feb Ct 1797

98 17 Jan 1797--John Landen to Abraham Curl...91 pds 16 sh...153
acres, part of three patents; one granted to Jesse Barnes and Cyprian

Cross 24 Oct 1786, one to Francis Speight 17 Jul 1748 and the third granted to Callum Ross 25 Feb 1738; land begins at pine in John Vann's corner that was formerly corner tree between Vann, Hargrove, Voight and Harrell, running to Odom's line, to Gum Swamp, to Hardy Cross' line, to Curl's line, to Long Branch and to pine landing...
Mills Landen   John Landen
James Landen
Feb Ct 1797

99 25 Feb 1797--James B. and Jethro Sumner have given power of attorney to Cyprian Cross to sell Negro girl Cloey for $200 and have received money...
David Harrell   James B. Sumner
Mills Eure   Jethro Sumner
Feb Ct 1797

100 23 Aug 1796--David and Nathaniel Riddick to Samuel Harrell... $1675...373 acres known as Horsepool and is ¼ of tract bequeathed to orphans of Mills Riddick, dec., beginning at pine in James Gordon's corner tree in side of desert and along desert S to Moses Brigg's line to patent line and crossing small branch, to said swamp and down middle, along said Gordon's line...
George Gordon   David Riddick
Leven Dure   Nath'l Riddick
Feb Ct 1797

101 4 Oct 1796--Nathaniel Riddick to his sister and brother-in-law, Elizabeth and William Carter...deed of gift...52 acres on W side of Horsepool Swamp, beginning at pine sapling near Mill Dam and Jacob Gordon's corner tree, with his line N to swamp, to sweet gum by road.
Jo. Ridick   Nath'l Riddick
Jacob Gordon
Feb Ct 1797

102 26 Jan--Samuel Taylor to his son, Nathaniel...15 pds...8 acres beginning at pine in branch running NW to Catherine Creek and up run to Roundtree's line and along line...
Richard Freeman   Samuel(X)Taylor
Feb Ct 1797

103 12 Dec 1796--Francis Saunders and wife, Ann, to Jethro Sumner of Nansemond Co., Va...$450...120 acres, plantation whereon they live on N side of Cypress Swamp, beginning at gum, running along line of marked trees binding on land said Sumners bought of Uriah and John Odom, along Henry Speight's line to John Lang's line, which he bought of William Saunders, to run of swamp...
Henry Goodman   Francis(X)Saunders
Isaac Pipkin Jr.
Law. Saunders
Feb Ct 1797

104 22 Nov 1796--John Odom to Jethro Sumner of Nansemond Co., Va... 130 pds...100 acres whereon he lives beginning at run of Cypress Swamp in mouth of Deep Branch between said Odom and Abigail King, up branch to corner of King's line and along her line to Plumb Tree Branch and down branch...
Timothy(X)Boyet   John Odom
Marthy(X)Boyet
Polly(X)Boyet
Feb Ct 1797

105 26 Jan 1797--John Powell of Jacob to Isaac Harrell Jr...$100...
50 acres beginning at sweet gum in Robert Powell's corner tree, James
Powell's, dec. line, with that line to main road and along road near
oald Tarkiln Bed, NW; being part of land Jacob Powell, dec. formerly
owned and gave to said John in his will...
Jo. Riddick
Robert Powell   John Powell
Feb Ct 1797

106 20 Dec 1796--James Baker Sumner to James Figg...$86...60 acres
formerly property of Loward, purchased by Col. Demsey Sumner and
given to his son, said James B., beginning at Honey Pot Swamp at
white oak, to foot of path that goes from said Figgs to main road,
a little above Williams' plantation, along road to Sumner's back
line...
Christ. Riddick
D. Duke   Jas. B. Sumner
Feb Ct 1797

107 3 Mar 1797--Luke Sumner to his daughter, Milicent Hunter Sumner...
deed of gift...300 acres where Mourning Sumner, widow of James Sumner, dec. lately lived, beginning on Orapeak Swamp binding on John
Powell's line near mill, up mill pond to Daniel Franklin's line and
along his line to Joseph J. Sumner's. Also, Negro woman Patients,
girl Rose and child Ester, 4 cows and calves and bed and furniture...
Miles Benton   Luke Sumner
Betsey Benton
May Ct 1797

108 1 Oct 1796--Lemuel Cotten of Hertford Co. to Elisha Felton...
1 sh...67 acres on N side of Chowan River beginning at cypress stump
and black gum, Joseph Dickerson's corner, up river to John Campbell's
corner tree, NE to juniper in his line, to said Dickersons, along
his line SW...
Moses Hare
Luke Hare   Lemuel Cotten
May Ct 1797

109 12 Mar 1796--Benjamin Crowell of Halifax Co. to James Knight...
70 pds...250 acres whereon Willis Wiggens Sr. now lives adjoining
land of Jacob Sumner, dec., Thomas Frazer, dec., John Darden, Edward Arnold and James Knight...
Seth Eason
Sally Bradford   Benj. Crowell
Patsey Bradford
Nov Ct 1796

110 17 Nov 1796--James Freeman to Timothy Freeman...150 pds...320
acres beginning at maple on side of pecosin in Robert Taylor's line,
by line of marked trees to Horse Pen Swamp, along swamp to Charles
Smith's line and along his line to Josiah Parker's...
John Darden   Seth Roundtree   James Freeman
Richard Freeman William Freeman   Selah Freeman
Nov Ct 1796

111 14 Oct 1796--Peter Parker and wife, Sarah, to Jesse Savage of
Nansemond Co., Va...47 pds 10 sh...125 acres beginning at county

line on Mill Dam Branch, down branch and by line of marked trees to Little Mare Branch, to mouth of Bay Branch and up branch to county line...
Caleb Savage   Peter Parker
Daniel Parker
Nov Ct 1797

112 15 Nov 1764--Amos Freeman and wife, Sarah, of Chowan Co. to Elisha Hunter...10 pds...130 acres on Chowan River in Hertford Co. that was granted to William Downing and given to his son, William, the second, and fell from him to William, the younger, and by him granted by deed of sale to R__ Freeman and by his will divided to his three children; tract begins at cypress on Chowan River, Sumner and Hunter's corner tree, up river to Beef Creek and up creek as patent runs to Bennetts Creek and down creek to Muddy Creek...
John Gordon   Amos Freeman
Elizabeth Hunter   Sarah Freeman
Thomas Hunter
Nov Ct 1797

113 13 Aug 1796--Jesse Eason to James Gordon...$150...128 acres on N side of Bass Creek and W side of Dismal Swamp and is land bequeathed to him by his father, Jesse, dec. beginning at white oak on winward point, NW to oak in John Small's line, W to pine, Ellis corner and along his line S to run of said swamp and down run E...
John Cowper   Nov Ct 1797
George Gordon
Nov Ct 1797

114 21 Nov 1796--Jacob Gordon to Kincheon Norfleet...134 pds...four tracts, each containing 20 acres, on S side of Crapeak Swamp and White Oak Springs Marsh, the first known as an island and is 3rd lot, in division by by Elisha Copeland and agreeable to will of John and Elizabeth Norfleet, dec. The second tract is Lot No. 1 and adjoins Jethro Ballard and the last two tracts are Lots 5 and 6 in the same division and join the first two tracts...
James Gordon   Jacob Gordon
David Riddick   Bathsheba Gordon
George Gordon
Nov Ct 1797

116 9 Nov 1796--Josiah Lassiter to Aaron Lassiter...100 pds, 78 acres whereon he lives, and being part of tract Aaron Lassiter, dec. bought of Elijah Harris, beginning at pine corner between said Josiah and Fullington's, along that line to new road and along road to William Hinton's and N...
David Rice   Josiah(X)Lassiter
Charles Jones
Humphrey Parker
Nov Ct 1797

117 15 Sep 1796--Stephen, Thomas and Willis Piland to William Baker 400 pds...349 acres beginning at John Lewis' corner pine on Scratchhall Branch, NE along line of marked trees to white oak, James Riddick's corner, to white oak, John Odom's corner, SW to post oak on John Parker's line to said branch...
Anthony Williams   Stephen(X)Piland
Henry Lee   Thomas(X)Piland
John Northcott   Willis Piland
Nov Ct 1797

119 19 Nov 1796--Michel Payne, marshall of districk of North Carolina, to James Granbery of Edenton, merchant...$716.50...land of Isaac Walters, whereon he lately lived, and recovered in court for debts of said Walters to Samuel Donaldson, surviving partner of firm of Gibson, Granbery and Donaldson...
Will. Blair   Mich'l Payne
Nov Ct 1797

120 15 Apr 1796--Joseph Jones of Hertford Co. to John Cowper...70 pds...Negro man Phill...
John Brewer   Joseph Jones
Peggy Brewer

121 19 Nov 1796--Jesse Eason to Jacob Gordon...150 pds...113 acres, N side of Bass Swamp, tract bequeathed to Elexander Eason by his father, Jesse, dec. in his will 29 Dec 1787, excepting 25 acres conveyed by said Alexander to him by deed 2 Dec 1795, and bought from Thomas Fullington, dec.; said land begins at mouth of branch near high bridge, crossing swamp at William Ellis' corner, N to large spruce pine in Benjamin Gordon's line, W to Miller's line. Also a tract of 25 acres beginning at red oak, said Gordon's corner to back of said Eason's desert patent and 181 acres of desert patent...
David Riddick   Jesse Eason
Daniel Duke
Nov Ct 1797

122 5 Dec 1794--Seth Eason and William Riddick to John Cowper...$280 Negroes Kate, Jack and Toney...
Benjamin Williams   Seth Eason
Chris. Cowper   Wm. W. Riddick
Christ'r. Riddick
Nov Ct 1796

123 17 Nov 1796--Jesse Ward to Timothy Freeman...160 pds...50 acres on N side of Horsepool Swamp, beginning at cypress along line of marked trees to red oak, corner of Jacob Outlaws, to Robert Taylor's line to said swamp...
Noah Hill   Jesse Ward
Frederick Blanchard
Nov Ct 1797

124 22 Nov 1796--Jethro and Miles Benton to Joseph Rooks...$220... Negro boy Baccus...
William Baker   Jethro Benton
Lewis Sparkman   Miles Benton
Nov Ct 1797

124 18 Oct 1796--Levin Dure to Robert Riddick...$100...Negro Phil...
Jethro Ballard   Levin Dure
Charles Jones
Nov Ct 1797

125 24 Mar 1796--John Lang of Pitt Co. to Henry Lee...80 pds... Negro man Boson...
Mary Goodman   John Lang
William Goodman
Nov Ct 1797

125 12 May 1797--Jesse Benton to William Doughty...80 pds...Negro

women Philes and Chloe and her child Harry...
Jethro Sumner   Jesse Benton
Edward Doughtie
May Ct 1797

126 14 May 1797--Aaron Harrell to his son, Willis Sparkman, deed
of gift...pot skillet, dish and bason, gun, froe, sheep shears,
coopers tools, ax, pine chest, bed, jug, 6 puter plates and 2 weeding
hoes...
Richard Freeman   Aaron Harrell
Ester(X)Green
Joseph(X)Morgan
May Ct 1797

126 12 May 1797--Jesse Benton to Charlotte Norfleet...deed of gift...
Negro boy Isaac...
Jethro Sumner   Jesse Benton
Edward Doughtie
May Ct 1797

127 17 Nov 1796--John Arnold to Micajah Reid...37 pds 10 sh...25
acres beginning at marked holly in Collage Branch, up branch to line
of marked trees to James Parker's line, along his line...
James Pruden   John Arnold
James Phelps
May Ct 1797

127 16 May 1797--Thomas Billups and Jonathan Roberts to Noah Harrell
Negro girl Seney...
James Hodges   Thomas Billups
John Roberts   Jonathan Roberts
May Ct 1797

128 20 Sep 1796--George Lassiter to Jonathan Lassiter...20 pds...10
acres beginning at white oak, line tree of Job Riddick's to pine by
line of marked trees to Watery Swamp and up swamp to mouth of Tobaco
House Branch, along said Riddick's line...
James Hodges   George Lassiter
Keziah(X)Davis
May Ct 1797

128 2 Jan 1794--Ester Parker to Moses Hines...36 pds...Negro girl
Cloah...
Robert F. Benton   Ester(X)Parker
John Parker
May Ct 1797

129 14 Jan 1797--Stephen Rogers of Glasgow Co. to James Jones...293
pds 18 sh...532 acres beginning at gum in run of Mills Swamp, James
Parker's corner, along his line SW to white oak, Col. Baker's corner,
W to white oak, John Odom's corner and along his line to James Gat-
ling's and on his line to John Lewis, to run of said swamp, down
run to Pipkin's corner, with his line to John Shepherd's white oak,
and along his line to run of swamp and down swamp...
John Shepherd   Stephen Rogers
James(‡)Parker
May Ct 1797

130 15 Feb 1797--Job Felton to Willis Piland...172 pds 10 sh...300 acres on W side of Coles Creek beginning at cypress at high point, up John Piland's line to gum, to branch of Jonathan Cullens', to pine on road and down road to side of Great Marsh and down marsh to ridge, to Jesse Harrell's line, running to said creek and up run.
Stephen Piland   Job (X)Felton
Thos. Collins   Sarah(X)Felton
John Piland
May Ct 1797

131 25 May 1797--William Williams, Jethro Slaven and Christian and Dorothy Williams to William Cleaves...50 pds 3 sh 6 pn...50 acres beginning on said Cleaves' line, binding on William Hinton's line, along patent formerly called Francis Pugh's and with line...
Humphrey Hudgens   William(X)Williams
Jesse Benton   Jethro(X)Slaven
Henry Smith   Christian(X)Williams
May Ct 1797   Dorothy(X)Williams

132 4 Feb 1797--Thomas Young and Norfleet Harris of Halifax Co. and Bethail Bell of Edgecomb Co. to Elisha Benton...84 pds...47 acres whereon said Benton lives beginning at marked beech, corner tree of Miles Benton, on side of Bennetts Creek, down creek S to red oak on side of road, E to hickory in field and S to burnt stump in Benton's field and along patent line...
Miles Benton   Thomas Young
John Duke   John H. Young
Elisha Benton   Bythal Bell
May Ct 1797   Norfleet Harris

134 18 Aug 1797--Demsey Jones to Fredric Lassiter...100 pds...50 acres beginning at Tarkil_ Branch, along branch to back line, along line of marked trees to swamp and down run to said branch and up branch...
Lassiter Riddick   Demsey(x) Jones
Abner(X)Lassiter
May Ct 1797

135 20 May 1797--Demsey Odom Jones to Winnefor Lassiter...5 bu. of corn per year...rent of 18 acres between said Demsey and Charles Smith, for two years...
James Hodges   Demsey(X) O. Jones
Absoley Lassiter
May Ct 1797

135 20 May 1797--Jesse Benton to Polley Norfleet...deed of gift... Negro Abram...
Jethro Sumner   Jesse Benton
Edward Doughtie
May Ct 1797

136 9 Dec 1796--George Lassiter to Abner Lassiter...25 pds...50 acres on W side of Deep Gut beginning at pine on old road on Flat Branch, along road to said gut and along gut...
James Hodges   George Lassiter
Samuel Green
James(X)Davis
May Ct 1797

137 12 Oct 1795--Demsey Jones, son of Hardy, to Charles Smith...$10
3 acres beginning at said Smith's line at red oak, E to a pine, by
strait course to red oak...
Abm. Riddick   Demsey(X)Jones
Joel Foster
May Ct 1797

138 8 Feb 1795--Luke Sumner to Daniel Franklin of Upper Parish of
Nansemond...16 pds 10 sh...40 acres partly in Nansemond Co. and
partly in Gates Co., beginning at ash in Jacob Brinkley's branch,
W to ded pine, corner tree of Josiah Franklin's, bounded by main
Edenton Road, to red oak near edge of said Sumner's oald field and
down edge of his mill pond to Poly Bridge Branch and adjoining land
of said Franklin, that he bought of said Sumner...
Abraham Morgan   Luke Sumner
Jonas(X)Franklin
William Knight
May Ct 1797

139 25 Aug 1797--Phillip Lewis and Henry Speight made oath that they
witnessed deed of gift of delivery of Negro Odom 21 Aug 1797 by Francis Speight to his son, Joseph...
                                                Henry Goodman

140 11 Jan 1797--Luke Sumner to William Mathias...$28...55 acres
known as Corapeak in Corapeak Swamp beginning at white oak on S side
in said Mathias' line, down swamp binding on high land to John Pow-
ell's line, along his line to Jethro Ballard's, with his line to Kedar
Ballard's, along his line running with swamp...
Jno. Powell   Luke Sumner
John Powell Jr.
John Brinkley
May Ct 1797

141 25 Nov 1796--David Harrell to Demsey Harrell...$25...25½ acres,
part of patent granted to Joseph Ballard 2 May 1722, beginning at
pine in patent line, running line of marked trees to Ready Branch,
along line of marked trees to patent line and along line...
Phillip(X)Stallings   David Harrell
James(X)Stallings
Thomas Harrell
May Ct 1797

142 23 May 1793--Francis Speight, planter, to Susannah Speight...10
pds...Negro Mary 9 years old...
Phillip Lewis   Francis Speight
Luten Lewis
Aug Ct 1797

142 21 Aug 1797--Jethro Sumner to John Odom...$200...Negro boy Pacel.
William Harriss   Jethro Sumner
Nov Ct 1797

143 21 Aug 1797--Henry Goodman to Jethro Sumner of Nansemond Co.,
Va...15 pds...1 acre, part of patent granted to him 28 Sep 1791,
beginning at cypress on side of Chowan River, William Crafford's
line to Barnes Creek and down run to gum, S to river and up side...
Open court   Henry Goodman
Aug 1797

143 16 May 1797--James Riddick to John Shephard...$42...14 acres beginning at sweet gum at lower end of ditch, up ditch and along his own line N to marked post oak in Shepherd's line and N...
P. Hegerty   James Riddick
Stephen Shepherd
Nov Ct 1797

144 10 Nov 1797--Samuel Smith, sheriff, to Isaac Hunter...27 pds... 30 acres formerly property of James B. Sumners, and sold by court order to satisfy court writ obtained by Bond Menchew; said land begins at Honey Pot Swamp, crossing swamp E to N side of road, to pine, James Figg's corner of land purchased of said Sumner, W to said swamp and down run...
Henry Smith   Samuel Smith
George Williams
Nov Ct 1797

145 28 Aug 1797--William Baker to Daniel Southall...$3000...two tracts, one of 202 acres begins on S side of Bennetts Creek, running NW to stump opposite tavern to branch joining Willis Parker, dec. line, to George Pilands, to Willis and James Brown, to George Williams' line and along his line to Troy Swamp and up swamp; second tract of 100 acres begins at maple of Spivey's patent on E side of Coles Creek, NE to 3 birches formerly Capt. Wiggens' corner, N to Troy Swamp, up side of Coles Creek to George Williams' line and W to creek and up run...
Isaac Hunter   William Baker
James Cross
Robert Wiggens

147 15 Feb 1797--Jesse Vann to Cyprian Cross...exchange of 15 acres beginning at pine in his patent line on side of pecosin, N to pine corner of said Cross and along his line to sand banks and by line of marked trees...
Riddick Cross   Jesse Vann
John Vann
Nov Ct 1797

148 15 Feb 1797--Cyprian Cross to Jesse Vann...exchange of 15 acres part of patent granted to him, beginning at two pines at corner, along line to Long Branch and by line of marked trees to side of Edenton Road and along road...
John Vann   Cyprian Cross
Riddick Cross
Nov Ct 1797

149 12 Nov 1797--James Knight to Ambrose Wiggens...50 pds...50 acres, whereon Willis Wiggens now lives on N side of Elm Swamp, beginning at walnut tree, up swamp to gum in woods patent line NE to branch and along branch to main road...
Pa. Hegerty   James Knight
Demsey Knight
Nov Ct 1797

150 22 Nov 1796--James Granbery of Edenton, merchant, to Jethro Sumner and Demsey Odom...458 pds 5 sh...land whereon Isaac Walters now lives or lately lived, purchased by said Granbery at public

sale from marshal of district of North Carolina...
Will. Blair   James Granbery
Isaac Pipkin Jr.

151 20 Nov 1797--Halon Williams to David Rawls...60 pds...100 acres
beginning at gum in George Williams, Jr. line on Hilly Swamp, along
his line to Turner's line, along that line NE and by line of marked
trees SW to said Williams' line...
Jesse Benton   Halon(H)Williams
Jonathan Parker
Nov Ct 1797

152 9 Aug 1797--Isaac Hunter to William Carter...200 pds...90 acres,
known as Maidenhead Neck, on S side of Bennetts Creek and formerly
property of William Sumner, sold by him to George Eason and bought
from him by said Hunter from Samuel Smith, sheriff, by virtue of
court execution of said Hunter; begins at mulberry tree, Bond's
corner, running NW along his line to Bennetts Creek and up creek
to dividing line between Timothy Lassiter, dec. and said land...
James Costen   Isaac Hunter
Jos. Granbery
Nov Ct 1797

153 10 Nov 1796--Levi Ownly to Edward Ownly...50 pds...25 acres be-
ginning at pine corner in James Prue's line, along his line to Thomas
Docton's line, E by line of marked tree in George Eason's line...
Norman King   Levi Ownley
William King

154 26 Aug 1797--James Jones to Isaac Pipkin Sr...72 pds 10 sh...
100 acres beginning at gum near run of Mills Swamp, John Lewis' corner tree, binding his line to maple in James Gatling's line, on his
line S to post oak, to white oak at head of branch, to said swamp and
along run...
Isaac Pipkin Jr.   James(X)Jones
Stephen Rogers
Nov Ct 1797

155 26 Feb 1796--Seth Eason to James Knight...$180...Negro girl
Ledely...
Demsey Knight   Seth Eason
James($)Jones
Nov Ct 1797

155 17 Feb 1797--Isaac Pipkin to Cyprian Cross...74 pds 10 sh 2 pn
Negroes Dinah, Cate, Sarah and Hannah...
Ja. B. Sumner   Isaac Pipkin Jr.
Sally Pipkin
Aug Ct 1797

156 15 Aug 1797--Joseph Taylor to Nathaniel Taylor...400 pds...100
acres beginning at white oak of William Freeman Sr. line near fork
of Great Branch that issues out of S side of Catherine Creek, running SE to pine in small pecosin, being corner tree of Thomas Garrett,
S to red oak on Old Town Road, along road to Charles Roundtree's
line to popular in Catherine Creek and down creek...
Wm. Volentine   Joseph(+)Taylor
Noah Trotman
Aug Ct 1797

157 12 Sep 1796--Pasco Turner of Nansemond Co., Va., executor of John Reid, dec., who was executor of Daniel Pugh, to Robert Parker...111 pds 10 sh...Negroes Agga and Leasor, sold by court order to satisfy writ of Luke Sumner in Nansemond court against said Pugh for debts...
Jethro Sumner   Pasco Turner
Aug Ct 1797

158 1 Jul 1797--Samuel Smith, sheriff, to Isaac Hunter...130 pds... 100 acres, property of George Eason, and sold by court order issued from Chowan County for judgment obtained by Thomas White against said Eason. Said land was part of tract given by Thomas Sumner of Nansemond to his son, William, who sold to said Eason, and begins at mulberry tree in line of orphans of Timothy Lassiter, dec., running S from Bennetts Creek to Richard Bond's corner white oak, along creek and Lassiter's line S...
Thomas Trotman   Samuel Smith
Moses Davis
John Arnold
Aug Ct 1797

159 22 Aug 1797--William Bennett to his daughter, Barsheba Speight... deed of gift...Negro woman Philis, girls Leah and Lucy and boys Burrell, Nelson and Jack...
William Harriss   William Bennett   William Bennett
Thomas Marshall   James H. Keys
Aug Ct 1797

160 12 Aug 1797--Joseph Taylor to Nathaniel Taylor...100 pds...black mare Litefoot, joke of oxen, cow, 3 feather beds and furniture, 2 chests, 2 trunks, 3 iron pots, crop of corn, peas and potatoes now growing on plantation...
William Valentine   Joseph(X)Taylor
Noah Trotman
Aug Ct 1797

161 15 May 1797--James Jones and wife, Sarah, to Jonathan Rogers... 135 pds 18 sh...172 acres beginning at pine, corner tree in William Gatling's line, on William Goodman's line to Edenton Road, to Cyprian Goodman's line and binding his line to Elisha Cross' corner pine, along Cross' line to said Rogers' corner pine in branch, binding on his line...
James(I)Parker   James(X)Jones
Judith(X)Parker   Sarah(X)Jones
Aug Ct 1797

162 28 Dec 1796--William Baker to Ebron Sears...$100...125 acres whereon he lives beginning at red oak at foot of Isaac Walters' path, along Billy Matthews' line to Demsey Williams' line, on his line to pine of Pa. Hegerty's corner, along his line to Kittrell's, with his line to Suffolk Road and down road...
Mills Lewis   William Baker
Reuben Williams
Aug Ct 1797

163 9 Mar 1797--Reuben Lassiter and wife, Elizabeth, to Willis Woodley...1 pd 13 sh...1 acre beginning at sweet gum at side of road to

oak, to swamp and along run; for purpose of building mill dam...
Richard Bond   Reuben(X)Lassiter
James Blanshard   Elizabeth Lassiter
Aug Ct 1797

164 15 Aug 1797--Samuel Smith, sheriff, to Anthony Matthews Sr...
32 pds 10 sh...Negro woman Poll, property of Joseph John Sumner,
and sold by court order by virtue of execution...
Aug Ct 1797   Samuel Smith

165 2 Mar 1797--Nathaniel Riddick to Samuel Harrell...116 pds...90
acres beginning at pine in Abraham Harrell's corner binding on his
line to Fullington's line, to corner pine near Suffolk Road, along
road to foot of path, by line of marked trees to water oak in branch
and down branch to maple in Carter's line, on his line to Jacob Gordon's line...
Pa. Hegerty   Nath'l Riddick
Jno. Davis
Aug Ct 1797

166 22 Nov 1796--James B. and Jethro Sumner to Isaac Pipkin Jr...
93 pds 4 sh 3 pn...Negroes Dinar, Cate, Sarah and Hannar...
David Riddick   J.B. Sumner
William W. Riddick   Jethro Sumner
Aug Ct 1797

166 12 Jan 1797--Richard Bond to Willis Woodley...deed of gift...
Negroes Jack and Abraham, Cherry and her son, Bob...
James Costen   Rich'd Bond
Elizabeth(X)Costen
Aug Ct 1797

167 4 Aug 1796--Peggy Rice to Willis Woodley...$40...Negro girl
Dinah...
Robert Riddick   Peggy Rice

167 2 Jun 1797--Stephen Copeland to his brother, Henry...deed of
gift...all goods and chattles, Negroes Mourning, Alex and Jack, and
money owed by Whit. Jones...
Henry (X) Winborn   Stephen Copeland
William Goodman

168 21 Aug 1797--Samuel Smith, sheriff, to Abraham Riddick...156
pds 10 sh...mill, utensils and 4 acres belonging to Luke Sumner,
and sold by court order to satisfy court writ against James Sumner's for debts...
Isaac Pipkin Jr.   Samuel Smith
John Parker
David(X)Benton

169 1 Jun 1797--James Freeman to Thomas Freeman...25 pds...169 acres
whereon said James lives, beginning at pine on Mill Swamp, along run
to bridge, along Jacob Outlaw's line to white oak in head of Poly
Bridge, down branch to gum and by line of marked trees...
James Walton   James Freeman
Charles Powell   Selah Freeman
Aug Ct 1797

170 1 Jun 1797--James Freeman to William Freeman...25 pds...125
acres on Poly Bridge Branch beginning at mouth and running up branch
to black gum and along line of marked trees to Catherine Creek...
James Walton   James Freeman
Charles Powell
Aug Ct 1797

171 15 May 1797--Jesse Eason to David Riddick...227 pds 10 sh...
Negro boys Mingo and Reuben...
James H. Key   Jesse Eason
John Vann
Aug Ct 1797

171 28 Dec 1796--Joseph Brady to William Baker...$100...125 acres,
tract whereon said Baker now lives, beginning at red oak at foot
of Isaac Walters' path, along Billy Matthews' line to Demsey Williams,
to Pa. Hagerty's corner, on his line to Kittrell's line, to Suffolk
Road and along road...
Blake Baker   Joseph(X)Brady
Reuben Williams
Aug Ct 1797

172 15 Oct 1796--Edward Briscoe to Eborn Sears...$200...50 acres
beginning at white oak, corner tree in Gordon's line, to red oak
corner tree in Robert's line, to pine corner on pecosin...
Joseph Parker   Edward(E.B.)Brisco
Lewis Carter
Aug Ct 1797

173 11 Aug 1797--James Hodges and wife, Delilah, to Willis Woodley...
60 pds...60 acres on N side of Bennetts Creek Road, beginning at red
oak along line of marked trees to Iron Mine Branch and up branch on
Hunter's line to corner white oak in Lassiter's line w to road...
James Barnes   James Hodges
James Small   Delilah Hodges
Aug Ct 1797

174 23 Jan 1798--Thomas Parker and Leah Riddick, who plan marriage,
to Daniel Southall...$500...to serve as trustee for the following
property: Negroes Jack, Margaret, Harry, Eadith, Edmund, Rachal and
Anakey, desk, black walnut table, looking glass, ½ doz. walnut chairs;
after marriage said Leah to retain full authority over property and
use for her benefit and her children. Should she die before said
Thomas, they agree her property will be delivered as she designates
in her will or if without will said Southall to deliver to her
children or legal representatives of said Leah and Thomas...
Jethro Haslet   Thomas Parker
John Miller   Leah Riddick
Feb Ct 1798   Daniel Southall

176 28 Dec 1797--George Gatling to David Harrell...11 bbls corn
and 2000 herring...Negro man Cary...
William Gatling Jr.   George(C)Gatling
Elisha Bond

177 1 Nov 1797--James Hodges and wife, Delilah, to Willis Woodley...
$500...250 acres beginning at cypress on creek, by line of marked
trees to mouth of Iron Mine Branch, up branch to Woodley's line, SE

to Lassiter's line, SW to Deep Gut, to Amos Lassiter's and up run of creek to corner marked tree...
Nath'l Newsom James Hodges
John Blunt Delilah Hodges
Feb Ct 1798

178 25 Jan 1798--George Gatling to David Harrell...$100...Negro woman Ester and children Suckah and Ned...
William Gatling Jr. George(X)Gatling
Peggy(X)Gatling
Feb Ct 1798

179 6 Feb 1798--James Jones to William Baker...$133 1/3...100 acres beginning at corner white oak of said Bakers and John Odom's, along Odom's line to corner gum in James Gatling's line, along line to corner pine stump, NE by line of marked trees to James Parker's line...
Isaac Parker James(X)Jones
Robert Wiggens
Jonathan Parker
Feb Ct 1798

180 18 Aug 1797--Myles Walton to Miles Roundtree...30 pds...10 acres beginning in main road in Daniel Stallings line, where it crosses, NE to persimmon tree and SW...
Jo. Riddick Myles Walton
Abraham(I)Spivey
Feb Ct 1798

181 6 Jan 1798--Henry Speight to Thomas Barnes...90 pds...Negro man Abram...
Joseph Freeman Henry Speight
Feb Ct 1798

182 1 Jan 1798--William Jr. and James Freeman to Riddick Trotman... $500...125 acres beginning at mouth of Poly Bridge Branch, up branch to black gum, to pine in side of mill pond, to hed of small branch, to Mill Race, down to Catherine Creek...
Jo. Riddick William Freeman
John Hoffler James Freeman
Feb Ct 1798

183 28 Nov 1797--Isaac Hunter to James Figg...27 pds 11 sh...50 acres on Honey Pot Swamp, beginning at road crossing, running E along N side to James Figg's corner pine of tract purchased of James B. Sumner, W to swamp and down run...
William W. Riddick Isaac Hunter
Thomas Riddick
Feb Ct 1798

184 9 Aug 1797--Thomas Smith Sr. to George Allen...10 pds...6 acres beginning at pine on said Allen's line in Mile Branch, up branch to Jethro Sumner's corner and along his line...
Hy. Hudgins Thomas Smith
William Harriss
Feb Ct 1798

185 20 Nov 1797--Amos Dilday to Henry Eborn Sears...50 pds...50 acres beginning at lightwood tree of Joel Goodman's and William Gatling's, to corner of Isaac Pipkins, to corner tree of William

Goodman and William Gatling and along Gatling's line...
James Hodges   Amos Dilday
Charity(X)Brady
Feb Ct 1798

186 10 Aug 1797--Seth Eason to James Gregory and Thomas Hunter...
25 pds...100 acres, ½ part of grant to Mrs. Mary Riddick, beginning
at black gum, Moses Briggs corner near old mill branch, along desert
E; includes two tracts of 18 acres and 82 acres...
William Baker   Seth Eason
Feb Ct 1798

187 2 Jan 1798--Thomas Hunter and Thomas Hofler to Moore Carter...
27 pds 1 sh...Negro boy Jeremiah 3 years old...
Law. Baker   Thomas Hunter
Feb Ct 1798   Thomas Hofler

188 22 Jan 1798--Jethro Sumner and Demsey Odom to Winborn Jenkins...
50 pds...50 acres beginning at red oak in John Doughtie's line, N by
line of marked trees to red oak, NE to said Doughtie and William Doughtie's line and along that line...
John Babb   Jethro Sumner
Isaac Walters Jr.   Demsey(X)Odom
Feb Ct 1798

189 23 May 1797--John Powell to son, John, deed of gift...1 acre,
saw mill, timber and all utensils belonging to mill before it was
blown up...
Nicholas Minor   John Powell
James(++)Jones
Feb Ct 1798

190 11 Jan 1798--Jacob Thomas to Seth Roundtree...$350...37½ acres
beginning at beech on Fox Branch, Thomas White's corner in Richard
Mitchell's line, along White's line to Jacob Spivey Jr., dec., with
his line to said branch and down branch...
Jo. Riddick   Jacob(J)Thomas
Riddick Trotman
Feb Ct 1798

191 7 Dec 1797--Samuel Harrell to Willis Woodley...56 pds 5 sh...150
acres, part of patent granted to Job Riddick, who conveyed to said
Harrell 27 Oct 1784, beginning at Thomas Sumner, dec. upper line,
formerly line between said Sumner and Timothy Lassiter on side of
Bennetts Creek Swamp, running to Richard Bond's line, down swamp to
end of said Bond's land just above mouth of Watry Swamp, Nw to run
of Bennetts Creek and along run to desert course...
John(W)Davis   Samuel Harrell
William Harrell
Feb Ct 1798

193 2 Feb 1798--Jacob Parker Jones to Isaac Harrell Jr...$100...50
acres beginning at post oak on E side of road at Dennis old field,
along road to Wards Folley, to pine in Levin Dure's line, SE to said
Harrells...
David Rice   Jacob Parker(X)Jones
James(++)Jones
Feb Ct 1798

194 18 May 1797--William Williams to Halon Williams...$100...80
acres, whereon he lives, beginning at pine at Thomas Smith's corner in William Cleaves' line, along his line to Jonathan Smith's
corner pine, then on his line to Figg's corner, to James Sumner's
corner and on his line to white oak of Thomas Smith's...
Jonathan Williams   William(X)Williams
Pa. Hegerty
Feb Ct 1798

195 4 Sep 1797--Jesse Eason to James Gordon...100 pds...543 acres
on S side of Great Dismal Swamp, beginning at black gum and pine,
Joshua Small's corner on W side, along his line NE to Luke Sumner's
line at the ridges, SW to Jacob Gordon's to corner of said Gordon's
and Seth Eason's line...
Pa. Hegerty   Jesse Eason
Jas. Gordon
Feb Ct 1798

196 8 Feb 1798--Robert Taylor and brother, Hilery, of Hertford Co.
to Elisha H. Bond...225 pds...160 acres on Bennetts Creek in Indian
Neck, beginning at maple, running to Timothy Freeman's and along Jacob Outlaw's to head of pond, along line of marked trees to Mirey
Branch, to Bennetts Creek Swamp...
Richard Bond   Robert(X)Taylor
Timothy Freeman   Hillery Taylor
Feb Ct 1798

197 16 Dec 1797--Brian Walters to William Gatling...31 pds 10 sh...
50 acres beginning at marked popular in Aaron Odom's line, N to
Great Branch, running to Henry Dilday's land sold to John Rawls in
same patent, to Gough Folly Branch and along branch...
Thomas Fryer Jr.   Briant(+)Walters
William(+)Gatling Sr.
Feb Ct 1798

199 13 Apr 1794--Simon Stallings, sheriff, to James Barnes...110
pds...150 acres belonging to estate of Docton Riddick, dec. and sold
by court order to satisfy writ of Boyd and William Bennetts against
him for debts; said tract begins at large mulberry tree near swamp,
running SW to Bennetts Creek, E to Moses Speight's line, to main
road, W to fork...
Luten Lewis   Simon Stallings
James Gatling
Feb Ct 1798

201 23 Sep 1797--John and William Cowper of Murfreesborough to William
Rea of same place...$1400...two tracts on Chowan River, one they bought of Mrs. Miriam Whitehead and one of William Arnold; including
fishery and Arnold's Ridge...
James Gordon   John Cowper
John Cowper   William Cowper
Anth. Williams
May Ct 1798

202 1 Nov 1797--Jesse Vann and Benjamin Barnes, planters, to William
Rea of Murfreesborough...$850...25 acres and fishery which they bought
of William Craford on the side of Chowan River, where said Vann, Barnes

and Crafford fished in spring of 1797 and which said Crafford patened 24 Oct 1786, beginning at cypress on river above Barnes Creek mouth, up river NW and then SW...
Thomas Wynn   Jesse Vann
Benjamin Roberts   Benjamin Barnes
James Palmer
May Ct 1798

204 13 Sep 1797--Thomas Fitt to William Rea, both of Murfreesborough...$3750...225 acres of Juniper Swamp and fishery on Chowan River with houses, saine rope, holyards, hogsheads, iron pot, vats and all fishing utensils, beginning at black gum at NE side of said river just below Speights Creek, NW to pine at Webbs Patent, crossing mouth of swamp, NE joining Rawls Patent to river and along run...
Benjamin Roberts   Thomas Fitt
James Palmer
May Ct 1798

205 4 May 1782--Clement Hill to Joseph Riddick...28 pds...50 acres on Horsepen Swamp beginning at gum, across land S to line in John B. Walton's line...
Charles Roundtree   Clement Hill
Simon Stallings
May Ct 1798

207 28 Aug 1797--Peter Marble of Nansemond Co., Va. to Elisha Cross and William Walters to insure payment of 500 pds as security for suit brought against him by James Gatling Sr...wagon, 3 horses, skillet, kettle etc...
Elijah Lewis   Peter Marble
May Ct 1798

208 16 Aug 1797--Miles Benton to Jesse Benton...35 pds 11 sh 1 pn...Negro man Carry...
Samuel Smith   Miles Benton
Jethro Sumner
May Ct 1798

208 28 Mar 1798--Mary Darden to Peggy Hare...deed of gift...her right in land that fell to her in husband, John Darden's estate; all Negro men, cattle, hogs, sheep, horses and other property...
James Knight   Mary(X)Darden
Demsey Knight
John Hare
May Ct 1798

209 7 Mar 1798--Thomas Hiatt to William Frost...56 pds...land, hogs and rest of estate...
Bray Saunders   Thomas(X)Hiatt
William(X)March

209 18 Jan 1798--Christopher Gayle to Isaac Pipkin Sr...90 pds...Negro man Harry 28 years old...
Isaac Pipkin Jr.   Christopher Gayle
Sally Pipkin
May Ct 1798

210 6 Mar 1797--Thomas Hunter to Timothy Freeman...15 pds...80 acres, part of patent granted 3 Dec 1720, to William Downing Sr., beginning

at mouth of Bennetts Creek, up marsh side to Timothy Walton's line, through middle of marsh...
John B. Walton
James Freeman   Thomas Hunter
May Term 1798

211 28 Nov 1796--Joseph John Sumner to Jethro Sumner...$150...80 acres beginning at pine on road leading from house where he now lives, along road to red oak at Hollow Bridge, up road N ...
William Arnold   Joseph John Sumner
Nath'l Griffin
May Ct 1798

211 3 Apr 1798--William Speight to Isaac Costen...$220...Negro Nancy and her three children: Mills, Milley and Percilla...
James Costen   William Speight
Hy. Hudgins
May Ct 1798

212 2 Dec 1795--Alexander Eason to Jesse Eason...22 pds 10 sh...25 acres beginning at red oak stump, corner in Thomas Fullenton's line, along said Jesse's line to run of Mills Swamp and up swamp to Seth Eason's line and along his line...
Edison Foster   Alex'r Eason
Richard(+)Foster
Morgan Hart, clerk of Orange Co. court certified that William Raney, justice of peace, attested to said signatures. 12 May 1798

214 2 Dec 1795--Alexander Eason and wife, Mary, of Orange Co. to Jesse Eason...141 pds 5 sh...113 acres beginning at mouth of branch near high bridge crossing Mill Swamp, up branch to path, to large spruce pine marked in Benjamin Gordon's line, up his line to Miller's line to patent line and along that line...
Edison Foster   Alex'r Eason
Richard(+)Foster   Mary Eason
11 May 1798

216 2 Dec 1795--Alexander Eason of Orange Co. to Jesse Eason...85 pds...181 acres of desert land beginning at dead pine and red oak, Jacob Gordon and Seth Eason's corner, along Eason's line E...
E. Foster   Alex'r Eason
Richard(+)Foster
May Ct 1798
Morgan Hart, clerk
William Raney, justice of peace

218 13 Feb 1797--Isaac Pipkin, sheriff, to James Gatling...109 pds 1 sh...75 acres belonging to Isaac Williams and sold by court order to satisfy suit against him for debts; said tract begins at old pine stump on riverside running John Rochel, dec. line to John Odom's line, along his line to Miles Benton's line and down his line to river...
Brian Saunders   Isaac Pipkin
David Lewis
May Ct 1798

220 27 Feb 1798--Miles Boyce to Moses Davis...250 pds...113 acres beginning on Bennetts Creek running along patent line to gum, corner

tree in Great Hawtree Swamp and down to said creek...
Hy. Hudgins   Miles Boyce
Richard Briggs
Jas. B. Sumner
May Ct 1798

221 1 Nov 1797--Thomas Hunter and Sarah Norfleet, who plan to enter
into marriage, agree that said Sarah shall have right to dispose of
her property that she now possesses without any hindrance of her husband and said Hunter will not lay claim to anything that she may give
away at her death; he shall have same authority over his property...
John Cowper Jr. Thomas W. Ballard   Thos. Hunter
May Ct 1798   Sarah Norfleet

222 30 Mar 1797--Thomas Hunter to John B. Walton...10 pds...50 acres
beginning at mouth of Bennetts Creek on E side of William Freeman's
corner pine on lower side of bridge to creek and down creek to another corner of said Freemans...
Thomas Freeman   Thos. Hunter
Timothy Freeman
May Ct 1798

223 23 Apr 1798--Jeremiah Speight to James Costen...705 pds 5 sh 6
pn...Negroes Isaac, George, Jac, Nanna, Cherry, Mourning, James and
Leah...
J.W. Voight   Jeremiah Speight
Hy. Hudgins
May Ct 1798

224 10 Nov 1797--William Speight to John Riddick...30 pds...40 acres
beginning at hickory near Cypress Swamp on N side of main road in William E. Webb's line, along said line to pine, along a new line to sweet
gum near main road and down road...
William Harriss   William Speight
Sally Riddick
May Ct 1798

225 13 Dec 1797--James Ransome to Jonathan Rogers...Negro man John
for 90 pds...
William King   James Ransome
Malacy(+)Streter
May Ct 1798

226 8 Feb 1798--Thomas Travis to David Harrell...225 pds...100 acres
beginning in center of two sweet gums and black gum in Jeremiah Jorden's line in Wireneck Branch, down and binding on said Jordans, Harrells and Doctor Nichols' line to John Hair's line, along his line
to water oak, Demsey Jones' corner, on his line and Kedar Hinton's
to marked red oak of said Hinton's and by line of marked trees SW...
Jonathan Roberts   Thomas Travis
Jonathan Nichols
May Ct 1798

227 24 Oct 1797--Henry Speight to Jesse Saunders...$28...14 acres
of woodland beginning at water oak in branch on said Saunders' line,
NW to pine, S to hickory on Deep Branch and down run to marked gum
in Saunders' line and by line of marked trees...
Lawrence Saunders   Henry Speight
Pa. Hegerty

228 7 Apr 1798--Joseph Brady to William Baker...$33...part of tract that James Brady Sr. lived on, beginning at road at Knotty Pine Swamp just below said Baker's mill, along road toward Sumerton, to foot of road leading to James Maney's Ferry and along road to run of Ready Branch and down run to said swamp...
Robert F. Wiggens   Joseph(I)Brady
John Vann
May Ct 1798

229 21 Dec 1797--Nathaniel Taylor of Chowan Co. to Joseph Taylor... 25 pds...117 acres beginning at white oak, William Freeman Sr. line near fork of Great Branch issuing out of S side of Catherine Creek, E to pine in small pecosin, a line tree of Seth Spivey, E to black oak in Old Town Road and along road to Charles Roundtree's red oak corner, to popular on Catherine Creek and down creek...
William Volentine   Nathaniel Taylor
Docton Bagley
May Ct 1798

231 23 Aug 1797--Samuel Smith, sheriff, to Levin Dure...618 pds... 125 acres, plantation belonging to James B. Sumner and whereon he lives, and sold by court order to recover debts, by James Sumner, executor of Seth Sumner, dec.; said land begins at Honey Pot Bridge on swamp, running along Mill Dam to Bennetts Creek and up creek to Thomas Smith Jr., and along his line to Capt. William Harris' line.
John Cowper   Samuel Smith
Hy. Hudgins
Anth. Williams
May Ct 1798

233 9 Feb 1798--Mills Riddick of Nansemond Co., Va. and Nathaniel and David Riddick to Jacob Gordon...$1400...533 acres known as Horsepool, part of three patents, two granted to Thomas Speight and the other to Mrs. Mary Riddick, partly in Dismal Swamp and being high land that Isaac Speight sold to Mills Riddick, dec. Said Mills, by his will appointed Jacob Hunter, David Rice and Jesse Eason, to divide his land among his sons and part now conveyed was allotted to son, Henry Riddick, dec., and begins at pine on side of desert, Samuel Harrell's corner tree, with his line SW to main road, to three gums in middle of Horsepool Swamp and up run to patent line, to William Carter's corner tree and along his line to Mill Dam and including dam, to said Harrell's desert patent...
James Gordon   Mills Riddick
Joseph Gordon   Nath'l. Riddick
May Ct 1798   David Riddick

235 18 May 1798--Seth Eason to William Harriss...120 pds...200 acres beginning at desert and binding on James Gordon's line to land of Willis Ellis, along Fullington's patent to Jacob Gordon's and back to desert...
Jethro Sumner   Seth Eason
K. Ballard
May Ct 1798

236 17 Apr 1798--Luke Sumner to Miles Benton...200 pds...600 acres on SW side of Dismal Swamp and known as White Oak Spring, beginning at red oak at head of land, line tree of John Brinkley, along his line W to William Mathias' line and along that line to William Ellis,

dec. to John Powell's line and along his patent to back line, to
line of patent granted to Richard Brothers, to John Cowper's land
to said Brinkley's line...
Simeon Brinkley   Luke Sumner
Elisha Brinkley
May Ct 1798

237 6 Jan 1798--Syprian Goodman to James Goodman of Upper Parish
of Nansemond Co., Va....148 pds 10 sh...180 acres beginning at
black oak by main road in Hardy Cross' line, along line of marked
trees to Elisha Cross, Jacob Walters and Hillory Willey's corner,
thence running Cross' line to Jonathan Rogers' line and along his
line to main road...
Henry Goodman   Cyprian Goodman
William Goodman Jr.
Bryan Saunders
May Ct 1798

239 19 Nov 1797--Robert Powell to William Powell $60...18 acres,
plantation whereon William Taylor now lives, beginning at Hinton's
corner pine, SW by line of marked trees to corner gum in John Powell's line, with his line NW...
Pa. Hegerty   Robert Powell
John Powell
May Ct 1798

240 3 Jan 1798--Luke Sumner to John Brinkley...$130...30 acres be-
ginning at red oak in said Brinkley's line on side of Marsh Road
to head of Sumner's lane, SW to Great Swamp, to John Cowper's line,
NW to William Ellis' line...
Thomas Brinkley   Luke Sumner
John Mathias
William(N)Mathias
May Ct 1798

241 16 May 1798--Richard Bond Jr. to Willis Woodley...50 pds...33
acres beginning at pine tree on side of main road leading from courthouse to head of small branch running across road and down run with
line of marked trees to gum near spring, to popular on side of hill,
S binding on Watery Swamp to large red oak, corner tree on road at
casway E to pine in head of branch...
William(X)Bond   Richard Bond
May Ct 1798

242 21 Jan 1797--Abel Cross to William Vann...33 pds 5 sh...Negro
girl Pat...
David Cross   Abel Cross
Edward Vann
May Ct 1798

243 3 Apr 1798--William Speight Sr. to Humphrey Hudgins...188 pds...
151 acres beginning near back of ditch at center of three oaks being
corner between William P. Jamerson and Pugh orphans, to Spanish oak
SW to road, NW to post oak between Jeremiah Speight and said William,
to Pugh's old patent...
J.W. Voight   May Ct 1798
James Costen
May Ct 1798

244 1 Jul 1797--Lawrence Baker by power of attorney from Dr. Eben-

ezer Graham 16 Jun 1795, to Mills Landen...46 pds 12 sh...Negro
girl Sarah...
John R. Cross   Law. Baker
May Ct 1798

245 20 Nov 1797--William Boyce and wife, Asle, to Miles Boyce of
Northampton Co...245 pds 1 sh...112 acres beginning at pine in Bennetts Creek, along patent line to corner gum in Hawtree Branch, down
swamp to said creek and down run...
Abner(R)Roundtree   William(+)Boyce
Abraham Riddick   Alce(AB)Boyce
May Ct 1798

246 12 Oct 1797--Timothy Freeman to James Baker...$24...½ of a
tract purchased of Thomas Hunter 6 Mar 1797 and containing 80 acres,
beginning at mouth of Bennetts Creek and running up marsh...
Norman King   Timothy Freeman
Ez'l(X)Trotman
May Ct 1798

247 10 Jan 1798--Luke Sumner to John Brinkley...$350...175 acres
beginning at pine in William Mathews line and Lewis Jones' corner,
along Jones' line N to pine near fork of Marsh Road and down road
binding thereon to large red oak at foot of road, along row of walnut trees and a desert course SW to said Mathews' line, on his line...
Pa. Hegerty   Luke Sumner
John Ellis
Miles Benton
May Ct 1798

248 11 Oct 1797--Luke Sumner to Lewis Jones...$100...50 acres beginning at gum at edge of Abraham Riddick's mill swamp, on side of
main road, along swamp to William Mathias' line, E along his line
to a pine, N to Marsh Road and along road...
John Brinkley   Luke Sumner
Elizabeth(X) (Brothers)
May Ct 1798

249 29 Dec 1797--John Brinkley to Elisha Brinkley...$80...31 acres
beginning at black gum in branch in said John's line, W on his line
to corner pine in fork of Marsh and Suffolk Road, down Suffolk Road
to water oak in branch and along run...
Thomas Brinkley   John Brinkley
Jacob Brinkley
May Ct 1798

250 20 Mar 1798--John Brinkley to William Brinkley of Nansemond Co...
60 pds...60 acres beginning at Lewis Jones' corner tree on edge of
Marsh Road, S on said Jones' line to William Mathias' line N to Marsh
Road...
Thomas Brinkley   John Brinkley
Selah(X)Brinkley
William Brothers
May Ct 1798

251 1 Feb 1798--Burrell Griffith of Hertford Co. to Jesse Vann...
$550...Negroes Jacob, Gill and Cate...
John Odom   Burrell Griffith
John Griffith

251 28 Feb 1798--Moses Davis to Isaac Harrell Jr...120 pds...185 acres beginning at a pine in a branch that is line of William Hinton and Josiah Granbery, NW to main road and by line of marked trees to John Walton's line, along his line to Soloman Briggs, to William Hinton's line; 100 acres was bought of Moses Hamilton and 85 from Josiah Granbery...
Samuel Harrell   Moses Davis
Henry Meroney
May Ct 1798

252 26 Feb 1798--Aron Harrell to John Harrell...50 pds...100 acres on E side of Coles Creek beginning at gum on side of creek, along Thomas Piland's line to beach on side of creek swamp and up creek and along Piland's line to Great Thicket Branch to black gum, corner tree on Edward Piland's and along his line to said creek...
Asa Harrell   Aron Harrell
Elijah Harress
May Ct 1798

254 20 Feb 1798--William Harriss to Jesse Benton...$305...Negro man Peter...
Jethro Sumner   William Harriss
Jethro Benton
May Ct 1798

254 5 Apr 1798--Richard Bond to Noah Harrell...28 pds 10 sh...34 acres beginning at pine on S side of road, to red oak and binding on Bety Bond's line to pine corner of Job Riddick's and on his line to Meazell's line...
Lassiter Riddick   Richard Bond
May Ct 1798

255 16 May 1798--Stephen Eure to Mills Eure...30 pds...50 acres on S side of Cypress Swamp and was formerly called Banks of Italy, beginning at marked gum in main Cypress Swamp near mouth of Little Branch, up branch and along line of marked trees to patent line, with line to Langston's corner tree, thence down Long Pond NE to pine in Lewis Sparkman's line and by line of marked trees to main swamp and down swamp...
Elisha Harrell   Stephen Eure
Peter Harrell
May Ct 1798

257 23 Dec 1797--John and Charity Ellis to Benjamin Barnes...132 pds 150 acres beginning at gum in Cyprian Cross' line and Aron Ellis' corner in Cabin Branch, formerly called John Hare's, along Everett's patent line to corner of 3 pines, to Ballard's corner and along William Everett's line to said Cross' line to Cabin Branch and up run...
Nathan Thompson   John(X)Ellis
Cypn. Cross   Charity(X)Ellis
Elisha Brinkley   Edith(X)Ellis
May Ct 1798

258 21 Feb 1797--State of North Carolina to Hardy Cross...50 sh per 100 acres...96 acres beginning at marked cypress in Grog Branch where it issues out of Beech Swamp, along branch to head, NE to pine in Demsey Odom's corner, on his line to main run of swamp and down

run... No. 115
J. Glasgow, sec.   Sam'l Ashe

259 2 Sep 1797--Patrick Hegerty and wife, Elizabeth, to Jesse Eason...
30 pds...1/3 of 181 acres tract of woodland survey made by Col. Jesse
Eason, dec. and bequeathed to his daughter, said Elizabeth, in his
will; bounded by said Eason on N, by Fountain on E, by Alexander
Eason on S and by Seth Eason on W...
Demsey Williams   Patrick Hegerty
Gabriel(X)Martin   Elizabeth(X)Hegerty
Aug Ct 1798

260 4 Aug 1798--Hezekiah Jones and wife, Gracy, to James Jones...$40
13 acres beginning at white oak, corner tree of James Jones and Jethro
Ballard, along Jones line S to mulberry tree in said Hezekiah's line,
SW to water oak in Lickingroot Branch, E to said Ballard's line and
NW...
Jethro Ballard   Hezekiah(X)Jones
John Powell
James Small
Aug Ct 1798

261 27 Jun 1798--William Taylor to James Benton...$100...Negro boy
George...
Jethro Benton   William Taylor
Samuel Harrell   Elizabeth(X)Powell
Abraham Benton
Aug Ct 1798

262 15 Jun 1798--Sarah Daniel to Lawrence Baker...$10...50 acres on
E side of Chowan River, left to her in will of Moses Spivey, dec.
and is out of tract patented by him...
Whitmil Eure   Sarah(X)Daniel
Betsey Glover
Aug Ct 1798

263 17 Sep 1797--Lemuel Powell of Perquimans Co. and John Powell Sr.
to Abraham Riddick of Nansemond Co., Va...$200...Negro man Kader...
William Hurdle   Lemuel Powell
Joseph Jno. Sumner   Jno. Powell
Lues Smith
Aug Ct 1798

264 17 Feb 1798--Joseph Riddick to son-in-law, Soloman Eason...deed
of gift...50 acres on W side of desert beginning at Abraham Hurdle's
corner tree in mouth of small branch running NW to side of desert
joining said Eason's line, to end of bridge and SW...
Reuben Riddick   Jos. Riddick
Myles Hill
Aug Ct 1798

265 27 Apr 1798--Luke Sumner to Henry Brinkley of Nansemond Co., Va.
24 pds...46 acres beginning at Jacob Brinkley's corner tree, N up
main road to Joseph John Sumner's line, SW to James Jones' corner
and along his line...
John Brinkley   Luke Sumner
Elizabeth(X)Brothers
Aug Ct 1798

266 28 Aug 1797--Daniel Southall to Seasbrook Wilson...far whereon he lives and all cleared land with privilege of fire and fence wood for his life...one ear of Indian corn yearly...
James Cross
Robert Wiggens   Daniel Southall
Aug Ct 1798

267 13 Jun 1798--Samuel Smith, sheriff, to Joseph Riddick...10 pds 40 acres belonging to George Eason Sr. and sold to cover court cost of suit he brought against Frederick Eason and others in Edenton; said land is known at Thomas Eason's pecosin or Old Womans Pecosin.
James Baker   Samuel Smith
Norman king
Aug Ct 1798

267 30 May 1798--William Rae of Murfreesborough to Benjamin Barnes... $400...fishery lying on E side of Chowan River in tract that he bought of John and William Cowper and called Whiteheads Fishery, beginning at cypress above upper windless, N to swamp, down line to river dividing said Rea and Hardy Murfree...
Jesse Vann   William Rea
Edward Vann
Aug Ct 1798

270 16 Aug 1798--Richard Briggs to Willis Woodley...100 pds...65 acres beginning at small white oak on side of road leading from Suffolk to Edenton near small slash at Robert Riddick's corner fence, along line of marked trees E to Brigg's line adjoining William Hinton's, S to cleared ground in gum pocosin to head of run and W to main road...
Robert Riddick   Richard Briggs
Nathaniel Newsom
Aug Ct 1798

272 10 Feb 1797--Nathaniel and David Riddick to Samuel Harrell... 100 pds...180 acres in Great Dismal Swamp beginning at gum on side of desert, Thomas Hunter and James Gregory's corner tree, joining said Harrell's high land running E to Moses Brigg's line to back of his land and along said Hunter's and Gregory's line to high land of Jacob Gordon's and along desert line...
Henry Meroney   David Riddick
William Harrell   Nathaniel Riddick
Aug Ct 1798

274 17 Sep 1798--State of North Carolina to Micajah Riddick...50 sh per 100 acres...100 acres beginning at gum on run of Middle Swamp, James Phelps corner tree, on his line NE to said Riddick's corner, SW to Noah Felton's line to run of swamp...
Will White, sec. No. 120.   W.R. Davis

275 13 Dec 1798--State of North Carolina to Demsey Parker...50 sh per 100 acres...90 acres beginning at white oak in Edwin Sumner's line in run of Knotty Pine Swamp, binding on his line NW to pine stump, SW to white oak, NW to run of swamp...
Will White, sec. No. 123   W.R. Davis

276 13 Dec 1798--State of North Carolina to Simon Stallings...50 sh per 100 acres...135 acres beginning at maple, a corner in Spivey's

patent SW to red oak corner in Blanchard's patent, NE to Bagley's line and along his line...
Will White, sec. No. 121   W.R. Davis

277 20 Oct 1794--Ann Piland, planter, to David Lewis...51 pds... Negro man, Bob, about 28 years old...
John Warren   John Lewis   Ann(X)Piland
Samuel Green   Elisha Harrell
May Ct 1799

277 May Ct 1799--Jeremiah Jordon and wife, Sarah, Henry Hill and wife, Elizabeth and Josiah Lassiter and wife (Mary) empower Armistead Russell of Cumberland Co. to commence suit against any person who may have Negroes which they are entitled to as children of William Russell and wife, Sarah, who died on or about 20 Mar 1796, under will of John Armstead, late of said county...
N. King   Jeremiah Jordan for himself and
John Hofler   wife, Sarah
May Ct 1799   Henry(X)Hill for himself and wife, Elizabeth
                                  Josiah(X)Lassiter for himself and wife (Mary)

278 8 Jan 1798--Richard Freeman of Orange Co. to John B. Walton... 100 pds...Negro woman Lewcy...
George Outlaw   Richard Freeman
Elizabeth Travis
Nov Ct 1798

279 2 Dec 1797--State of North Carolina to William Watkins...30 pds per 100 acres...900 acres beginning at James Jones' corner in Capt. Cowper's line, to Col. Riddick's line E to his juniper, SW to county line...No. 117
J. Glasgow, sec.   Samuel Ashe

280 2 Dec 1797--State of North Carolina to Joseph Riddick...10 pds per 100 acres...1000 acres beginning at James Jones' corner in desert, E to juniper, SW to out edge of desert and along desert...
J. Glasgow, sec. No. 118   Samuel Ashe

281 14 Dec 1798--State of North Carolina to Lawrence Baker...30 sh per 100 acres...67 acres on E side of Chowan River beginning at Daniel Spivey's patent corner below the mouth of Sarum Creek on edge of river, along Spivey's line NE to Beef or Cow Creek to river...
Will. White, sec. No. 119   W.R. Davis

282 20 May 1798--Isaac Hunter and Lewis Thompson, executers of William Hinton, dec., to Amos Lassiter...25 pds...100 acres beginning at Samuel Smith's corner gum in Francis Pugh's line, NW along his line to James Knight's corner tree, N to William Boyce's corner pine, to his new line, to said Pugh's and along that line...
George Gordon   Isaac Hunter
Willis Woodley
Nov Ct 1798

283 5 Jan 1798--John B. Walton to Richard Freeman...$100...Negro Peny and child Agatha...
Geo. Outlaw   Jno. B. Walton
Elizabeth Travis
Nov Ct 1798

283 4 Oct 1797--Samuel, Thomas and Jonathan Smith to Henry Smith...
25 pds...12 acres beginning at chinquipen oak in run of watery Swamp,
along said Thomas' line to said Samuel's road, NW to Horsepen Branch
and up run to water oak in Micajah Riddick's line, NE to Jeremiah
Speight's corner post oak in said Samuel's line in Watery Swamp...
Hy. Hudgins   Samuel Smith
Pa. Hegerty   Thomas Smith
Nov Ct 1798   Jonathan Smith

284 30 Aug 1798--Isaac Walters to John Babb...50 pds...50 acres
whereon said Babb lives beginning at small branch at forked water
oak, NE by line of marked trees to forked pine, S to William Walter's and Sion Boyce's, NW along Boyce's line to said branch...
Isaac Walters Jr.   Isaac Walters
Elizabeth Walters
Nov Ct 1798

285 29 Aug 1798--Jethro Sumner and Demsey Odom to Isaac Walters...
460 pds...600 acres where said Walters lives, purchased by James
Granbery of Edenton at public sale of marshall of district of North
Carolina 19 Nov 1790 and sold to said Sumner and Odom 22 Nov 1790;
excepting 50 acres of tract was sold to Winborn Jenkins...
John Babb   Jethro Sumner
Isaac Walters Jr.   Demsey(O)Odom
Nov Ct 1798

287 29 Jun 1796--Thomas Granbery of Bertie Co. to John Campbell...
50 pds...640 acres, patented to Kedar Powell 18 Aug 1783 by Alex.
Martin, gov., beginning at two gums and maple, Joshua Small and Jesse
Eason's corner tree in desert, NW to Jethro Ballard's corner, to said
Eason's line and along it...
John Askew   Thos. Granbery
Fred. Francis

289 27 Oct 1798--Jacob Spivey to Ezekiel Trotman...$250...Negro
man Samuel, formerly property of Jesse Spivey, dec...
John Hofler   Jacob Spivey
Docton Bagley
Noah Trotman
Nov Ct 1798

290 19 Nov 1798--David Rawls and wife, Penina, to John Langston,
all of Upper Parish of Nansemond Co., Va...77 pds 10 sh...100 acres
beginning at gum in line of George Williams Jr. on Hilly Swamp, a-
long his line to Turner's line, NE along row of marked trees W to
George Williams Sr. line...
Isaac Miller Jr.   David Rawls
Jesse Savage   Pina(+)Rawls
Jethro Riddick
William Goodman, justice of peace, testified said Penina signed
deed freely. Nov Ct 1798

292 21 Sep 1798--Ann Hill to Abraham Spivey...10 pds...feather bed
and furniture, chest, 2 iron pots, 3 plates, 2 basons, dish, all
puter, 12 spoons, wool wheel, linen wheel, 2 tubs, 2 pails, ax, 3
baskets and 5 hogs...
Simon Stallings   Ann(X)Hill
Elijah Lyons
Nov Ct 1798

293 16 Jan 1798--William March to John March of Nansemond Co., Va...
134 pds...Negro woman Chase, 17 years old last June, 8 or 9 year old
sorrel mare, 2 feather beds and furniture, 50 bbls corn, fodder, 2
bbls pork, 3 sows and pigs, red cow with white face, yearling, 12
earthen plates, puter dish, 2 puter basins, man's bridle and saddle,
linen wheel, woolen wheel and 10 bu peas...
Richard Brown   William(X)March
Bray Saunders
Nov Ct 1798

294 1 Oct 1798--Elisha Norfleet to his nephew, Kinchen Norfleet...deed
of gift...Negroes Tarty, Luke and Tom, household furniture and stock...
Elisha Hare   Elisha Norfleet
Nicholas Minor
Nov Ct 1798

295 4 Mar 1798--John, Josiah and James Granbery, sons of the late Mrs.
Christian Cowper, 200 pds...126-acre Brick House Plantation, which
was purchased of Elisha Hunter by the said Mrs. Cowper, alias Doeber,
according to survey by John Moran in September 1787, beginning at
marked pine at Mill Pond S along James Costen's line by schoolhouse,
to red oak, corner tree of James Gregory's line, SE to Staffords
Branch, to Mill Swamp and down swamp...
James Gordon   John Granbery
Mills Riddick   James Granbery
W. Slade   Josiah Granbery
William Harriss
Nov Ct 1798

297 8 Aug 1798--Elisha Brinkley to Cyprian Cross...$100...50 acres
beginning at pine in Cyprian Cross's patent, corner of Jesse Vann's,
along Cross' line to said Vann's, to outside swamp and across it to
Demsey Harrell's and along his line to James Landen's, on his line
to Aaron Ellis' and along his line to said Cross'...
Joseph Smith   Elisha Brinkley
Riddick Cross   Elizabeth(X)Brinkley
Nov Ct 1798

298 21 Sep 1798--Ann Hill to son-in-law, Abraham Spivey, deed of
gift...37 acres, her 1/3 of land that fell to her by her husband,
Abraham Hill, dec. joining Moses Hill, dec line and Kedar Hill's
land, on N side of Catherine Creek...
Simon Stallings   Ann(X)Hill
Elijah Lyon
Simon Stallings Jr.

300 5 Oct 1797--Soloman Hobbs to Levi Eason...54 pds 10 sh...36 acres,
1/3 of land of Jacob Hobbs, dec. on N side of Cabin Creek, beginning
at sweet gum, running to Flat Branch and down branch and joining lines
of William King, William Berryman and Amos Trotman...
Will. King   Soloman(+)Hobbs
Samuel(+)Hobbs, son of John

302 20 Aug 1798--Barnaby Blanchard to Samuel Brown...$78...13 acres
on Beaver Dam Swamp beginning at corner black gum in said Brown's
line, up branch to corner water oak, NW to pine on S side of Great
meadows and by line of marked trees...
Moses Lassiter   Barnaby Blanchard
Pa. Hegerty
Nov Ct 1798

303 10 Feb 1798--Joseph John Sumner to Patty Meroney...$200...Negro women Rose and Siller...
Thomas Parker   Joseph Jno. Sumner
Harriss Spence
Nov Ct 1798

304 13 Nov 1797--Elisha Norfleet to Kincheon Norfleet...90 pds... 84 acres, lots 8,9,10 and 11, in tract formerly belonging to John Norfleet, dec. and given to his 11 children in his will, beginning at mouth of Orapeak Swamp at stake in John Norfleet's head line on W side of an island, running NE to back line of patent, to Powell's line to said island and S...
Jethro Ballard   Elisha Norfleet
Mourning Norfleet
Moses(M)Small
Nov Ct 1798

305 8 Aug 1798--Elisha Brinkley to Cyprian Cross...$400...150 acres beginning at pine in Cabin Swamp, said Cross' line tree, along his line to John Odom's corner tree, along Odom's line to pine of Cross and Gatling...
Joseph Smith   Elisha Brinkley
Riddick Cross   Elizabeth(+)Brinkley
Nov Ct 1798   Martha(+)Brinkley

306 19 Nov 1798--John Robbins of Perquimans Co. to Cader Hinton... 15 pds...71 acres on Bennetts Creek beginning at cypress, along line of marked trees to corner oak on Sharps Island, to corner pine in patent line and along patent to said creek and up run...
Thomas Hofler   John Robins
Jethro Meltear
Nov Ct 1798

307 15 Jan 1798--Luke Sumner to Jethro Ballard...150 pds...Negro men Tom and Reuben...
John Nerney   Luke Sumner
Thos. W. Ballard

307 16 Mar 1798--Samuel Harrell to Jonathan Roberts...$180...119½ acres beginning at water oak in James Hayse' line in Flat Branch, up his line to corner of said land, across to Kedar Hinton's line, to gum stump in said branch and down branch; said tract is part of tract William Lewis and said Harrell bought of Chowan Indians...
Jos. Granbery   Samuel Harrell
David Harrell
Nov Ct 1798

309 26 Jan 1799--Isaac Walters Sr. to Isaac Walters Jr...$500... 250 acres called Broadneck, beginning at post oak on Blackbird Hill, corner tree of Sion Boyce and said Walters and joining lands of Demsey and Jonathan Williams...
Jethro Sumner   Isaac Walters
John Babb
Feb Ct 1799

310 21 Jul 1797--James Freeman to Jethro Lassiter...12 pds...8 acres whereon Robert Ward now lives, beginning at maple in branch, running to pine and along line of marked trees...
Willis(X)Sparkman   James Freeman
Daniel(X)Eoyer
Feb Ct 1799

311 21 May 1798--William Harriss to Seth Eason...1000 pds bond on condition of execution of deed on lands on which said Eason lives as security to said Eason for 250 pds...
Jethro Sumner   William Harriss
Kedar Ballard
Feb Ct 1799

312 20 Feb 1799--Joseph Riddick and Elisha Hunter, executors of will of Thomas Hunter, dec. to William Baker...$275...Negro Sam in which said Thomas owns 2/3 and Thomas Hofler claims 1/3 interest...
Law. Baker   Jo. Riddick
James Gordon   Elisha Hunter
Feb Ct 1799   Thomas Hofler

314 14 Feb 1799--Henry Hill to Daniel Powell...45 pds...35 acres in Indian Neck beginning at pine corner of Seasbrook Hinton and said Powell's line at Indian Road, running E to corner of said Hill and Hinton, along James Robbins' line to gum, SW to road...
Mills R. Field   Henry(H)Hill
Guy Hill
Feb Ct 1799

315 5 Jun 1798--Luke Sumner to John Powell...1 pd 10 sh...20 acres beginning at gum on edge of swamp, along edge and binding on land of John Powell Jr. to William Mathias' line, NW to land said Sumner gave to his daughter, to road and S...
H. Powell   Luke Sumner
Mills Ellis
James(+)Jones
Feb Ct 1799

316 6 Feb 1799--Abraham Riddick to Humphrey Hudgins...20 pds...22 acres at flax landing on S side of Bennetts Creek, along swamp and up creek on high land of John Hudgins to old orchard, to branch between said Riddick and Hudgins and down branch to creek...
Jas. B. Sumner   Abm. Riddick
William Hayse
Feb Ct 1799

317 12 Feb 1799--John Shepherd to William Shepherd...100 pds...175 acres, part of two patents, one granted to Thomas Duke Jr. of Nansemond 28 Oct 1702 and the other to Ruth Barfield 20 Apr 1694, beginning at cypress on N side of Mills Swamp near mouth of Deep Branch, down main run to mouth of James Brady's mill swamp and up run to N side of Bear Garden to marked gum, by line of marked trees between said Brady and Shepherd to Phillip Lewis' line and along his line to Isaac Pipkin Sr.'s corner post oak and down dividing line between said Pipkin and Shepherd to Bear Garden and S...
James Hodges   John Shepherd
Elizabeth Savage
Feb Ct 1799

319 18 Jan 1799--James Bristow and wife, Mary, of Northampton Co. to Lawrence Baker...$17...17 acres on N side of Bennetts Creek road, beginning at white oak, said Baker's corner tree on Trumpet Marsh Branch, along his line SE to said road and down road NW...
William Brooks   James Bristow
Jno. B. Baker   Mary Bristow
Warner Bristow
Feb Ct 1799

321 15 May 1797--Demsey Jones Sr. to Sarah Jones...$30...6 acres, part of tract formerly property of Gabriel Lassiter, dec., beginning at red oak, corner tree near Joseph Parker's fence, down his line to Kader Hinton's line, along his line to said Demsey's...
Demsey Jones Jr.   Demsey(X)Jones
Abraham Riddick
Feb Ct 1799

322 9 Feb 1799--James Jones to William Baker...$161... 2/3 of 97 acre tract beginning at water oak, said Baker's corner in James Parker's line, by line of marked trees Nw to post oak in James Gatling's line on path side, to said Baker's purchase of said Jones and along that line...
Demsey Parker   James(X)Jones
Robert A. Wiggens
Feb Ct 1799

324 10 Sep 1797--Joseph John Sumner to Kedar Ballard...250 pds... 250 acres, half of plantation whereon said Sumner lives and given to him by his father, beginning at swamp side near William Arnold's line, W by row of apple trees to W door of dwelling house, through entry and to road that leads to Brothers by Virginia line to bound of land...
Ambrose(X)Wiggens   Joseph Jno. Sumner
Cadar(X)Wiggens
William Arnold
Feb Ct 1799

325 15 Nov 1798--Lewis Sumner to Josiah Sumner...12 pds...1/3 of 150 acres beginning at cypress stump, corner tree of John Lang's in Cypress Swamp and down swamp...
Henry(X)Saunders   Lewis(+)Sumner
Joseph(X)Saunders
Feb Ct 1799

326 29 Jan 1799--Edward Allen and wife, Elizabeth, and Caty Reid of Nansemond Co., Va. to Micajah Riddick Jr...$1200...563 acres known as Francis Pugh's patent...
Jethro Sumner   Edw. C. Allen
Noah Felton   Eliza. Allen
David Riddick   Caty Reid
Robert M. Riddick and Jno. C. Cohoon testified
said Elizabeth signed deed freely 18 May 1799 in Nansemond Co.

328 19 Dec 1798--Noah Trotman to Seth Trotman...566 pds...56 acres beginning at marked tree in Catherine Swamp, running to fork and binding on Jacob Bagley, dec. line, down swamp to head of branch near bridge binding on Miles Hill's line to land of orphans of Moses Hill, dec, cornering at ditch and by orchard...
Abraham Spivey   Noah Trotman
Miles Walton
Feb Ct 1799

330 26 Jan 1799--Hugh and Purnel King to Mills Eure...150 pds...100 acres beginning at corner pine of Samuel Taylor's, running his line to Elisha Harrell's line, along his line to Stephen Eure's line to out pecosin, to corner pine and down pecosin to said Stephen's, with his line to said Taylor's and along his line. Said land is part of patent granted to John Alston 12 Jul 1725...
Blake Eure   Hugh King
Willis Piland   Purnel King
Pleasant Harrell
Feb Ct 1799

331 10 Dec 1798--Seth Trotman and wife, Sarah, to Noah Trotman...
490 pds...56 acres, which they heired, on Catherine Creek beginning
at marked tree, up swamp to said creek and up creek to fork binding
on land of orphans of Jacob Bagley, dec., down swamp to branch near
bridge, along Henry Walton's land to head of branch near road, to
red oak corner tree of Miles Hill and along line of orphans of Moses
Hill, dec., then through orchard...
Miles Walton   Seth Trotman
Abraham(+)Spivey   Saley(X)Trotman
Feb Ct 1799

332 4 Jan 1798--William Hayse, administrator of Wright Hayse, dec.
to Jonathan Lassiter...by court order...Negro boy Silas...
Samuel Smith   William Hayse
Thos. Walton
Feb Ct 1799

333 25 Nov 1798--Samuel Smith, sheriff, to John Cowper...61 pds 8
sh...50 acres of desert land that belongs to John Fontain of Virginia...to secure revenue due to state; said property is part of
larger tract that fell to said Fontain by heirship, beginning at
his line where it intersects said Cowper's, formerly James Sumner's
line and then N...
James Walton   Samuel Smith
Henry Smith
David Riddick
Feb Ct 1799

334 19 Jan 1799--Timothy Freeman to Josiah Parker...200 pds...200
acres beginning at maple in side of pocosin in Robert Taylor's line,
by line of marked trees to Horsepen Swamp and along swamp to Charles
Smith's line and along his line to Timothy Walton's, along his line
to said pocosin...
James Williams   Timothy Freeman
John Marshall
Feb Ct 1799

335 15 Jun 1798--William Rea to Benjamin Roberts, both of Murfreesborough in Hertfort Co..$1200...½ of fishery and 25 acres granted
24 Oct 1786, beginning at cypress on E side of Chowan River above
mouth of Barnes Creek, up run NW...
H. Murfree
Jas. Maddrey
John Vann Jr.
Feb Ct 1799

336 24 Oct 1797--William Crafford to Benjamin Roberts of Hertford
Co...$850...½ of fishery and 25 acres granted 24 Oct 1786, beginning at cypress on side of Chowan River above mouth of Barnes Creek,
up river NW and then S...
Jesse Stallings   William Crafford
Willis(+)Stallings
James Rae
John Vann
Feb Ct 1799

338 2 Mar 1797--Luke Sumner to Levin Dure...$220...Negro woman Pat
and her child Aggy...
K. Ballard   Luke Sumner
Miles Benton
Feb Ct 1799

338 20 Jan 1798--William Speight to John Duke Jr...$250...100 acres on SE side of Bennetts Creek beginning at white oak in mouth of branch running NE along line of marked trees to John Riddick's line, along his line to William E. Webb, orphan of John Webb, dec. and along that line to Cypress Swamp, to Bennetts Creek...
Miles Benton   William Speight
Betsey Benton
William Phelps
Feb Ct 1799

340 9 Feb 1798--Charles Eure to Levi Eure...60 pds...two tracts, one of 50 acres was bought of Elisha Ellis, who purchased of Daniel Ellis 2 May 1789 and the other tract, also bought of said Elisha, and was purchased by James Ellis from Aron and John Odom 7 Sep 1751 and containing 150 acres; first tract begins at gum on S side of Cypress Swamp, corner tree between Elisha and Daniel Ellis, up small branch to John Parker's line, along his line to William Ellis' line, along that line to said swamp; the other tract begins at gum at said Parker's line, along his line to said Charles' line in branch in Levi Lee's patent, down branch...
Open Ct Feb 1799   Charles Eure

342 5 Jun 1799--State of North Carolina to William Rea...50 sh.. per 100 acres...75 acres beginning at Benjamin Harrell's line on NE side of Mud Creek along his line to William Arnold's W along his patent to William Crafford's line, S to creek...
Will. White, sec. No. 124   W.R. Davis

343 1 Jan 1799--Willis Woodley to Andrew Woodley of Isle of Wight, Va...$600...250 acres on S side of Bennetts Creek and purchased of James Hodges, and lying on S side of main road to courthouse and adjoining John Hunter and Amos Lassiter, begins at cypress, running N by line of marked trees to mouth of Iron Mine Branch, up branch to corner tree to said road and along road S to Deep Gut adjoining land of Mrs. Minnard's and said Lassiter, along run to Bennetts Creek and up creek...
Abel Garrison   Willis Woodley
Harrison(+)Chapman
Sam'l Woodley
8 Oct 1799

345 8 Jun 1799--Willis Woodley to Andrew Woodley...$1000...1500 acres beginning at white oak near main Edenton Road, along line of marked trees adjoining Richard Briggs land, E to Moses Davis land to corner tree of Soloman Briggs, NE to Josiah Lassiter's and along his line of marked trees S to new road, to Abraham Harrell's line W to Isaac Harrell's, across main road to Edenton to Josiah Granbery's land, along swamp W to Bennetts Creek, along Moses Speight's line to Aron Speight, to road to Winton, to Robert Riddick's to main road to Suffolk. Also small piece of mast land beginning at Isaac Reid's, running to Webbs land, to Ellis' place where Mourning Ellis lives, adjoining Robert Powell and Zilpha Powell, to tract occupied by said Willis, to beginning of land Woodley got by marriage to his wife, Mary, whereon he lives and where William Hinton formerly lived.
Abel(X)Garrison   Willis Woodley
Harrison(+)Chapman
Sam'l Woodley
John Lewis Taylor, justice of supreme court

Vol. 5

2 9 Mar 1799--Jethro Sumner of Nansemond Co., Va. to William Goodman...$130...1 acre, part of patent granted to Henry Goodman 22 Sep 1791, beginning at cypress on side of Chowan River, William Crafford's corner tree, along his line to Barnes Creek and down creek to gum, S to river and up run...
Henry Hare   Jethro Sumner
Pheraba Hare
May Ct 1799

3 23 Mar 1799--John and William Cowper of Northampton Co. to William Rea of Murfreesborough, Hertford Co...$900...250 acres, swamp and fishery on E side of Chowan River, beginning at holly tree, William Arnold's corner, S to side of river and up river to mouth of Mud Creek, up creek NE to said Arnold's line and SE; being tract that Benjamin Harrell and James Parker conveyed to John Whitehead, dec. formerly of Southampton Co., Va., who in his will directed his executor, Miriam Whitehead to sell and in December 1791 she sold to said Cowpers...
Jethro Ballard   John Cowper
Thomas Cowper   William Cowper
James Rae
King Parker
May Ct 1799

5 23 Mar 1799--John and William Cowper of Northampton to William Rea of Murfreesborough...$500...300 acres containing Juniper and another swamp, which they brought of John Bruner and conveyed by William Arnold to them 12 Aug 1796, on E side of Chowan River beginning at holly tree, Whitehead's corner, SW to Whitehead's other corner and N...
Jethro Ballard   John Cowper
Thomas Cowper   William Cowper
King(X)Parker
May Ct 1799

7 16 May 1799-Willis Piland to James Piland...182 pds 10 sh...300 acres on W side of Coles Creek beginning at cypress on side of run, to John Piland's line and along his line to Cullen's line, to main road that leads to Sarum Creek, along road to S side of Great Marsh, along marsh to branch, to Jesse Harrell's line, to run of creek and up middle...
John Piland   Willis Piland
Thomas(+)Felton
May Ct 1799

8 9 Nov 1798--Thomas Smith to son, Richard...deed of gift...100 acres, part of land purchased of Zadoc_ Hinton, beginning at corner maple in Bennetts Creek, running by line of marked trees NW to run of Mile Branch and up run to branch issuing out of Watery Swamp and along run to mouth of Bennetts Creek...
Sam'l Smith   Thomas Smith
Henry Smith
Anthony Mathews Sr.
Pa Hegerty
May Ct 1799

10 2 Feb 1799--William Polson to John Polson...50 pds...34 acres beginning at gum on Half Way Run Branch, up run NW to Bennetts Creek Road, E to said John's line, SW along said William's line to road...
James Williams   William Polson
John Marshall
May Ct 1799

11 22 Jan 1799--George Outlaw to Nathaniel Taylor of Chowan Co...
12 pds 10 sh...5 acres on NW side of Old Town Road, N along Joseph Taylor's line to post oak in road and along road...
Joseph(X)Morgan   George Outlaw
Thomas(X)Baker

12 18 Apr 1799--Dempsey Jones Sr. to Kader Hinton...120 pds...30 acres beginning at water oak on John Hare's line, along line of marked trees to said Hintons, to Joseph Parker's line and along his line to said Hares...
Mills R. Fields   Demsey(X)Jones
Guy Hill
May Ct 1799

14 11 Mar 1799--Thomas Hurdle and wife, Judith, to Simon Stallings...
$520--75 acres on S side of Catherine Creek, beginning at several saplings in Josiah Roundtree's line N of old path, E to gum in branch to line above plantation whereon Miles Hurdle now lives, up branch to clearing by William Robinson's, SE to pine in Thomas Hobbs' line, along his line W to near said Roundtree's dead woods and NW...
Jo. Riddick   Thomas Hurdle
Betsey Bagley   Judith(X)Hurdle
Nathan Riddick

16 10 Apr 1799--Moses Briggs and Tamor Hill, who intend marriage in deed of trust to Joseph Riddick convey her dower in lands of Moses Hill, dec. and following: horse, 13 hogs, 2 feather beds and furniture, 7 chairs, chest, 2 earthen dishes, 9 plates, set of cups and saucers, 3 bowls, coffee pot, pewter basin, 9 spoons, iron pot and hooks, skillet, frying pan, 2 tables, ax, 2 hoes, plow, 2 glass tumbler,..
May Ct 1799

18 13 Feb 1799--Henry Griffin to Jonathan Parker...100 pds...58 acres beginning at main road which leads from Knotty Pine to Suffolk in Edwin Sumner's line, by line of marked trees SE to pine corner, NE to pine on said road and up road...
James Tuggle   Henry(X)Griffin
Pa. Hegerty   Elizabeth Griffin
May Ct 1799

20 1 Jun 1798--Henry Griffin and wife, Elizabeth, to John B. Walton 62 pds 10 sh...60 acres beginning at red oak, a corner on his line formerly called Blanchards, by line of marked trees to post oak on line of children of Nan Robbins, along their line to Seasbrook Hinton's, up his line to Bennetts Creek road and down road...
George Eason   Henry(X)Griffin
Guy Hill
May Ct 1799

21 4 May 1799--Micajah Riddick Jr. to Humphrey Hudgins...56 pds 5 sh

45 acres beginning at red oak, corner tree between said Hudgins and William Harriss, in head of Wild Cat Branch, W to main road and along road to Hudgin's line, along his line NE...
Noah Pelton   Micajah Riddick Jr.
Caleb Savage Jr.
May Ct 1799

22 24 Aug 1797--Jeremiah Speight to Watson Stott and Co. of Suffolk, Va...420 pds...600 acres beginning at mouth of Major Camp Branch at white oak, running along line of marked trees to line of orphans of David Sumner and William Pugh, to maple in head of Dogwood Neck patent, along said line to Sam'l Smith's line, to Watery Swamp, to Bennetts Creek and up creek, deducting 150 acres agreeable to William Speight's deed; also 84 acres beginning at blazed pine in Henry Smith's line, to said Harris' line, to Reid's line, to post oak...
William Fisher   Jeremiah Speight
Josiah Speight
William Speight
May Ct 1799

24 18 May 1799--Isaac Fryer and wife, Mary, Judith Harrell, Hetty Crafford and Rebekah Ellis to David Harrell...3 pds...5 acres beginning at white oak on S side of Outside Swamp in Josiah Harrell's line, to corner maple, S across ridge to gum in branch, down main run to mouth, E to patent line, to said Josiah's line and S; said tract is part of one formerly belonging to Epaphoditaus Jones...
Josiah Harrell   Isaac(X)Fryer
Samuel Harrell   Judith(X)Harrell
James Crawford   Hetty(X)Crafford
May Ct 1799   Rebekah(X)Ellis

25 9 Dec 1798--George Lasitor to Abner Pearce...27 pds...40 acres of woodland beginning at white oak, Abner Lassiter and Aron Blanchard's corner, along Blanchard's line NW to Theopulis Hunter's corner, on his line to old road and along road and by line of marked trees...
Pa. Hegerty   George Lassiter
Jonathan Lassiter
Aron(X(Lassiter
May Ct 1799

26 9 Feb 1799--Joseph John Sumner and Kedar Ballard to Micajah Riddick Jr...$100...Negro Boy Gilbert...
Jethro Sumner   Jos. Jno. Sumner
Isaac Miller Sr.   K. Ballard
May Ct 1799

27 18 Apr 1799--Dempsey Odom Jones to Dempsey Jones Sr...150 pds...69 acres beginning at Jeremiah Jordon's corner tree, along David Harrell's to Kedar Hinton's in Flat Branch, up branch to gum, corner between said land and Charles Smith, S by line of marked trees to maple in Cypress Branch and along branch and said Smith's line...
Mills R. Field   Demsey Odom(X)Jones
Guy Hill
May Ct 1799

28 15 Feb 1799--Josiah Parker to James Baker...$425...140 acres beginning at mouth of Crooked Branch where it issues out of Bennetts Creek, up creek to pine, Seth Roundtree's corner, by line of marked

trees NE to corner pine on side of Horsepool Swamp and down swamp to pine in George Outlaw's line, S to head of branch and down branch.
Pa. Hegerty
Timothy Freeman
May Ct 1799
                        Josiah(X)Parker

28 8 Dec 1798--George Lassiter to Abner Pearce...100 pds...77 acres beginning at pine, Aron Blanchard's corner in run of Deep Gutt, on his line SW to Walton's line, to Bond's corner, to branch and running branch to said gut...
Pa. Hegerty
Jonathan Lassiter   George Lassiter
Aron(X)Lassiter
May Ct 1799

30 27 Feb 1799--James B. and Jethro Sumner to Micajah Riddick Jr... $265...Negro Mike...
Anthony Mathews   Jas. B. Sumner
William Baker
May Ct 1799

30 29 Jun 1799--William Freeman to Daniel Riddick of Nansemond Co., Va...$1750...295 acres on S side of Catherine Creek, including part of creek, beginning at sweet gum, Charles Powell's corner in branch, along his line to red oak, Lemuel Taylor's, dec. corner tree, to said swamp and down swamp to pine in Richard Rawl's line, SW to his high land at end of point, to patent dividing said land and said Powell's, to middle of branch...
Jo. Riddick   William Freeman
Nathan Riddick   Sarah Freeman
William Goodman, justice of peace, testified said Sarah signed deed freely...
Aug Ct 1799

33 22 Mar 1798--John Baker to Lawrence Baker...$100...850 acres on E side of Chowan River, beginning at mouth of Sarum Creek, down run to Beef or Cow Creek and up creek to Spivey's patent, to include claim said John has from purchase made by them of Abner Roundtree and wife, Sarah and Priscilla Spivey...
Hen. Baker   Jno. Baker
Seth Williams
Aug Ct 1799

34 16 May 1797--William Freeman to Richard Rawls...350 pds...150 acres beginning at large red oak on side of old orchard, SW to large persimmon tree, to swamp and holding high land called Freemans Point, to Catren Swamp, to Lemuel Taylor's line...
James Freeman   William Freeman Sr.
William Freeman Jr.   Sarah Freeman
Aug Ct 1799

36 20 May 1799--Willis Wiggens Sr. to sons: deeds of gift to Willis feather bed and furniture, Kedar cow, yearling, bed and furniture, Thomas feather bed and furniture, Pugh cow and calf, Jacob yoke of oxen, desk, feather bed and furniture and cross cut saw; other property to be divided equally...
William Hurdle   Willis Wiggens Sr.
Ambrose(X)Wiggens
Treasy(X)Wiggens
Aug Ct 1799

36 1 Aug 1799--Willis Brown to Michael Lawrence...$250...100 acres,
a patent to William Daniel, beginning at gum in James Hayes' line,
running to red oak in William Riddick's line, to hickory in James
Raby's line and along his line to white oak in Moses Spivey's line...
Miles Gatling   Willis Brown
Law. Baker
Aug Ct 1799

38 17 Aug 1799--Henry Goodman to Thomas and Richard Barnes...$200
25 acres beginning at mouth of Speights Creek, up river to gum and
N along creek...
Isaac Pipkin Jr.   Henry Goodman
William Goodman
Aug Ct 1799

39 5 Feb 1799--Levin Duer to David Riddick...583 pds 6 sh 8 pn...
200 acres known as Folly, on S side of Loosing Swamp, beginning at
marked white oak, Larcum and Harriss corner tree, SE to land of Jacob
Powell, dec. and Moses Davis, to marked gum by branch, N to land of
John Miller, dec. running to Jethro Ballard and Benjamin Gordon's
corner, to S side of swamp...
Isaac Hunter   Levin Duer
James Gregory
Aug Ct 1799

40 19 Aug 1799--James Small to Theopheulis Harrell...92 pds 10 sh...
Negro girl Fanny...
John Small   James Small
John Cowper Jr.
Aug Ct 1799

41 28 May 1799--Benjamin Baker to H. Eborn Sears...12 pds...55 acres
beginning at center of three maples, gum and bay, Moses Boyce's corner
of his new survey, SW to pine in Moses Kittrell's line, N to pine in
Samuel Baker's line and along his line NE...
James Hodges   Benjamin Baker
Jonathan Lassiter
Aug Ct 1799

43 31 May 1799--Jesse, Samuel, Albridgeton and John Browne of Southampton Co., Edward Browne of Nansemond Co., Va., James Browne of Norfolk Co., Va. and Anthony Browne of Person Co., to William Baker...
200 bbl of cut herring...769 acres beginning at cypress in upper side
of Sarum Creek on E side of Chowan River, running up river and including Great Island to mouth of Barnes Creek, up creek NE to gum in
Enos Eure's line, on side of pocosin and down pocosin W to head of
Little Creek, to Sarum Creek and including entry made by William
Crafford, Patrick Garvey and Dr. Samuel Browne for 400 acres, 2/3
of which was conveyed to said Samuel by said Crafford and Garvey;
and all entries made by said Samuel during his lifetime...
William Sturgeon   J. Browne
Benjamin Barnes   Sam'l Browne
Francis Murfee   Albt. Browne
Thomas Newsome Jr.   Edward Browne
Robert Wiggens   Jas. Browne
Caleb Ward   Anthony Browne
Jasper Gaskins
Aug Ct 1799

45 31 May 1799--Jesse, Samuel, Albridgeton and John Browne of Southampton Co., Edward Browne of Nansemond Co., Va., James Browne of Norfolk Co., Va. and Anthony Browne of Person Co. to William Baker... all lands possessed by Dr. Samuel Brown Sr. at the time of his death including patent granted to Patrick Garvey, William Crafford and said Browne for 400 acres, 2/3 of which was sold to said Browne later. Said Crafford and said Garvey not having made a suffieient deed, they are now requested to do so with Patrick Hegerty, Gates Co. surveyor, making out the plats; returning to secretary's office...

William Sturgeon	J. Browne
Benjamin Barnes	Sam'l Browne
Francis Murfee	Albt. Browne
Thomas Newsome Jr.	Edward Browne
Robert Wiggens	Jas. Browne
Caleb Ward	Anthony Browne
Jasper Gaskins	

Aug Ct 1799

46 20 Aug 1799--Israel Beeman to Abraham Beeman...34 pds 8 sh...122 acres joining land of John Parker, Charles Eure and said Israel, beginning at small pine in said Charles' line, W along said Israel's line to dead pine in said Parker's line and along his line to small pine, along line of marked trees to said Eure's line and S...
Benjamin Beeman   Israel Beeman
Aug Ct 1799

47 17 Apr 1799--Abraham Riddick of Nansemond Co., Va. to John Powell Sr...$200...Negro man Kedar...
Jacob Sumner Powell   Abraham Riddick
K. Ballard
Aug Ct 1799

48 10 Feb 1799--Joseph Riddick to Soloman Eason...10 pds...40 acres, Thomas Eason's pocosin, and sold to said Riddick by Samuel Smith, sheriff, to comply with court order. Said land, patented by George Eason, begins at William Berriman's corner, along his line to Jacob Pearce's line, to Elisha Hunter's line, to Hardin Eason's line and along bounds of his land...
David Rice   Joseph Riddick
Simon Stallings
Aug Ct 1799

49 3 Apr 1799--Willis Woodley to Jethro Sumner and Miles Gatling... 225 pds...Negro man Toby, Negro woman Lucy and girl Hetty...
Jesse Benton   Willis Woodley
Nath'l Newsom
Aug Ct 1799

50 5 Mar 1799--Sarah Hunter to Joseph Gordon...150 pds Jen mare and colt, stock of cattle, sheep and hogs, feather bed and furniture, riding chair and all other property...
Benjamin Gordon   Sarah Hunter
Sarah Norfleet

50 9 Jan 1799--James Freeman and wife, Selah, to Charles Powell 37 pds 10 sh...25 acres bought of Jesse Ward, beginning at pine

on George Outlaw's line, along his line to said Ward's, with his
line to Jacob Outlaw's land and along his line to Poly Bridge Branch,
down run...
Riddick Trotman   James Freeman
Aug Ct 1799   Selah Freeman

52 11 Nov 1799--William King to Isaac Pipkin Sr...375 pds...500
acres beginning at popular near run of Cypress Swamp, Dunn's corner,
NE on said line and Sumner's line to litewood stake, corner of John
Lang's land, thence SE to post oak, Henry Speight's corner, to main
road and crossing to Thomas Barnes' corner, SW to aforesaid swamp and
down run...
Isaac Pipkin Jr.   William King
Henry Lee
Henry Goodman
Nov Ct 1799

53 19 Dec 1797--Timothy Walton to Levin Duer...60 pds...Negro Savory.
William Volentine   Tim'y Walton
Alex. Volentine
Nov Ct 1799

54 22 Aug 1799--Mathias Willey of Bertie Co. to Hillory Willey...$480
163 acres left to him in his father's will, beginning at corner of
Jonathan William's land near mouth of branch issuing out of Knotty
Pine Swamp, up run and binding on said Williams' line to Elisha Cross'
line, on his line to Jacob Walters , dec. corner popular, to said
Hillory's own line and along swamp and down run...
Henry(X)Griffin   Mathias Willey
Jitty Griffin
Nov Ct. 1799

55 1 Nov 1799--James B. and Jethro Sumner to Thomas Riddick...55 pds
50 acres beginning at persimmon tree marked for corner in said James'
line on SE side of Honey Pot Road, along Honey Pot Swamp to White Pot
Swamp, running to Beaverdam Swamp and to Bennetts Creek, to said
Riddick's line and on his line to his brother, James' line...
Mills R. Fields   James B. Sumner
Nov Ct 1799

56 21 Aug 1799--William Harriss to Peggy Cunningham...100 pds...Neg-
ro man Volentine...
John Glover   William Harriss
Milly Odom
Nov Ct 1799

57 27 Feb 1799--Aaron, Milley, Levi, Leviney and Aaron Maner Jr.
of Edgecomb Co. to Charney Curl...$100...57 acres allotted to Mary
Maner, wife of Aaron Maner Sr., out of real estate of Demsey Langston, dec., beginning at corner maple on N side of Cypress Swamp,
running by line of marked trees NE to corner red oak in James Gatling's line, NW to corner black oak, SW along row of marked trees
to corner ash in aforesaid swamp and down run...
William Vann   Aaron Maner
Zachariah Maner   Milley Maner
Nov Ct 1799   Levy Maner
                                             Levinia Maner
                                             Aaron Maner

58 14 Jan 1799--George Lassiter to Aaron Lassiter...$85...70 acres on W side of Deep Gutt beginning at water oak above Pearces' corner, down gut to old road binding on Moses Lassiter's line and Bond's land to said George's line and along his line to black gum and along Abner Pearces' line...
Rich'd Bond
Hance Lassiter   George Lassiter
Nov Ct 1799

60 20 Mar 1799--Richard Odom and wife, Elizabeth, of Edgecomb Co. to Isaac Langston...50 pds...47 acres beginning at water oak in Rogers Branch, along row of marked trees to corner pine in old line and along that line to branch, to corner pine in John Parker's line and along branch to Rogers Branch, to main run and down branch...
William Vann   Richard(O)Odom
Levy Maner   Elizabeth(X)Odom
Elisha Landen
Nov Ct 1799

61 3 Jun 1797--Joseph Dilday of Hertford Co. to Isaac Pipkin Jr... 50 pds...Negro woman Amey...
William Goodman   Joseph Dilday
Benjamin Barnes
Nov Ct 1799

62 7 Nov 1799--John Ellis to Nathaniel Newsom...150 pds...Negro women Hannah and Ledday and girl Amey...
Henry Meroney   John Ellis
Willis Woodley
Nov Ct 1799

63 7 Nov 1799--John Ellis to Nathaniel Newsom...horse $60, mare and colt $75, bed and furniture $30, bed and furniture $22, yoke of oxen $40, cow and yearling $15, 23 head hogs $100, 60 bbls. Indian corn $120, beaufat $10, 12 plates $4 and 4 basons $2...
Henry Meroney   John Ellis
Willis Woodley
Nov Ct 1799

64 7 Nov 1799--John Ellis to Nathaniel Newsom...100 pds...100 acres known as White Oak Neck beginning at gum at ditch adjoining John Brinkley's line, NE along Elisha Brinkley's to maple adjoining Sim. Brinkley, down ditch E to maple adjoining John Cowper's land and SE...
Henry Meroney   John Ellis
Willis Woodley
Nov Ct 1799

65 7 Nov 1799--John Ellis to Nathaniel Newsom...75 pds...50 acres of desert land known as Third Ridge on SW side adjoining John Small's land...
Henry Meroney   John Ellis
Willis Woodley
Nov Ct 1799

66 5 Nov 1799--Micajah Riddick Sr. and Micajah Riddick Jr. to Anthony Mathews...120 pds...80½ acres, two tracts beginning at pine in Timothy Lassiter's line, corner tree in Moses Kittrell's new patent, NE to

Lewis Walters and along his line SE to Isaac Miller's line, to Timothy Lassiter, dec. line and running W; other tract joins land of said Walters, Samuel Baker, dec. and others...
Hy. Hudgins   Micajah Riddick Sr.
James Small   Micajah Riddick Jr.
J.W. Voight
Nov Ct 1799

68 15 Jan 1799--Jesse Parker to Willis Brown...100 pds...56 acres beginning at white oak and running SE to stake, thence NE to gum in back swamp, to corner tree of Polson's, to road and down it to Bennetts Creek...
John Marshall   Jesse Parker
Thomas Marshall
Nov Ct 1799

69 18 Nov 1799--David and Elizabeth Bullock to Timothy Walton...$180 100 acres beginning at new road near William Draper's line, running W to Old Bennetts Creek Road and down it to red oak in George Williams' corner, SE to new road and along it...
John S. Parker   David Bullock
Docton Bagley   Elizabeth(X)Bullock
William Baker testified said Elizabeth
signed deed freely. Nov Ct 1799

71 1 Oct 1799--Thomas Trotman to Henry Walton...$160...80 acres joining road at Long Causway, beginning at pine in said Walton's line, by line of marked trees to a pine, formerly Demsey Trotman, dec. line, to Jacob Bagley, dec. corner pine near road and along road...
Elisha Trotman   Thomas Trotman
Noah Hill
Nov Ct 1799

72 1 Mar 1799--Amos Lassiter to Thomas Smith...25 pds...50 acres beginning at sweet gum, corner tree between William Cleaves and said Amos, being known line of Micajah Riddick Jr., to corner pine of Timothy Lassiter and along his line to corner pine in White Pot, by line of marked trees and through pecosin to Jonathan Williams' line, to black gum in said Cleaves' line; being survey taken by Samuel Smith.
Richard Smith   Amos(X)Lassiter
Anthony Smith
Nov Ct 1799

74 16 May 1799--Micajah Riddick Jr. to Thomas Smith...25 pds...25 acres on head of Cypress Pond, beginning at white oak, George Allen and William Cleaves corner, binding Cleaves' line N to gum, SE along row of marked trees to water oak, Henry Smith's corner and along said Thomas' line...
Richard Smith   Micajah Riddick Jr.
Sam'l Smith
Pa. Hegerty
Nov Ct 1799

75 1 Jun 1798--Caleb Polson to his son, John...deed of gift...150 acres whereon said Caleb lives...
Jethro Benton   Caleb(X)Polson
Joseph Jno. Sumner
Noc Ct 1799

76 14 Mar 1798--Amos Parker to Jethro Benton...30 pds...26 acres be-
ginning at popular corner of said Benton's, along small branch near
public road, SW and along line of marked trees NW to a marked sass-
afras in run of said branch...
Miles Benton
Jethro Sumner   Amos(+)Parker
James B. Sumner
Nov Ct 1799

77 19 Nov 1799--John Polson to Timothy Walton...25 pds...30 acres
beginning at red oak on side of main road that leads to Winton, binding on Gen'l. Lawrence Baker's line, to old Bennetts Creek Road and
down road to fork near William Polson's and along road...
Richard Rawls   John Polson
George Outlaw
Nov Ct 1799

78 22 Jan 1798--Moses Lassiter to Demsey Jones...25 pds...20 acres
beginning at water oak in branch near path, up path to Abner Lassi-
ters, NW by line of marked trees to gum in branch...
Pa. Hegerty   Moses Lassiter
Frederick(X)Lassiter
Nov Ct 1799

79 24 Dec 1799--Jonathan Lassiter and Demsey Jones to Sarah Riddick
of Perquiman Co...105...Negro girl Selah...
Lassiter Riddick   Jonathan Lassiter
Job Riddick   Demsey(X)Jones
Feb Ct 1800

80 17 Feb 1800--Jethro Sumner, sheriff, to Josiah Collins of Edenton
...165 pds 4 sh 8 pn...Negro Kitt belonging to Josiah Granbery and
sold by court order to satisfy William Felton's writ against him
for debts...
Thomas Johnson   Jethro Sumner
Feb Ct 1800

81 5 Jul 1799--Joseph John and Jethro Sumner to Kincheon Norfleet...
$250...Negro woman Dinah and her child Patt...
Almedia Godwin   Joseph Jno. Sumner
Polley Sumner
Feb Ct 1800

82 31 Dec 1799--Jonathan Roberts, guardian of heirs of William Lewis,
dec. to William Hinton...180 pds...88 acres beginning at popular near
branch near Hinton's house on S side of main road, along road to Booths
line, along that line to post oak, Thomas Marshall's corner on land of
said Marshall and Murphy, to George Outlaw's corner, to Jethro Mel-
tears, to David Harrells corner gum, NW to road and along it to
courthouse, thence running SW...
John Hudgins   Jonathan Roberts
John Roberts
Feb Ct 1800

84 20 Dec 1799--Jethro Sumner, sheriff, to Josiah Ellis of Nansemond
Co., Va...7 pds 2 sh 6 pn...land of Kedar Wiggens joining line of
James Knight and Joseph Hare, and sold by court order to satisfy debts.
Jesse B. Benton   Jethro Sumner
James(X)Ellis
Feb Ct 1800

86 15 Feb 1800--John Eure to Jesse Taylor...52 pds 10 sh...25 acres
called Little Cypress on S side of Cypress Swamp, beginning at black
oak, corner tree of Mills Landen, W on said Taylor's line to corner
tree of said Eure, along his line of marked trees to corner pine
and along Israel Beeman's line of marked trees to said Taylors...
Benjamin Beeman   John(X)Eure
Polley Beeman   Ann(X)Eure
Feb Ct 1800

87 19 May 1798--Soloman Hobbs to Simon King...35 pds...16 acres, part
of tract belonging to Jacob Hobbs, dec...
George Eason   Soloman(X)Hobbs
Samuel (X)Hobbs
Feb Ct 1800

89 20 May 1799--William Rea of Murfreesborough to William Crafford Jr.
5 bbls apple brandy...5 acres for fishery and part of tract bought of
John and William Cowper and patented by Benjamin Harrell, beginning at
mouth of Mud Creek at marked black gum, through pecosin to water edge...
William Crafford   William Rae
Joseph Crafford
Jesse(X)Brittain
Feb Ct 1800

90 20 Jul 1799--Hertford Co., William Rae of Murfreesborough to
William Crafford to clear and make landing with free access...½ acre
patent out of 70 acres at head of Mud Creek on right hand side as
one goes toward Barfield's Fishery into Gates Co....
Jesse R. Cross   William Rae
Joseph Crafford
Feb Ct 1800

91 24 Nov 1798--Richard Bond to Levin Dure...$300...Negro man Abram...
Jos. Granbery   Rich'd Bond
John Granbery
Feb Ct 1800

92 16 Aug 1798--Henry Eborn Sears to Jethro Sumner...65 pds...Negro
girl Mason...
William Walters   Eborn Sears
Jesse B. Benton
Feb Ct 1800

93 20 Sep 1799--William King to David Cross...$100...67 acres be-
ginning at elm in said Cross' line, Hooks Patent, N to white oak
on edge of low ground, NW to hill, SW to Pine Swamp and along Cross'
line; being patent granted to Thomas Barnes...
Demsey Williams   William King
Peggy(X)Cross
Abel Cross
Feb Ct 1800

94 23 Dec 1799--David Small to James Small...$___...yoke of oxen,
cart and wheels, 18 hogs, 10 bbl. corn, crop of corn, gun, work tools,
tarkiln, 2 feather beds and furniture, household and kitchen furniture...
K. Ballard   David Small
Sam'l. Harrell
Feb Ct 1800

95 23 Mar 1799--James and Jethro Sumner to Thomas Riddick...55 pds...
50 acres on N side of Bennetts Creek beginning at persimmon tree at
road on N side of Honey Pot Swamp, down side of swamp, by line of
marked trees to White Pot Swamp and up swamp to N side of crossing,
to said Riddick's line...
John Roberts   Jas. B. Sumner
David Bullock   Jethro Sumner
Feb Ct 1800

96 1 Feb 1800--Andrew Woodley of Virginia to James Costen...$500...
200 acres bought of James Hodges, lying on Bennetts Creek on S side
of main road leading to courthouse and adjoining John Hunter and
Amos Lassiter, running by line of marked trees to mouth of Iron Mine
Branch to line of Willis Woodley, to Deep Gutt and along run W to
Bennetts Creek...
Robert Riddick   Andrew Woodley
Isaac Costen
Willis Woodley
Feb Ct 1800

98 13 Feb 1800--Sion Boyce of Northampton to Matta Mathews...$160
67 acres beginning at pine, William Walters' corner, running by line
of marked trees NE to black oak stump, Isaac Walters' corner, on his
line NW to corner post oak...
Hy. Hudgins   Sion Boyce
Nicholas Nerney
Abraham Smith
Feb Ct 1800

99 17 Jan 1800--Timothy Freeman to Willis Sparkman...$100...50 acres
beginning at cypress on N side of Horsepen Swamp, along line of marked
trees to red oak corner in Jacob Outlaw's line, to corner pine in Elisha H. Bond's line, to said swamp...
James Walton   Timothy Freeman
James Freeman
Feb Ct 1800

101 19 Feb 1799--John Hudgins of Perquiman Co. to John Roberts...105
pds...105 acres beginning at beech and chinkapen in side of Bennetts
Creek Pecosin above Hinton's old landing, SE to small gum and ash in
Jonathan Nichol's line, along his line NW to Demsey Jones' line, to
popular in Abraham Riddick and said Jones' corner, down branch to
Bennetts Creek...
Seth Roundtree   Jno. Hudgins
Jo. Riddick
Feb Ct 1800

102 27 Dec 1798--John Hayse to Miles Lassiter...1/3 Indian corn
yearly for rental on 20 acres for 10 years, beginning at pine sapling
on main road on S side of Bennetts Creek, down William Hayes' line,
to creek swamp, to mouth of branch and up branch...
Abm. Riddick   John(J H) Hayse
John Phillips
Feb Ct 1800

104 18 Feb 1800--Jesse Taylor to Kindred Parker...43 pds 15 sh...12½
acres beginning at black oak, corner tree of Mills Landing and said

Taylor, thence running line of marked trees with said Landing's line to red oak, corner tree, along Taylor's line to white oak, corner tree of said Taylors to a water oak, another corner...
John Parker   Jesse Taylor
Whitmill Eure
Elisha Harrell
Feb Ct 1800

105 15 Feb 1799--Jacob Spivey to Miles Hill...$200...50 acres beginning at white oak on branch on N side of road that leads from Timothy Freeman's to Bennetts Creek Road, NW across small neck of land to said branch, to John B. Walton's line and along his line S to land of heirs of Polly Freeman, dec. with their line NE...
Timothy Freeman   Jacob Spivey
Guy Hill
Feb Ct 1800

107 2 Feb 1798--William Harriss to Judah Phelps...spinning yearly of one pound of 700 thread for rental on 5 acres beginning at foot of John Duke's path...
John Riddick   William Harriss
Salley Riddick
Feb Ct 1800

108 14 Mar 1800--James Baker to Jesse Rogerson of Perquiman Co...18 pds 10 sh...75 acres of desert land, part of patent of 650 known as Pine Noles, joining SE most corner on Joseph Hurdle's line...
Josiah(I)Rogerson   James Baker
Norman King
May Ct 1800

109 1 Apr 1800--Blake Baker to Henry Eborn Sears...150 pds...100 acres beginning at white oak, William Matthew's corner, on his line to Lassiter's, to Benjamin Baker's corner pine, along his line to Demsey William's line and along his line...
William Kittrell   Blake Baker
Pa. Hegerty
May Ct 1800

110 13 Nov 1799--William King to Henry Goodman...$850...620 acres beginning at white oak, corner tree of Francis Speight's, along his line SE to chinquepin oak, along line to Burrell Griffin's corner, on his line SW to line of David Cross' to his elm corner, to corner pine on Sand Banks, to Pine Swamp and down it to gum in Abel Cross' line, to Blake Baker's black oak corner tree, N along Cross' line to swamp, NE to Henry Speight and Jesse Saunders' corner...
Elizabeth(X)King   William King
William Goodman
May Ct 1800

111 21 Feb 1800--William Harriss to Richard Brothers...100 pds... Negro Man Stephen...
Nicholas Nerney   William Harriss
John(X)Duke Sr.
May Ct 1800

112 17 May 1799--Abraham Curle to John Vann...110 pds...150 acres, part of three patents, one granted to Jesse Barnes and Cyprian Cross

24 Oct 1756, one to Francis Speight 17 Jul 1743 and the third to
Callum Ross 21 Feb 1738, beginning at a pine in said Vann's corner,
that was formerly a corner between Vann, Hargrove, Vaughan and Harrell, thence along Vann's line to corner pine in Odom's line, along
that line to gum in Cross Swamp, down swamp and across at black gum,
to Cross' holly corner, up line of marked trees to said Curle's corner and along his line to head of Long Branch, to a black gum, James
Landing's corner, to his pine corner and along line of marked trees
to Vann's corner pine...
James(Ja.)Curle   Abraham(X)Curle
Riddick Cross
May Ct 1800

114 17 Mar 1800--Benjamin Gordon to David Rice...75 pds...Negro
girl Bridget...
James Gregory   Benj'm. Gordon
K. Ballard
May Ct 1800

114 20 Oct 1798--Henry Hobbs to Icabod Jordon..$2 per acre...50 acres
beginning at post oak, corner of William Hurdle and Thomas Hobbs, along Hurdle's line to William Kelly's, to George Eason's, along Levy
Eason's line to marked pine by side of broad path that runs across
Hobbs' fence, to William and Thomas Hobbs' line...
John Kelley   Henry(X)Hobbs
May Ct 1800

115 16 Jun 1800--Thomas Smith to James Bond...50 pds...50 acres beginning at run of Bennetts Creek on N side binding on Jethro Sumner's
land, along his line to post oak, line tree between him and said
Smith, to sweet gum in branch, to said creek and down run...
Henry Smith   Thomas Smith
Richard Smith
Hy. Hudgins
May Ct 1800

117 11 Feb 1800--Hance Hayes to Mills R. Field...30 pds...23 acres
on NW side of Bennetts Creek beginning at gum in swamp, along Thomas
Riddick's line W to pine corner of said Riddick and James Hayes, SW
to black oak, corner tree of Harmon Hayes, to swamp and up swamp...
William Hayes   Hance Hays
Elisha Hayes
May Ct 1800

119 17 Apr 1800--Jethro Sumner, sheriff, to Hardy Murfree of Hertford Co...203 pds...fishery and 225 acres sold by court order from
Halifax Co. to satisfy writ for debts brought by William Amis against
said Murfree and William Rae and signed by Lovat Burges, Halifax Co.
clerk. Said fishery is located on Chowan River...
Riddick Cross   Jethro Sumner
David Dickinson
May Ct 1800

121 1 Apr 1800--Henry Eborn Sears to Blake Baker...100 pds...125
acres beginning at Kittrell's line on side of main road, to Patrick
Hegerty's corner sweet gum, along his line to William Matthew's line,
to Demsey Williams' line, to main road and along road; also tract of

55 acres in pocosin taken up by Samuel Baker, dec., adjoining Moses Boyce and Kittrells...
William Kittrell
Pa. Hegerty
              H. Eborn Sears

122 10 Jun 1799--Bond Minchew to Kedah Hinton...$50...20 acres of woodland beginning at pine in Hinton's line, by line of marked trees to post oak, said Bond's corner, on said line to corner white oak of Isrel Minyard's and along his line...
              Bond Minchew
Jacob Hinton
Pa. Hegerty
May Ct 1800

123 4 Feb 1800--Andrew Woodley of Virginia to Isaac Costen...$300...
44 acres on Watery Swamp beginning at pine tree on side of main road at head of branch, down run to gum near spring, through cornfield S and bordering on swamp to large oak on side of road at foot of bridge and up swamp to William Bond's fence, to branch near cosway N to main road...
Jethro Sumner
James Costen   Andw. Woodley
May Ct 1800

125 17 May 1800--Elisha Hunter to Abraham Hurdle...$1500...518 acres on W side of main desert beginning at James Jones corner tree in mouth of Great Branch, along run to pine, formerly Mills Riddick's now Josiah Briggs, along his line to Moses Briggs' line, to Cypress Branch and down branch and binding on Jacob Pearces' to Soloman Eason's, to Hardy Easons, to Frederick Easons, to fork of Watery Branch, to desert and excluding 1 acre for mill...
Tim. Walton
David Bullock   Elisha Hunter
May Ct 1800

127 1 May 1800--Joseph Riddick to Elisha Hunter...160 acres patented 2 Dec 1797 to comply with agreement made by said Riddick and Col. Thomas Hunter who paid entry money and said Thomas by his will gave land to said Elisha; beginning at James Jones corner tree in mouth of Great Branch on W side of desert, running E to juniper and SW to desert...
David Rice   Jo. Riddick
Simon Stallings
Abram. Hurdle
May Ct 1800

128 9 Sep 1799--Miles Benton to Seth Morgan...$300...Negro woman Siller...
John Gwin   Miles Benton
Abraham Benton
May Ct 1800

129 4 Mar 1799--David Jones to Jacob Parker Jones...$150...farm let for 10 years of plantation whereon said David now lives...
Jacob Sumner Powell   David(X)Jones
John Powell Jr.   Jacob Parker(X)Jones
John Powell
May Ct 1800

130 3 Mar 1800--Frederick Blanshard to Timothy Freeman...$450...150
acres given to him in will of Absolum Blanshard, on side of Pond Bra-
nch, binding on Timothy Walton's mill swamp and John B. Walton's line
and down Pond Branch...
John Hofler   Frederick Blanshard
John Marshall
Thos. Marshall
May Ct 1800

131 10 Mar 1800--William Powell to William Sumner...50 pds...18 acres
on S side of Loosing Swamp, beginning at pine stump in Hinton's line,
running SE to water oak in said line, NE to pine in James Powell's
line, E to pine in Robert Powell's line and NE...
John Small   William Powell
John Powell
May Ct 1800

133 12 Mar 1800--William Gatling Jr. to William Gatling Sr...30 pds...
50 acres beginning at popular in Aron Odom's line as he sold to Arthur Willey, dec., from thence running N to Great Branch, up branch
to line of marked trees and along that line to land that Henry Dilday, dec. sold to John Raws, running that line to Gough Folly Branch
and up branch...
Amos Dilday   William Gatling Jr.
Henry Goodman
May Ct 1800

134 21 Jan 1800--Demsey O. Jones to Frederick Lassiter...50 pds...20
acres beginning at water oak, corner in Deep Gut, running old road
and binding on Abner Lassiter and Abner Pearce's line, to said gut...
Mills R. Field   Demsey(X)O. Jones
Kedar(X)Hinton
May Ct 1800

134 10 May 1799--Joseph Jno. Sumner to Abraham Morgan...$60...Neg-
ro man Tartey...
Micajah Riddick Jr.   Joseph Jno. Sumner
Jethro Sumner
May Ct 1800

134 1 Sep 1800--State of North Carolina to John Cowper...10 pds per
100 acres...10 acres beginning at cypress, said Cowper's corner tree,
on John Norfleet's marsh survey, E to Jethro Ballard's, SW to forked
maple, Ballard's corner, to Cowper's line, patented by William Jones
and NW...
Will White, sec. No. 133   B. Williams
Isaac Pipkin, clerk

136 18 Aug 1800--Samuel Taylor and wife, Sarah, to Jonathan Williams...
$500...133 acres beginning at Halon Williams' corner in Knotty Pine
Swamp, on his line to main road, to Sumner's line, to said swamp and
along swamp...
Pa. Hegerty   Samuel Taylor
Lewis Walters   Sarah(X)Taylor
Jethro Sumner testified said Sarah
signed deed freely. Aug Ct. 1800

137 14 Jul 1800--Jeremiah Speight and James Costen to William Baker...

$300...Negro man George...
Mary(X)Duke
John Speight   Jeremiah Speight
Aug Ct 1800   James Costen

138 26 May 1800--Jonathan Williams to John Cuff Jr...40 pds...100 acres beginning at red oak, Jonathan Smith and Micajah Phelps' corner, binding on Phelps' line to Cleaves' line, along Thomas Smith and James Knight's land on White Pot to Gen'l Baker's line and along his line...
Pa. Hegerty   Jonathan Williams
Elisha Williams
Jesse Arline
Aug Ct 1800

139 23 Dec 1799--James Piland to Willis Piland...100 pds...100 acres beginning at cypress on main run of Coles Creek, along Brooks' line to white oak stump, thence along Baker's line to corner pine, along Peter Piland's line to line of James Piland's orphans, to Thomas Piland, dec. and along his line to water oak on main run of creek...
Asa Harrell   James Piland
Thomas Cullens
Aug Ct 1800

140 5 Nov 1799--Micajah Riddick Sr. to Micajah Jr...60 pds...Negro women Cate and Sall...
Hy Hudgins   Micajah Riddick Sr.
Ruth(X)Duke
Aug Ct 1800

140 12 Aug 1800--Andrew Woodley of Isle of Wight, Va. to Robert Riddick...$250...50 acres on main road from Edenton to Suffolk, adjoining Richard Briggs, being tract Willis Woodley bought of said Briggs, 8 Jun 1799, beginning at oak on side of road, to large white oak, along line of marked trees and across large ditch to cleared ground, to corner tree between William Hinton and said Briggs, N to road, to slash near said Riddicks...
Alex'r. Miller   Andw. Woodley
Henry Goodman
Aug Ct 1800

142 31 Jul 1800--Peter Harrell to Elisha Harrell...100 pds...50 acres, part of patent granted to Capt. Henry Baker 1 May 1728, beginning at gum near run of Cypress Swamp, near Samuel Taylor's corner tree, with his new line to pond in Stephen Eure's line and along his line to a branch and down it to main run of said swamp and along swamp...
Lewis Sparkman   Peter Harrell
Samuel Taylor
Annis(X)Harrell

143 10 Jun 1800--David Jones of Chowan Co. to Jacob Parker Jones...$243...150 acres, whereon his father lived and willed to him, beginning at sweet gum, line tree of John Cowper in Flatt Branch near Dogwood Neck, running N to pine in Kinchen Norfleets, binding his line to Elisha Hare's line, to patent granted to John Powell
Kedar Ballard   David(+)Jones
James Small
Henry Meroney
Aug Ct 1800

145 19 Mar 1799--Ezekiah Jones to Edward Parker...72 pds...Negro boy Stephen...
Thomas Parker   Ezekiah(X)Jones
Seth Eason
Aug Ct 1800

146 14 Aug 1800--Israel Beeman to Abraham Beeman...92 pds 10 sh...
80 acres beginning at sycamore in John Umphlet's former line, SW to post oak, E along road as Fort Island Road goes, to Little Cypress, to mouth of Hawtree Branch, to John Parker's line and up his line to corner tree, E along Job_e_ Umphlet's former line...
Benjamin Beeman   Israel Beeman
Charles Eure
Aug Ct 1800

147 8 Oct 1799--Jethro Sumner, sheriff, to Jacob Powell...34 pds 7 sh...Negro boy Kedar belonging to John Powell, and sold by court order to satisfy execution issued at instance of Levin Duer against him for debts...
Kedar Ballard   Jethro Sumner
Aug Ct 1800

147 14 Aug 1800--Hezekiah Jones to James Jones...$72½...14½ acres beginning at mulberry tree between said parties, running S to gum, E to red oak in Loosing Swamp, to Jethro Ballard's line, to water oak, line tree of said Ballard and James and W...
K. Ballard   Hezekiah(X)Jones
John Powell
Washington Jones
Aug Ct 1800

148 31 Jan 1800--Esther Jones to Abraham Morgan...130 pds...Negro woman Rose...
Micajah Riddick   Esther(X)Jones
Simon Hare Jones
Aug Ct 1800

149 3 Apr 1800--Jethro Sumner, sheriff, to Esther Jones...$100...
Negro boy Peter, belonging to Willis Woodley, and sold by court order to satisfy execution against him issued by Levin Duer for debts...
Micajah Riddick   Esther(X)Jones
Abraham Morgan
Aug Ct 1800

150 1 Sep 1800--State of North Carolina to Jethro Sumner...30 sh per 100 acres...60 acres beginning at red oak in Thomas Smith's line on N side of Bennetts Creek Swamp, down swamp to George Williams' line, S up run and NW...
Will White, sec.   B. Williams
Isaac Pipkin, PR No. 132

151 11 Dec 1800--State of North Carolina to Henry Goodman...10 pds per 100 acres...100 acres beginning at pine on N side of Outside Swamp near Fort Island Bridge, Stephen Eure's corner, with his line NW and along pocosin side to pine, Isaac Langston's corner, thence along pocosin to center of 3 pines near Little Island Path, into pocosin SW to cypress in branch of Outside Swamp and down branch...
Will White, sec.   B. Williams
No. 136

152 10 Jun 1799--State of North Carolina to John Saunders...30 sh per 100 acres...35 acres beginning at pine corner of said Saunders and Barrs, SE to pine in James Parker's corner, on his line NW to William Barr's corner...No. 126
Will White, sec.   William R. Davie

153 1 Sep 1800--State of North Carolina to John Powell...30 sh per 100 acres...50 acres beginning at Luke Sumner's line below Powells Mill on N side of Orapeak Swamp, crossing swamp and binding on Sumner's patent, S to Norfleet's line, up run NE to marked pine on N side and binding on high land...
Will White, sec. No. 129   E. Williams
I. Pipkin, PR

154 11 Dec 1800--State of North Carolina to William Baker...30 sh per 100 acres...20 acres, balance of an island in Chowan River, opposite petty shore not surveyed by William Crafford and called Great Island, beginning in Crafford's corner, across island, up Cow Island Creek to W side...
Will White, sec. No. 134   B. Williams

155 11 Dec 1800--State of North Carolina to William Baker...10 pds per 100 acres...5 acres beginning at low corner of tract granted to Patrick Garvey, William Crafford and Dr. Brown_ on E side of Chowan River, on side of island creek...
Will White, sec. No 135   B. Williams

156 1 Sep 1800--State of North Carolina to John Baker...10 pds per 100 acres...170 acres on E side of Coles Creek beginning at maple, Spivey's patent corner, NE crossing mouth of Troy Swamp, up swamp to hickory, George Williams and Pilands corner, into run, SW to main road.
Will White, sec. No. 131   B. Williams

157 10 Jun 1799--State of North Carolina to Amos Speight...30 pds per 100 acres...48 acres beginning at pine, Judith Hill's corner in Coleman's patent, on her line SE to Ephriam Blanshards and on his line W to Indian line, NE to run of branch to Coleman's patent...
Will White, sec. No. 125   Wm. R. Davie

158 1 Sep 1800--State of North Carolina to Abraham Riddick...30 sh per 100 acres...250 acres beginning at Willis Brown's line, running up side of swamp binding on high land to gum in George Williams and Jethro Sumner's line, into swamp SW and down run to Lassiter's patent to Jacob Hease's line and down run to said Browns...
Will White, sec. No. 127   B. Williams

159 1 Sep 1800--State of North Carolina to James B. Sumner...10 pds per 100 acres...50 acres beginning on E side of Honey Pot Swamp in main road, along road to W side, to Bennetts Creek, thence crossing mouth of Honey Pot to high land and up side to said Sumner's line...
Will White, sec. No. 128   B. Williams

160 20 Jun 1800--Robert Powell to William Sumner...26 pds...26 acres of woodland beginning at red oak in John Powell's line, on his line and by line of marked trees to pine, Sumner's corner, on his line to pine stump in Hinton's line and along ditch E...
David Small   Robert Powell
Hezekiah(X)Jones
Nov Ct 1800

161 5 Aug 1800--Josiah Parker to Riddick Trotman...$500...200 acres on E side of Bennetts Creek pocosin in Robert Taylor's line, along line of marked trees to Horsepen Swamp and along swamp to Seth Roundtree's line, to pocosin and down side...
Thos. Freeman   Josiah(J.P.)Parker
Daniel(X)Eure

162 6 Jun 1800--John S. West, marshall for district of North Carolina, to Josiah Collins, the elder, of Edenton...$1540...170 acres belonging to Josiah Granbery and sold by order of court for debts recovered by John Field and Son 13 Nov 1799 in circuit court in Raliegh, Oliver Elsworth, chief justice and Francis Hawks, clerk. Said land is on W side of road leading from Edenton to Suffolk and S of said Granbery's dwelling house, and beginning at stake in lane, running SW and along road...
P. Browne
Arthur Jones   John S. West,
Alex. Miller   Marshall of North
Nov Ct 1800   Carolina

164 6 Sep 1800--Jethro Sumner to Luten Lewis...5 pds...Negro girl Mason...
Riddick Cross   Jethro Sumner
Edward Vann
Nov Ct 1800

165 23 Aug 1800--Benjamin Edwards of Northampton Co., guardian of William E. Webb, orphan, by order of court of Halifax Co. in 1799, to John Riddick...105 pds 11 sh...133 acres, part of said Webb's estate to satisfy demands against said estate. Land begins at pine, said Riddick's corner tree, running NE to Docton Riddick's corner red oak, SW to said John's corner pine stump, to pine and past fence.
Jo. Riddick   Benjamin Edwards
William Harriss
Jas. Barnes
Nov Ct 1800

166 16 Sep 1800--Hezekiah Jones to his children, deed of gifts, Daughter Mary Jones bed and furniture purchased from his father's estate and mare; to Son Benjamin plantation whereon he lives, reserving portion for his use until he arrives at age 21...
John Cowper Sr.   Hezekiah(X)Jones
Simeon Hare Jones
Mourning(X)Ellis
Nov Ct 1800

168 8 Aug 1800--Bray Saunders of Hertford Co. to Briant Saunders...$100...200 acres beginning at cycamore on side of creek, a corner tree of Barnard March and said Saunders, along March's line to Henry Lee's line and along his line to Jacob Walters, to John March's line, to Somerton Creek and down creek...
John Cross   Bray Saunders
Isaac Pipkin Jr.
Nov Ct 1800

169 11 Aug 1800--Priscilla Spivey to Abner Roundtree...$125...½ of 140 acres, formerly property of Moses Spivey, dec., beginning at

pine in Henry Baker's Buckland line in Wiggens Branch, up branch
to William Daniels' line to gum, NW to center of 3 trees and NW...
William Polson   Priscilla(X)Spivey
William Draper
Moses Davis
Nov Ct 1800

170 1 Sep 1800--James Sumner of Hertford Co. to Thomas Riddick...55
pds...50 acres beginning at persimmon tree marked for corner in James
B. Sumner's line on S side of Honey Pot Road, down side of swamp to
sweet gum and maple, to Beaverdam Swamp, to said Thomas' own line
and along his and his brother, James Riddick's line, to Honey Pot
Road...
Jethro Sumner   James Sumner
Jesse Southall
Nov Ct 1800

171 6 Jun 1800--George Lassiter to William Williams...37 pds 10 sh...
20 acres on W side of Watery Swamp beginning at tree, along Joseph Alphin's line to head of Rooty Branch, down run and by line of marked
trees to said Lassiter's line and along his line...
William Jas. Nuttall   George(X)Lassiter
John(X)Stepto   Rachal(X)Lassiter
Nov Ct 1800

173 21 Dec 1799--James Freeman to Thomas Freeman...1000 pds...150
acres beginning at mouth of Juniper branch, up branch to Aaron Blanshard's Bridge to gum at head, along Thomas Garrett's line to head
of Gum Swamp and down swamp to Cathren Creek and down creek...
Daniel(X)Your   James Freeman
James Outlaw
Nov Ct 1800

174 31 Oct 1800--Henry Hill to John B. Walton...30 pds...18 acres in
Indian Neck beginning at white oak, corner tree of James Robins, along
line W to maple corner of Richard Freeman, dec. and along said Walton's
line...
James Freeman   Henry(H)Hill
Matthew Murphy
Jethro Meltear
Nov Ct 1800

175 14 Nov 1800--Jesse Harrell to his son, Jesse...deed of gift...
100 acres, part of Horns Patent of 1718, NW side of Coles Creek, be-
ginning in patent between head of Sarum Creek and mouth of Cypress
Swamp, SW to Mile Pecosin binding on N side and along row of marked
trees to Coles Creek, to Sarum Creek, to patent line...
Asa Harrell   Jesse Harrell Sr.
Reuben Harrell
Nov Ct 1800

177 19 Aug 1800--Hardy Cross to son, John, both of Nansemond Co., Va.
deed of gift...180 acres purchased of Enos Rogers and Eborn Sears, be-
ginning at pine, formerly Joel Goodman's, now William Goodmans in
Goffs Folly Branch, along Goodman's line to pine, Brady's corner, along
Brady's line to William Warren's corner E along Warren's line to Elisha
Odom's, dec., thence along Odom's line to land of Walters' corner, to

James Goodman's corner pine, formerly Joel Goodman's and along his
line to main road...
Elisha Parker   Hardy Cross
Jesse Savage
Nov Ct 1800

178 11 Oct 1800--Samuel Taylor to Noah Morris...20 pds...10 acres
on Long Pond beginning at corner oak in Isaac Green's line, along
his line and said Taylor's line to corner pine of Mills Eure's and
along Eure's line and Elisha Harrell's line by line of marked trees...
Mills Eure   Samuel(X)Taylor
Mary(X)Eure
Lewis Eure
Nov Ct 1800

179 5 Feb 1800--John Hunter to William Lassiter...56 pds 5 sh...50
acres beginning at run of creek to black gum on side and binding on
Reuben Lassiter's line to Thoplas Hunter's line to run of creek...
William Bond   John Hunter
John Hill
Nov Ct 1800

180 6 Sep 1800--Cyprian Cross to Jethro Sumner...5 pds...Negroes
Dinah, Hannah and Flowar...
Edward Vann   Cyprian Cross
Riddick Cross
Jn. B. Sumner
Feb Ct 1801

181 2 Feb 1801--William Goodman, deputy sheriff, to Levin Duer...45
pds 10 sh 6 pn...Negro girl Tizzy, sold by court execution won by
Benjamin Gordon against Noah Hill...
Norman King   William Goodman
Feb Ct 1801

181 24 Nov 1800--Elijah Lyons to Ann Walton...$66...33 acres that
belonged to his wife, Melison, and given to her in division on Kat-
hren Creek...
Rach'l(+)Morgan   Elijah Lyons
Sarah(+)Lank   Milison(X)Lyons
Easter(X)Lilley
Feb Ct 1801

182 23 Aug 1800--Benjamin Edwards, guardian of William E. Webb, of
Northampton Co. to Levin Duer...265 pds 1 sh...318 acres part of said
Webb's estate beginning on E side of Bennetts Creek at a pine in Wal-
nut Neck Patent, William Hinton's, dec. corner tree near Isaac Read's
fence, with Hinton's line NE to holly in small branch, John Riddick's
fence, to Cypress Branch or Speight's Branch to John Duke's corner
tree just below road and down road to Walnut Neck Patent...
Jo. Riddick   Benj'n. Edwards
William Harris
Feb Ct 1801

184 27 Nov 1800--Josiah Granbery and Josiah Collins of Edenton,
Chowan Co. to Levin Duer...$384...Slave Mulatto named Lucy, 18 years...
Benja. Gordon   Josiah Granbery
Feb Ct 1801   Josiah Collins

185 29 Nov 1800--Josiah Granbery and wife, Ann, to Josiah Collins of Edenton...5 sh...231 acres, said Granbery having defaulted on conditions of indenture made 18 Apr 1789 for $4000, and purchased by said Collins at sale of marshall of district of North Carolina 23 May last, to satisfy judgment obtained by John Field and Son of Philadelphia. Said land is on E side of main road leading from Hunter's Mill to Folly, along road N to Hinton's or Woodley's line, to Mirey Branch and W to Bennetts Creek and along creek to beech, corner tree of said Collins...
John Granbery   Jos. Granbery
Alexn'r. Miller
Feb Ct 1801

187 29 Nov 1800--Inventory of goods and chattels of Josiah Granbery: bed bolster and pillows, pair of sheets, pillow case, 2 blankets, counterpane and bedstead in N room; bed bolster, pillow case, pair sheets, pillow, 2 double blankets, counterpane, 4 poster bedsteads with curtains, N room upstairs; bed bolster, pillows, pair sheets, cases, 2 double blankets, counterpane and bedstead in S room upstairs; bed, mattress, bolster, 2 pillows, pair sheets, pillow case, 2 blankets, coverlets and bedstead in S shed room; bed bolster, 2 pillows, pair sheets, 2 pillow cases, 2 blanket coverlets and beds in W room; bed bolster, pillow, pair sheets, pillow cases, pair blanket coverlet and bed in furthest W room; small table, cloth, dressing glass in N room upstairs; small table, cloth and glass in S shed room; table, cloth and glass in S room upstairs; candlesticks, bureau and looking glass in near W room; round table, square table, 14 black walnut chairs, 10 windsor chairs, arm stool chair, looking glass, 2 dining tables and chairs, 2 clothes chests, 11 pictures, queensware, earthen ware in closet, candlesticks, knives, large pot, 2 small pots with hooks, 2 pair andirons, 2 pair tongs, 2 shovels, poker, pair kitchen andirons, frying pan, shovel, pair tongs, spit, griddle, large iron pot, small pot, 2 Dutch ovens, kettle, frying pan, 2 gridirons, fork, kettle and stand, chaffing dish, 2 pine ironing tables and blanket, 2 smoothing irons with stands, 2 trays, tub, 3 pewter dishes, queens china dishes, everything in milk house, all kitchen furniture, 9 silver table spoons, large silver soup spoon, pair silver tongs, 6 silver teaspoons, tumbling cart and cart and apparatus theretoo, gridstove...
John Granbery   Jos. Granbery

188 29 Nov 1800--Inventory of Josiah Granbery: crop of fodder peas, flax cotton, potatoes, work tools, 34 head cattle, 30 head sheep, 100 hogs, 3 horses, yoke of oxen, cart with furniture, double riding chair, still, large pitch kettle, pr. large scales, 100 empty barrells, 3/4 seine and salt barrell delivered to Alexander Miller...
John Granbery   Jos. Granbery

190 29 Nov 1800--Inventory and husbandry of Josiah Granbery to Josiah Collins of Edenton by deed 18 Aug 1789...$3000...Slaves Ben, Will, Tartey, Sam, Jacob, Merrick, Dick, Lewis, Jerry, Ned, Jim, Isaac, Jack, Tom, Myles, Jude, Binah, Liza, Aggy and child Peg, Patt, Venus and child Amy, Amy Younger, Sciller, Susy, Hannah; said Myles having been delivered to Alexander Miller for use; Also for $1500... household furniture, crops and stock, bay horse having been delivered to said Miller. Said Collins having possessed himself of slaves Ned,

Jerry, Jacob, Isaac, Liz, Sarah, Amy, Benah and child, Hannah. Personal items...10 sh...
                Jos. Granbery
John Granbery
Alex'nr. Miller
Feb Ct 1801

194 29 Nov 1800--Josiah Granbery & Josiah Collins of Edenton, Chowan Co. to Alexander Miller, also of Edenton...$192.50...Negro Claressa.
John Granbery   Jos. Granbery
Nov Ct 1800   Josiah Collins

195 6 Oc6 1800--Richard Bond to Isaac Costen...$88...22 acres beginning at black gum in branch, down branch to run of Watery Swamp and up run to cycamore on side of main road to said Costen's corner...
Pa. Hegerty   Richard Bond
John Speight
Feb Ct 1801

196 16 Feb 1801--John Cowper to Benjamin Gordon...$18 2/3...3 3/4 acres, part of plantation whereon said Cowper lives, beginning on said Gordon's road at small post oak and gum, running SE down branch to N side of road and along road...
Open ct Feb 1801   John Cowper

197 17 Feb 1801--William Speight Jr. to Humphrey Hudgins...150 pds...
Negro Naney and her two sons, Jack and George...
Jesse Benton   William Speight
Noah Felton
Feb Ct 1801

197 17 Feb 1801--Thomas Freeman to Josiah Freeman...500 pds...125 acres beginning at pine on Mill Swamp, along line of marked trees to gum in Poler Bridge Branch, up run to oak on Outlaw's line, to gum in Juniper Branch and along branch...
Timothy Freeman   Thos. Freeman
Mills R. Fields

199 26 Jan 1801--William Harriss to Humphrey Hudgins...150 pds...
Negro George, the younger...
Levin Duer   William Harriss
Feb Ct 1801

199 30 Aug 1799--George Outlaw to James Baker...$105...15 acres in Indian Neck beginning at small red oak in old Ferry Road, along line of marked trees to Parkers, W down Parkers' line and S to road and along road...
Charles Powell   George(X)Outlaw
Riddick Trotman   George Outlaw Jr.
Feb Ct 1800

201 8 Dec 1800--George Lassiter to William Williams...50 pds...
40 acres beginning at gum in run of Bennetts Creek, Job Riddick's corner tree, along his line to corner tree on end of Richard Bond's Island, up side of Watery Swamp to branch issuing out of said swamp that divided said George and Jonathan Lassiter's land, into run of swamp and down to Bennetts Creek...
William Walters   George Lassiter
Feb Ct 1801

202 7 Jan 1799--Holoday Walton of Chowan Co. to Joseph Parker...62 pds 10 sh...Negro girl Penny...
Kedar(X)Hinton   Holloday Walton
Jeremiah Jordan
Feb Ct 1801

203 22 Dec 1800--Thomas and Timothy Freeman to James Jackson...$225... Negro man Soloman...
John Felton   Thos. Freeman
William Jackson   Timothy Freeman
Feb Ct 1800

203 28 Jan 1800--Moses Lassiter to Kedar Hinton...80 pds...80 acres beginning at post oak in Willis Woodley's road, running to pine, corner tree in Frederick Lassiter's line, along his line to gum in Deep Gut and up gut to water oak in Abner Lassiter's, down old road to Aaron Lassiters, to pine, corner tree in Demsey Bond's line, to pine corner of Israel Minyard's, to post oak in bottom, to water oak in gut and along gut...
John Hare   Moses(X)Lassiter
Jethro Meltear
Feb Ct 1801

205 12 Dec 1799--Levin Duer to Isaac Harrell...75 pds...Negro woman Pat...
Henry Meroney   Levin Duer
Feb Ct 1801

206 12 Dec 1800--William Mathews Sr. to Anthony Mathews...150 pds... 50 acres where he now lives and which he bought of William Walters, and 35 acres which he took up by survey, beginning at head of White Pot Pecosin at gum in Samuel Smith's, to corner tree in pecosin near Mathews Path, NE to white oak in Edward Sumners and Samuel Baker's corner, SW to Demsey Parker's line and along his line to said Smiths.
Clement R. Mathews   William(W)Mathews
Dread Mathews
Feb Ct 1801

208 21 Jan 1800--Frederick Lassiter to Demsey O. Jones..100 pds... 50 acres beginning at Tarkiln Branch and along run to back line and along line of marked trees...
Mills R. Fields   Frederick(X)Lassiter
Kedar(X)Hinton
Feb Ct 1801

209 3 Feb 1801--Noah Hill to Levin Duer...$333 1/3...Negro man Fill, 20 years old...
John Hoffler   Noah Hill
Rich'd Briggs
Feb Ct 1801

210 6 Oct 1800--Isaac Costen to William Speight Sr...300 pds...Negro woman Nancy and three children Mills, Milley and Perceller...
James Lassiter   Isaac Costen
Rich'd Bond
John Speight
Feb Ct 1801

210 10 Feb 1800--Abraham Pearce to William Pearce...175 pds...100

acres on S side of Fox Ridge Pecosin beginning at pine in Isaiah Riddick's line, corner tree of said William's, along his and Joseph Riddick's line, SE to line dividing tract sold and land whereon said William lives...
Jo. Riddick   Abraham(X)Pearce
Joseph Trotman
Nathan Riddick
Feb Ct 1801

211 17 Feb 1801--Alexander Miller of Edenton, Chowan Co. to Miss Nancy Granbery...5 sh...Negro slave Clarissa about 12 years, purchased at sale of Josiah Granbery's estate...
Thomas Johnson   Alex'r. Miller
Feb Ct 1801

212 6 Oct 1800--Mordecai Perry to Hardy and Soloman Eason...170 pds 16 sh 11 pn...200 acres whereon he lives joining lands of William Hurdle, Shadrack Felton, dec., Thomas Hobbs, Richard Mitchell, Edmund Hobbs and William Kelly running to Warwick Swamp...
Jo. Riddick   Mordecai Perry
Nathan Riddick
Joseph Trotman
Feb Ct 1801

213 27 Dec 1800--Samuel Harrell to Elisha Harrell...150 pds...85 acres known as Fort Island, part of patent granted to John Webb 1 April 1723, beginning at corner gum in Great Branch, running E to Cowpen Swamp, by line of marked trees to upper end of said Branch and down run...
Mills Eure   Samuel Harrell
Mary(X)Eure
Feb Ct 1801

214 6 Oct 1800--Mordacai Perry to Hardy and Soloman Eason...254 pds 12 sh...Negroes Cherry, Dick, Zade, Venus and Medrick...
Jo. Riddick   Mordecai Perry
Nathan Riddick
Joseph Trotman
Feb Ct 1801

215 1 Dec 1800--Aron Lassiter to William Speight Sr...106 pds 5 sh... Negro woman Hulday...
Allen Lassiter   Aron Lassiter
John Speight
Thomas Costen
Feb Ct 1801

215 16 Sep 1800--David Riddick to Isaac Harrell Sr...Negro woman Pheba and her child Adder...
Elisha Hunter   David Riddick
Feb Ct 1801

216 14 Feb 1801--Abraham Riddick to Robert Parker...5 pds...43 acres on N side of Bennetts Creek beginning in Willis Brown's line, running E up side of creek to main run to said Brown's line...
Ann(A.P.)Parker   Abraham Riddick
William(W.P.)Parker
Feb Ct 1801

217 1 Sep 1800--James Tugwell to James Vann...$300...50 acres whereon he lives on Knotty Pine Swamp, beginning at pine at mouth of a branch, up run and by line of marked trees to William Vann's line, along his line to corner, formerly a maple but now persimmon, to said swamp and up swamp...
Jonathan Parker   James Tuggel
James(P)Parker   Mary(X)Tuggel
Thomas Fryer
Feb Ct 1801

218 31 Dec 1800--William Speight Sr to Aron Lassiter...106 pds 5 sh...Negro girls Milley and Perciller...
Thomas Costen   William Speight
Allen Lassiter
John Speight
Feb Ct 1801

218 21 Oct 1800--Henry Smith to Abraham Smith...10 pds...2 acres beginning at hickory, line tree between said Henry and Jeremiah Speight, along Speight's line to said Henry's, to mulberry tree in field and along his line...
Jonathan Smith   Henry Smith
Nicholas Nerney
George(X)Allen
Feb Ct 1801

220 2 Sep 1800--William Harriss to Isaac Harrell Sr...75 pds...Negro man Will...
Samuel Harrell   William Harriss
Isaac Harrell Jr.
Feb Ct 1801

220 13 Mar 1800--Sarah Jones to Kedar Hinton...22 pds 10 sh...6 acres beginning at red oak in said Hinton's line, E to Joseph Parker's line, along his line SW to red oak in said Hinton's line, to black jack...
Jethro Meltear Jr.   Sarah(X)Jones
Demsey(X)Jones
Feb Ct 1801

222 28 Dec 1800--William Cleaves to Micajah Phelps...100 pds...two tracts of woodland; first one of 80 acres is on White Pot Swamp beginning at sweet gum on NE side of main road in William Williams' line, down road to pine corner, by line of marked trees to water oak in said Phelps' line, down run to other piece of 20 acres which begins at sweet gum in John Cuff's line and runs S to Phelps' line...
Wm. W. Riddick   William Cleaves
William Phelps
Feb Ct 1801

224 9 Oct 1800--Humphrey Hudgins to William Speight Sr...188 pds 15 sh...151 acres beginning near bank at center of three oaks, being corner between William P. Jamerson and Pugh's Orphans, SE on Pugh's line to Spanish oak, SW to road to post oak, corner tree between Jeremiah Speight and said Hudgins, N to Pugh's old patent and S...
Isaac Costen   Humphrey Hudgins
Rich'd Bond
John Speight
James Lassiter
Feb Ct 1801

225 28 Apr 1801--John Swan Parker and wife, Zilphia, to Simon Stallings...$130...32 acres on W side of Tuckalow Branch, beginning at red oak, Timothy Walton's corner tree, along his line to pine, corner made by division in said land, running line of marked trees between them and Mary Walton, to black gum in said branch to said Stalling's line...
Richard Rawls   John S. Parker
Mary(X)Walton   Zilpha(X)Parker
Amely(X)Rawls
May Ct 1801
Isaac Pipkin testified said Zilpha signed deed freely.

227 21 Mar 1801--Jethro Sumner, late sheriff, to John Cowper...7 pds 17 sh...128 acres of a larger tract of desert land belonging to John Fontain of Virginia, beginning at Camden Co. line near Sumner's back line and running SE to said line and NW; said land sold by court order to secure revenue for taxes...
May Ct 1801   Jethro Sumner

228 5 Mar 1801--Bray Saunders and Mary Bethea to Joseph Freeman...
227 pds 10 sh...105 acres beginning at pine corner tree in Henry and William Goodman and Henry Lee's lines, along said Goodman's lines to corner pine blowed up, to corner pine in Lee's line and along his line to persimmon tree in branch and down branch...
Abel Cross   Bray Saunders
David Freeman   Mary(X)Bethey
Mary Bethey
May Ct 1801

229 20 Feb 1801--Israel Minard to Moses Lassiter...60 pds...70 acres beginning at white oak, corner tree in Deep Gut, W along Amos Lassiter's line to post oak, corner tree in Bond Minchew's, along his line to Kedar Hinton's white oak in Demsey Bond's line, E to post oak in bottom, to white oak in Deep Gut and up gut...
Kedar(X)Hinton   Israel(X)Minyard
Thomas Marshall
May Ct 1801

231 18 Sep 1796--Willis Sparkman to Noah Morris...50 pds...25 acres in Cypress Swamp beginning at chenkerpin running SE through plantation to _simmon tree, to pine on branch, by line of marked trees to pine in Jesse Harrell's line to said swamp...
Stephen Harrell   Willis(X)Sparkman
Samuel Green
Aaron Harrell
May Ct 1801

232 1 Dec 1800--Sarah Forrest to Thomas Forrest...37 pds 10 sh...
1/3 of 100 acres which her husband, Henry Forrest, dec. died possessed..
William Speight   Sarah(S)Forrest
May Ct 1801

233 10 Jan 1801--Ann Parker to James Cross...$330...110 acres beginning at red oak on side of new road to Hawtree Branch, up branch and along line of marked trees SW...
Daniel Southall   Nancy(X)Parker
John Riddick
Robert Parker
May Ct 1801

235 14 Feb 1801--Israel Beeman to Benjamin Beeman...90 pds...100 acres beginning at sycamore by side of road that goes to Fort Island Bridge near Abraham Beeman's house, running E to pine corner in Charles Eure's line, S on his line to red oak, to Jesse Taylor's line, N to John Eure's, to run of Little Cypress Swamp, to Ft. Island road and up road...
Elijah Harrell   Israel Beeman
May Ct 1801

236 4 Nov 1800--William Harris to Jesse Benton..$230...Negro boy Jack...
Miles Benton   William(X)Harriss
Hy. Hudgins
May Ct 1801

237 25 Jul 1800--Josiah Parker to Timothy Freeman...50 pds...3 acres of high land, part of tract whereon he lives joining Cos_ Bridge of said Freeman's...
William Harriss   Josiah(#P)Parker
John B. Walton
May Ct 1801

238 20 May 1801--Miles Benton to David Cross...$60...30 acres on E side of Chowan River beginning at said Cross' line on river pecosin, down to Boyces Branch and up branch to little pecosin, to Cross' line.
Jesse R. Cross   Miles Benton
Cypn. Cross
May Ct 1801

239 9 Dec 1800--George Lassiter to David Harrell...10 pds...18 acres beginning at post oak, Bond's corner tree, along his line to corner pine in John B. Walton's line, along Abner Pearce's line to black gum, thence along Aaron Lassiter's line...
Jonathan Roberts   George(X)Lassiter
Jethro Meltear
James Baker
May Ct 1801

240 17 Jan 1801--Demsey Jones Sr. to Nathaniel and Joseph Jones... $100...69 acres, retaining rights of lifetime for himself and wife, Rachael, beginning at Jeremiah Jordon's corner tree, along David Harrell's line to Kedar Hinton's, up Flat Branch to gum corner between said land and Charles Smith, W to black gum in Cypress Branch and by line of marked trees to Deep Branch and up run...
Ann Parker   Demsey(X)Jones
Abraham Riddick
May Ct 1801

241 18 Oct 1800--Edith Walters to Mary Walters...100 pds...Negroes Ben and Vilot...
William Gatling Jr.   Edith(X)Walters
Jos. T. Morgan
May Ct 1801

242 8 Apr 1801--William Harriss to Micajah Riddick Jr...425 pds... 300 acres beginning at pine stump at head of Wildcat Branch, called Francis Pugh's corner on ridge land purchased of Edward Allen, running along main road to Dabseys Run, to said ridge land, to run of Bennetts Creek to said branch and up run...
Hy. Hudgins   William Harriss
John Harriss Johnson
May Ct 1801

244 2 Oct 1800--Seth Trotman to Joseph Parker...125 pds if found on other side of Rownoake River, if found on this side 150 pds...Negro man Sam...
John Hoffler
Jacob Spivey   Seth Trotman
Aug Ct 1801

245 11 Dec 1800--State of North Carolina to Abel Cross...30 sh per 100 acres...30 acres beginning at pine in run of Gum Swamp, Watsons corner in Winburn's line, up that line SE to pine, William King's corner, SW to edge of swamp, binding high land to run...
Will White, sec. No. 137   B. Williams

246 10 Dec 1801--State of North Carolina to James Norfleet..30 sh per 100 acres...45 acres beginning at pine on E side of Suffolk Road in Norfleet's line, SE to pine stump, Capt. Cowper's line, SW to Benjamin Gordon's N to Cowper's piney woods...
Will White, sec. No. 141   B. Williams

247 26 Dec 1801--State of North Carolina to Henry Goodman...10 pds per 100 acres...200 acres beginning at marked gum at head of Sarum Creek, Col. Baker's corner, on his line to head of Little Creek, to pine and by desert course and line of marked trees to beach ridges, up side of Outside Swamp, NE to pine, Peter Harrell's corner, down swamp to head of Cypress Swamp...
Will White, sec.   B. Williams

248 21 Mar 1800--John S. West, marshall for district of North Carolina, to Peter Brown_, attorney of Halifax Co. by virtue of execution from circuit court...$300 which was recovered by Samuel Pleasants and Sons against William Wynns and Jonathan Brickell...300 acres beginning at cypress in corner on Chowan River opposite land Cpt. John Campbell formerly owned on W side of river in Hertford Co., NW and 60 acres of swamp land below mentioned tract and purchased by said Wynns of Noah Cotton...
Isaac Lee Guion   John S. West

250 1 May 1801--Peter Browne of Halifax Co. to Edward Kilbee of Hertford Co., merchant...$125...two tracts of 300 acres and 60 acres and described in above deed...
William Rea   P. Browne
Daniel Southall

251 16 May 1801--William Cleaves to Jethro Williams...90 pds...60 acres on N side of Bennetts Creek beginning at chinquamin oak in Hilly Swamp running E binding on Isaac Langston's line to white oak, corner tree, along Jethro Sumner and George Allen's lines to Maple Branch and down branch to said swamp and along main run...
Wm. W. Riddick   William Cleaves
Aug Ct 1801

252 15 Aug 1801--Mary, Nancy, Willis and Elizabeth Brown to Willis Brown Sr...$63...28 acres beginning at post oak in Southall's line, said Brown's corner, NW to stake, SW to marked hickory in Daniel Southall's line and along his line NE...
Mary(X)Parker   Mary(X)Brown
Pa. Hegerty   Nancy(X)Brown
Aug Ct 1801   Willis Brown
                                                          Elizabeth Brown

253 18 Aug 1801--Henry Goodman, sheriff, to David Harrell...66 pds 1 penny...land known as Whiteheads Tract of Arnolds belonging to William Rea and Hardy Murfree on E side of Chowan River and sold by writ from supreme court of Halifax Co. to pay debts recovered by William Amies against them...
David Riddick   Henry Goodman
Simon Stallings
Nov Ct 1800

254 8 Aug 1801--Demsey Harrell to David Harrell...5 pds...3 acres beginning at black gum on S side of Cypress Swamp, running SW by line of marked trees to corner gum in Great Branch, down branch to main county road and along road...
Willis(X)Stallings   Demsey Harrell
Miles(X)Wallis
Aug Ct 1801

256 12 Nov 1800--Joseph Riddick to Edward Ownley...$15...2½ acres beginning in crossroads at James Baker's line, along Sandy Ridge Road to Austin Nickson's line, S along his line to pine, said Ownleys corner tree, with his line...
Joseph Trotman   Jo. Riddick
Joanna(X)Riddick
Aug Ct 1801

257 3 Jun 1801--Abraham Smith to Anthony Matthews...$16...2 acres beginning at hickory, corner tree in Henry Smith's line, along his line to white oak, to corner mulberry tree...
John Matthews   Abraham Smith
Dread Matthews
Aug Ct 1801

258 21 May 1801--William Blanshard to Timothy Freeman...57 pds 10 sh...40 acres on S side of Pond Branch and NE of main road, being part of land Absolum Blanchard gave to him in his will...
Jo. Riddick   William Blanshard
Reuben Riddick
Mills Hill
Aug Ct 1801

259 17 Aug 1801--David Cross to Meedy Azel...$100...33 1/3 acres beginning at pine in Flat Branch that runs down branch to mouth of Old Orchard Branch, down center of run and along line of marked trees...
Benjamin Stuckey   David Cross
Nancy Cross
William Benson
Aug Ct 1801

260 18 Jun 1801--James Baker to Timothy Freeman...$455...140 acres beginning at Riddick Trotman's line, along his line to Seth Roundtree's and along his line to Boar Swamp, along swamp to said Baker's, to George Outlaws and along his line to Juniper Swamp and up run...
Charles Powell   James Baker
George Outlaw
Aug Ct 1801

261 17 Aug 1801--Meedy Azel to David Cross...$100...Negro boy Jack.
Riddick Cross   Meedy(X(Azel
John Roberts
Aug Ct 1801

262 15 Aug 1801--Charles Eure to Whitmill Eure...100 pds...100 acres beginning at pine in Abraham Beeman's, along his line N to forked white oak, Stephen Eure's corner tree, along his line N to pine corner, S to large sweet gum in prong of pecosin, thence S...
Benjamin Beeman   Charles Eure
Levi Eure
Aug Ct 1802

263 10 Dec 1800--Willis Piland to John Worrell...$80...40 acres of woodland beginning at water oak sapling in or near William Brook's line, with his line SE to center of a few blazed trees, corner in Gen. Baker's line, SW on Bakers and orphans of Peter Piland, to litewood stake in Pilands Old Field, being corner of orphans of Thomas Piland, with his line NW and along line of marked trees...
Pa. Hegerty   Willis Piland
Thomas(X)Felton
Aug Ct 1801

264 4 Aug 1801--Josiah Jones to Abraham Riddick of Nansemond Co., Va...47 pds...47 acres beginning at water oak near swamp at Milly Ellis' line, on her line to white oak, corner tree between said Josiah and William Jones, down line of marked trees to swamp to pine in said Jones' line...
William Hurdle   Josiah(X)Jones
Mills Ellis
Nathaniel Brinkley
Aug Ct 1801

264 10 Sep 1796--Peggy Rice to Josiah Granbery...$170...Negro woman Sarah, 2 beds and furniture, iron pot, kettle, copper teakettle, iron skillet, large coffee pot, 6 walnut chairs, 2 tables, mahogany candlestand, brass candlesticks, 2 spinning wheels, large chest, 2 trunks, 6 teaspoons, set of china, fat pot, gilt looking glass, flour tub, case of knives and forks...
Christ. Cowper   Peggy Rice
Aug Ct 1801

265 19 Feb 1801--Henry Goodman, sheriff, to James H. Keys of Hertford Co...47 pds...500 acres whereon James B. Sumner's now lives, excepting such parts sold by James Sumner, dec. during his lifetime. Said land sold by court order to satisfy writ of William W. Riddick against said James...
W. Slade   Henry Goodman
Jethro Benton
Nov Ct 1801

266 12 Oct 1801--Henry Hill to Daniel Powell...30 pds...35 acres beginning at maple, corner tree of John B. Walton and Richard Freeman, dec., along Walton's line N to white oak, corner tree of said Walton and Robins, along Robins' line to white oak and maple, corner of Daniel Powell, along his line to Indian Town Road, down road to said Freemans...
James Lassiter   Henry(X)Hill
Miles(X)Lassiter
Nov Ct 1801

267 4 Sep 1798--Noah Morris to Thomas Collins...42 pds 10 sh...33

acres beginning at pine, corner tree in Nathan Cullens and Samuel Green's line, along Green's line to chinquamin tree on side of Cypress Swamp, Peter Harrell's line, along his line to pine in Jesse Harrell's line, along his line to pine corner of Nathan Cullens and along his line...
Timothy Walton   Noah(X)Morris
Willis Brown
Nov Ct 1801

269 11 Sep 1801--Henry Goodman, sheriff, to James Barnes...750 pds... 500 acres belonging to Joseph J. Sumner and sold by court order to satisfy execution won by Levin Duer against him; said land beginning at line of orphan of Luke Sumner, along her line to Henry Brinkley's line, on his line to Josiah Frank line running his line to Abraham Riddick's line, on his line to James Jones and Ellen Sketer's line, thence John Knight's line to William Hurdles, on his line and including land he now lives on...
Daniel Southall   Henry Goodman
Pa. Hegerty
Nov Ct 1801

270 22 Aug 1801--William Warren Sr. to John Rooks (alias)Warren... 100 pds...300 acres, two tracts, one known as Piney Woods and the other whereon said William lives...
Pa. Hegerty
Mills Lewis   William Warren
Nov Ct 1801

271 8 Aug 1801--William Crafford to Jesse Stallings...72 pds...70 acres, part of patent granted to Jacob Odom for 640 acres 21 Feb 1738, beginning at corner gum, Josiah Harrell's line in Cypress Swamp, down line of marked trees NW to corner gum in main run of river, W across island, by line of marked trees SE to corner gum in main run of Cypress Swamp...
David Harrell   William Crafford
Jose(X)Ellis
Nov Ct 1801

273 16 Nov 1801--Henry E. Sears to Elizabeth Burges...100 pds...50 acres purchased of Amos Dilday, beginning at lightwood tree, corner of Joel Goodman, dec. and William Gatling, along Goodman's line to corner lightwood of Isaac Pipkin's, along his line to corner tree of William Goodman and William Gatling and along Gatlings line...
James Hodges   Henry E. Sears
David(X)Brown
Nov Ct 1801

274 1 Nov 1801--Henry Goodman to David Harrell...25 pds...80 acres beginning at large corner pine of Isaac Langston's on pecosin side, running to center of three pines near Little Island Path, in pecosin SW to cypress in branch of Outside Swamp and down branch to swamp to opposite beginning...
Jesse B. Benton   Henry Goodman
Demsey Harrell
Nov Ct 1801

275 7 Dec 1795--Zachariah Copeland to Watson Stott, both of Nansemond

Co., Va...218 pds 5 sh...437½ acres being land conveyed by James Copeland and Charles Jenkins to Henry Copeland, beginning at cypress on river, through swamp and by line of marked trees to gum in Flatt Cypress, along patent line to pine corner between said Jenkins and Copeland, to edge of river and through swamp...
Willis Fisher   Zachariah Copeland
Thomas Baker
John Hatersley
Nov Ct 1801

276 16 Feb 1801--John Odom to Seth Morgan...166 pds 13 sh 4 pn...
Negro man Peter...
Micajah Riddick   John Odom
Edward Vann
Nov Ct 1801

277 10 Apr 1801--Nathaniel and Esther Newsom to John Ellis...$100...
31 1/3 acres known as White Oak Neck...
John Brothers   Nathaniel Newsom
John Mathias   Esther Newsom
Nov Ct 1801

278 29 Aug 1801--Mills Ellis to Thomas Parker...$72.50...14½ acres beginning at E corner of land he purchased of William Jones yesterday, running NE to gum sapling, SE to holly in Norfleet's line, SW to water oak and by line of marked trees E to Rich Thicket Road...
Edward Parker   Mills Ellis
Pa. Hegerty
Nov. Ct 1801

279 28 Aug 1801--William Jones to Thomas Parker...$96...32 acres beginning at Mills Ellis' line at public road, NE to corner pine, SW to road and along road...
Pa. Hegerty   William Jones
Mills Ellis
Nov Ct 1801

280 21 Dec 1797--Nathaniel Taylor of Chowan Co. to Joseph Taylor...
100 pds...mare, yoke of oxen, cow and calf, feather bed and furniture, 2 chests, 2 trunks and 2 pots...
William Volentine   Nathaniel Taylor
Docton Bagley
Nov Ct 1801

281 9 Oct 1801--James Baker to Thomas Marshall...825 pds...½ of tract of marsh land purchased of Timothy Freeman, who bought of Thomas Hunter 6 Mar 1799, lying at mouth of Bennetts Creek running to post oak on creek side, to Timothy Walton's line and through middle of marsh...
Joseph Trotman   James Baker
Jethro Meltear
Feb Ct 1802

282 13 Feb 1802--Josiah Collins of Edenton, Chowan Co. to John Cowper...$5000...three tracts purchased at public sale by Marshall John S. West of District of North Carolina 23 May 1800 and sold to satisfy judgment obtained by John S. Field and son of Philadelphia against Josiah Granbery for debts. Said land included tracts of

401,170 and 231 acres; the last tract lies in Gates Co. on W side of main road leading from Hunter's Mill to Folly, and known as Sunsbury occupied by the late Josiah Granbery, running to Mirey Branch and E of swamp to Isaac Hunters near mill dam...
Alexr. Miller   Josiah Collins
Will. Carter Jr.
Feb Ct 1802

284 20 May 1801--Inventory of property that Capt. Jonathan Roberts got by Sarah Riddick: 620 acres of land, 4 beds and bedsteads, desk, walnut table, pine table, 5 walnut chairs, 6 chairs, looking glass, trunk, 2 pots, Dutch oven, 11 knives and forks, 2 books, 2 earthen dishes, decanter, parcel of earthenware, parcel of books, 6 silver teaspoons, 2 puter plates, dishes, whip saw, parcel of wheels and beehives, 3 candlesticks, fire dogs, meal sifter, 2 trays, parcel of hogsheads and barrells, leather for all Negro shoes, 2 jugs, churn, 3 plows, parcel of hoes, fat tub, hand saw, 5 guns, 2 pair traces, saddle, cart and wheels, 2 waiters, glass tumbler, boufat, still, loom and stays, apple mill, fire tongs, parcel of tools, hone, iron wedge, money scales, 6 spoons, flat iron, hand mill and grindstone. Negroes: Pompey, George, Jacob, Sam, Mark, Hannah, Phebe, Zilpha, Isaac and Demsey. Also 3 horses, ox, 11 cattle and 21 sheep...
                                                     Miles Gatling for
J. Hamilton   Sarah Riddick
                                                     Jonathan Roberts

284 20 May 1801--Jonathan Roberts to Miles Gatling, planter, all rights in Negroes and other property herein annexed, according to will of late Christopher Riddick, late husband of his wife, Sarah, and promises to support and maintain children of said Sarah and pay all her debts...
J. Hamilton   Jonathan Roberts

285 18 May 1801--Memo: There are 5 sows and pigs, 2 little Negroes Chester and M___ given to Zilla Riddick and Penny Roberts, which are not included in bill of sale and Jonathan Roberts to hold manner plantation, still and Negroes working in crops and during cyder time and after crops deliver to said Gatling...
                                                     Jonathan Roberts
                                                     Miles Gatling for
J. Hamilton   Sarah Riddick

285 18 May 1801--Lawrence Baker, court clerk, appoints Benjamin Gordon, Samuel Harrell, John Powell of Jacob, Robert Riddick Jr. and John Small with county surveyor to make division of real estate of John Miller, dec. agreeable to his will...
                                                     L. Baker

286 3 Jun 1801--Division of estate of John Miller, dec. is made as follows: Survey No. 1--Robert Miller...74 acres, the manner plantation. No. 2--Reuben Miller...92 acres. No. 3--William Miller... 70 acres...
Pa. Hegerty, county surveyor   Benj. Gordon
Feb Ct 1802   Samuel Harrell
                                                     Robert Riddick
                                                     John Small

286 7 Apr 1801--Henry Baker of Halifax Co. to Cyprian Cross by

power of attorney given to him by John Baker of Montgomery Co.,
Tn...100 pds...Negro man Will, property of said John...
L. Baker   Henry Baker
Feb Ct 1802

287 10 Feb 1801--John Doughtie to William Walters...$84...28 acres
beginning at marked pine in Isaac Walter's line, NE to corner pine,
to persimmon tree on side of Merry Hill Pecosin and running SW...
Pa. Hegerty   John(X)Doughtie
Bray Baker
Feb Ct 1802

288 31 Jul 1795--Abraham Riddick to William Hayse...$16...20 acres
on Bennetts Creek beginning at John Hayse' line at mouth of Deep
Bottom Branch, up bottom to side of creek to William Gordon's line,
to main run of creek, to Thomas Riddick's line, to Wright Hayes'
line and down swamp...
John Simons   Abraham Riddick
Feb Ct 1802

289 29 Jul 1795--Abraham Riddick to William Hayse, administrator
of estate of Wright Hayse, dec...5 pds...20 acres on N side of Bennetts Creek beginning in William Hayes' line, to main run and down
run including island and swamp between James and William Hayes...
Sarah(SR)Riddick   Abraham Riddick
John Simons
Feb Ct 1802

290 Feb 1802--Simmons Hare Jones to Abraham Benton...6 pds 10 sh...
25 acres of woodland beginning at water oak, corner in Hare's patent on David Benton's line, NE to pine and SE...
Jethro Sumner   Simmons H. Jones
Miles(X)Benton
Feb Ct 1802

291 19 Nov 1801--Josiah Collins to John Cowper, esq...$181...Negro Liz, formerly property of Josiah Granbery...
Samuel Harrell   Josiah Collins
Feb Ct 1802

291 22 Jan 1802--Dempsey Parker to William Gatling Sr...$90...90
acres near Honey Pot Pecosin beginning at black gum, corner in Christopher Riddick's line, NW to pine in Sumner's line, binding on said
line to post oak at Hughs Old Road, on road to post oak in Cuff's
line, S to sourwood in Riddick's line and NW...
Pa. Hegerty   Demsey Parker
John Vann
Feb Ct 1802

292 28 Dec 1801--Samuel Riddick of Pasquotank Co. to James Barnes...
600 pds...350 acres so as to include track belonging to Docton Riddick, dec. and patent of 325 acres of swamp land granted to said Docton 27 Oct 1784, beginning on S side of main road on Bennetts Creek
at run called Cypress Binding on Speight's land, along his line to
Jamerson's line, E to Bennetts Creek and along run to Aron Speights
to main road and NW. Also a patent of 100 acres to said Docton by
deed from John Powell 20 Sep 1799 and beginning at red oak near
main road binding on William Hinton's line, along Robert Riddick's

line to Richard Briggs, to John Riddicks...
Moses(X)Speight   Samuel Riddick
Feb Ct 1802

294 15 Feb 1802--John Arnold to James Pruden...16 pds...8 acres on E side of Gum Branch, along line of marked trees to said Pruden's line and along his line to stump...
James Matthews   John Arnold
Nathaniel Pruden
Feb Ct 1802

295 23 Nov 1801--James Knight to Demsey Knight...40 pds...Negro boy Mac...
William Arnold   James Knight
Thomas(X)Wiggens
Feb Ct 1802

296 1 Feb 1802--John Vann Sr. to Edward Burges_...$400...100 acres beginning at white oak on NE side of Peters Swamp, James Brady's corner, NW to Henry Eborn Sears' line, on his line to corner gum on run and down run...
James(X)Brady   John Vann
Patrick Hegerty
Feb Ct 1802

297 23 Mar 1801--David Jones of Chowan Co. to John Cowper...110 pds Negro woman Patt about 35 years old...
Wills Cowper   David(X)Jones
Feb Ct 1902

297 8 Apr 1801--David Umphlet to William Umphlet...10 pds or $20... 15 acres beginning at sassafras, corner tree, running along James Costen's line to an overcupt oak, corner tree on Lickingroot Branch, up run to corner water oak, along John Parker's line to red oak, corner tree and along his line to said Umphlet's...
Josey(X)Ellis   David(+)Umphlet
Feb Ct 1802

298 30 Dec 1801--Aaron Lassiter to Isaac Harrell...$350...60 acres whereon Henry Meroney lives, beginning at white oak, corner of said parties, W along Harrell's line to branch, up branch to white oak, E to pine, Holloday Walton's corner, S along his line...
Isaac Harrell Jr.   Aaron Lassiter
Allen Lassiter
Feb Ct 1802

299 5 Mar 1801--Mary Riddick to Samuel Harrell...36 pds 18 sh... 36 acres of woodland beginning at pine on right side in Jacob Gordon's line, along main road to William Carter's corner, on his line SW to maple in branch, binding Harrell's line to water oak and along path...
Jacob Gordon Jr.   Mary Riddick
Jno. B. Bennett
Feb Ct 1802

301 16 Feb 1802--John Rooks Warren to H. Eborn Sears...10 pds...7 acres beginning at pine, along Sears' line to Gum Swamp or Mill

Swamp, down swamp to Sears' line and along branch...
James Hodges   John Warren Rooks
William Sears
Feb Ct 1802

302 10 Feb 1802--Jethro Sumner, sheriff, to Abraham Benton...30 pds...
land belonging to Hezekiah Jones and whereon he lives...to pay three
court writs for debts recovered by Levin Duer...
Simmons H. Jones   Jethro Sumner
Miles(X)Benton
Feb Ct 1802

303 10 Feb 1802--Isaac Walters to Anthony Mathews...$125...180 acres
on Merry Hill Pecosin and known as Coles Island, which belonged to
Isaac Walters, dec. and left in his will to be sold...
William Barr   Isaac Walters
Dread Mathews
Riddick Mathews
Feb Ct 1802

305 21 Nov 1801--Richard Bond to Isaac Costen...$132...24 acres be-
ginning at black gum in Spring Branch, by line of marked trees E to
corner dogwood in Lassiter's line, by line of marked trees and along
patent line S to main road and down road to said Costen's corner pine
and down run of branch...
Pa. Hegerty   Richard Bond
John Hunter
Jonathan Lassiter
Feb Ct 1802

306 2 Feb 1801--Demsey Parker to Anthony Mathews of Nansemond Co.,
Va...3 pds...10 acres beginning at pine, corner tree of said Matt-
hews on S side of Edwin Sumner's line on side of White Pot Pecosin,
W along Sumner's line to post oak, corner tree on E side of Huses'
road, E along road as it formerly ran to John Cufe's line and along
his line to corner in edge of said pecosin, along William Vann's
line to corner tree, to said Matthews' line...
Miles Parker   Demsey Parker
Mary Parker
Feb Ct 1802

307 25 Nov 1801--David Riddick of Hertford Co. to John Cowper...
$333 1/3...Negro man Mingo about 20 years old...
Wills Cowper   David Riddick
Feb Ct 1802

308 15 Nov 1801--Jacob Pearce to John Delany...9 pds...12 acres
beginning at white oak, corner tree joining Moses Brigg's line, a-
long line of marked trees to red oak, to large corner pine of Christopher Pearces' and along path...
Josiah Briggs   Jacob Pearce
Isaac(X)Pearce
Feb Ct 1802

309 16 Feb 1802--Capt. Jonathan Roberts to William Hayse...37 pds...
20 acres beginning at pine, Bond Minchew's corner binding on Jacob

Hayse and said William's line to water oak in Flat Branch and up branch NE to pine in Minchew's line...
Pa. Hegerty
Richard Barnes   Jonathan Roberts
Feb Ct 1802

310 23 Nov 1801--James Knight to Demsey Knight...60 pds...170 acres beginning at walnut tree on road on Ellum Swamp, down road NW to small branch, N to pine at path, to white oak called Kedar Wiggen's corner, NE to county line, to run of Orapeak Swamp, down run to Ellum Creek and SW...
William Arnold   James Knight
Thomas(X)Wiggens
Feb Ct 1802

312 24 Dec 1801--Abraham Riddick of Nansemond Co., Va. to Josiah Jones...47 pds...47 acres in lower end of Gates Co. on Orapeak Swamp, joining land of Mills Ellis, beginning at water oak, running S along to line of marked trees, to William Jones and said Riddicks, to pine in swamp...
William Hurdle   Abraham Riddick
Mills Ellis   Penny(X)Riddick
Humphrey Parker
Feb Ct 1802

313 29 Dec 1801--Josiah Jones to Humphrey Parker...100 pds...47 acres whereon said Jones lives in lower end of Gates Co. and lying on Orapeak Swamp...(described in above deed)
K. Ballard
Cader Parker   Josiah Jones
James Parker
Feb Ct 1802

315 11 Sep 1801--Henry Goodman, sheriff, to David Benton...7 pds 16 sh...50 acres belonging to heirs of Moses Hare, dec. and sold by court writ won by said Benton for debts. Said land begins at pine in Abraham Benton's corner in said David's line, SE to red oak in Thomas Parker's line and along patent line...
Simons Hare   Henry Goodman
Thos. Barnes
Feb Ct 1802

316 10 Sep 1801--John Powell to John Gwin...1 sh per year for 9 years...let of 15 acres bounded on E by main road, S by Isaac Harrell and by branch...to clear ground sufficient to contain 50 apple trees 20 feet apart...
Wills Cowper   John Powell
Hister(X)Gwin   John Gwin
Feb Ct 1802

318 11 Dec 1801--Aaron Lassiter to Holloday Walton of Chowan Co... 320 pds...100 acres whereon he lives and old plantation whereon his father formerly lived, being part of patent of Joseph Booth, beginning at pine, Isaac Harrell's corner tree, along his line to David Rice's and along his line SW to Samuel Harrell's and W...
Samuel Harrell   Aaron Lassiter
Feb Ct 1802

319 14 Mar 1801--Noah Hill to Jacob Eason...120 pds...42½ acres beginning in middle of swamp joining Whitmill Hill's line, running up middle to Guy Hill's line, to public road and along said Whitmill's line of marked trees and swamp...
Barnaby Nixon
Joseph Davis   Noah Hill
Guy Hill
Feb Ct 1802

320 3 Jan 1802--Jesse Stallings to David Harrell...50 pds...75 acres at Little Islands on N side of Cypress Swamp beginning at corner gum in river pecosin swamp, John Odom's corner, across islands and along Odom's line of marked trees S to corner gum in said swamp and along swamp...
                                                       Jesse Stallings
Willis(X)Stallings   Priscilla(X)Stallings
Feb Ct 1802

321 30 Mar 1802--Amos Lassiter to Michael Lawrence...$40...50 acres beginning at pine, corner in Timothy Lassiter's line, along his line to corner tree in Boyces' old line to corner pine in James Knight's line and along his line to pine in John Cuff's line and along his line to Thomas Smith's line...
Lawrence Baker   Amos(X)Lassiter
May Ct 1802

322 1 Apr 1802--Jonathan Roberts of Nansemond Co., Va. to John Roberts...1000 pds...340 acres beginning at cypress in side of Bennetts Creek, Jethro Meltier's line, by line of marked trees to pecosin, to pine, Briscoe's corner tree, along his line to Meltear's line to Maple Branch and down run to mouth of Mirey Branch, up branch to William Hinton's line, to Forrest's line, to pecosin, to Mill Race and down race to creek and up creek...
Hy. Hudgins   Jonathan Roberts
Wm. W. Riddick
Nicholas Nerney
May Ct 1802

324 22 Mar 1802--Henry E. Sears to Eborn Brisko...$200...50 acres beginning at pine, corner tree in Jonathan Robert's line, to red oak, corner tree on Jethro Meltear's line and along his line to white oak, corner tree in Thomas Marshall's line, to pecosin and down pecosin...
Jesse Southall   H. Eborn Sears
Rich'd Bond
May Ct 1802

325 27 Feb 1802--William Baker to James Brady...200 pds...100 acres formerly owned by Demsey Rooks Sr., beginning at black gum, corner tree of William Warren Sr., along line of marked trees to run of small branch, up branch to Mills Lewis' line and along his line to oak, corner tree of James Brady's, down branch to run of Peters Swamp and down run to Mills Swamp...
May Ct 1802   William Baker

326 15 May 1802--Jonathan Roberts, guardian to orphans of William Lewis, dec. to David Harrell of Isaac...93 pds 7 sh 7 pn...73 acres

beginning at Edenton Road SE of schoolhouse, along Jonathan Lassiter's line, N to side of Bennetts Creek Road to small branch, to Edenton Road...
Jo. Riddick   Jonathan Roberts
Pa. Hegerty
May Ct 1802

328 3 Oct 1800--Jacob Hayse to son, Elisha...deed of gift...50 acres on SE side of Bennetts Creek beginning at poppaw gum, corner tree on said creek at mouth of a bottom, up bottom S to Bennetts Creek Road, to post oak in William Gordon's line, to said creek and down creek...
Mills R. Field   Jacob(X)Hays
William Hays
May Ct 1802

329 25 Mar 1802--Holloday Walton to Isaac Harrell Jr...$100...30 acres beginning at persimmon tree on side of old field by graveyard, S to Harrell's line and along his line...
David Rice   Holloday Walton
Hannah(X)Stallings
May Ct 1802

330 8 Dec 1802--State of North Carolina to Mary Walters...50 sh per 100 acres...36 acres beginning at pine stump, Col. Goodman's and March's corner, on March's line NW to pine, Saunders' corner, SW to dead pine...No. 145...
Will White, sec.   J. Turner

331 29 Dec 1801--John Small to John Cowper Sr...$50...50 acres, part of tract granted to Luke Sumner in Great Dismal Swamp, beginning at maple on N side of ridge at E end of Moses Small's ridge called Rice Patch, S to maple, N to end of two small islands and S...
Wills Cowper   John Small
Gilbert Gray
Samuel Hodges
May Ct 1802

332 12 Jun 1801--Andrew Woodley of Isle of Wight, Va. and Willis Woodley and wife, Mary, to Henry Meroney...yearly rent or $5... part of tract left to said Mary by her late husband, William Hinton, beginning at post oak in Moses Speight's line, along his line to Bennetts Creek, to Mirey Branch, to Josiah Granbery's line, up branch as his line runs...
Samuel Harrell   Willis Woodley, agent
Benjamin Gordon   for Andrew
May Ct 1802   Mary(X)Woodley

333 8 Mar 1802--Mary Riddick to her daughter, Elizabeth Carter, wife of William Carter...deed of gift and 5 sh...378 acres known as Horsepool for their life and after their death to go to their son, Thomas Mills Carter...
Richard Bond Jr.   Mary Riddick
Isaac Costen
May Ct 1802

334 1 Mar 1801--Jethro Sumner, sheriff, to Benjamin Roberts of Hertford Co...4 pds 5 sh...70 acres, property of William Rae, to secure revenue for taxes owed on 1000 acres, beginning in Benjamin Harrell's

line on NE side of Mud Creek, along his line N to William Arnold's
line, binding his line W to William Crafford's S to Mud Creek...
May Ct 1802   Jethro Sumner

335 20 Mar 1802--Richard Bond to Isaac Costen...$198...33 acres
beginning at gum in branch, said Costen's corner, N to persimmon
tree, to dogwood and by line of marked trees to mulberry in Lassiter's line S to Costen's corner...
Pa. Hegerty
May Ct 1802   Richard Bond

336 4 Jan 1802--Aaron Lassiter to John Hinton...$360...78 acres
whereon Joseph Lassiter formerly lived, beginning at pine, corner
tree between Lassiter and heirs of Thomas Fullenton, along his line
to new road and along road to William Hinton's heirs, running their
line N; being part of patent that Aaron Lassiter, dec. bought of
Elijah Harriss...
David Rice   Aaron Lassiter
William Harrell
Henry Meroney
May Ct 1802

337 26 Oct 1801--David Riddick to Thomas W. Ballard...800 pds...300
acres known as the Folly, where said David now lives and which he
purchased of Levin Duer...
Jas. B. Sumner   David Riddick
John Small
Theophelus Harrell
May Ct 1802

338 19 Sep 1801--James Brown to Miles Parker...$30...feather bed
and furniture, boufatt and furniture, trunk, pine table, ½ doz chairs,
iron pot, iron teakettle and all other goods...
Pa Hegerty   James Brown
May Ct 1802

338 4 Jan 1802--Jethro and Miles Benton to Abraham Morgan...$330...
Negro man Spencer...
Jethro Sumner   Jethro Benton
Micajah Riddick Jr.   Miles Benton
May Ct 1802

339 17 Nov 1801--Theophelus Harrell to David Harrell...1050 pds...Ne-
groes Robin, Sid, Fanny, Willis and Sam, 3 feather beds and furni-
ture, household and kitchen furniture, livestock and fodder...
Jethro Ballard   Theophelus Harrell
Thomas W. Ballard
May Ct 1802

340 22 Mar 1802--Thomas Hurdle Sr. to Barnaby Nixon...95 pds 5 sh...
75 acres beginning at James Baker's line, running his line to Edward
Onley's line, along his line to Osten Nixon's line, on it to Indian
Branch and down branch to said Hurdle's and across to said Bakers...
Zadock Ownley   Thomas Hurdle
Moses(X)Hurdle
Aug Ct 1802

341 2 Apr 1802--Bray Baker to William Matthews...$60...20 acres of
woodland beginning at pine by main path on N side of Crane Pond, to

pine in Moses Boyce's line, along his line and line of marked trees to pine stump, Isaac Walters' corner and on his line to said path...
Matt. Matthews
Bray Baker
Aug Ct 1802

342 24 Nov 1790--Patrick Garvey to Samuel Browne of Southampton Co., Va...1/3 of land opposite said Browne's fishery on Chowan River, which was entered by William Crafford, Joseph Riddick and said Garvey...
Jas. Maney
Pa. Garvey
William Brickell
Aug Ct 1802

342 17 May 1802--Samuel Harrell to Millicent Walton...40 pds...Negro girl Rose...
William Harrell
Samuel Harrell
Aug Ct 1802

343 6 Mar 1802--Jethro Benton to Jacob S. Powell...$24...4 acres known as Crossroads, whereon meeting house stands, beginning at fork of road and along road to said Benton's, SW to new road...
Jethro Sumner
Jethro Benton
Aug Ct 1802

344 29 Apr 1802--Moses Haynes to Capt. Kedar Powell...65 pds...52 acres of woodland beginning at pine in Jesse Savage's line of marked trees to white oak on Bay Branch, up run to corner black gum in mouth of small branch and up branch and by path w...
Pa. Hegerty
Moses(X)Haynes
Jesse Savage
Aug Ct 1802

345 22 Feb 1802--Kedar Wiggens to Willis Brinkley, both of Nansemond Co., Va...6 pds...55 acres beginning at red oak in Joseph Hare's line in Virginia line, E to woods patent and along patent SW to Hare's line and NW...
William Hurdle
Kedar(X)Wiggens
Thomas(X)Wiggens
Abraham Riddick
Aug Ct 1802

346 25 Mar 1802--Isaac Harrell Jr. to Holloday Walton...$100...30 acres beginning at small gum near branch at Samuel Harrell's house, being corner tree between said Harrell and David Rice, up run of branch NE to fork, to main road that leads from Perquimans Road to Edenton, to said Rice's line at mouth of lane leading to Samuel Harrell's and S...
David Rice
Isaac Harrell Jr.
Hannah(X)Sumner
Aug Ct 1802

347 7 Jan 1801--Samuel Taylor to Samuel Jr...49 pds...65 acres, patent granted to John Aulston, beginning at corner pine at side of small branch on Peter Harrell's line, along said line to corner tree of Stephen Eure's, along Eure's line to corner pine at head of Cypress Pond and along said Taylor's line to Long Pond and down it...
Mills Eure
Samuel Taylor
Elisha Harrell
Blake Eure
Aug Ct 1802

348 12 Mar 1802--James Baker to Ezekiel Trotman...$800...three tracts 4 acres at Sandy Cross whereon dwelling house stands, 28¼ acres on W side of road opposite Society Chapple joining Thomas Hurdle, Edward Ownley and main road and 100 acres, part of land said Baker bought of Edward Berriman on S side of road binding line of Thomas Trotman, William Berriman, Austin Nickson and Joseph Riddick's ditch and running to road and along it...
Jo. Riddick James Baker
Abraham Hurdle
Nov Ct 1802

349 2 Sep 1803--William Carter to Jesse Twine...$550...90 acres known as Maidenhead Neck, formerly property of William Sumner, who sold to George Eason and was sold by Samuel Smith, sheriff by court writ to Isaac Hunter, who sold to said Carter; lying on S side of Bennetts Creek and beginning at mulberry tree, Bond's corner, running NW along his line to Bennetts Creek, to dividing line between Timothy Lassiter, dec. line and land sold, S along line...
Isaac Hunter William Carter
James Costen
Nov Ct 1802

350 8 Aug 1802--Benjamin Meltear to Robert Smith...150 pds 10 sh... 105 acres beginning at beech and chinquipen tree on side of Bennetts Creek above Hinton's old landing, S to small gum and ash in Jonathan Nichols' line, along his line to Demsey Jones' line, N to popular of Abraham Riddick and said Jones' corner, to creek and down creek...
George Freeman Benjamin Meltear
Joel Foster
Nov Ct 1802

352 5 Aug 1802--John Roberts to Benjamin Meltear...142 pds 10 sh... 105 acres described in above deed...
Aaron Blanshard Nov Ct 1802 John Roberts

354 26 Feb 1802--Samuel Godwin of Hertford Co. to Daniel Southall... $225...Negroes Patience and Cate...
Jesse Southall Samuel Godwin

354 14 May 1802--Abraham Parker to Daniel Southall...$240...80 acres, part of land allotted to him by his father, Robert Parker, dec. and beginning at white oak on Bennetts Creek old road that leads to house, E to stake in new road and up new road to branch, up branch and by line of marked trees to old road and along it...
Jesse Southall Abraham Parker
William Brooks
Robert Parker
Nov Ct 1802

356 4 Jun 1802--James Vann to John Vann and Isaac Parker Jr...$250 50 acres whereon he lives, beginning at Mill Swamp in said Parker's line and following known bounds and devised to him in his father's will...
Jonathan Parker James Vann
Pa. Hegerty
Nov Ct 1802

357 1 Jun 1802--Moses Haynes to his daughter, Elizabeth Phelps... deed of gift...50 acres known as Old Place, adjoining Baytree Branch

and binding on Jesse Benton's land, Jesse Savage and tract where
said Haynes lives...
Jesse B. Benton   Moses(X)Haynes
Pa. Hegerty
Aaron Smith
Nov Ct 1802

357 30 Nov 1801--Lewis Morgan and wife, Abagail, to Daniel Southall...
$10...50 acres, part of said Abagail's dower, beginning at gum on
new road, a little this side of plantation of Robert Parker, dec.,
being corner tree between Abraham Parker and Willis Parker's orphans,
thence along said Abraham's line to corner red oak on main road opposite dwelling house of Willis Brown, along road to fork above Gates
Courthouse and along new road...
Jesse Southall   Lewis(X)Morgan
Willis Brown Jr.   Abigail(X)Morgan
Nov Ct 1802

358 8 Oct 1802--Benjamin and Barnaby Blanchard to Samuel Brown...$280
226 acres of pecosin and meadow ground beginning at water oak in Pa-
latiah Blanchard's line, on his line N to pine in Menchia's line, on
Abner Pearce's line to Aaron Blanchard's corner, on his line to Dem-
sey Blanchard's, to stake in said Brown's line and NW...
Mary(X)Jones   Benjamin Blanchard
Patrick Hegerty   Barnaby Blanchard
Nov Ct 1802

360 9 Oct 1802--Ameriah Blanchard to Samuel Brown...$105...34 acres
beginning at Hollow Bridge where it crosses run of Beaverdam Swamp
in main public road, along road to Benjamin Blanchard's line, on his
line to said swamp and down run...
Patrick Hegerty   Ameriah Blanshard
Benjn. Blanshard

361 20 Jan 1802--George Lassiter to Abner Pearce...150 pds...28 acres
beginning at Watery Swamp at mouth of Middle Branch, running branch
to Jonathan Lassiter Sr., along his line to red oak in Job Riddick's
line and along his line SE to said swamp...
Aaron Blanshard   George Lassiter
Joseph Alphin
Nov Ct 1802

362 9 Nov 1802--William Hinton to Jacob Hinton...500 pds...75 acres
in Indian Neck beginning at gum in Juniper Branch, along middle to
popular in Thomas Hoffler's line and along his line NW to head of
Mare Branch, down branch and S by line of marked trees...
John B. Walton   William(X)Hinton
John Roberts
Thos. Forrest
Nov Ct 1802

363 1 Jun 1802--Moses Haynes to his grandson, Moses Wilkins...deed
of gift...50 acres purchased of Jesse Benton, whereon Jacob Wilkins
now lives, after lifetime of said Haynes' daughter, Judith...
Jesse B. Benton   Moses(X)Haynes
Pa. Hegerty
Aaron Smith
Nov Ct 1802

364 8 Sep 1802--William Doughtie Jr. to Elisha Parker...105 pds...
Negro man Hardy...
William Doughtie Sr.   William Doughtie
Edward Doughtie
Nov Ct 1802

364 28 Apr 1801--David R. Sumner of Hertford Co. to his nephew, Jethro W. Sumner...deed of gift...Negro boy Sunnon...
Jethro Sumner   David R. Sumner
Nov Ct 1802

365 9 Nov 1802--William Hinton to John Hinton...500 pds...75 acres in lower part of county in Indian Neck, beginning at head of Juniper Branch at gum, running SW to pine in Forrest's line, down swamp and binding on said Forrest's line to Morris' line and along that line to Thomas Hoffler's corner popular and up Juniper Branch...
J.B. Walton   William(X)Hinton
John Roberts
Thos. Forrest
Nov Ct 1802

366 10 Nov 1802--Isaac Miller Sr. to Isaac Jr...deed of gift...115 acres whereon he lives, binding on Lewis Walters, heirs of Timothy Lassiter, dec. and Micajah Riddick Jr., retaining use of said land for Isaac Sr. and his wife, Elizabeth, for their lifetime...
Micajah Riddick Jr.   Isaac Miller Sr.
Hy. Hudgins
Hy. D. Hudgins
Nov Ct 2802

367 15 Nov 1802--Isaac Miller Jr. to Fanny Miller...$120...all rights in Negroes left to his mother, Elizabeth Miller, by his grandfather's will; after death of said Fanny Negroes and their increase to go to said Elizabeth's daughter, Jiney H. Miller...
Micajah Riddick Jr.   Isaac Miller Jr.
Hy. D. Hudgins
Nov Ct 1802

368 5 Jul 1802--Jacob Spivey to Langley Billups...$164½...41 1/8 acres beginning at white oak on side of branch in Miles Hill's line, along his line to beach, John B. Walton's line, NE to old road and along road SW...
Miles Hill   Jacob Spivey
Nov Ct 1802

368 17 Sep 1802--James Baker to Jethro Lassiter...$50...15 acres known as Poverty Hall...
Norman King   James Baker
Nov Ct 1802

369 19 Nov 1801--Josiah Collins to Louedicia Harrell...$50...Negro woman Sarah...
Thomas Granbery   Josiah Collins
Nov Ct 1802

370 7 Aug 1802--Elisha Cross to Abraham Parker Jr. of Nansemond Co., Va...200 pds...4 Negroes Kessiah, Silvey, Chaney and Jone; to use as his security for matter of controversy now depending between

said Cross and Cambel and Whealer in Nansemond Co. Court...
William Goodman
Pa. Hegerty   Elisha Cross
Nov Ct 1802

370 3 Feb 1802--John Hunter to James Lassiter...150 pds...100 acres
beginning on S side of Bennetts Creek at corner cypress between said
Hunter and James Costen, up Iron Mind branch to Spanish oak, corner
tree between sd. John and Theopolus Hunter, E to William Lassiter's
line and along line of marked trees running N to Bennetts Creek...
Lassiter Riddick   John Hunter
Aaron Blanshard
Nov Ct 1802

372 14 Oct 1802--Stephen Eure to Elisha Harrell...17 pds 12 sh...88
acres of woodland beginning at sweet gum, Charles Eure's corner, SW
to pine, gum and red oak in Abram Beeman's line, E to corner white
oak in said Charles' line or Whitmil Eure's line, on their line...
Pa. Hegerty   Stephen Eure
Benjn. Beeman
Abraham Beeman
Nov Ct 1802

373 16 Sep 1802--Holoday Walton to Isaac Harrell Jr...$200...30 acres
beginning at water oak in branch, along branch and parcel of marked
trees to said Harrell's and along his line...
Isaac(X)Harrell Sr.   Holoday Walton
David Rice
Nov Ct 1802

373 7 Aug 1802--Elisha Cross to Abraham Parker Jr. of Nansemond Co.,
Va...682 pds...115 acres purchased of the Arline Family, for said
Parker to use as security in matter of appeal of controversary in
county court of Nansemond between said Cross and Cambel and Wheeler...
Pa. Hegerty   Elisha Cross
William Goodman
Nov Ct 1802

375 30 Jan 1803--Thomas Hurdle to Abraham Hurdle...300 pds...200
acres joining Indian Branch and given to James Price by Thomas Docton 11 Apr 1752 and sold by him to Job Riddick 5 Mar 1762, who sold
to said Hurdle, excepting 75 acres sold to Barnaby Nixon, beginning
on N side of Indian Branch at mouth, up branch and by line of marked
trees to head line...
Joseph David   Thomas Hurdle
Henry Hurdle
Isaac Griffin
Feb Ct 1803

376 22 Oct 1802--Jethro Sumner, sheriff, to James Gordon...438 pds...
plantation belonging to Seth Eason, whereon he lives, to satisfy writ
of Mary Riddick's against said Eason and William Harriss for debts...
Jos. B. Skinner   Jethro Sumner
Feb Ct 1803

378 23 Aug 1802--Levin Duer of Hertford Co. to Arthur Jones of Edenton...750 pds...318 acres on E side of Bennetts Creek beginning at
pine in Walnut Neck Patent, William Hinton, dec. corner tree near

Isaac Reed's fence, with Hinton's line NE to several small saplings, SE to small branch by John Riddick's fence, down branch to Speight's or Cypress Branch, down it to gum in John Speight's corner just below road, on his line NW to dead pine, SW to branch by Duke's fence and down branch to Walnut Neck Patent...
David Riddick
Seth Perry   Levin Duer
Feb Ct 1803

380 8 Nov 1802--Levin Duer of Hertford Co. to Arthur Jones of Edenton...600 pds...100 acre Juniper Pecosin between Catherine Creek and Bennetts Creek and called Bennetts Creek Pecosin and is tract Henry Hill purchased from Chowan Indians in 1758 and mentioned in his will as lands deeded by Henry and Himrick Hill to William Lewis and from William Lewis to James Baker, from Jonathan Nichols and wife, Mary, to said Baker and from Levin Duer to James Baker, all of which were sold to said Duer 1 Oct last; also land purchased by said Duer from Timothy Freeman 6 Jan 1801 and being part Clement Hill heired from his father, Henry Hill...
Jacob Perry   Levin Duer
W.H. Boyce
Feb Ct 1803

382 15 Jan 1803--John Dorlon to Edward Howell Sr...$1250...500 acres known as Wianock beginning at state line on N side of Somertin Creek, down run to Chowan River and up river to Black Water, along state line; reserving to said Dorlan land from point opposite Warrens Seine Place to marsh below seine place, called Pumpkin Patch...
Abram Parker Jr.   John Dorlon
John Darden
Jesse Parke_
Elias Daughtery
Feb Ct 1803

383 13 Jan 1803--Thomas Hurdle to Abraham Hurdle...$800...Negroes Prince, Isaac and Judey, yoke of oxen, 6 sows and pigs, 3 feather beds, mare, bridle, 8 head cattle, 1000-wt. bacon, 50 bbl. corn, loom and gear, 6 chairs, 2 chests, 6 dishes, 5 basons, 12 plates, whip saw, 5 head sheep, 2 pots, pan, linen wheel and woolen wheel...
Joseph Davis   Thomas Hurdle
Henry Hurdle
Isaac Griffin
Feb Ct 1803

384 18 Jun 1802--Jesse Saunders to son, Lawrence...deed of gift... 100 acres purchased of William King, Joseph Speight, Joseph Parker, Elizabeth Dwyer and Sarah Saunders 1 Oct 1791 and whereon said Lawrence lives and 100 acres purchased of Abraham and Charity Saunders 3 Mar 1790 and adjoining first tract...
Pa. Hegerty   Jesse($\frac{I}{}$)Saunders
Mary Saunders
Feb Ct 1803

385 6 Feb 1802--Willis Piland to John Piland...$300...60 acres on E side of Coles Creek, beginning at cypress on main run, along Brooks' line to white oak, Worrell's corner and along his line, formerly belonging to Thomas Piland, dec. and along that line to main run...
George Williams   Willis Piland
Soloman Green
Feb Ct 1803

386 18 Jan 1802--Jesse Saunders to son, Lawrence...deed of gift...
Negroes George and Rachal and children Joe, Jim, Willis, Nelly and
Sally...
Pa. Hegerty   Jesse(|)Saunders
Feb Ct 1803

387 6 Jan 1803--Elizabeth Lewis to Henry Copeland...$ per acre...
34 acres beginning at her corner tree, red oak in head of small
branch, along her line to Isaac Pipkin's line and along his line to
main road, along road to small red oak, new line tree, to branch and
up branch...
Jas. Gatling   Elizabeth Lewis
John Odom
Feb Ct 1803

388 8 Mar 1802--Jethro Sumner, sheriff, to James Gordon...90 pds...
mill and 2 acres belonging to Seth Eason and William Harriss and
sold to satisfy writ for debts recovered in court by Thomas Brinkley, guardian of orphans of John Barr, dec...
Feb Ct 1803   Jethro Sumner

390 19 Feb 1803--Delilah Ming to daughter, Pennellopy Ming...deed
of gift...Negro boy Dick, 2 feather beds and furniture, walnut dining table, mahogny tea table, walnut case and bottles, blue painted
chest, 2 cows and calves, kitchen furniture; reserving until her
death...
Jo. Riddick   Delilah(+)Ming
Nathan Riddick
Feb Ct 1803

391 26 Jan 1803--Miles Benton to Henry K. Benton...20 pds...610 acres
granted to Epaphroditus Benton 1 Mar 1720 and conveyed to Jethro Ben-
ton, who conveyed by deed of gift to said Miles, lying on E side of
Chowan River, beginning at cypress and running NE to maple in Mirey
Branch, NW and along patent line to David Cross' line, to river and
along river...
Jethro Benton   Miles Benton
Jesse Benton
William Benton
Feb Ct 1803

393 28 Jul 1802--George Outlaw to Thomas Marshall...143 pds...44
acres beginning at side of pecosin in Edward Briscoe's line, along
his line NE to white oak, Jethro Meltear's corner in William Hinton
Jr. line, SW to pecosin...
James Outlaw   George Outlaw
Benjn.(X)Hayse
Feb Ct 1803

394 2 Apr 1802--William Matthews to Bray Baker...$60...20 acres be-
ginning at pine on side of broad path near Crane Pond, running path
to main road and by line of marked trees NW to corner post oak and E.
Pa. Hegerty   William Matthews
Matt. Matthews
Feb Ct 1803

395 16 Feb 1802--Abraham Riddick to Samuel Harrell...$100...100
acres granted to him 1 Sep 1800 on N side of Bennetts Creek, beginn-

ing at Thomas Riddick's line, along high land and up creek to dividing line between George Williams and Jethro Sumner, thence S to main run of Bennetts Creek and down run N...
Moses Davis							Abraham Riddick
Dorothy(X)Davis
Feb Ct 1803

397 6 Jan 1801--Timothy Freeman to Levin Duer...$____...200 acres so as to include that part of Juniper Pecosin that Henry Hill gave to his son, Clement, who conveyed to James Freeman, who conveyed to said Timothy...
James Walton							Timothy Freeman
John Hofler
Feb Ct 1803

398 1 Oct 1802--James Baker to Leven Duer...670 pds. 16 sh 1 penny... 1000 acres of Juniper Swamp purchased of William Lewis 12 Jan 1796, of Jonathan Nichols and wife, Mary, 12 Sep 1795 and of said Duer 12 Nov 1795, lying on Bennetts Creek Pecosin...
Samuel Harrell							James Baker
Edward(X)Onley
Feb Ct 1803

400 18 Sep 1802--James Baker to Joseph Riddick...500 pds...Negroes Sam and Fillis and those that may fall to him by death of Willis Trotman, dec.3 feather beds and furniture, 3 cows and calves, yoke of oxen and buffet...
John Polson							James Baker
George Freeman
Feb Ct 1803

401 23 Feb 1803--Jethro Sumner, sheriff, to Arthur Jones of Edenton... 100 pds...Negro girls Rachel and Becky, belonging to Josiah Granbery and sold by court order to satisfy judgment against said Granbery by Warren Ashley for debts...
Jos. B. Skinner							Jethro Sumner
Feb Ct 1803

402 1 Jan 1803--Josse Ellis to Levi Eure...41 pds 5 sh...27½ acres, part of tract that James Carter bought of said Ellis, on S side of Cypress Swamp beginning at white oak in run, along Levi Eure's line W to pine corner of John Parker's, along his line N to prong of swamp, formerly called Francys Langston's corner, down main run...
Benjamin Beeman							Josse(X)Ellis
Timothy Langston
Jesse Taylor
Feb Ct 1803

403 1 Jan 1803--Josse Ellis to James Carter...$406...102 acres beginning at birch, to main run of Cypress Swamp, up run to corner gum of Francis Langston's, NE to corner pine in John Parker's line, down branch to water oak, corner tree in Lickingroot Branch and down branch...
Benjamin Beeman							Josse(X)Ellis
Jesse Taylor
Feb Ct 1803

405 18 Aug 1802--David Harrell to William Hinton...26 pds...13 acres at head of branch on Edenton Road, along road NE to foot of path near schoolhouse, up path to pine in Robert Lassiter's line, NW to Bennetts Creek Road and along road to small branch...
Benjamin Meltear
Feb Ct 1803
David Harrell

406 19 Feb 1800--Samuel Taylor to Jesse Taylor...4 pds 16 sh...6 acres, part of patent granted to William Horn 22 Jan 1718, on N side of Cypress Swamp beginning at Taylor's or Norris' corner gum, running that line to path that goes over swamp to run and down run...
Benjn. Beeman
Abraham Beeman
Feb Ct 1803
Samuel Taylor

408 17 Jan 1803--Henry Eborn Sears to Demsey Odom...$510...100 acres purchased of Blake Baker, beginning at white oak in William Matthews corner, on his line to Lassiters and along that line to Benjamin Baker's corner, on his line to Demsey Williams, along his line...
James Brady
Britian Odom
Edward Burgess
Feb Ct 1803
H. Eborn Sears

409 17 Feb 1803--Benjamin Baker to Demsey Odom...$525...122 acres beginning at marked hickory in Demsey Williams line, Eborn Sears' corner, along Sears line to corner pine in Timothy Lassiter, dec. line, along his line to pine corner in Boyce's new survey, to dead pine, Samuel Smith's corner near Bakers Folly on White Pot Pecosin, along Anthony Matthew's line and N...
Blake Baker
Patrick Hegerty
Feb Ct 1803
Benjamin Baker

411 25 Jun 1801--William Freeman to his son, James T....deed of gift...tract formerly given by Thomas Trotman to his daughter, Mary Roundtree, joining crossroads...
Josiah Freeman
Timothy Walton
William Blanshard
Feb Ct 1803
William Freeman

421 22 Aug 1801--Josiah Freeman to his parents, James Freeman and wife, Selah...deed of gift...land whereon they live for their natural lives...
Timothy Freeman
Charles Powell
Feb Ct 1803
Josiah Freeman

413 19 Feb 1803--Samuel Taylor to Jesse Taylor...20 pds...50 acres, part of patent granted to Henry Hackley 22 Jun 1722, beginning at run of Reedy Branch in Cearom Creek Road, N on Samuel Eure's line to white oak, corner tree, W up Crach Hall Branch, by line of marked trees to holly, corner of More Carter and Charles Eure, along said Charles' line to run of Reedy Branch and down branch...
Benj. Beeman
Abraham Beeman
Feb Ct 1803
Samuel Taylor

414 18 Feb 1803--William Jones to Humphrey Parker...24 pds 7 sh 6 pn 19½ acres joining said Jones' beginning at pine in bottom on S side of Orapeak Swamp, being line tree of said Jones, S along Jones and Parker's line to tree called Norfleet's line tree, to sweet gum, another corner of Norfleet's and Elizabeth Parker's, N along her line...
Jo. Powell Jr. William(+)Jones
Mills Ellis
Feb Ct 1803

416 21 Oct 1802--John Doughtie to Benjamin Baker...$540...135 acres whereon Jonathan Parker now lives beginning at William Doughtie's corner in Riddick Hunter's line on Merry Hill Pecosin on Doughtie's line, to Winborn Jenkins corner pine in Parker's Marsh, on his line and Isaac Walters, to William Walters on side of pecosin and along pecosin line... John Doughtie
Leah(+)Doughtie
Patrick Hegerty
Feb Ct 1803

417 25 Feb 1800--Thomas Marshall to his friends, John B. Walton and Joseph Riddick...deed of gift...400 acres whereon he lives and small tract of marsh land at mouth of Bennetts Creek, whereon is a fishery...
David Harrell Thomas Marshall
Timothy Freeman
6 Oct 1803 Edenton

419 25 Feb 1803--Thomas Marshall to his friends, John B. Walton and Joseph Riddick...deed of gift...Negroes Dave, Chloe, Edith, Jerry, Salley, Anice, Cadah and Trease...
David Harrell Thomas Marshall
Timothy Freeman
George williams
David Harrell
6 Oct 1803

420 30 Nov 1801--State of North Carolina to John Duke...50 sh for 100 acres...30 acres beginning at elm in run of Cypress Swamp in James Barnes' line, down run to 3 gums in Bennetts Creek, up run to Humphries Beaver Dam at mouth of small branch issuing out of run and along it and binding on Gregory's line to edge of swamp...
Will. White, sec. N. 138 B. Williams

421 10 Dec 1801--State of North Carolina to Charles Powell...50 sh per 100 acres...40 acres beginning in mouth of Pond Branch in Riddick's line, down side of swamp and along Powell's line to Grog Branch and along run to creek and SW...
Will White, sec. No. 148 B. Williams

422 10 Dec 1801--State of North Carolina to Patrick Hegerty...50 sh per 100 acres...55 acres beginning at red oak in Joseph Hare's line in Virginia line, E on patent line and SW...
Will White, sec. No. 142 B. Williams
20 Feb 1802--Patrick Hegerty and Josiah Ellis endorse all rights in tract to Kedah Wiggens...
Jethro Sumner Pa. Hegerty
  Josiah(X)Ellis

423 22 Aug 1803--Thomas Marshall to John Little of Edenton, merchant...680 pds 12 sh 10 pn...40 acres beginning at cypress at end of Sharps Island on E side of Bennetts Creek at Gabriel Lassiters, to end of Beach Island, to creek and along Chowan Indian line to white oak, along Piland's line to head of Sandy Bottom joining high land in Phelp's line to said creek. Also, Negro man Dave, woman Chloe, Boys Kader and Jerry and Girls Sally, Anarchy, Treacey and Edith...
Jo. B. Littlejohn
Edenton 14 Oct 1803
Thomas Marshall

424 8 Dec 1802--State of North Carolina to Samuel Eure...50 sh per 100 acres...86 acres beginning at end of new road which intersects Sarum Creek Road near John Piland's house, NW to post oak, SW to pine and oak, binding on Uriah Eure's line SW to hickory, Nathan Cullen's corner, SE to run of Lickingroot Branch and up road...
Will White, sec. No. 146
Jas. Turner

425 10 Dec 1801--State of North Carolina to Patrick Hegerty...50 sh per 100 acres... 8 acres beginning at gum in run of Elm Swamp in Woods' patent line, up run to chenquipen oak, Houses Patent, to gum in Woods' Patent, on his line S... Josiah Ellis endorses his claim to said land 20 Feb 1802...
22 Apr 1804--Patrick Hegerty makes over said tract to Joseph Hare.
John Hare
Pa. Hegerty

427 8 Dec 1802--State of North North Carolina to James Piland... 50 sh per 100 acres...150 acres beginning at cypress at run of Coles Creek on E side of High Hill Island in George Williams' line, W to John Piland's, on his and Cullen's line NW to maple in March Branch and up branch and by line of marked trees W to James Piland's to gum in Jesse Harrell's line, E to Coles Creek and up run...
Will White, sec. No. 147
J. Turner

428 23 Nov 1802--State of North Carolina to Jesse Harrell Sr... 50 sh per 100 acres...411 acres beginning at gum on side of Sarum Creek, running E to pine in Uriah Eure's line, to gum in Cypress Swamp, to cypress on run of Coles Creek, down run and binding on Spivey's patent to Herring Creek, to Sarum Creek and along it...
Will White, sec. No. 144
B. Williams

429 8 Dec 1802--State of North Carolina to John Piland...50 sh per 100 acres...125 acres beginning at pine on N side of Lickingroot Branch, Capt. David Lewis' corner, on his line SW to Uriah Eure's corner, on his line SE to new road where it intersects Sarum Road and along road to Licking Root Branch...
Will White, sec. No. 150
J. Turner

430 8 Dec 1802--State of North Carolina to Hillery Willey and William Warren Sr...50 sh per 100 acres...32 acres on W side of run of Knotty Pine Swamp beginning at pine in Richard Odom's patent corner on W side, binding on Warrens and Willeys, to pine in Jonathan Williams' line, on his line and down swamp...
Will White, sec. No. 149
J. Turner

431 27 May 1800--Benjamin Roberts of Hertford Co. to John Pipkin

of Northampton ...$1487...25 acres and fishery on E side of Chowan
River and granted to him 24 Oct 1786, beginning at cypress on side
of river above mouth of Barnes Creek and up creek NW...
Edwin Liles   Benjn. Roberts
John R. Cross
J. Thomas
May Ct 1803

432 18 Feb 1803--John Lang to Sarah Butler...deed of gift...10 acres
joining John Sumner's line, during her natural life, and 2 cows, sow
and pigs, pot, feather bed and furniture, puter bason, dish, 2 plates
and 2 spoons...
Jas. Ransone   John Lang
Thomas Collins

432 20 Jan 1803--Thomas Harrell and wife, Nancy, to Henry Goodman...
7 pds 10 sh...151 acres beginning at pine corner of John Rawls' patent, SE to gum in edge of pecosin and NE...
Joseph Speight   Thomas(X)Harrell
William Goodman   Nancy(X)Harrell
May Ct 1803

434 7 Mar 1803--William Warren to John Warren...27 pds...14 cattle,
30 hogs, 8 sheep, feather bed and furniture, 2 iron pots, pan, trunk,
chest and other goods...
Edwin Warren   William Warren
David(X)Brown
May Ct 1803

435 14 May 1803--Austen Nixon to Reuben Nixon...$___...15 acres beginning at main road at persimmon stump, E to black oak, on line of
marked trees to Abraham Hurdle's, S to main road...
Norman King   Austen Nixon
Barnaby Nickson
May Ct 1803

435 18 Apr 1803--James Riddick of Nansemond Co., Va. to Isaac Pipkin
Sr...$1110...370 acres on Mills Swamp beginning at main run, by line
of marked trees S to 2 white oaks at Minqua Pond, SE to corner tree
of Col. Will Baker and Miles Gatling, NE to stooping pine of Henry E.
Sears, to red oak in Deep Branch, down branch NE to corner gum of
said Sears and John Shepherd, down Shepherd's line NW and up swamp;
is part of patent of Henry Mills 20 Apr 1685...
Isaac Pipkin Jr.   James Riddick
Rich'd Barnes
May Ct 1803

437 25 Aug 1800--Benjamin Edwards, guardian of William E. Webb of
Northampton Co., to James Gregory...1778 pds 3 sh 9 pn...532 acres,
part of Webb's estate, on E side of Bennetts Creek, beginning at cypress, SE to 3 saplings, William Hinton's corner in Walnut Neck Patent,
along line to Hinton's corner, SW to branch by side of John Duke's
fence, to Bennetts Creek...
Jo. Riddick   Benj. Edwards
Reddick Trotman
Elisha Hunter
May Ct 1803

439 5 Mar 1803--Willis Sparkman to Elisha H. Bond...40 pds...44 acres

whereon he lives, beginning at gypres on N side of Horsepool Swamp, along line of marked trees to pine, to Jacob Outlaw's line, to said Bond's line and running to swamp...
Rich'd Bond
Thomas Bond   Willis(X)Sparkman
May Ct 1803

441 1 Mar 1803--Henry Hill to Benjamin Meltear...$140...35 acres beginning at run of branch at Acrons Bridge, Hinton's corner on Daniel Powell's line, NW to run of Gabriels Swamp, to line of marked trees, SW to run of branch...
Patrick Hegerty
_____ Meltear   Henry(H)Hill
May Ct 1803

442 13 May 1803--Moses Hines & Kedar Wiggens, both of Nansemond Co., Va... to Demsey Knight...$35...55 acres beginning in Joseph Hares and Ambrose Wiggens lines near Ellum Swamp, N on Hare's line to county line, to Demsey Knight's and along his line...
Pew Wiggens
Abraham Riddick   Willis(X)Brinkley
Thomas(X)Wiggens   Kedar(X)Wiggens
May Ct 1803

446 6 Mar 1803--Seth Roundtree to Joseph Taylor...20 pds...15 acres beginning at maple at run of swamp, along said Taylor's line S to Old Town Road, NE to run of swamp...
Seth Spivey
Mills Hurdle   Seth Roundtree
May Ct 1803

447 14 Jan 1803--Jeremiah Benton of Northampton Co. and Mary Benton to Maj. Jesse Benton...80 pds...81 acres, part of 125 acre tract, being land their brother, Robert, died possessed of, on W side of Bennetts Creek, beginning at corner gum, Jesse Benton Jr.'s corner, by line of marked trees W to Jacob Wilkins' corner, on his line to creek and up run...
Jesse B. Benton
William Doughtie   Jeremiah Benton
Winburn Jenkins   Mary Benton
May Ct 1803

449 5 Jan 1803--Elijah Harrell to Asa Harrell...71 pds...50 acres beginning at white oak, corner tree in Alse Green's, running his line E to Coles Creek, along creek to mouth to said Green's line...
Benjamin Beeman   Elijah Harrell
Abraham Beeman
May Ct 1803

451 22 Mar 1803--Isaac Carter to James Gatling...$708.75...315 acres beginning at marked pine on patent line on S side of Doctors Road, N to corner pine stump, to N side...
Luten Lewis   Isaac(X)Carter
John Parker   Charity Carter
Aug Ct 1803

453 19 Feb 1803--Meedy Azel to David Cross...$100...33 1/3 acres beginning at pine on Flat Branch that runs into Pine Swamp, William

Hooks' corner, on Hooks' patent line, down branch to Old Orchard Branch and up it...
Abel Cross   Medy(X)Azel
Zilpha Cross
Charity Cross
Aug Ct 1803

454 13 Aug 1803--Stephen Eure to his son, Demsey of Bertie Co... deed of gift...Negroes Cloe and Peag...
Abraham Beeman   Stephen Eure
Levi Eure
Benjamin Beeman
Aug Ct 1803

454 20 May 1803--George Gatling to David Harrell...100 pds...100 acres purchased of Moses Odom, on S side of Beaverdam Swamp, beginning at gum, corner tree between said Gatling and Jesse Saunders, up swamp to oak, corner tree of George and William Gatling, up their dividing line, to said Saunders' line...
William Goodman   George(X)Gatling
William Goodman Jr.
Aug Ct 1803

456 22 Feb 1802--Patrick Henry Fontaine of Henry Co., Va. to John Cowper...$803.50...803½ acres, an undivided fourth part of tract belonging to heirs of John Fontaine, joining 2000 acre tract...
Wills Cowper   P.H. Fontaine
Seth Eason
Thos. Cowper
Aug Ct 1803

457 13 Aug 1803--Stephen Eure to daughter, Mary Langston, of Hertford Co...deed of gift...Negro girls Lettis and Kate...
Abraham Beeman   Stephen Eure
Benjamin Beeman
Levi Eure
Aug Ct 1803

458 20 May 1803--David Harrell is bound to George Gatling and wife, Susanna, for $100 for land whereon they live; they are to have possession for lifetime and if Susanna survives said George she is to have 1/3...
William Goodman   David Harrell
William Goodman Jr.
Aug Ct 1803

459 15 Mar 1803--Jacob Odom of Hertford Co. to Richard Martin... $124...31 acres on Lady of Honour Branch, beginning at pine, corner on head of branch issuing out of said branch, up its run to mouth of Marsh Branch to corner gum and running E...
Etheldred Odom   Jacob Odom
William Goodman
Aug Ct 1803

460 8 Jul 1803--Richard Martin of Hertford Co. to Jonathan Williams Jr....$130...31 acres joining Lady of Honour Branch, beginning at corner pine on head of branch in Hillory Willey's line, down to

Lady of Honour Branch, up its run to Marsh Branch, to corner gum
in dividing line, running E...
Jonathan Williams   Richard(X)Martin
Pa. Hegerty
Aug Ct 1803

461 19 Mar 1802--William Wallis to James Crafford...$20...50 acres
known as Pine Swamp beginning at gum in mouth of Cross Swamp, called
Joseph Runnell's corner, E binding on James Curl's line to Cyprian
Cross' line, up swamp to John Odom and Benjamin Barnes' corner, on
Odom's line to chinkapin oak called Callum Ross's corner, binding
on high ground and down to swamp...
David Harrell   William(X)Wallis
Milley(X)Harrell
Aug Ct 1803

463 6 Oct 1802--Nathaniel Jones, Charles Smith and Joseph Jones to
James Trevalthan...$34.50...10 acres of woodland beginning at red
oak in Charles Smith's line, on his line to pine sapling in said
Joseph's line, NE to white oak, SE to Flatt Branch and along branch.
Elisha Trevathan   Nathaniel Jones
Pa. Hegerty   Charles Smith
Aug Ct 1803   Joseph(X)Jones

464 5 Apr 1803--Mary Garrett and William Speight Jr., who intend
marriage shortly, to William Speight Sr. as trustee...5 pds...
Negro Sam and household furniture belonging to said Mary; 5 pds...
1/3 of estate of personal items of said William...
                                                 Mary(X)Garrett
John Speight   William Speight Jr.
Thomas Speight   William Speight
Nancy(X)Speight
Aug Ct 1803

INDEX

Albright, Jacob 3
Allen, Betty 47,186
  Edward 47, 186,217
  George 123,169,197,215 218
  John 44
  Joshua 47,83,116
Alphin, James 3
  John 43
  Joseph 10,51,96,139,153, 209,233
  Sarah 42
  Soloman 1,3,10,83
Alston, Clabourne 111,124
  Col. John 2
  John 2,46,68,76,89,186, 231
  Rachael 124
  Soloman 47,83,116
  William 2
Amies, William 202,219
Anderson 56,67,147
Arline, James 32,92
  Jesse 112,205
  John 4,92,110
  John Jr. 59
Armistead, John 181
Arnold, Edward 3,9,11,38,43,49, 53,54,71,81,133,151,158
  Edward Sr. 3
  Elizabeth 67,69,71
  John 11,38,43,45,49,58,71, 110,129,136,138,139,148,161, 166,225
  Kizia 43,54
  Patsy 58
  Richard 46,67,69
  William 3,9,24,30,43,49,53, 54,57,62,63,65,66,67,69,71, 73,90,95,99,110,125,135,137, 138,139,142,145,151,152,171, 173,186,189,225,227, 230
Ashbury, Francis 49
Ashe, Samuel 179,181
Ashley, William 15,60,67,238
Askew, John 182
Atkinson, John 76
Auston, Richard 19
Azel, Meedy 219,243, 244

Babb, James 87
  John 11,126,170,182,184
Bagley, Betsy 190
  Docton 175,182,197,222
  Jacob 8,9,18,24,27,30,32, 34,37,40,41,47,50,54,59, 72,84,85,186,187,197

Bachelor, William 151
Baker, Absala 101
  Agatha 144
  Benjamin 52,61,82,99,121,125, 133,193,201,239,240
  Blake 168,201,202,239
  Bray 121,224,230,231,237
  Col. 161,218 Gen'l 205,220
  Henry 7,12,74,122,124,137,148, 192,205,209,223,224
  James 34,53,60,91,98,101,111, 120,129,134,146,150,152,177, 180,191,201,217,219,222,230,232, 234,236,238
  John 22,45,58,119,120,126,129,130, 133,142,145,149,192,224
  John B. 185
  Lawrence 13,30,44,46,53,57,61, 72,92,93,108,144,146,170,176, 179,181,192,193,198,223,224, 228
  Nancy 45
  Richard 61,98,99,117
  Samuel 7,19,22,68,71,73,79,81, 129,193,197,203
  Sarah 68
  Thomas 190,222
  William 13,18,22,51,52,53,81, 83,84,94,98,101,121,122,124, 129,132,141,145,146,149,151, 152,159,160,164,166,168,169, 175,183,185,186,192,193,197, 204,207,228,242
  William H. 125
Ballard, Jethro 16,18,19,20,43,59, 60,66,71,74,79,82,87,88,92, 93,94,96,101,103,104,122,126, 127,131,140,144,146,149,151, 159,160,163,179,182,184,189, 193,204,206,230
  Joseph 26,44,52,163
  Kedar 16,57,62,77,96,131,136, 141,163,175,185,186,187,191,194, 199,202,205,206,227
  Thomas W. 174,184,230
Banrone, James 83 (See Ransone)
Barnes, Benjamin 18,42,43,77,123, 145,171,172,180,193,194,196,245
  Demsey 14,42,44,60,62,65,68,90, 91,126, 130,136,147,150
  James 168,171,208,221,224,240
  Jesse 7,19,30,44,46,60,64,68, 95,101,116,120,156,201
  Prudence 147
  Richard 70,100,115,125,133,139, 193,227,242

Barnes, Thomas 38,40,45,46,
   65,104,105,123,125,130,
   133,139,140,169,193,195,
   199,227
   William 46,62
Barfield, Ruth 185
Barr, John 29,237
Barrett, John 6,15,31
Barrow, Sherrard 52
Bachelor, William 151
Beeman, Abraham 49,194,206,217,
   220,235,239,243,244
   Benjamin 194,206,217,220,
   235,238,239,243,244
   Israel 2,14,34,35,40,49,
   57,77,78,87,88,106,113,125,
   137,138,148,199,206,217
   Polley 199
   Rachael 40
Beesley, Mary 141
   William 44
Bell, Bythal 162 W. 26
Benbery, Richard 151
Bennett, Boyd 171
   George 83,98
   James 56,77
   John B. 225
   Joseph 83,98
   William 166,171
Benson, William 219
Bentley, John 93
   William 166
Benton, Abraham 179,203,224,226,
   227
   Betsy 158,188
   Elisha 81,162
   Epaphratitus 25,237
   David 138,167,224,227
   James 179 James B. 198,221
   Jeremiah 113,243
   Jesse 11,35,50,96,102,103,
   108,135,141,160,161,162,
   165,172,178,194,212,217,233,
   237,243
   Jesse B. 199,233,243
   Jesse Jr. 35,243
   Jethro 9,11,50,64,78,108,
   109,112,127,141,147,153,
   160,178,179,187,197,198,
   220,230,231,237
   Jethro Jr. 11,49
   Jethro Sr. 11,73
   John 11,13,35,96,129,141
   John Jr. 11
   Josiah 11,48
   Henry K. 237
   Isaac 3,9

Benton, Mary 141,243
   Miles 52,73,81,84,93,112,141,
   158,160,162,172,173,175,177,
   187,188,198,203,217,224,230,237
   Milley 73
   Moses 9,18,50,71,73
   Robert 129,243
   Robert F. 135,141,161
   Robert S. 117
   William 237
Berryman, Edward 134,146,232
   Richard 43,49,54
   William 30,134,146,232
Bethey, Elisha 5
   James 100,105,112,147
   Jesse 36
   John 4,5,8,9,15,21,27,36,81,
   147,148
   Mary 4,216
Best, David Rice 21
Billups, Langley 234
   Thomas 117,122,141,145,161
Bird, Penelope 146
Blair, Will 160,165
Blade, Law 4
Blanchard, Aaron 1,3,12,32,56,63,64
   83,84,96,98,132,191,192,209,232,
   233,235
   Aaron Jr. 1,84
   Aaron Sr. 1,92
   Abner 1,24,26,63,233
   Absolum 8,30,204,219
   Absalah 84
   Amariah 1,63,127,128
   Amos 51,153
   Ann E. 63
   Barnaby 183,233
   Benjamin 56,233
   Capt. 126
   Demsey 1,3,26,32,47,64,92,108,
   136,143,150,233
   Elizabeth 1
   Ephriam 56,83,98,107
   Frederick 102,160,204
   Henry 92
   James 167
   Keziah 51,153
   Monicua 30
   Monijay 51
   Moses 24,28,30,47,54,94
   Micajah 126
   Palatiah 92,151,233
   William 93,219,239
Blunt, John 169
Bond, Demsey 23 26,47,73,94,143,151,
   213,216
   Elizabeth (Betty)178

Bond, Elisha Hance 73,84,124,
   125,132,168,171,200,242
   James 5,202
   Mary 84,122,127
   Rachael 73
   Richard 30,33,37,46,47,57,
   63,84,92,94,97,100,107,115,
   122,125,127,132,133,138,155,
   166,167,170,171,178,196,199,
   212,213,215,216,228,229,230,
   243
   Richard Jr. 114,176
   Richard 114
   Selah 73
   Thomas 73,243
   William 84,114,155,176,203,
   210
Bonner, Henry 56
Boothe, Henry 11,14,16,17,22,25
   Elizabeth 46
   James 99
   Joseph 24,227
   Margaret 17,25
   William 22,23,25,34,47,55,
   70,88,89,122
Bosworth, Obediah 107
Boyce, Alse 177
   Jonathan 44,64,77
   John 27
   Miles 140,173,174,177
   Moses 39,71,73,112,126,142,
   193,203,231
   Sion 126,181,184,100
   William H. 23,29,37,39,65,
   66,68,78,80,81,91,94,96,
   100,103,109,119,140,148,177,
   181,236
Boyette, Marthy 157
   Polly 157
   Timothy 157
Bradford, Patsy 158
   Sally 158
Brady, Charity 170
   James 7,22,25,35,45,59,61,
   67,77,78,80,91,124,132,152,
   185,225,228,239
   James Jr. 21,104,175
   Joseph 41,123,152,168,175
   Mary 80
Brewer, John 60
   Peggy 160
Brickell, Jonathan 218
   Thomas 10,17,23,28,29,36,48,
   69,70
   William 231

Breashear, Abraham 12
   John 35,59
Bridges, John 155
Briggs, John 13,20,55,59
   Josiah 33,143,203,226
   Moses 18,19,36,38,40,71,111,
   131,143,156,157,170,180,190,
   203,226
   Richard 13,126,131,174,180,188,
   205,213,225
   Nancy 104
   Soloman 33,39,87,178,188
Brinkley, David 50,90,129
   Elizabeth 52,184
   Elisha 21,119,122,124,129,142
   176,177,178,184,196
   Francis 5,21,29,123,130
   Henry 179,221
   Jacob 129,163,177,179
   John 12,51,58,119,122,142,163,
   175,176,177,179,196
   Joseph 26,28,29
   Josiah 24,128
   Levina 124
   Martha 184
   Nancy 58
   Nathaniel 220
   Peter 19
   Sarah 90
   Selah 127
   Simeon 51,90,119,147,153,176,
   196
   Thomas 176,177,237
   William 177
   Willis 231
Briscoe, Edward 77,79,80,115,116,
   168,237
   James 72,94,100,117,185
   Mary 185
   Warner 185
   William 84
Britt, Etheldred 133
Brittian, Jesse 199
Brittianham, Mary 133
Brooks, George 108,119,136,150
   Ludowick 113,134,135
   William 17,30,55,72,104,108,
   113,119,135,136,185,220,232
Brothers, Elizabeth 177,179
   John 12,129,144,222
   Richard 176,201
   William 177
Brown, David 221,242
   Elizabeth 218
   Hardy 22,70,113
   Happy 55

Brown, James 1,2,3,11,17,22,80,
   91,106,145,151,164,230
   Jesse 2,14,42,70,76
   Joseph 25,55
   Joseph Jr. 1
   John 153
   Mary 52,56,76,218
   P.(?) 5
   Nancy 218
   Richard 182
   Samuel 11,16,17,18,26,43,
   45,52,56,58,63,68,72,118,
   130,142,183,233
   Samuel Sr. 67
   William 80
   Willis 11,17,22,57,85,91,
   107,109,117,130,145,151,
   164,193,197,207,214,218,
   221,233
   Willis Jr. 233
   Willis Sr 218
Browne, Albridgeton 193,194
   Anthony 193,194
   James 193,194
   Jesse 193,194
   John 193,194
   Peter 208,218
   Samuel Dr. 15,193,194,207,
   221
Bullock, David 197,200,203
   Elizabeth 197
Bruner, John 189
Buren, Lew 111
Burges_, Edward 225,239
   Elizabeth 152,221
   John 69,152
   Lovatt 81,202
   Thomas 21
Burlton, John 125
Butler, Sarah 242

Campbell, John 158,182,218
   Nancy 55
   Thomas 55,182
Carber, William 114
Carter, Ann 79
   Elizabeth 72,157,229
   Charity 243
   Isaac 79,121,127,148,243
   James 97,125,144,149,238
   John 7,15,74,97,122,125,
   137,144
   Keziah 144
   Lewis 168
   Moore 7,8,10,19,43,45,72,
   76,77,80,96,97,148,170,239

Carter, Thomas Mills 229
   William 145,157,165,175,225,229,232
   William Jr. 223
Caldwell, Spencer 52
Casey, John 15
Caswell, Richard 64,65
Chapman, Harrison 188
Clark, will 17
Cleaves, William 14,16,17,35,37,38,
   78,118,123,140,147,162,171,197,
   215,218
Coffield, Edward 109
   Job 109
   Mary 109
Cole, Abraham 61,81,82
   James 81,82
Cohoon, Jno. C. 186
Collins, John 77,88
   Josiah 75,76,92,95,97,98,153,
   198,208,210,211,212,222,223,
   224,234
   Josiah Jr. 75,76,153
   Lemuel 80
   Sarah 149
   Thomas 162,220,242
Coak, Thomas 49
Colley, Marget 50
   Samuel 50
Conners, Lewis 46
Copeland, Demsey 105
   Elisha 22,35,48,51,55,71,78,
   88,159
   Elisha Sr. 78
   Henry 59,61,64,74,78,81,82,90,
   96,102,113,120,121,122,123,124,
   128,130,136,143,154,167,222,237
   James 18,26,35,48,55,69,90,112
   James Sr. 35
   Jesse 55,137,
   John 55,69,90
   Mary 55
   Sarah 120,121,122,123,124,
   Silas 55,137
   Stephen 167
   William 39
   Zachariah 35,48,51,90,128,221,
   222
Costen, Elizabeth 132,133,167
   Demsey 51,52,61
   James 13,51,52,54,63,100,165,
   167,173,174,176,183,200,203,204
   205,225,230,232,235
   Isaac 46,54,63,100,173,200,203,
   Thomas 215
Cotton, Demsey 37
   James 26,37,61

Cotton, Lemuel 158
   Noah 218
Cowper, Capt. 181,218
   Christ. 121,140,153,160,220
   John 103,105,106,107,121,
   141,145,151,152,153,159,160,
   171,175,176,180,187,189,193,
   196,199,204,205,208,212,216,
   222,224,225,244
   John Jr. 174
   Thomas 189,214,244
   Mrs. 183
   William 13,61,151,152,171,
   180,189,199,244
   Wills 225,226,227,229
Crafford, David 41
   Hetty 191
   James 13,42,64,120,191,245
   Joseph 199
   William 5,9,19,25,26,30,34,
   41,42,50,57,59,61,62,79,84,
   85,95,97,104,111,112,116,
   118,124,129,130,135,145,163,
   171,187,188,189,193,194,199,
   207,221,130,231
Creecy, Christopher 52
   W. 41
Croom, Ann 52
   Isaac 52
   Mary 52
   Richard 52
Crowell, Benjamin 81,151,158
Cross, Abel 22,44,50,69,81,
   84,90,91,112,115,123,150,
   176,199,201,216,218,244
   Benjamin 108
   Charity 244
   Cyprian 2,21,41,52,53,60,
   64,68,73,77,88,90,91,95,101,
   111,116,120,130,133,157,164,
   165,178,183,201,210,217,223,245
   Christian 41,46
   David 41,44,50,60,64,69,90,
   91,112,120,123,128,138,176,
   199,201,217,219,237,243
   Elisha 15,81,111,115,125,
   129,166,172,176,195,234,
   235
   Hardy 4,20,76,90,117,136,143
   143,157,176,178,209,210
   James 164,180,216
   Jesse R. 199,217
   John 76,208,209
   John R. 177,242
   Mary 77

Cross, Nancy 219
   Peggy 199
   Priscilla 111
   Penelope 128
   Riddick 112,164,183,184,202,208,
   210,219
   Samuel 77
   Stephen 32,60
   Zilpha 244
Cuff, John 215,226,228
Cullens, Jonathan 13,31,105,111,138,
   162
   Nathan 105,134,138,221,241
   Thomas 205
   Zilphia 106
Culley, William 6,18
Cunningham, John 132,133,142,143
Curle, Abraham 201,201
   Charney 195
   Edy 125
   James 16,64,95,116,202,245
Daniel, Sarah Sarah 179
   William 109,193,209
Darden, David 82,87,141
   Elisha 56,61,96
   Esther 56
   Jacob Jr. 96
   John 38,49,67,71,81,92,95,106,
   113,117,126,127,135,151,158,172,
   236
   Isaac 91,100
   Jethro 56
   Mary 172
   Sally 56
   Sarah 100,128
   Theresa 127
Davie, William R. 10,14,54,57,180,207
Davis, Dorothy 238
   James 103,108,132,136,153,162
   John 6,9,33,167,170,242
   Joseph 134,146,156,227,235
   Kezia 136,161
   Marmaduke 10,14
   Mary 9,14
   Moses 13,33,39,59,87,88,140,155,
   156,166,173,178,188,193,209,238
   Rachal 6,9,10,14
   Seney 134
   Thomas 74
Davidson, William 45,46,52,56,58,
   64,66,72,88,97
   William Jr. 64
Dawn, Bridget 56
Delany, John 99,226
Deloach, John 24

Denby, John 70,86
Dickins, Robert 139
Dickerson, David 202
    Joseph 26,112,158
Dilday, Amos 69,101,108,169,
    170,204,221
    Elizabeth 60
    Henry 19,42,60,80,91,100,
    108,136,143,171,204
    Henry Sr. 32
    Jesse 19,42
    Joseph 196
    William 129
Docton, Jacob 37,93,105,146
    John 133
    Thomas 72,92,165,235
Doeber, ___ 183
Donaldson, Samuel 160
Douglas, Robert 80
Dorlan, John 236
Doughtery, Aaron 103
    Daniel 99
    Edward 2,32,161,162,234
    Elias 236
    Jacob 61
    Leah 99,240
    Margaret 2
    John 170,224,240
    Robert 80
    William 2,94,99,116,136,
    160,170,234,240,243
    William Sr. 233
Downing, William 139
    William Sr 172
Drake, Edward 59,70
Draper, Thomas 51,136
    William 23,58,197,209
Driver, Willis 70
Drury, Charles 105
    John 27
Duke, Daniel 143,158,160
    Francis 36
    John 3,6,9,27,53,67,96,103,
    152,155,162,210,240
    John Jr. 4,10,15,133,188
    John Sr. 201
    Mary 204
    Ruth 205
    Thomas Jr. 185
Dunn, George 24,40,48,104,105,
    133,139
    Sarah 24
Dunsford, William 59,79
Durian, Elisha
Dure, Levin 102,103,114,132,140
142,146,153,155,156,157,160,170,
175,187,193,195,206,210,212,213,
221,226,230,235,236,238

Dwyer, Elizabeth 100,101,104,105,236
    Morgan 46
Eason, Abner 37,41,100
    Abraham 5,35,72,73,79,91,102,
    111,112,139
    Alexander 9,10,14,21,25,43,71,
    74,99,101,104,119,120,160,173
    Anseneth 111
    Betsy 126,152
    Elizabeth 10
    Frederick 109,110,180
    George 31,45,73,89,93,100,101,120,
    126,139,152,165,190, 194,198,202
    George Sr. 135,180,232
    Hardin 194
    Hardy 120,214
    Isaac 93,98,99
    Jacob 4,5,6,23,31,37,61,73,89,
    100,228
    James 4,5,6,23,61,175
    Jesse 10,14,19,20,21,33,35,38,
    39,41,66,74,82,85,104,111,112,
    130,155,156,159,160,168,171,
    173,179
    John 6,23,31,93,109,114,126,132,
    135
    Levi 4,23,31,61,183,202
    Mary 74,173
    Moses 14,66,71,103
    Seleca 100
    Seth 14,20,21,35,39,71,73,74, 81,
    85,93,99,101,103,104,113,129,130,
    131,149,151,158,160,165,170,171,
    175,179,185,206,235,237,244
    William 18,40,65,75,89
Edwards, Benjamin 208,210,242
Elem, Thomas 114
Ellen, Thomas 92
Ellis, Aaron 21,46,178,183
    Charity 21,178
    Daniel 9,95,102,103,135,188
    Edith 178
    Elisha 14,69,102,103,188
    James 188,198
    John 3,8,46,80,117,141,145,150,
    177,178,196,222
    Jose 221,225,238
    Josiah 198,240,241
    Mary 60,88,140
    Mills 67,69,138,185,220,222,240
    Milly 220
    Mourning 30,188,208
    Rebekah 191
    William 5,15,25,35,57,60,62,69,88,
    92,103,109,117,119,122,136,140,141,
    142,145,153,160,175,176,188
    Willis 175
Elsworth, Oliver 208

Eoyer, Daniel 184
Eure, Ann 199
   Benjamin 12,22,33,137,138
   Blake 186,231
   Charles 8,11,16,22,40,43,45,
   52,77,86,87,88,97,102,120,
   125,128,137,144,188,194,206,
   217,220,235,239
   Daniel 10,16,63,94,120,208,
   209
   Demsey 244
   Enos 97,118,193
   James 7,45,52,66,75,125
   James Jr. 70,86
   John 16,22,33,40,125,137,
   148,199,217
   Levi 128,148,188,220,238,244
   Lewis 210
   Mary 210,214
   Mills 58,77,135,137,146,157,
   178,186,210,214,231
   Samuel 17,45,52,53,66,67,
   73,77,106,148,151,239,241
   Stephen 9,11,16,17,19,25,
   33,56,58,61,66,68,76,86,
   87,88,133,138,178,186,205,
   206,220,231,235,244
   Ruth 137
   Uriah 63,64,70,83,106,120,
   131,151,241
   Vires 10
   Whitmill 179,201,220,235
      46
Evans, William 111
Everett, William 44,130,178

Farmer, Nicholas 140
Farrow, Jesse 5
Faulk, Demcy 17,36
   Joel 131
   John 35
   Mary 16
   William 16,90
Felton, Elisha 158
   Elizabeth 31
   Job 131,138,162
   John 31,32,26,42,53,56,
   213
   Judith 89
   Noah 7,36,85,89,99,110,125,
   139,140,144,147,155,180,191,
   212
   Richard 35,83
   Sarah 13,138,162
   Shadrack 4,5,24,61,69,89,
   100,214

Felton, Thomas 32,53,83,138,189,220
   William 6,7,31,56,70,198
Farrow, Jesse 5
Field, John 153,208,211,222
   Mills R. 156,185,190,191,195,
   202,204,212,213,229
Figg, James 158,164,169
   Joseph 28,135
Finney, Mary 99
   Thomas 99
Fisher, Robert 56
   Thomas 56,68
   Willis 222
Fitt, Thomas 116,172
Fontaine, Patrick Henry 244
   John 66,85,151,187,216,244
   William 106,107
Fiveash, Peter 61
Foreman, James 47
   John 36
Forrest, Anna 83
   Henry 47,78,83,84,88,93,115,122,
   130,149,216
   Sarah 216
   Thomas 233
Foster, Edison 173
   Elizabeth 104
   Joel 55,65,88,102,140,141,150,
   163,232
   Peter 135
   Richard 173
   Rosannah 141
Foote, John 152
Franklin, Daniel 129,134,158,163
   Jonas 163
   Josiah 163,221
Francis, Fred 182
Frazier, Marget 38
   Thomas 67,81,151,158
Freeman, Amos 159
   David 216
   Demcy 10,66,137,148
   George 155,232,238
   James 8,10,12,20,27,50,60,68,
   74,76,85,86,94,107,118,138,158,
   167,168,169,173,184,194,195,100,
   209,220
   James T. 239
   John 27,58
   John Jr. 10
   Joseph 169,216,239
   Josiah 212
   Polly 201
   Richard 20,115,126,148,157,158,
   159,161,181,209,220
   Sarah 94,159,192

Freeman, Soloman 48
   Thomas 167,174,208,209,212,213
   Timothy 50,158,160,171,172,174,177,187,192,200,201,204,213,217,219,222,236,238,239,240
   William 8,43,60,66,85,86,94,148,155,156,158,168,174,192,239
   William Jr. 169
   William Sr. 165,175
Fryer, Isaac 25,96,138,191
   Mary 191
   Thomas 38,215
   Thomas Jr. 171
   William 8,12,95,97,152
Fullington, Thomas 21,38,39,87,94,101,160,178,230
Frost, William 172

Garrett, Everard 3
   James 1,3,5,8
   James Sr. 2
   Jesse 44,137
   Mary 245
   Rachael 13
   Thomas 17,21,58,165,209
   Thomas Jr. 5,58
   Thomas Sr. 5,56
Garrison, Abel 188
Gaskins, Jasper 193,194
Garvey, Brown 97
   Patrick 61,116,118,193,194,207,231
Gatling, Edward 62,67,77,79,93,99,111,121
   George 51,99,168,169,244
   James 86,117,124,134,139,142,143,144,145,148,149,161,165,169,171,173,186,195,237,243
   John 4,10,34,93,121,146,148,152
   Miles 121,124,148,152,193,194,223,242
   Peggy 169
   Susaner 99,244
   William 41,50,60,65,67,75,80,89,91,108,134,137,166,168,169,170,171,221,244
   William Jr. 60,75,148,204,217
   William Sr. 171,172,204,224
Gay, John 44,136

Gayle, Christopher 121,156,172
   Isaac D. 119
Gibbons, John 116
Gibson, Ann 1,6,25,40,81
Giles, Elender 82
   John 82
Glover, Betsy 179
   John 195
   Polly 142
Glasgow, James 18,25,26,27,28,37,57,61,64,65,71,75,84,85,87,94,95,97,98,107,112,113,115,118,129,130,133,139,145,179,181
Gills, Pilvey 75
Godwin, Almeda 198, Samuel 232
Gooden, Andrew 70
   William 103
Goodman, Cyprian 137,166,176
   David 91
   Edith 15,78,91
   Henry 5,15,51,55,58,60,67,89,91,97,100,102,105,110,111,112,124,157,163,176,189,195,201,204,205,206,218,219,220,221,227,242
   James 115,125,176,210
   Joel 80,91,100,108,117,136,143,169,209,210,221
   John 5,15,53,55,67
   Mary 160
   Sarah 78
   Soloman 100
   William 5,15,17,18,51,53,55,58,60,67,80,91,93,100,110,112,120,121,122,123,130,137,148,160,166,167,169,182,189,192,193,196,201,209,210,216,221,229,235,242,244
   William Jr. 5,176,244
   William Sr. 5,15
Gordon, Benjamin 6,25,38,43,62,65,87,109,119,120,140,154,160,173,193,194,202,210,212,218,223,229
   Bathsheba 159
   George 146 149,154,157,159,181
   Jacob 15,20,35,38,39,46,60,66,74,85,87,101,126,127,135,149,157,160,171,173,175,180,224
   Jacob Jr. 135,225
   James 131,155,157,159,171,175,183,235,237
   John 6,10,14,20,28,46,65,66,71,79,103,127,155
   John Jr. 129,131,149
   Joseph 156,175,185,194
   Mrs. Joseph 118
   William 47,50,53,60,88,90,101,

Gordon, William 10,109,110,
    114,115,116,139,142,156,
    229
Graham, Dr. Ebenezer 113,134,
    135,177
Granbery, Ann 75,211
    J. 101
    James 160,164,165,182,183
    John 13,132,183,199,211,
        212
    Josiah 2,20,30,33,53,54,59,
        62,63,67,71,75,84,92,93,95,
        97,98,103,127,128,132,136,
        153,154,156,165,178,183,184,
        188,198,208,210,211,212,214,
        220,222,223,229,238
    Nancy 214
    Thomas 92,95,97,103,182,234
Gray, Gilbert 229
Green, Abraham 65,105
    Alse 148,243
    Ester 161
    Isaac 46,63,70,75,118,210
    John 17,19
    Martha 148
    Mary 82
    Mathias 17,32
    Milly 154
    Richard 10,13,46,83,106,120
    Samuel 10,18,31,32,39,40,46,
        63,64,65,66,68,70,75,86,89,
        91,118,131,134,138,139,143,
        152,155,162,181,216,221
    Selah 13
    Soloman 10,12,86,118,120,134,
        236
    Thomas 42,76,77
    William 10,13,31,64,83,106,
        111
    Zeruah 32
Gregory, James 10,13,15,16,21,
    22,31,49,71,73,91,98,101,
    103,106,107,114,130,146,
    170,183,193,202,242
    Jane 21
    Jeam 22
    John 62
    Priscilla 76,153
    Thomas 76,153
Griffin, Burrell 177,201
    Elizabeth 190
    Ephriam 8,24,32,34
    Henry 23,32,127,190,195
    Hugh 90,129
    Isaac 235
    Jitty 195
    John 177

Griffin, Joseph 8,18,26,34
    Nathaniel 173
    Sarah 8,32
Guion, Isaac Lee 218
Gwin, Charlotte 80
    Daniel 25,43,74
    Hister 227
    John 227
    Mary 79,80
    Roland 100,105
    William 73,79,80,111
Hackley, Henry 8,10,43,45,63,64,66,
    72,120,239
Hall, Henry 110
    John 43
    Judith 91
    William 135
Hare, Edward 4,10
    Elisha 62,89,127,142,183,205
    Henry 189
    Jean 62
    Jesse 105
    John 20,25,45,99,146,172,174,
        190,241
    Joseph 126,151,198,231,240,241,
        243
    Luke 158
    Moses 3,9,25,28,41,53,59,62,89,
        90,92,96,113,114,119,127
    Moses Jr. 50,62,92,95,117
    Peggy 172
    Pheraba 189
    Simmons 227
    Thomas 4
Hambleton, Andrew 16,17,22,40,56
    J. 223
    James 24
    Moses 33,178
Hamilton, George 68
Hargrove, Amelia 34
    George 12,34,49,52,73,78
Harrell, Aaron 8,11,45,52,60,66,
    178,216
    Abraham 51,94,135,161,167,188
    Andrew 39
    Anne 11,52,124
    Annis 205
    Asa 12,13,17,22,32,35,53,56,77,
        106,111,115,148,178,205,209,243
    Asenah 149
    Benjamin 56,62,65,66,85,95,139,152,
        188,189,199
    Charles 136
    David 51,52,60,80,92,95,97,99,
        114,122,132,135,149,157,163,
        168,174,184,191,197,217,218,

Hardy, Robert 78
Harrell, David 219,228,229,
    239,240,244,245
  Demsey 34,70,79,80,95,
    103,135,163,183,218,
    219,221
  Elijah 178,217,243
  Elisha 42,43,58,76,88,110,
    115,120,121,123,124,178,181,
    186,201,205,210,214,231,
    235
  Elizabeth 60
  Henry 52,108
  Isaac 7,18,24,30,51,83,136,
    142,149,213,227,228
  Isaac Jr. 83,135,142,149,
    158,170,215,225,229,231
  Isaac Sr. 242,215,235
  Jesse 7,12,13,14,15,16,17,
    22,25,31,32,34,42,58,72,
    73,81,131,134,155,162,188,
    189,209,216,221,225,235,241
  Jesse Jr. 67
  Jesse Sr. 209,241
  Jethro 8,49
  John 4,7,49,52,64,78,122,
    178
  Josiah 14,95,96,111,138,191,
    221
  Lemuell 7
  Louedicia 234
  Mary 13,80,115
  Milley 80,245
  Nancey 78,242
  Noah 51,83,106,161,178
  Osiah 80
  Peter 11,17,40,
  Pleasant 186
  Rachael 111
  Rebeckah 7
  Reuben 70,102,122,124,209
  Ruth 81
  Samuel 16,18,24,34,63,67,83,
    87,92,94,98,101,102,104,107,
    109,114,128,135,142,143,147,
    154,156,157,167,170,175,178,
    179,180,184,191,199,214,215,
    223,224,227,229,231,237,238
  Stephen 36,56,66,83,111,151,
    216
  Theophilus 135,193,230
  Thomas 7,124,125,138,148,168,
    242
  William 170,180,215,230,231
Harrison, Anna 35
  Henry 35

Harrison, John 139
Harriss, Amelia 103
  Easter 111
  Elijah 159,230
  John 6,9,14,17,32
  Norfleet 162
  William 23,26,27,28,30,32,33,49,
    78,79,82,87,95,97,103,107,119,
    126,130,132,133,134,136,140,142,
    143,147,149,155,163,166,169,174,
    175,178,183,185,191,201,208,210,
    212,217,235,237
Hart, Morgan 173
Haslet, Jethro 168
Hatersley, John 222
Hawks, Francis 208
Hayes, Benjamin 237
  Daniel 43,53,90,115
  David 24
  Elisha 202,229
  Hance 202
  Harmon 202
  Henry 55
  Jacob 43,93,140,156,227,229
  Jack 135,200
  James 1,2,34,55,56,57,93,109,
    135,140,146,147,148,156,184,
    193,202
  John 147,156,224
  Jonathan 93
  Mary 95
  Sarah 135
  Thomas 4
  William 14,43,93,110,135,140,
    146,147,149,156,185,187,200,
    202,224,226,229
  Wright 55,70,93,146,156,187,224
Haynes/ Hines, Moses 11,48,96,134,
    141,161,231,233,243
Hease, Jacob 207
Hedgepeth, Charles 56
Hegerty,Elizabeth 120,179
  Patrick 72,79,81,84,94,96,98,
    99,101,108,113,115,116,117,119,
    120,121,122,124,126,127,129,
    131,134,136,141,142,144,152,
    164,166,167,168,171,176,179,182,
    183,189,190,192,198,201,202,203,
    204,205,212,218,220,221,222,223,
    224,225,226,227,229,230,231,233,
    235,236,237,239,240,241,243,245
Hiatt/Hyatt, Jesse 9
  Soloman 51,78
  Elisha 77,78
  Thomas 77,172
Hill, Abraham 53,59,79,183

Hill, Ann 182,183
    Clement 54,76,172,236,238
    David 16,22,42,146,147
    Elizabeth 23,59,86,181
    Guy 28,32,79,185,190,191,
      201,227
    Henry 4,15,16,18,20,21,22,
      23,47,50,59,72,79,80,86,
      100,112,127,128,131,132,
      139,146,147,181,185,209,
      220,236,238,243
    Henry Sr. 4
    Himrick 16,20,22,42,79,
      131,132,146,236
    Isaac 21
    John 210
    Judith 207
    Kador 8,30,32,37,38,47,54,
      79,86,183
    Mary 50
    Moses 5,7,32,37,41,78,137,
      183,186,187,190
    Myles 179,186,187,201,219,
    Noah 160,191,210,213,228
    Tamor 190
    Whitmill 227
Hinton, Elisha 8
    Jacob 4,6,18,42,56,203,233
    James 7,8,55,141
    John 10,149,230,234
    Kedar 20,25,47,99,106,117,
      128,132,138,150,154,174,
      184,186,190,191,203,204,
      213,215,216,217
    Leah 84
    Mrs. 118
    Nancy 114
    Oner 114
    Seasbrook 16,22,23,42,114,
      185,190
    William 6,8,19,20,23,30,33,
      39,51,57,83,84,87,88,94,99,
      147,159,162,178,180,181,188,
      198,205,210,224,228,229,
      230,233,234,235,237,239,242
    Zadock 83,84,104,113,114,
      116,120,189
Hofler, Christian 126
    James 5,44
    John 32,47,86,96,105,126,
      137,169,181,204,213,218
    Thomas 10,20,21,22,33,94,
      115,126,170,184,185,233
      234
Holland, Daniel 35,49
    Elizabeth 35,111

Holland, Henry 24,25,35,44
    Joseph 67,111
    Joseph John 130
    Joseph Jr. 121
    Joseph Sr 121
Hobbs, Aaron 37,50,78,156
    Amos 50,100
    Edmond 155,214
    Guy 6,37
    Henry 4,6,202
    Jacob 182,199
    John 60,85,183
    Samuel 183,199
    Soloman 183,199
    Thomas 1,10,31,152,190,202
    Reuben 58,155
    William 202
Hooks, John 82
    William 90,123,138
Hodges, Delilah 168,169
    James 93,103,132,140,142,153,
      154,161,162,168,169,170,188,
      193,200,221
    John 142,150
    Samuel 229
Holt, Thomas 101,102,154
Hogens, James 136,147,226
    Lem 50
Horn, William 31,33,75,125,239
    William Sr. 70,86
Horton, Charles 1,43
    Daniel 55
    Willeford 83
Howard, Ann 71
    Hardy 71
Howell, David 22
    Edward 22,69,128
    Edward Sr. 236
    Michal 22,69
    ___son 42
Hubbart, John 3,53,67
    Matthew 3,53,67
Hudgins, Humphrey 32,37,48,65,73,
    87,95,96,102,103,108,113,114,
    116,118,135,136,162,175,176,
    185,190,212,215
    Hy. 125,127,169,173,174,182,
      197,200,202,205,217,228,234
    Hy. D. 234
    John 65,102,148,185,198,200
    William Jr. 52
Hughes, Sarah 77
    William 67,77,135
    William Sr. 35
    Willis 61,70,119,135,145

Hunt, J. 98
Hunter, Chloe 86
   Col. 139
   Elisha 5,10,13,18,20,24,26,
   28,30,32,40,47,54,65,66,74,
   97,111,159,183,185,194,203,
   214,242
   Elizabeth 159
   Isaac 18,21,41,45,48,53,62,
   63,77,87,118,154,164,169,
   181,193,223,232
   Jacob 20,21,37,39,41,63,175
   John 66,74,86,107,109,139,
   188,200,210,226,235
   Kedar 64
   Nicholas 65,74
   Riddick 105,128,240
   Sarah 194
   Sele 8,107
   Theolopus 139,191,210,235
   Thomas 3,20,28,30,38,40,
   50,59,73,79,86,91,92,107,
   111,115,118,126,130,137,138,
   143,155,170,172,173,174,177,
   180,184,185,190,203,222
   Timothy 82,92,127,144
   William 32,42,65,74,86,105,
   107,118,126,149
   44
Hurdle, Abraham 52,74,91,133,152,
   179,203,235,236,242
   Hardy 148
   Henry 235,236
   Harmon 110
   Joseph 39,72,73,75,85,89,91,
   129,139,201
   Judith 190
   Martin 58,148
   Miles 110,190,243
   Moses 230
   Thomas 32,50,72,85,89,98,101,
   232,235,236
   Thomas Sr. 230
   William 3,4,5,6,35,70,100,
   179,192,202,214,220,221,227,
   231
Hutches, William 133

Jamerson, Peggy 103,132,133
   Samuel H. 103,107,142
   William Pugh 107,176,215
Jackson, James 213
   Jeremiah 78
   William 213
Jernigan, Thomas 60

Jenkins, Charles 137,222
   Winborn 107,128,170,182,240
Johnson, Gab. 56,60
   Jacob 72,131
   John Harriss 217
   Thomas 198,214
Johnston, Sam. 65,75,84,85,87,139
Jones, Arthur 105,208,235,236
   Benjamin 208
   Benton 73
   Charles 62,82,93,94,96,159,160
   Christian 132
   Chloey 151
   David 54,56,59,62,65,88,90,99,
   127,203,205,225
   Demsey 9,16,25,55,63,84,124,125,
   127,129,132,133,136,141,147,150,
   162,163,174,198,213,215,217,232
   Demsey Jr. 47,156,186
   Demsey Sr. 186,190,191
   Demsey Odom 162,191,200,204
   Edith 69
   Epaphoditous 191
   Esther 206
   Even 89,117,119,120
   Hardy 2,150,163
   Hezekiah 25,79,80,111,179,206,
   207,208,226
   Henry 35
   James 2,15,25,29,35,41,54,57,
   59,62,63,76,107,112,119,122,
   127,139,143,151,153,161,165,
   166,169,170,179,181,185,186,
   203,206,221
   James Parker 151
   Jacob Parker 170,203,205
   Gracy 179
   John 1,9,30,36,59,63,103,106,117,
   132,138, 153
   Joseph 3,9,160,217,245
   Josiah 63,220,227
   Joshua 81
   Judith 59,63,76,153
   Jesse 80
   Kiat 124
   Lewis 30,50,51,73,90,153,177
   Mary 51,208,233
   Moses 15,30,31,85,90,91,120,123
   Nathaniel 217,245
   Olde David 119
   Phelishia 1
   Rachael 115,132,133,217
   Sarah 215
   Simons Hare 206,224,226
   Treasy 72

Jones, Washington 206
    William 9,54,69,71,105,124,
    204,220,222,227,240
    William Sr. 9
Jordon, David 89
    Elisha 89
    Icabod 202
    Jeremiah 17,31,72,97,117,
    132,138,174,181,191,213,
    217
    Josiah Jr. 17,29
    Ple___ 63
    Sarah 181
Keaton, John 46
    John Jr. 101
Keen, James 16,58
    Lemuel 58,133,138
    Will 4,5
Kelly, David 115
    Edward 71,136,151
    John 202
    William 23,202,214
Keys, James H. 166,168,220
Kilbee, Edward 218
King, Abigail 157
    Bersheba 24
    Betsy 56,58
    Cathren 4,18,24
    Charles 8,140
    Elizabeth 120,201
    Henry 2,4,18,29,36,38,40,48,
    52,56,70,76,81,104,105,108,
    134
    Hugh 134,186
    John 78,82,84,102,104,
    125
    Mary 124
    Nicholas 36
    Norman 165,177,180,181,201,
    210,234,242
    Pernell 76,186
    Phereby 81
    Simon 199
    Soloman 24,53,82,87,93,100,
    106,131
    William 46,92,100,101,104,
    105,123,165,174,183,195,
    199,201,217,236
Kinne, R.M. 98
Kittrell, John 36,81,91,107,
    116,128,141,144
    Luize 144
    Moses 41,58,59,65,66,68,70,
    71,79,97,124,193,196

Kittrell, Jonathan 71
    Standley 144
    William 117,120,128,141,201,203
    Willis 128
Knight, Demsey 128,131,164,172,
    225,227
    Demsey Jr. 151
    James 23,38,43,67,69,73,81,
    131,151,158,164,165,172,181,
    198,205,225,227,228
    John 67,81,128,129,221
    Jon___ 38
    William 163
Knox, James 4,121,123,124,136
Lamb, Abner 142
Landen, Elisha 95,116,138,196
    James 5,9,13,16,42,59,61,
    64,79,82,95,101,111,116,125,
    157,183,202
    John 16,101,116,156,157
    Levina 138
    Mills 101,116,125,157,177,
    199,200
Lang, Elizabeth 147
    James 4,5,32,55,100,105,147
    John 5,117,134,147,157,160,
    186,195,242
    Mary 53
Langston, Ann 6,7
    Catherine 12
    Demsey 2,6,7,18,35,59,64,83,
    88,122,195
    Elizabeth 7
    Francis 238
    Isaac 2,6,17,64,93,120,121,122,
    137,141,148,149,196,206,218,221
    Jemmima 6
    John 12,86,88,182
    Luke 6,59,64,83,93,120,121,123,
    124,130,131
    Mary 244
    Thomas 6,7,12,59,64,83
    Timothy 238
    William 7,17
Lank, Sarah 210
Larkum, John 6,9,14
Lassiter, Abisha 3,108
    Abner 162,191,198,204,213
    Absoley 162
    Aaron 18,20,24,27,30,39,41,51,
    62,67,84,87,144,159,191,192,
    196,213,214,215,217,225,227,
    230
    Allen 214,215,225

Lassiter, Amos 1,10,31,49,64,
    101,102,110,154,169,181,
    188,197,200,228
  Christian 24
  Elizabeth 166,167
  Ezekiel 144
  Frederick 2,150,162,198,
    204,213
  George 27,42,96,97,98,107,
    109,143,154,161,162,191,
    192,196,209,212,217,233
  George Sr. 47
  Gabriel 55,140,186,241
  Hance 196
  Jacob 76
  James 31,49,101,102,117,138,
    140,146,213,215,220,235
  Jean 144
  Jeremiah 24,72
  Jethro 21,24,53,184,234
  John 18,43,49,54
  Jonathan 17,25,31,42,48,69,
    88,97,98,106,107,108,122,
    132,136,150,161,187,191,
    192,193,198,212,226
  Jonathan Sr. 233
  Joseph 230
  Josiah 39,94,159,181,188
  Jothom 64
  Mary 140,181
  Miles 138,200,220
  Moses 51,96,143,183,196,198,
    213,216
  Mourning 108
  Persiler 1,3,33
  Prisiller Jr. 84
  Rachael 33,209
  Robert 42,61,109,239
  Rubin 3,33,109,139,166,167,
    210
  Sarah 144
  Seanar 32
  Seth 94
  Timothy 24,26,37,42,46,53,
    63,67,68,84,165,166,170,196,
    197,228,232,234,239
  William 65,210,235
  Winnefor 162
Lawler, Patrick 10,69,77,83,
  98,122,139
Luke, William 41,45
Lawrence, Charles 17,28,36,37,
    70,122
  George 55
  John 51
Lawrence, Michael 51,193,228
  Peggy 55
  Polly 55
  Rachael 48
  Richard 100,105
  Sawyer 55
Ledsom, Thomas 122,126,129
Lee, Henry 9,27,51,117,119,142,
    147,154,159,160,195,208,216
  John 12,82,87,106,150
  Levi 103,149,188
  Sam. 114
Lewis, David 64,70,75,83,86,118,
    125,134,151,181
  Elijah 172
  Elizabeth 237
  Fielding 105
  John 35,67,78,105,124,152,
    161,165,181
  Lemuel 114
  Luten 45,111,121,124,145,152,
    163,171,208,243
  Mills 35,67,78,111,121,132,159,
    166,221,228
  William 48,69,83,88,98,107,122,
    128,129,131,142,146,184,198,228,
    236,238
Liles, Edwin 242
Lilley, Easter 210
  Eddy 23,29
Little, John 241
  Jo. B. 241
Lupton, John 83
Lyons, Elijah 182,210
  Melison 210
Lyunce, Mich'l 92,106

Maddrey, Jas. 187
Majen, Stephen 128
Maner, Aaron 195
  Aaron Jr. 195
  Aaron 195
  Levinia 195
  Levy 195,196
  Mary 7,195
  Milly 195
  Robert 59
  Zachariah 195
Maney, James 56,68,175,231
Mann, Thomas 105
Mansfield, Samuel 56
Marble, Peter 172
Markum, John 12
March, Barnard 142,208
  Daniel 51

March, John 42,117,142,183,208
    William 172,183
Marshall, James 190
    John 187,204
    Permelia 83,98
    Thomas 55,69,79,80,88,98,
      106,109,122,129,146,147,
      166,198,204,216,222,228,
      237,240,241
Martin, Abel 10
    Alexander 18,28,37,71,97,
      112,113,115,118,182
    David 11
    Elizabeth 11
    Presse 153
    Richard 244,245
Matthews, Anthony 1,45,85,121,
    132,192,196
    Anthony Sr. 167,189,213,219,
      226,239
    Clem. R. 132,213
    Dread 219,226
    Elizabeth 132
    Esther 29,87,145
    James 73,117,142,144,145,
      225
    John 122,176,219,222
    Matt 200,231,237
    Sarah 1,142
    Riddick 226
    William 19,29,30,65,108,121,
      131,137,141,145,152,163,166,
      168,175,176,185,201,202,230,
      237,239
    William Sr. 213
McCabe, John 61
McCoy, Willoughby 76,77
McCullock, Robert 53,83,90
McDonald, William 58
McKesend, William 129
McKinsey, ___ 50
Meltier, Benjamin 115,116,232,
    239,243
    Elizabeth 97
    Jethro 2,20,21,22,27,31,42,
      50,60,63,90,91,114,115,122,
      152,184,198,209,213,215,217,
      222,228,237,243
Meroney, Elizabeth Cheney 77
    Henry 51,149,156,178,180,
      196,205,213,225,229,230
    Nancy D. 119
    Patty 54,119,184
Milfield, Charles 29
Meredith, Lewis 62
Mizell, Moses 5,42

Miller, Alexander 75,92,98,153,205,
    208,211,212,214,223
    Elizabeth 234
    Francis 33
    Isaac 33,35,37,38,39,55,57,59,
      65,66,77,78,85,102,106,135,155,
      156,168,191,197
    Isaac Jr. 182,234
    Isaac Sr. 127,140,142,147,234
    Jiney H. 234
    James 133
    John 6,9,10,14,26,30,44,48,
      59,65,66,87,145,156,193,223
    Reuben 223
    Robert 223
    Thomas 53
    William 223
Milner, Thomas 3,67
Mills, Henry 242
Minard, Ann 31, 188
    Israel 64,108,142,203,216
Ming, Delilah 237
    Pennellopy 237
Minchew, Augustus 47,49,114,143,
    154
    Bond 24,83,109,110,134,142,
      154,156,164,203,216,226
    Dinishus 31,47
    Hanna 47
    Jacob 82,108,134
    John 31,82,108
    Richard 1,10,102
    Zaccraiah 83,110
Minor, Nicholas 156,170,183
Mitchel, Richard 127,170,214
Modling, Sarah 68
Moore, Benjamin 89
    Charles 127
    James 129
    Rachael 89,91
    Randel 6
    Thomas Allen 36
    William 53,89
    Willis 60,107
Moran, Charles 149
    John 54,149,183
Mor, William Ware 111
Morgain, Abagail 233
    Abraham 43,45,49,54,58,84,110,
      112,113,133,163,204,206,230
    John 1,48,53
    Joseph 161,190
    Joseph Trader 74,217
    Lewis 233
    Mathias 54
    Rachael 210

Morgain, Ruth 45
    Seth 148,203,222
Morris, Charity 146,147
    Cherry 84
    Ephram 63,84,88
    Noah 210,216,220,221
    William 58
Morley, John 6,9,14
Murdaugh, James 89
Murfree, Evan 17,22,55,88,122
    Francis 193,194
    Hardy 139,152,180,187,202,219
Murphy, Matthew 209
Muse, Will. T. 92

Napier, Robert 92,112,129
Nerney, John 184
    Nicholas 200,201,215,228
Newby, Thomas 79
Newsom, Esther 222
    Francis 124
    Nathaniel 169,180,194,196,222
    Thomas Jr. 193,194
Neverson, William 78
Nichols, Doctor 99,174
    Frederick 144
    Jonathan 2,3,16,20,22,23,25,34,55,65,72,97,99,117,140,143,146,174,200,232,236,238
    John 54,120,123
    Mary 146,236,238
Nixon, Austin 52,219,230,232,242
    Barnaby 227,230,235,242
    Reuben 52,242
Norfleet, Abraham 35,36,121
    Charlotte 161
    Elizabeth 11,36,45,46,53,60,69,159
    Elisha 45,74,96,126,127,129,135,183,184
    Henry 35,36
    Hezekiah 45,46
    Jacob 2,3
    James 46,66,82,96,99,103,121,139,144
    John 16,17,20,45,46,56,60,66,92,93,96,126,127,159,184,204,218
    Joseph 14,86,87,95,96,113
    Judah 46
    Kicheon 141,146,151,153,159,183,184,198,205

Norfleet, Marmaduke 105,145
    Mary 45,46
    Mourning 184
    Polly 162
    Sarah 35,36,174,194
    Thomas 38,105
Norris, John 95
    Sarah 22,125
    Thomas 11,16,17,22,63,70,75,86,95,96,114,125,134
Northcutt, John 159
Noures, Joseph 116
Nuttall, William James 209

Odom, Aaron 9,27,36,42,102,171,188,204
    Absila 32
    Abraham 19
    Britian 127,239
    Benjamin 127
    Cador 4,5,12
    Demsey 4,15,19,20,21,27,36,81,92,100,105,112,115,119,127,129,148,164,170,178,182,239
    Elisha 209
    Elizabeth 121,196
    Etheldred 244
    Jacob 4,14,35,59,60,64,70,79,80,95,122,221,244
    Jemima 114
    John 12,21,31,39,42,43,44,46,52,60,61,64,68,70,71,77,78,80,82,83,84,86,88,101,102,103,106,113,114,120,121,122,123,124,125,130,134,136,138,139,144,147,149,150,154,157,159,161,163,169,173,177,184,188,222,228,237,245
    Kedar 35,77
    Mills 92
    Milly 195
    Moses 244
    Monica 78
    Richard 12,59,86,88,196,241
    Sarah 8
    Uriah 26,53,70,82,134,147,150,154,157
    William 26,44,48,53,55,71,82,106,114,142
Opdyke, Bartholomew 74
Outlaw, George 8,44,47,60,74,85,94,97,104,117,122,128,137,144,148,156,181,190,192,195,198,212,219,237

Outlaw, George Jr. 137,212
   George Sr. 212
   Jacob 1,2,8,10,20,27,44,
   60,85,94,160,167,195,200,
   237
   James 44,50,68,76,85,109,
   137,171,209
   Lewis 68
   (P) 47
   Zilphia 68
Overman, Morgan 90
Owens, Alce 89
Ownly, Edward 165,219,230,232,238
   John 6,89
   Levi 165
   Penelope 6,46
   Zadock 230

Palmer, James 172
Parker, Abgall 13,78
   Abraham 232,233
   Abraham Jr. 234,235,236
   Amos 3,24,136,198
   Amelia 104
   Ann 214,216,217
   Benjamin 4,34,106
   Cader 102,227
   Catren 92
   Daniel 36,112,159
   Demsey 7,14,15,19,21,28,
   29,36,39,41,100,180,186,
   213,224,226
   Edward 206,222
   Elisha 2,11,33,48,59,107,
   112,116,128, 144,154,210,
   234
   Elisha Jr. 107,154
   Elizabeth 62,240
   Esther 154,161
   Feroby 101
   Francis 4,52,55,70,84
   Humphrey 159,227,240
   Isaac 36,169
   Isaac Jr. 232
   James 11,24,25,34,44,60,61,
   62,66,72,110,121,129,137,
   148,152,161,166,169,186,
   189,207,215,227
   James Sr. 9
   Jesse 197,236
   John 10,25,33,34,54,59,64,
   69,70,77,83,86,87,88,103,107,
   121,123,125,133,138,143,
   146,147,148,149,152,159,
   161,167,188,194,196,201,
   206,115,238,243

Parker, John Jr. 120,137
   John Swan 137,197,216
   Joseph 20,25,47,101,104,105,
   150,168,186,190,213,215,218
   Josiah 49,72,73,97,121,138,
   158,187,191,192,208,217
   Josiah Jr. 72
   Josiah Sr. 44
   Judith 166
   Kedar 11,35,125
   Kindred 148,149,200
   King 189
   Mary 33,36,226
   Miles 14,36,91,119,226,230
   Moses 11
   Nancy (Ann) 216
   Omy (Naomi) 121
   Peter 23,35,48,154,158,159
   Rebecca 106
   Richard 2,23,102
   Robert 1,2,13,14,15,17,32,53,
   57,76,77,81,100,105,115,116,
   121,165,214,216,232,233
   Robert Jr. 1,27
   Robert Sr. 12,27,30,42,78
   Ruth 61,62
   Sarah 158
   Thomas 3,49,53,62,67,69,71,
   140,168,184,206,222,227
   William 3,35,41,53,67,130,214
   William Sr. 9
   Willis 22,23,27,79,80,99,145,
   164,233
   Zilphia 216
Parnall, John 78
Payne, Michel 160
Pearce, A. 37
   Abner 96,191,192,196,204,217,
   Abraham 85,99,152,213,214
   Christopher 18,19,20,36,38,40,
   41,107
   Isaac 10,38,226
   Jacob 5,18,19,20,28,36,41,52,
   105,107,139,194,203,226
   Moses 10,39,40,111
   Richard 37,112
   Sarah 38
   Thomas 21
   William 3,27,33,34,96,99,105,
   152,213
Peal, Joseph 10,50
Per___, John 63
Perry, Jacob 236
   Mordecia 69,70,100,109,214
   Penina 150
   Robert 150

Perry, Sarah 69,70
   Seth 236
   William 150
Pelt, Daniel 142
Phelps, Christian 125
   Demsey 28,29,88,130
   Elizabeth 232
   James 13,43,49,110,111,125,
   132,133,139,180
   James Jr. 125
   James Sr. 125
   Jesse 137
   Judah 201
   Micajah 58,118,205,215
   Renthy 132
   Trentha 111
   William 3,188,215
   Wo_ 123
Phillips, Demsey 70
   John 200
   Majer 123
   Soloman 59,127
Piland, Ann 77,148,181
   Catherine 72
   Charity 53
   David 96
   Edward 24,46,70,72,86,
   95,96,134,178
   George 1,2,3,11,17,72,149,
   151,164
   James 42,56,109,119,189,
   205,241
   John 56,76,111,115,148,151,
   162,189,236,241
   Peter 17,24,28,29,30,46,
   53,60,70,72,220
   Sarah 17
   Stephen 35,46,86,88,159,
   162
   Thomas 8,35,44,49,76,86,88,
   96,114,134,135,159,178,
   205,220,236
   Willis 151,159,162,186,189,
   205,220,236
Pinder, Paul 150
Pipkin, Isaac 5,8,15,16,21,41,
   51,53,54,55,60,67,91,95,
   96,100,105,108,117,120,
   121,123,134,169,173,185,
   195,204,206,207,216,221,
   237,242
   Isaac Jr. 105,126,152,
   157,165,167,193,208,242

Pipkin, Isaac Sr. 105,165,172
   Jennett 95
   John 5,41,44,51,55,67,68,75,
   79,83,93,94,241
   Sarah 134,165,172
Pitman, Samuel 81,151
Pleasants, Samuel 218
Porlet, Robert 113
Pope, Richard 71
Polson, Caleb 96,197
   John 17,109,190,197,198,238
   William 53,60,190,198,209
Porter, John 9
   Joseph 51
   William 51
Powell, Benjamin 55,147
   Charles 107,128,144,148,167,
   168,192,194,212,219,239,240
   Daniel 114,185,220
   Elizabeth 122
   Isaac 15,139,140,155
   Jacob 56,85,87,94,122,140,156,
   158,193,194,206,223
   Jacob S. 203,231
   James 69,124,138,140,158
   John 3,15,17,30,42,66,72,77,85,
   88,93,94,122,140,141,145,158,
   163,170,176,179,185,194,203,
   204,205,206,207,223,224,227,
   240
   John Jr. 185,203
   John Sr. 179
   H. 185
   Kedar 20,103,182,231
   Lemuel 43,49,54,153,179
   Mary 94
   Robert 13,88,158,176,188,
   204,207
   Sarah 15
   William 6,15,39,54,65,68,85,
   95,133,140,155,176,204
   William Sr. 6,49
   Zilpha 188
Pratt, Kimbell 35,78
Price, James 235
   James Jr. 72
   Noah 72
Pruden, Jacob 142
   James 43,45,58,110,112,129,
   137,145,154,225
   John 33,225
   Nathaniel 225
Prue, James 165
Pugh, Daniel 1,6,13,88,113,165

Pugh, Francis 23,26,32,39,62
    147,162,181,217
    Orphans 176,215
    William 108,191
Purvis, Teberus 108,127

Ra__, John 19
Raby, Adam 43,49
    Jacob 2,104
    James 193
    John 43,49,51,94,109
    Kedar 51,94
    Kedar Sr. 94
    Lemuel 94
    Sarah 94
Raney, William 173
Ransone, James 84,105,120
    174,242
    Thomas 135
Rawls, Amelia 216
    David 165,182
    James 90,111
    John 15,25,89,111,172,242
    John Jr. 124
    Penina 182
    Richard 192,198,216
Rayne, Joshua 150
Reid, Catey 47,186
    Hardy 126
    Isaac 188,210,236
    John 165
    Mary 47
    Micajah 161
Redding, John 129,142
Rea, James 187,189
    William 171,172,180,187,
    188,189,199,202,218,219,
    229
Realy, Elisha 142
Rhodes, John Jr. 37
Rice, David 10,20,24,41,62,69,
    76,82,87,92,113,114,117,122,
    124,127,131,144,146,159,170,
    175,227
    James 61,72,104
    John 17,21,23,24,27,41,60,
    62,63,76,113,153
    Peggy 62,76,153,167,220
Riddick, Abraham 55,65,76,90,
    109,131,136,139,140,141,
    147,150,156,163,167,177,
    179,185,186,194,200,207,
    214,217,220,221,224,227,
    231,232,237,238,243
    Christopher 3,7,15,21,28,
    57,72,75,106,107,109,117,
    145,158,160,223,224

Ridddick, Col. 181
    Daniel 134,139,144,192
    Demsey 1
    David 72,126,127,131,143,155,
    156,157,159,160,168,175,180,
    186,187,193,214,219,226,230,
    236
    Docton 3,39,171,208,224
    Elizabeth 93,94
    Edward 59
    Isiah 109
    James 9,14,51,57,90,96,114,117,
    121,134,159,164,209,242,
    Jethro 51
    Job 27,37,42,46,51,54,63,67,
    97,101,108,136,150,161,170,
    178,198,212,233,235
    John 1,2,9,106,126,143,144,
    174,188,201,208,210,216,225,
    236
    Joseph 4,5,6,9,14,23,24,25,
    28,37,39,40,54,65,66,67,72,
    73,75,85,89,91,94,98,101,105,
    115,119,129,132,134,138,139,
    144,146,151,152,157,158,169,
    170,172,179,180,181,185,190,
    194,200,203,208,219,231,232
    Julia 79
    Jo. 98,109,110,111,210,214,229,
    238,240,242
    Joanna 219
    Kedar 14,51,57,94
    Lassiter 162,178,198,235
    Leah 168
    Lemuel 87,140
    Henry 175
    Mary 2,39,71,72,85,107,170,175,
    225,229,235
    Micajah 1,42,55,58,59,66,68,
    72,99,125,133,139,144,180,182
    Micajah Jr. 155,190,191,196,
    197,204,205,217,230,234
    Micajah Sr. 134,196,197,205,206,
    222
    Mills 19,36,39,40,72,111,112,
    131,143,155,156,157,175,183,
    203
    Nathan 190,192,214,238
    Nathaniel 72,94,126,127,131,
    143,155,156,157,167,175,180
    Nathaniel Sr. 78
    Orphans 38
    Penney 227
    Reuben 54,57,89,90,111,146,
    152,179,219

Riddick, Robert 39,47,73,86,90,
  92,119,126,151,154,160,
  167,180,188,200,205,223,
  224
  Robert Jr. 223
  Robert M. 186
  Sally 201
  Samuel 224,225
  Seth 23,27,28,40,57,59,91
  Sophia 28
  Thomas 109,140,156,169,
    195,200,202,209,224,238
  William 1,109,160,193
  William W. 167,215,218,220,
    228
  Zilla 223
Richards, John James 135,136
Right, Nathaniel 17
  William 16 (See Wright)
Ritter, William 96,147
Roberts, Christian 132
  Benjamin 172,187,229,241,242
  John 4,5,6,23,24,152,161,198,
    200,219,228,232,233,234
  Jonathan 3,8,13,25,26,28,31,
    50,60,63,88,89,92,93,97,99,
    102,114,122,132,146,151,161,
    174,184,198,217,223,226,228
  Penny 223
Robertson, Margaret 88
  Thomas 24,86,95,113,114,134
Robins, Bashford 96,106
  Christian 21
  Darkis 21
  Benjamin 21,83,98
  Elizabeth 21
  James 21,83,98,127,133,185,
    209
  John 20,22,25,34,72,77,98,
    99,106,117,184
  John Jr. 22,34
  John Sr. 97,106
  Ma___ 20
  Nancy 21,23,190
  Pashents 21
  Rachel 98,99,106
  Sarah 21
Robinson, William 190
Rochell, John 61,73,81,82
  Judith 82
Rogers, Ely 116
  Enos 29,32,116,117,143,
    144,209
  Jonathan 115,116,124,143,
    144,147,166,174,176

Rogers, Joseph Jr. 98
  Lot 29,148
  Phillip 34,100,105,116,120,144
  Robert 32,60,86,88,144,148
  Sarah 116
  Stephen 35,94,122,124,147,148,
    149,161,165
  Timothy 108
  Zilpha 148
Rogerson, Jesse 111,129,201
  Josiah 89,201
Rollin, Richard 100
Rooks, Charles 83
  Demsey 45,104
  Demsey Sr. 132,145,228
  Edith 104
  John (Warren) 225,226
  Joseph 45,61,160
Ronals, Mary 13
Ross, Callum 16,116,120,157,202,
    245
  Elizabeth 136
  John 7,42,104
  Soloman 136,143
Roundtree, Abner 130,177,192,208
  Charles 9,24,37,40,41,50,52,
    56,61,165,172,175
  John 24,56,61,102
  Josiah 190
  Mary 239
  Miles 110,169
  Sarah 130,192
  Seth 50,56,58,66,102,128,137,
    138,156,158,170,191,200,203,
    219,243
  Thomas 37
Runnels, Joseph 19,60,84,245
  William 181
Russell, Charles 7,12,72,73
  Armistead 181
  James 92
  John 13
  Sarah 181
Ruters, William 138

Saunders, Abraham 52,55,71,82,236
  Ann 150,157
  Bray 44,82,99,142,172,183,
    208,216
  Benjamin 26,29,44,70
  Briant 154,173,176,208
  Charity 82,236
  Charles 44,55,70,108,114,154
  Francis 4,26,52,82,147,150,157
  Henry 26,29,101,108,186

Saunders, John 49,207
   Joseph 70,186
   Lawrence 128,157,174,236,237
   Mary 236
   Richard 150
   Sarah 26,29,100,101,104,105,108,236
   William 134,157
Savage, Caleb 34,106,159
   Caleb Jr. 191
   Elizabeth 185
   Jesse 158,182,210,231
Sawyer, Samuel 151
Scott, Joseph 54,59,76,103,132,153
   Mary 54,59,76,103,132,153
   Watson 88
Sears, Delilah 143
   Henry Eborn 78,80,91,136,143,152,154,166,168,169,193,199,201,202,203,209,221,225,228,239,242
   Mary 143
   William 226
Sharp, Starky 89
Sheppard, John 10,21,49,161,164,185,242
   Joseph 44
   Stephen 40,44,49,73,164
   William 95,185
Sedgley, John 67
Simons, John 85,110,111,136,137,140,142,148,156,224
   Nancy 137
Sketer, Ellen 221
Sketo, James Jones 15,99
Skinner, James 7,21,31,44,45,64,68,71,77
   Jos. B. 235,238
   Lewis 36
   John 11,17
   Mills 79
   William 12,53,90,93,220,121
Slade, W. 183,220
Slaven, Jethro 162
Small, Charity 9,10
   David 21,79,80,136,151,199,207
   Elizabeth 90
   James 10,71,79,90,117,118,127,136,146,151,168,179,193,197,199,205

Small, John 8,25,43,74,119,136,151,159,193,196,204,223,229,230
   Joshua 6,9,10,14,20,38,43,71,74,79,80,82,103,171,182
   Josiah 72
   Moses 183,229
   Rachael 13
Smith, Aaron 233
   Abraham 200,215,219
   Amos 1,26,108,133
   Anthony 197
   Charles 138,140,141,150,158,162,163,187,191,217,245
   Charles M. 54,76
   Elizabeth 48,93
   Henry 19,26,37,47,48,83,113,116,162,164,182,187,189,191,197,202,215,219
   Jonathan 9,27,35,37,38,47,48,95,118,123,130,134,171,182,205,215
   Joseph 68,77,183,184
   Lewis 179
   Richard 197,202
   Richard R. 129,136,189
   Robert 232
   Samuel 9,19,23,27,29,35,37,38,39,41,48,54,65,66,86,87,93,108,116,121,127,147,164,165,166,167,172,175,180,186,189,191,194,197,213,232,239
   Sealy 7
   Stephen 48
   Thomas 7,9,15,20,21,23,28,29,33,35,37,38,39,47,48,87,93,95,113,115,123,140,171,182,189,197,202,206,228
   Thomas Jr. 118,175
   Thomas Sr. 116,118,169
   William 70,75,86
Southall, Daniel 164,168,180,216,218,221,232,233
   Jesse 209,228,232,233
Sparkman, Ann 118
   Lewis 7,45,52,74,91,122,124,133,137,160,178,205
   Rachael 137
   Reuben 13,63,81,118
   Selah 22,52
   Thomas 7,12,74
   Willis 31,81,134,161,184,200,216,242,243

Sparling, George 78
Speight, Aaron 188,224
  Amos 207
  Barsheba 166
  Francis 26,48,49,62,63,73,
  100,101,104,105,108,134,
  141,145,157,163,201,202
  Henry 26,29,35,44,48,100,
  101,104,105,108,141,142,145,
  154,157,163,169,174,195,201
  Isaac 175
  Jeremiah 26,27,28,30,32,47,
  81,83,87,96,108,113,116,
  127,144,174,176,181,191,
  201,205,215
  Joseph 4,8,18,26,29,35,40,
  44,48,92,100,101,104,105,
  236,242
  Josiah 191
  John 205,212,213,214,215
  Nancy 245
  Richard Dobbs 129,130,133,
  139,145
  Susannah 163
  Thomas 103,175,245
  Turlington 45
  William 3,44,91,114,144,150,
  173,174,188,191,216
  William Jr. 212,245
  William Sr. 176,213,215,245
Spence, Harriss 183
Spivey, Abraham 28,169,182,186
  Abner 38
  Ann 40
  Champion 7,37,40
  Daniel 22,95,181
  Elizabeth 41
  Elijah 50
  Jacob 50,52,58,137,155,182,
  201,218,234
  Jacob Jr. 170
  Jesse 13,52,109,182
  Moses 22,41,51,57,94,109,
  130,179,193,208
  Nathaniel 7,9,24,37,40,41,
  50,68
  Priscilla 109,130,192,208,
  209
  Sarah 40,109
  Seth 68,175,243
  Thomas 30,40,51,137
  William 41,68
Stallings, Daniel 85,118,126,169
  James 163

Stallings, Hannah 229
  Jesse 85,187,221,228
  Josiah 14,69,95
  Phillip 163
  Rachael 50,119
  Priscilla 228
  Seth 7,37,41,50,119
  Simeon 30,37,38,40,50,51,58,
  79,86,110,150,151,171,172,
  180,182,183,190,194,203,216,
  219
  Simeon Jr. 183
  Willis 85,95,187,219,228
Standen, John 149
Stott, Watson 191,221
Stead, Green 144
Stepto, John 209
Street, Richard 50
Streator, Malico 120,174
Stewart, James 151
Stroud, Anderson 109
Suggs, Stephen 112
Sumner, Abraham 3,25,39,40,48,65,
  72,73,75,85,89,90,91,92,93,
  102
  Ann Streater 131
  Betsy 134
  David 191
  David R. 234
  Dempsey 4,7,43,104,128,131,
  158
  Edwin 19,32,35,50,62,65,71,
  141,180,190,213,226
  Hannah 231
  Jacob 2,3,23,38,81,158
  James 8,15,23,25,29,30,38,40,
  54,57,58,66,67,82,113,127,141,
  144,151,158,167,171,175,187,
  200,209,220
  James B. 50,74,81,86,104,113,
  123,131,134,135,140,144,149,
  157,158,164,165,167,169,174,
  175,185,192,195,198,207,209,
  210,220,230
  Jethro 8,11,18,29,32,33,35,
  46,50,57,70,82,92,94,95,108,
  113,117,123,126,127,128,129,
  131,135,150,154,155,157,161,
  162,166,170,172,173,175,178,
  182,185,186,189,191,192,194,
  195,198,199,200,202,203,206,
  207,208,209,216,218,224,226,
  229,231,234,235,237,238,240
  Jethro W. 234

Sumner, John 101,104,108,242
   Joseph John 47,54,57,62,
   99,113,119,131,134,158,
   166,167,173,179,184,186,
   191,197,198,204,221
   Josiah 186
   Judith 141,153
   Luke 11,12,19,20,29,38,39,
   40,57,60,82,85,87,88,90,
   92,93,94,104,108,113,119,
   122,127,129,131,134,136,141,
   142,147,153,158,163,166,167,
   175,176,177,179,184,185,187,
   207,221,229
   Lewis 186
   Mary 72
   Mourning 38,99,153,158
   Millicent Hunter 158
   Polly 198
   Martha 87
   Samuel 54,57
   Sarah 23,131
   Seth 175
   Teresa 131
   Thomas 37,42,63,166,207
   William 11,12,42,100,165,
   166,204,207,232
Swann, William 34,57

Taylor, Hilery 171
   James 50,60
   Jesse 74,137,138,199,200,
   201,238,239
   John 49
   John Lewis 188
   Joseph 137,156,165,166,175,
   222,243
   Judah 12
   Isaac 150
   Lemuel 192
   Lydia 137
   Nathaniel 13,110,157,165,
   166,175,190,222
   Robert 4,15,21,76,77,84,
   150,158,160,171,187,207
   Samuel 8,11,12,13,17,33,
   43,46,52,56,58,66,68,74,
   76,137,156,157,186,204,
   205,210,231,239
   Samuel Jr. 231
   Thomas 22,55
   William 21,176,179
Thomas, Elizabeth 21
   J. 242
   Jacob 170

Thomas, James 49,109
   John 5,7,21
   Mary 70
   Robert 34
   Samuel 42,43,49,52,61,70,78,
   109,133
   William 49,78
Thompson, Lewis 181
   Joseph 51,73
   Lewis 181
Thurston, William 8
Thorburn, James 78,88
Trader, Jonathan Army Trader 12,30
Trevathan, Elisha 245
   James 109,245
   William 33,43,49
Travis, Elizabeth 25,72,181
   Thomas 25,72,97,98,174
Trotman, Amos 9,26,29,183
   Ann 6
   Christian 13
   Demsey 13,18,26,30,32,34,47,
   50,51,56,74,86,118,126
   Emiley 13
   Ezekiel 32,40,65,66,74,149,
   155,177,182,232
   Elisha 197
   Joseph 212,214,219
   Riddick 86,169,170,195,207,
   212,219,242
   Sarah 187
   Seth 186,187,218
   Thomas 6,13,32,24,47,50,54,
   98,101,134,155,166,197,232,
   239
   Noah 155,165,166,182,186,187
   Willis 238
Tugwell, James 100,190
   Mary 215
Turlington, Miles 145
Turner, J. 241
   Miles 96
   Pap 14
   Pasco 89,113,166
Twine, Jesse 15,102,232
   John 15
   Pleasant 15
   Thomas 15,110
Tyne, Elizabeth 87
   Thomas 24

Umphlet, Asal 149
   Benjamin 88
   David 24,138,149,225
   Job 24,77,87,88,206

Umphlet, John 206
  William 40,46,148,149,225
Vann, Bryant 104,136
  Charles 2,54,55
  Edward 176,180,208,210,222
  Henry 152
  James 215,232
  Jesse 2,5,7,8,21,31,52,68,
  73,78,79,82,86,101,130,133,
  136,164,171,172,177,180,183
  John 39,73,77,112,120,126,
  145,147,150,152,157,164,168,
  175,187,201,202,224,232
  John Jr. 187
  John Sr. 225
  Joseph 12
  Liles 91
  Nancy 70
  Sarah 31
  Thomas 27,67,95,96,104,111,
  121,132,145
  William 16,21,23,29,32,34,
  36,41,45,52,67,80,91,100,
  136,176,195,196,215,226
Varnall, Benjamin 120,123,136,138
  Jim 13
  John 16,46,84,136,138,147
Vaughn, Charles 49
  Nancy 49
  William 49
Vick, Jo. 128
Voight, J.W. 144,174,176,197
Volentine, Abigail King 82,87,
  106
  Alexander 195
  Joseph 87,93,114
  Rebecca King 106
  William 60,111,118,137,165,
  166,175,195,222

Wa_fe, Thomas 109
Walker, Elkanah 62
Walters, Bryant 136,171
  Edith 217
  Elizabeth 29,182
  Edey 136
  Isaac 45,121,126,128,144,
  152,154,160,164,166,168,
  182,200,224,226,231,240
  Isaac Jr. 68,71,170,182,184
  Isaac Sr. 132,184
  Jacob 27,42,51,117,142,143,
  176,208
  James Bray 4,18,29

Walters, John 35
  Lewis 66,68,71,155,197,204
  Mary 217,229
  William 4,18,29,39,45,73,98,
  99,112,123,126,136,138,142,
  154,172,182,200,212,213,224,
  240
Wallis, Ann 123
  Edith 123
  James 44
  John 24,44,90,91,109,123
  John Sr. 123
  Miles 74,148,219
  William 30,31,44,46,74,90,91,
  109,120,123,245
Walton, Ann 210
  Esther 51,115,128,129
  Henry 8,13,18,24,28,30,32,
  34,47,54,92,187,197
  Hanah 111
  Holloday 45,128,135,154,213,
  225,227,229,231,235
  Isaac 1,154
  James 40,50,51,56,76,97,110,
  117,118,128,167,168,187,200,
  238
  John 8,21,22,30,32,33,34,42,
  43,178
  John B. 40,50,51,54,56,59,
  73,84,86,102,110,115,125,126,
  127,128,129,130,132,145,151,
  173,174,181,190,201,204,209,
  217,220,233,234,240
  Mary 30,216
  Mills 156,169,186,187
  Millicent 231
  Pallatial 13,28
  Prescilla 30,38
  Richard 37,58
  Sarah 8
  Thomas 13,52,187
  Timothy 52,59,76,94,97,102,
  110,126,151,187,195,197,198,
  203,204,216,221,222,239
Ward, Caleb 193,194
  Jesse 160
  John 70
  Robert 47,184
Warren, Bray 67,96,123,124,154
  Edward 29,34,38,65
  Edward Jr. 34
  Edwin 242
  John 45,70,143,181,221
  John Rooks 225,226

Warren, Priscilla 123
    William 45,61,67,77,79,80,
    93,111,117,121,123,125,130,
    139,243,209,242
    William Sr 221
Watkins, William 181
Washington, General George 19,
    66,103,105
Watson, David 8,44,69,78,90,
    91,115,128,141,150
    John 22,69,112
    Rachael 150
    William 128
Weatherly, Isaac F. 87
    John 125
Webb, John 1,8,16,27,33,34,101,
    188
    William E. 126,174,188,208,
    210
West, John W. 208,218,222,242
Whels, John 49
White, Bethary 58
    George 58
    John 58,68,86,88
    Joshua 58,117,118
    Meedy 72
    Thomas 58,155,170
    will 180,181,204,206,207,
    218,229,240,241
Whitehead, John 62,152,189
    Miriam 152,171,189
Widbee, John 117
Wiggens, Ambrose 164,192,243
    Andrew 186
    James 88,90
    Jacob 192
    John 118
    Jesse 36
    Kedar 186,192,198,227,231,
    240,243
    Mary 38
    Noah 3
    Pugh 192,243
    Robert 164,169,180,193,194
    Robert F. 175,186
    William 14
    Willis 23,38,73,104,153
    Willis Jr. 43,81,151,192
    Willis Sr. 57,67,81,151,158
    Thomas 11,12,28,153,192,225,
    227,231,243
Wilkins, Jacob 96,233,243
    Judith 233
    Moses 233

Wilkins, Shadrack 12
    will 26
Wilkinson, John R. 12,29,30,71,
    78,88,141
    Mills 11,12,153
    William 12
    Willis 12,15,153
Willey, Arthur 42,204
    Hillory 176,195,241,244
    Mathias 195
Williams, Absolom 125
    Anthony 132,141,145,149,159,
    171,175
    Benjamin 107,160,206,207,240
    Christian 162
    Demsey 36,41,44,48,96,116,
    117,120,121,141,144,152,166,
    168,179,184,199,201,239
    Dorothy 162
    Elisha 204
    George 1,3,8,17,22,27,35,38,
    49,70,72,107,120,145,148,151,
    164,165,197,206,207,236,238,
    240,241
    George Jr. 14,16,119,182
    George Sr. 70,182
    Halon 119,165,171,204
    Hardy 34
    Hezekiah 119,140
    Isaac 102,173
    James 187,190
    Jonathan 9,11,23,35,39,79,
    81,93,117,144,171,184,195,
    197,204,205,241,244,245
    Jethro 218
    Judeah 29,30,71,88
    Mack 119
    Moses 140,147
    Seth 192
    Samuel 36,70,81,113,114,119
    William 46,72,80,140,162,171,
    209,212,215,218
    Whitmel 43
    Reuben 166,168
Wilson, Capt. 95
    James 17
    Seasbrook 1,2,3,11,13,17,21,
    22,76,149,151,180
Wills, Hardy 105
    John 114
    James 124,154
    Matthew 82
Wisler, Bryant 132

Winburn, Ham 154
   Henry 167
   James 16,35,90
   John 103
   Nancy 16
   Sarah 124,154
   Thomas 26
Woodley, Andrew 188,200,203,205,229
   Mary 188,229
   Samuel 188
   William 87,167
   Willis 168,170,176,180,181,194,196,200,205,213,229
Wood, Jimmia 48
   Tomas 48
Wright, James 62
   Jane 62
   John 62
   Henry 62
   Sarah 62
Wynns, George 103,153
   Judith 103,153
   Thomas 172
   William 128
Young, John H. 162
   Thomas 81,162

LOCATIONS

Acrons Bridge 243
Alphins Line 27
Alstons Line 22
An Hill Pecosin 40
Arline Family Land 235
Arnolds Ridge 171,219
Ashleys Path 26

Bakers Folly 29,65,66,71,239
Bakers Patent/Mill 72,175
Bakers New Survey 239
Ballards Line 145,178
Ballards Patent 104,130
Banks of Italy 74,178
Bare Garden 185
Barfields Fishery 199
Barnes Creek 58,62,74,104,118,130,163,172,187,189,193,194,242
Barnes Old Landing 108,134
Basses Creek/Swamp 33,38,39,87,101,119,120,130,159,160

Bay Branch 48,158,159,231
Bay Tree Branch 232
Beach Swamp 4,19,20,27,36,51,81,92,100,105,112,117,129,178
Beach Island 55,241
Beaverdam Swamp 15,27,47,51,63,84,94,99,104,122,125,127,129,183,195,209,244
Beef Creek 159,181,192
Bentons Line 22,91,137
Bennetts Creek 1,2,3,5,6,8,11,14,17,19,21,22,23,25,26,27,31,32,34,36,37,38,39,42,43,46,47,49,53,55,60,63,64,76,77,78,79,80,83,84,85,86,88,89,90,92,93,95,96,97,98,101,102,107,108,109,110,112,114,115,116,117,122,125,128,130,132,135,136,139,140,141,142,145,146,147,148,149,154,155,156,159,162,164,165,166,168,170,171,173,174,175,177,185,188,189,190,191,200,201,202,206,207,208,210,211,214,217,218,222,224,228,229,232,235,236,238,239,240,241,242,243
Bennetts Road 13
Bertie County 4,10,46,53,85,89,140,182,195,244
Big Flat Branch 119,120
Blanchards Old Patent 115
Blanchards Line 20,23
Blackbird Hill 184
Black Fish Hole 135
Berrymans Patent 129
Black Water 236
Bonds Line, Swamp 37,165,192,217
Bonds Island 63,110,232
Booths Line 198
Bradys Line 10,117,209
Boar Swam 219
Briscoes Line 115,228
Brogadon Branch 21
Brothers Line 57,186
Boyces Branch/Line 217,228
Brooks Line 205,236
Broadneck 184
Brickhouse Plantation 183
Bucklands 94,209
Buckhorn Creek 97,139
Bull Pocosin/Bridge 38,46

Carters Line 167
Cabin Swamp/Branch 21,46,115,126,130,132,178,183,184
Camden Co. 66,216
Cambel & Wheeler 235

Caletes Dowry 25
Catherine Creek, 1,3,6,7,9,14,
23,26,27,31,40,44,47,49,50,66,
79,83,92,98,104,114,127,128,
132,137,144,146,156,157,165,168,
169,175,183,187,190,192,209,236
Channers Line 50
Chowan Co. 1,2,3,5,6,7,8,10,12
31,35,37,38,42,54,56,58,63,72,
76,77,92,93,95,97,98,121,125,
153,166,175,205,210,212,213,
214,222,224,227
Chowan Indians 4,47,55,83,98,
132,146,184,236,241
Chowan Indian Line 1,27,77,97,
128,254
Chowan River 22,24,35,40,56,
58,61,62,64,66,67,68,69,71,
72,73,78,82,83,91,95,97,100,
102,103,108,112,116,118,128,
130,133,134,139,144,150,152,
154,158,159,163,171,172,179,
180,181,187,189,192,193,194,
202,207,217,218,219,231,236
237,242
Coleman Branch 96
Colemans Patent 207
Coles Creek 17,19,22,32,42,53,
56,77,95,119,120,145,148,162,
164,173,189,205,207,209,236,241,
243
Coles Island 1,209,226
Collage Branch 110,129,137
Conellor Ditch 26
Cool Springs 133
Copelands Line 93,154
Cottons Ferry 144
Cow Swamp 73,97,146,207
Cleaves Line 205
Crooked Branch 97,191
Cowpers Swamp 214
Cos__Bridge 217
Cross Swamp 16,245 Corner 202
Corapeak Swamp 163
Crane Pond 230,237
Cullens Line 118,189
Cuffs Line 224
Cumberland Co 7,181
Cumberland Settlement 142
Cypress Swamp 2,4,5,11,14,26,
29,33,39,40,46,52,54,55,59,
61,63,64,69,70,74,75,80,81,
86,95,96,102,104,117,118,122,
124,125,134,138,140,141,147,
150,157,174,178,186,188,189,
191,194,195,199,205,209,210,

Cypress Swamp 216,217,219,221,
224,227,236,239
Cypress Pond 68,111,197,231

Dabseys Run 217
Davis Line 20
Davidson Co. 149
Deep Branch 4,5,11,14,24,25,28,
45,55,69,156,157,174,185,204,216
Deep Cypress Swamp 4,52
Deep Gut 31,101,102,114,131,136,
138,140,154,157,162,169,192,196
Deep Run 40,204,216,242
Deep Bottom Branch 224
Dennis Old Field 122,170
Dildays Line 29
Dickersons Patent 145
Dismal Swamp 38,52,59,111,155,
159,175
Dobbs Branch 85,155
Dobbs Co. 52
Doctors Road 243
Dunns Corner 195
Dukes Clearing 33 Fence 236
Dukes Seine Place 150
Dowry 115

Easons Line 131
Edenton 58,69,75,76,92,122,130,
133,145,153,160,163,164,166,180,
181,182,188,198,205,207,210,211,
212,213,229,231,235,239
Edgecomb Co. 2,15,24,53,83,127,
195,196
Elizabeth Co., Va. 50
Elm Swamp 38,67,164,241
Ellum Swamp 227,243
Ellis Corner 159

Feltons Line 42,81,106,117,118
Flat Branch 25,34,35,44,59,147,
162,183,184,191,205,217,219,245
Flat Cypress Branch 48,52,137,
141,222
Figgs Line 171
Flat Pond 21
Folly 87,140,193,211,223,230
Foreman Swamp 59
Forrests Line 228
Fort Neck Branch 4,21,42,63,67,
84,130
Fort Island 7,15,16,25,34,67,72
111,206,214,217
Fredericksburg, Va. 105
Freemans Point 192
Fullingtons Line 159,167,175
Fox Branch 170

Fox Ridge Pecosin 214
Gabriel Branch 16,114
Garretts Line 17
Gates Road 53,59
Gibson, Granbury & Donaldson 160
Glasgow Co. 161
Gatlings Corner 133
Gaul Bush Branch 44
Goff Folly Branch 29,42,117,143, 171,204, 09
Goodmans Line 65
Gordons Line 8,79,86,168
Granville, Earl of 82
Grog Branch 240
Great Dismal Swamp 66,153,171, 180,229
Great Hawtree Branch 57,78, 148,174
Great Meadows 183
Great Thicket Branch 178
Great Pocosin 48,171,219
Great Island 193,194
Greens Pocosin 39
Gregorys Line 240
Griffins Line 133
Grate(Great)Marsh 3,19,20,26, 29,33,34,42,58,106,111,162, 165,175,176,189,203,204,207, 214
Gum Branch/Swamp 7,8,12,16,19, 20,33,34,35,43,45,49,50,58,60, 64,66,68,70,73,78,79,85,95,101, 109,110,116,120,150,157,209,218, 225
Gum Pecosin 39,43,42
Gut Landing 35

Hackleys Swamp/Patent 18,31
Hagertys Corner 152
Halifax Co. 1,6,81,134,151,158, 162,202,208,218,219,223
Halfway Run Branch 13,17,53,60, 72,107,189
Hampton River/Town 50
Hanover Co., Va. 106
Hares Old Patent 77,130
Hars Clearing 141
Harrells Line 20,62, 202
Hares Patent 64,130
Hargroves Line 157,202
Harriss Line 57,87,88,101,193
Hawtree Branch 2,34,40,76,138, 177,206,216
Henry Co., Va. 244

Hertford Co. 1,2,7,26,27,28,44,48, 59,61,62,63,70,77,81,89,91,94,103, 111,116,133,150,152,158,159,160, 171,177,187,189,196,199,202,209, 218,220,226,229,232,234,235,241, 244
High Hill Island 241
Herring Creek 22,95,241
Hilly Bridge Branch 18,
Hickory Neck Branch 3,40
Hilly Swamp 14,16,70,119,140, 165,182,218
Hill Pecosin 65
Hintons Line 16,89,176,207,211,243
Hinton Landing 65,232
Hintons Path 115,126
Hintons Mill Pond 63
Hobbs Branch 20
Hollands Line 45,61,77
Holly Island 18,105
Hop Pecosin 57
Hollow Bridge 173,233
Honey Pot Swamp 15,135,158,164, 169,200,207,209,224
Honey Pot Bridge 173
Honey Pot Road 195,209
Holly Tree Branch 110
Honour Branch 117
Hooks Patent 123,199,244
Horns Patent 209
Horse Swamp 133
Horsepen Swamp 54,97,138,158,182, 187,200,229
Horsepool Swamp 20,39,72,76,131, 157,160,175,192,207,243
Hughs Old Road 224
Hughs Road 226
Hughs Patent 241
Humphries Beaverdam Swamp 240
Hunters Mill 211,223
Hunters Corner 43,168

Indian Gut 27,60,77
Indian Branch 85,118,230,235
Indian Old Field 56,77
Indian Line 24,55,90,115,207
Indian Road 16,185
Indian Neck 16,56,94,104,133,138, 171,185,209,234
Indian Town/Road 22,76,220
Indian Swamp 47,83,84,94,98,122, 132
Iron Mine Branch 1,10,31,101,109, 139,154,168,188,200,235
Isle of Wight 11,12,188,205,229

Jacks Branch 46,70,113,135
Jamersons Line 224
Johnston Co. 72,139,155
Jordens Neck 127
Juniper Branch 116,127,132,146, 209,233
Juniper Swamp 4,10,12,35,47,49, 56,59,73,76,85,101,146,150,151, 153,172,189,219,233,234,236,238

Kelleys Branch 129
Keatons Branch 54,63
Kings Line 69,90,128,131
Kings Patent 112
Kittrells Line 111,152,166,168, 202
Knotty Pine Swamp 18,100,111, 121,175,180,190,204,215,241

Lady of Honour Branch 29,244
Langstons Corner 74,178
Larcum & Harriss 140,151
Larcums corner 57,87,88,101, 193
Lassiters Branch 18
Lassiters Line 21,201,207,280
Lewis Patent Line 108
Lickingroot Branch 19,42,77,83, 111,125,138,148,151,179,225, 238,241
Licking Hole 125
Liberty Co. S.C. 148
Line Branch 69
Little Branch 178
Little Cypress 40,138,199,217
Little Dam 39
Little Hawtree Swamp 34,57
Little Mare Branch 23,48,159
Little Island 14,42,59,103, 206,221,227
Little Creek 118,218
Little Reedy 71
Long Branch 5,24,34,70,72,91,92, 100,105,113,115,116,119,123, 125,130,133,135,152,157,164,202
Long Marsh 99
Long Pond 46,68,210,231
Long Beaverdam 9
Long Causeway 8,197
Long Ridge 80
Loosing Swamp 6,9,10,14,18,36, 43,57,65,79,87,88,89,140,193, 204,206
Lowards 158

Mair Desert 40 Road 61
Maiden Hair Neck 46,100,165
Maidenhead Branch 67,101,232
Major Camp Branch 191
Mare Branch 2,4,10,18,29,99,102, 115,233
Martin Co. 62,95
Maneys Ferry 104
Maple Swamp/Branch 2,8,13,99,149 218
Marsh Road 122
March Branch 241,245
Marchs Line 229
Mathews Co., Va 102,135 Path 39
Meherrin Swamp 18,19,20,25,26, 32,37,39,40,54,63,66,82,86,103, 107,118,132,153
Menchews Line 24,53,90,115,233
Middle Swamp 36,39,85,110,117, 133,139,141,144,155,180,233
Middle Ridge 39,155
Mile Bridge 123 Branch 189
Mile Pecosin 209
Methodist 49
Millers Line 49,160,175
Mill Dam 157,159,175
Mill Dam Swamp 48,232
Mill Gutt 84
Mill Race 169,228
Mills Swamp 132,161,167,173,183, 185,228,242
Minqua Pond 242
Minyards Land 110
Mirey Branch 223,228,229,237
Miry Hill Pocosin 1,39,56,65, 71,110,112,129,138,142,154,224, 226,240
Miry Branch 13,15,35,63,73,99, 106,115,120,126,149,171,211,
Mizells Line 178
Mizells Mill Branch 71
Mongses Plantation 103
Morleys Point 79
Morgans Line 112
Morris Pecosin 26,33,134,189,230
Morris Line 150
Muddy Creek 26,30,62,65,112,159, 189,199
Muddy Gutt 127,144,152,188
Murfreesborough 171,172,180,187, 189,199
Murphys Line 198
Montgomery Co., Tn. 224

Nansemond 1,2,4,10,12,16,17,22, 24,29,34,35,42,46,47,48,49,50, 55,68,69,71,72,73,81,89,90,94, 100,104,105,106,109,111,113,115, 116,118,121,125,128,129,131,133, 135,137,143,145,154,157,163,166, 172,175,176,177,179,182,183,185, 186,189,193,194,198,209,220,221, 226,227,228,231,234,235,242,243
Newborn 98
Norfleets Line 207,240
Norfolk Co., Va. 46,76,155,193, 194
Norris Line 33,239
Northampton Co. 93,117,122,177, 200,208,210,242,243
Norwest Northwest Branch 36,65, 99,125,139,144
Notte(Knotty)Pine Swamp 16,18, 36

Oald Indian Line/Road 2,114,133
Oald Swamp 13
Oald Indian Patent/Place 80,127, 232
Old Bennetts Creek Road 197,198
Old Brakes 40
Old Field 47,132,134
Old Indian Town 42
Odoms Line 34,157,202
Old Ferry Road 212
Old Indian Town 42
Old Mill Swamp 48
Old Quarter 47,83,116
Old Orchard Branch 219,244
Old Tarkiln Bed 66
Old Town Neck 44
Old Town Road 41,68,74,109, 156,165,175,190,243
Old Woman's Pocosin 180
Orapeak Swamp 9,11,12,15,20, 29,30,69,92,93,141,158,159, 184,207,227,240
Onslow Co. 152
Orange Co. 2,109,173,181
Outside Swamp 191,206,218,221
Ownleys Line 91,98,101,152

Parkers Line 26, 46,154,212
Parkers Old Field 45,240
Painter Ridge 19,32
Pasquotank Ridge 39,155
Pasquotank Co. 224
Pearces Line 131
Peniboa Island Bridge 111

Panters Island 17,32
Perquimans Co. 6,11,15,19,47,89, 96,105,111,117,132,179,200,201
Person Co. 193,194
Perquimans Road 143,231
Perquimans River 39
Peters Swamp 5,10,19,21,45,55, 61,77,79,80,91,100,123,124,132, 179,200,201
Phelps Line 1,2,22
Philips Old Field 39,102,241
Philadelphia 211,222
Pilands Line/Corner 17,55,120, 207,241
Pine Noles 129,201
Pine Box Island Swamp 106
Pine Swamp/Branch 17,32,41,60,90, 120,123,147,199,201,245
Piney Woods 30,221
Pipkins Line 150,161
Pitch Kittle Road 134
Pitt Co. 76,77,160
Plumb Tree Branch 99,150,157
Plumb Tree Patch 51
Pond Branch 204,219,240
Popular Branch 6,10,69,79,152
Poverty Hill 234
Powells Mill Pond 141
Powells Line 61,84
Poly Branch 27,64,129,163,167,168
Pughs Line 37,84,112,144
Pughs Bridge 108
Pumpkin Patch 125,236
Poket Branch 110,137

Raleigh 208
Randolph Co. 92,144
Rawls Line 57,116,172
Red Hill 73
Reedy Branch/Swamp 7,19,24,34,35,44, 52,53,70,82,90,96,103,109,111,115, 121,128,139,147,148,154,163,175, 239
Reid Line 191
Rice Patch 229
Ridges 82,116 Ridge Pecosin 37
Riddicks Line 99,240
Rich Thicket Swamp 9,11,222
Roanoke River 218
Roberts Line 168
Robertson Line 52,54,115
Robins Line 220
Rogers Branch 59,74,196
Rogers Line 35,41,44,74,102

Rooty Branch 209
Rogers Pocosin 12
Rowan Co. 79
Sandy Ridge/Road 89,91,146,219 232,241
Sand Bank Land 7,56,58,64,83, 114,201
Sand Hill 68
Schoolhouse Branch 94,115,125, 126,132
Scratchall Branch 8,152,159, 239
Seine Beach 134
Sarum Creek 17,22,46,95,130, 181,189,192,209,239
Sarum Road 13,131,241
Sarum Swamp 24,95,113,134
Short Beaverdam 9
Sharps Island 55,184,241
Snake Branch 28
Somerton Creek 26,82, 133,142, 175,193,194,208,218
Society Chapel 98,101,232
Southampton Co. 54,59,62,67,72, 81,82,96,103,125,193,194,231
Snake Branch 28,126
Speights Creek 57,61,116,172, 192,210,236
Speights Mill Pond 48,151
Speights Patent Line 64,97,113, 117,154,172
Spivey Branch 9
Spivey Patent Line 47,145,164, 192,241
Spring Branch 10,17,23,31,226
Stallings Branch 39
Starffords Branch 61
Suffolk 5,49,51,72,88,121,122, 124,130,133,134,145,166,167, 177,180,205,208
Sumners Line 36,116,224
Sumners Mill Swamp 108
Sussex Co. Va 141
Tarkiln Branch 12,47,158,162, 213
Tar Landing 130
Taylors Line 1
The Trap 50
Thicket Road/Swamp 53,69,71
Thick Neck Branch 15,124
Third Ridge 196
Tennessee 142
Tobacco House Branch 161
Trotmans Corner Tree 28
Troy Swamp 3,22,89,95,145,164 207

Trumpet Marsh 185
Tucklow Bridge 110,216
Turners Land 16,70,119,165,182
Turnip Patch 53
Upper Parish 24
Vinyards Point 130
Vaughns Patent Line 64,73,202
Virginia 1,24,133,152,187,202, 216,240
Virginia Line 19,38,57,81,151, 186,231
Virginia Road 51,137
Voights Line 157
Waltons Old Mill 37
Waltons Line 192,218
Watering Hole Branch 65,141
Warwick Plantation 58,155
Watery Swamp 1,3,27,31,33,37,47, 49,52,63,83,96,97,136,150,161, 170,176,182,191,203,209,212,232
Walnut Neck Patent 210,235,236, 242
Warrick Swamp 4,5,6,23,24,41,58, 61,68,69,109,214
Waters Landing 22,130
Warrens Line 135
Warrick Co. 75
Wallis Corner 91
Wards Folly 170
Watsons Patent 150
Webbs Patent 61,97,116,172,188
Webbs Branch 19
Watering Hole Branch 65
Watsons Patent 150
White Oak Neck 70,141,196,222
White Oak Spring Marsh 19,29,45, 56,60,93,97,105,127,141,159,175
White Pot Pocosin 7,15,19,23,35, 37,38,39,56,65,66,71,197,200, 205,213,215,226,239
Wianock 236
Wild Cat Branch 32,191,217
Whiteheads Fishery 180 Tract 219
Wiggens Swamp/Branch 18,164,209
Wire Neck Branch 17,22,25,34,39, 97,99,106,141,174
Winton 5,53,61,93,130,133,188, 198
Windborns Deed 69,218
Woodleys Patent 101,211
Wolf Pit Ridge 74
Wynns Ferry 9,30,62,66,135

www.ingramcontent.com/pod-product-compliance
Lightning Source LLC
Chambersburg PA
CBHW030424020526
44112CB00044B/229